WILD
Utah

by
**Bill Cunningham
and Polly Burke**

FALCON®

HELENA, MONTANA

A FALCON GUIDE ®

Falcon® is continually expanding its list of recreational guidebooks. All books include detailed descriptions, accurate maps, and all the information necessary for enjoyable trips. You can order extra copies of this book and get information and prices for other Falcon guidebooks by writing Falcon, P.O. Box 1718, Helena, MT 59624 or calling toll-free 1-800-582-2665. Also, please ask for a free copy of our current catalog. Visit our website at http:\\www.falconguide.com.

Cover photo: Pale Evening Primrose in the Henry Mountains, San Rafael Desert, by Bruce Jackson

Back cover photo: Coyote Gulch, a tributary of the Escalante River, by Larry Carver

Color section by Scott Smith

All black-and-white photos by authors, except where noted.

Library of Congress Cataloging-in-Publication Data

Cunningham, Bill.
    Wild Utah / by Bill Cunningham and Polly Burke.
       p. cm.
    "A Falcon guide."—T.p. verso.
    Includes index.
    ISBN 1-56044-616-1 (pbk.)
    1. Outdoor recreation—Utah—Guidebooks. 2. Wilderness areas—Utah—Guidebooks. 3. Utah—Guidebooks. I. Burke, Polly. II. Title.
GV191.42.U8C86 1998
917.9204' 33–dc21
                                                      97-38573
                                                        CIP

 Text pages printed on recycled paper.

CAUTION

Outdoor recreational activities are by their very nature potentially hazardous. All participants in such activities must assume the responsibility for their own actions and safety. The information contained in this guidebook cannot replace sound judgment and good decision-making skills, which help reduce risk exposure, nor does the scope of this book allow for disclosure of all the potential hazards and risks involved in such activities.

Learn as much as possible about the outdoor recreational activities in which you participate, prepare for the unexpected, and be cautious. The reward will be a safer and more enjoyable experience.

To the thousands of citizens from Utah and elsewhere, past and present, who have fought for the freedom of Utah's profound and irreplaceable wildness. May the uncluttered expanse of untamed deserts, plateaus, mountains, and canyons remain so forever. And to the memory of Ed Abbey, whose writings inspired so many of us to become defenders of the remarkable landscape he so deeply loved.

CONTENTS

North-Central MIDDLE ROCKY MOUNTAINS AND CENTRAL PLATEAUS

FOREWORD

One cannot imagine a state more beautiful or interesting to explore than Utah. From the slickrock canyons and roaring rivers of the Colorado Plateau, to the "island" mountains and isolated valleys of the Great Basin, to the alpine basins and 13,000-foot peaks of the High Uintas, Utah offers an incredible array of wild country.

Unfortunately, Utahns have been remiss when it comes to protecting these world-class treasures. Of the 11 western states, only Nevada has less designated wilderness than Utah. Most of the other states have four to five times as much protected land. Forget about the excuse that the state already has five national parks—all five combined would fit with room to spare in Glacier, Grand Canyon, or Death Valley. Where Utah reigns supreme is in its bounty of public lands that still qualify for formal wilderness designation. But these wildlands are vulnerable, subject to the same mindset of exploitation that eroded our nation's once grand, sea-to-shining-sea wilderness into the fragments of wild country we still have today.

A legacy of grazing, mining, timbering, and wildlife mismanagement has already taken its toll. Fifty years ago, in his conservation classic, *A Sand County Almanac*, Aldo Leopold dedicated his chapter on Utah to cheat, the exotic Asian grass that dominates much of the state. Cheat proliferated as a result of too many cattle and sheep devouring the native grasses and trampling the soil, leaving the land raw and open to a weedy invasion. Ten years before Leopold's treatise, wilderness explorer Bob Marshall had proposed the creation of an 8-million-acre national monument in the wild Escalante-Canyonlands country. Today, the wilderness Marshall worked for is fragmented by hundreds of miles of roads, one result of the post-World War II rush for lands that might yield uranium, oil, or coal. Only a few large pieces of the pre-war wilderness remain. Not surprisingly, Utah's wildlife haven't fared much better. Gone are the grizzly and the wolf, and probably the wolverine, the lynx, and the fisher. Bighorn sheep have been swapped for domestic sheep. Exotic rainbow, brown, and brook trout have replaced the native cutthroat.

We can do better. We must treat the land and its inhabitants not as a storehouse of material wealth for human exploitation, but rather as a rich biological and spiritual heritage to be shared with all living things. By living in this way, we can make the wilderness of Bob Marshall's time, fragmented by decades of abuse, whole again.

The Utah Wilderness Act of 1984 marked the first major citizen victory in the fight to secure permanent protection for Utah wildlands. That law brought 12 new areas and 750,000 acres into the National Wilderness Preservation System, lands permanently set aside by law for preservation in their natural condition. There are now 15 areas totaling more than 800,000 acres of designated wilderness in Utah. But that is just a start. There are millions of acres managed by the Bureau of Land Management, National Park Service, and USDA Forest Service that deserve permanent protection. It takes an act of Congress to designate wilderness, and that can only happen with strong, unwavering public support. These are public lands—*our* lands—and we should insist that they be preserved for generations to come.

Wild Utah introduces you to many of these remarkable places, some of the most beautiful lands in the world. Be forewarned, however, this is just a primer. In 30-plus years of wandering Utah's backcountry I've found that every canyon leads to a dozen more waiting to be explored. I hope this effort to share some of Utah's wild places will not only show you the beauty of the state, but will encourage you to enlist in the efforts to protect it. There is much to see, and much to do.

> —*George Nickas*
> *Policy Coordinator*
> *Wilderness Watch*
> *August 1997*

ACKNOWLEDGMENTS

A book of this magnitude would have been impossible without the able assistance of someone intimate with the history, politics, and values of Utah's bountiful treasure of wildness. In short, a guide for the guidebook. This crucial help was cheerfully provided by our consultant, George Nickas, whose knowledge of wild Utah, gained by growing up in the state and working many years as a staffer for the Utah Wilderness Association, proved invaluable. George offered dozens of innovative trip ideas, most of which worked out and some of which were, well, interesting. When our own travel plans were unrealistic, George would rub his chin and say, "Well, you might be able to do that." Fortunately, you won't find any of those questionable trips in this book.

We are especially grateful to George for helping us keep our focus on unprotected wildlands within each complex. Our collective hope is that after exploring these special places you will raise your voice in their defense when the opportunity arises.

Like a breath of fresh air from the north, five young people blew down from Montana and gave an immense boost to our exploration of Wild Utah. Bryn Cunningham, Megan Sarnecki, Justin Cunningham, Mark Matule, and Kerry Patton backpacked, hiked, and laughed with us in some of southern Utah's wildest canyon country. As a senior in recreation management at the University of Montana, Bryn wrote a lively description of our extended backpack in Dark Canyon (see complex 25 in the Colorado Plateau section).

We want to give special thanks to Cecil and Annette Garland who put us up at their historic ranch house on the sunrise side of the Deep Creek Range. With spring snowstorms blasting over the mountains, their warm hospitality was especially welcome. We hope that a bit of Cecil's conservation ethic and vast knowledge of Utah wildlands is somehow reflected in the following pages.

Dozens of federal public lands offices throughout Utah provided up-to-date material on resources, land status, road conditions, and non-motorized recreation. This enabled us to put together the wealth of information about Utah wildlands you will discover in the following pages. Although we had far too much help to name everyone individually, several agency folks deserve special thanks: Marty Ott, Utah Coordinator for the National Park Service; Margaret Kelsey, Wilderness Coordinator for the Bureau of Land Management (BLM) in Utah; and Phil Zieg of the BLM District Office in Richfield. Phil led us to several obscure trailheads in the Pahvant Range one cloudy morning, saving us hours of fruitless searching.

Enormous credit is due the Utah Wilderness Coalition for its 1990 publication, *Wilderness At The Edge*. This superb book contains detailed descriptions, maps, and photos of 5.7 million acres of citizen-proposed BLM wilderness in Utah. Using principles of conservation biology, the proposal combines roadless areas into larger ecological complexes rather than fragmenting and isolating them, as was done in the BLM wilderness inventory. We relied upon these complexes for much of the geographical framework for *Wild Utah*, which we gratefully acknowledge. With *Wilderness At The Edge*, the Utah Wilderness Coalition has published the most thoroughly documented case for BLM wilderness in the nation. Another indispensable publication is the *Utah Handbook*, by Bill Weir and Robert Blake (Moon Publications, 1995). We used the handbook to get from place to place during our extensive travels throughout Utah. We are also grateful to the staff of the University of Montana library for their help in locating the myriad Utah topographic and surface management maps needed for our pre-trip research.

Lastly, we are grateful to those citizens of Utah who for decades have fought a sometimes lonely battle for the freedom of their wild country. Without their continued efforts we would have had little to write about.

LEGEND

Interstate	
Paved Road (U.S., State, or County)	
Gravel Road (County or Forest)	
Graded Dirt Road	
Unimproved Road	
Railroad	
Trail, Trail Number, Trailhead	102T
Pass or Saddle	
Bridge	
Lake, River, Falls	
Intermittent Stream	
Marsh or Wetland	
Spring	
Site Location	Utah

Mountain	5,281 ft.
Elevation Point	5,281 ft.
Mesa/Tableland	
Campground	
Ranger Station	
Gate	
Mine	
Cabin or Building	
City or Town	Escalante
Urban Area	
State or International Boundary	UTAH COLORADO
Orientation	N
Map Scale	0 0.5 1 Miles

WILD UTAH

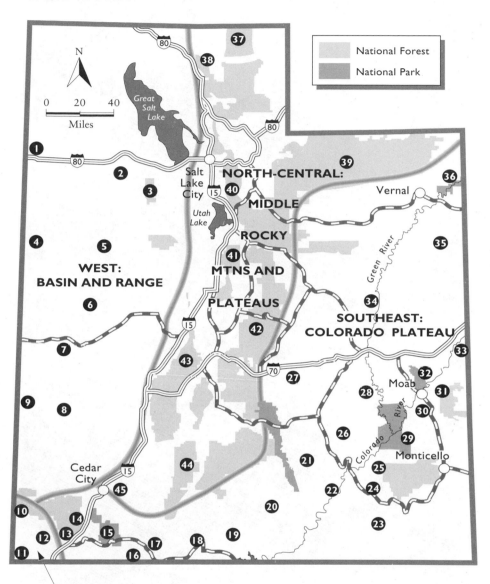

National Forest
National Park

N

0   20   40
Miles

Great
Salt
Lake

80

80

80

37

38

39

36

Vernal

35

Green River

NORTH-CENTRAL:

MIDDLE

ROCKY

MTNS AND

PLATEAUS

SOUTHEAST:
COLORADO PLATEAU

34

33

32

Moab

31

30

29

Monticello

Colorado River

Salt
Lake
City

15

40

Utah
Lake

41

42

43

70

27

28

26

25

24

23

22

21

20

WEST:
BASIN AND RANGE

1

2

3

4

5

6

7

8

9

10

11

12

13

14

15

16

17

18

19

44

45

Cedar
City

15

SOUTHWEST:
HOT DESERT

The cliffs of Fisher Towers, in the La Sal Canyons complex.

INTRODUCTION

Nearly one million acres of Utah's landscape are designated as federal wilderness, and millions more are under consideration for wilderness designation. Visitors to these wildlands should appreciate the meaning and value of wilderness, if for no other reason than to better enjoy their visits with less impact on the wildland values—such as unspoiled vistas, open space, and solitude—that attracted them in the first place.

Those who know and love wild country have their own personal definition of wilderness, heartfelt and often unexpressed. But because Congress reserved for itself the exclusive power to designate wilderness in the historic Wilderness Act of 1964, it is important that we also understand the *legal* meaning of wilderness.

The fundamental purpose of the Wilderness Act was to provide an *enduring* resource of wilderness for this and future generations so that a growing, increasingly mechanized human population would not occupy and modify every last wild niche. Just as important as preserving the land is the preservation of natural processes, such as naturally ignited fire, erosion, landslides, and other forces that shape the land. Before 1964 the whims of administrative fiat were all that protected wilderness. During the 1930s the "commanding general" of the wilderness battle, Wilderness Society co-founder Bob Marshall, described wilderness as a "snowbank melting on a hot June day," though in the Utah desert the analogy might be closer to a sand dune shrinking on a windy day.

The act defines "wilderness" as undeveloped federal lands "where the earth and its community of life are untrammeled by man, where man is a visitor who does not remain." The word *trammel* means "a net" in Middle English, so that Modern English "untrammeled" conveys the idea of land that is "unnetted," or uncontrolled, by humans. Congress recognized that no land is completely free of human influence, going on to say that wilderness must "generally appear to have been affected primarily by the forces of nature, with the imprint of man's work substantially unnoticeable." Further, designated wilderness must have outstanding opportunities for solitude or primitive and unconfined recreation, and be at least 5,000 acres in size or large enough to preserve and use in an unimpaired condition. Lastly, wilderness may contain ecological, geological, or other features of scientific, educational, scenic, or historical value. The expanses of Utah's mountains, canyons, and deserts described in the following pages meet and easily exceed these legal requirements. Any lingering doubts are removed by the distant music of a coyote beneath a star-studded desert sky, or by the soothing rhythm of an oasis waterfall in a remote canyon.

The Eagle Crags and Zion National Park as seen from Canaan Mountain, at the head of South Creek Canyon.

In general, wilderness designation protects the land from development: roads, buildings, motorized vehicle and equipment use, and commercial uses other than preexisting livestock grazing, outfitting, and the development of mining claims and leases validated before the 1984 cutoff date in the federal Wilderness Act (or the date of designation for areas added after 1984). The act set up the National Wilderness Preservation System and empowered three federal agencies to administer wilderness: the USDA Forest Service, the U.S. Fish and Wildlife Service, and the National Park Service. The Bureau of Land Management (BLM) was added to the list with passage of the 1976 Federal Land Policy and Management Act. The addition of the BLM as a wilderness management agency was especially important to Utah, where millions of acres of qualified BLM wildlands await congressional action. These agencies can and do make wilderness recommendations, as any citizen can, but only Congress can set aside wilderness on federal lands. This is where politics enters in, as epitomized by the kind of grassroots democracy that eventually brought about passage of Utah's first statewide attempt at protecting national forest wilderness, in 1984. The formula for wilderness conservationists has been, and continues to be, "endless pressure endlessly applied."

But once an area has been designated wilderness, the unending job of wilderness stewardship is just beginning. The managing agencies have a special responsibility to administer wilderness areas in "such manner as will leave them unimpaired for future use and enjoyment *as wilderness*." Wilderness can remain unimpaired over time only through partnership between concerned citizens and the agencies.

Wilderness is the only truly biocentric use of land, where the needs of flora and fauna take precedence over human interests. We make wilderness off-limits to intensive human uses with the objective of preserving the diversity of non-human life, with which Utah is richly endowed. As such, the preservation of wilderness is our society's highest act of humility. These are the places where we deliberately slow down our impulse to drill for the last barrel of oil, mine the last vein of ore, build a parking lot on top of the last wild peak. The explorer of Utah's desert wildlands can take genuine pride in reaching a remote summit under his or her own power, traversing a narrow serpentine canyon, or walking across the uncluttered expanse of a vast, high desert plateau. Hiking boots and self-reliance replace motorized equipment and push-button convenience, allowing us to find something in ourselves we feared lost.

Utah's Wilderness History

With the Wilderness Act of 1964 Congress reserved the authority to designate suitable federal lands for inclusion in the National Wilderness Preservation System. It also defined the characteristics necessary for such designation (see above). Initially the USDA Forest Service, U.S. Fish and Wildlife Service, and the National Park Service were directed by the act to inventory their roadless units and submit a list of qualified lands for Congress to consider. Later, with the Federal Lands Policy and Management Act of 1976, the U.S. Bureau of Land Management (BLM) was included in the wilderness designation process and was likewise instructed to evaluate its lands for wilderness suitability, leaving to Congress the authority to designate wilderness.

In 1978 the first designated wilderness in Utah was established. Lone Peak, on the Wasatch Front, was included in the omnibus Endangered American Wilderness Act after a 15-year lobbying effort. Lone Peak's 30,000 acres constituted a mere pinpoint in the more than 35.8 million acres of federal lands in Utah, but it was a start.

In 1984, the Utah Wilderness Act grew out of the Roadless Area Review and Evaluation (RARE II) process. The act set aside 12 new wilderness areas on national forest lands: Mount Naomi, Wellsville Mountain, Deseret Peak, Mount Olympus, Twin Peaks, Mount Timpanogos, High Uintas, Mount Nebo, Pine Valley Mountains, Ashdown Gorge, Box Death Hollow, and Dark Canyon. As a result, the amount of protected wilderness in Utah's national forests rose to a total of 775,000 acres. Many roadless areas in Utah's national forests remained unprotected as wilderness, however, and these face an uncertain future while awaiting further action by Congress. Even now these areas are shrinking due to mining, logging, and road and utility development.

The National Park Service also inventoried its wildlands in response to the 1964 act. Managers at the eight national parks and monuments in Utah individually recommended 80 to 99 percent of their lands for wilderness designation, and the total came to 1.3 million acres. Thus far Congress has taken no action on the Park Service's wilderness proposal for Utah.

The BLM, which manages 23 million acres of federal land in Utah, began its wilderness process in 1977 with a statewide inventory of its holdings. Lands that, in the BLM's judgment, did not "clearly and obviously" contain wilderness characteristics, were dropped. In November 1980 the BLM established 83 wilderness study areas in the units that "might have those characteristics as specified in the Wilderness Act." The wilderness study areas covered 2.6 million acres, 11 percent of the BLM lands in the state. According to federal statute, wilderness study areas are to be managed to protect their wilderness values until Congress decides their fate. When the 1980 decision was announced, conservation groups in Utah and throughout the nation arose in an uproar over the wildlands that had been omitted by the BLM. Led by the Utah Wilderness Association, conservationists filed the largest appeal ever with the Interior Board of Land Appeals. The largely successful appeal gained wilderness study area status for an additional 600,000 acres of public wildlands. The fury intensified when, in a 1990 final environmental impact statement, the BLM recommended designation of 1.9 million acres as wilderness—a mere eight percent of BLM lands in Utah.

The Utah Wilderness Coalition was formed in response to the BLM's process and its decision. This alliance of 19 grassroots conservation organizations conducted extensive field work and research, and put together a counterproposal for a Utah wilderness bill covering 5,710,600 acres. Nearly half of this land (2.5 million acres) had been dropped from wilderness study area status by the BLM. Currently only 26,000 acres of BLM land in Utah are protected by wilderness designation. These consist of two fragments—the Beaver Dam Mountains and the Paria Canyon–Vermilion Cliffs—that were included in the 1984 Arizona Strip Wilderness Act. Legislation for BLM wilderness in Utah remains at a standstill in Congress, leaving millions of acres vulnerable to roads, mining, and other development. Only 801,000 acres of wilderness are presently protected in Utah. Lovers of wilderness have a challenging task: to include *all* of Utah's wildlands in the Wilderness Preservation System.

In 1996 President Bill Clinton used executive authority to establish the 1.7 million-acre Grand Staircase–Escalante National Monument. From Bryce Canyon National Park on the west to Capitol Reef National Park and Glen Canyon National Recreation Area on the east, the monument includes Circle Cliffs, the Cockscomb, part of the White and Vermilion Cliffs, the massive Kaiparowits Plateau, and the Escalante's canyons. All preexisting uses continue, but new mining claims have been halted. Although a big step forward, monument status is not a substitute for the protection afforded by the Wilderness Act. The monument is unique because it is to be managed by the BLM, a first for that agency. It remains to be seen whether the BLM can shed its resource bias and focus on conserving the environmental integrity of the monument. Meanwhile, as the monument's creation indicates, the national constituency supporting protection of federal wildlands in Utah grows stronger. Within Utah, however, anti-wilderness voices have also become more strident. Visitors to wild Utah are urged to become involved in protecting its pristine and primitive lands, for passivity means an irretrievable loss.

Leave No Trace Etiquette

Utah's popularity has put the state's beautiful wildlands at risk of being trashed and trampled by hordes of thoughtless visitors. The preservation of wild Utah depends on every person following the guidelines of the leave-no-trace ethic, whether day hiking or backpacking.

PLAN AHEAD. Get maps, information, and regulations from the appropriate agency. If possible, avoid high-use areas and peak seasons. Keep your group small; some areas have group size limits.

PREPARE. In assembling your gear (see Appendix A), repackage food to reduce your trash load; what you don't consume you will be carrying out. Carry a trowel to bury human waste and zip-locked bags for packing out used toilet paper and feminine hygiene products. In areas that require human waste to be packed out, carry a "poop tube" or other portable waste container. Avoid flashy colors in clothing and equipment to be considerate of other backcountry travelers who appreciate Utah's solitude.

TREAD LIGHTLY. Our goal is to pass through the land without altering it in any way. Stay on existing trails wherever possible. In trailless areas, travel on bedrock, slickrock, or sandy wash bottoms. Avoid stepping on the delicate soil crust—known as cryptobiotic soil—of cyanobacteria, algae, mosses, and lichens that is essential to preserve scarce desert soil. If you cannot avoid this delicate surface, follow one set of footprints to minimize damage.

CAMP LIGHTLY. If possible, stay at an established campsite. Otherwise, select a site where vegetation and soil won't be damaged, such as slickrock. Avoid delicate alpine areas for camping. When in camp, spread your travel broadly to avoid creating new trails. Don't remain in one site too long.

FOREGO FIRES. Use a backpacking stove for cooking. If you must have a fire, use an established fire ring, or, if there isn't one, make your fire spot invisible to future campers by using a firepan or fire blanket to prevent soil scarring. Do not mar the landscape with broken off branches when gathering wood: use only downed wood. Firewood diameter should be no larger than your wrist. Douse all fires thoroughly and scatter the dead ashes broadly.

KEEP WATER CLEAN. Water is a precious commodity for Utah's wildlife and vegetation. Treat it accordingly. Never bathe or wash dishes directly in a water source. Even "biodegradable" camp soap must not be used in or near surface water—do all your washing at least 300 feet (one football field) away from lakes and streams. Likewise, disperse your dirty water far from the source, in a cat-hole if it contains speckles of food, or broadcast it widely and away from vegetation. Carry your food waste out with you.

RESPECT WILDLIFE. One of the thrills of remote backcountry travel is enjoying the sight of wildlife. Special care, however, is required to prevent your presence from disturbing the animals for which this is home. Keep your distance—use binoculars and telephoto lenses. If your presence affects an animal's behavior, you are too close. In the desert, camp well away from and out of sight of water holes, seeps, and springs. Your presence will frighten away wildlife that may have no other water source. Pets are best off at home and may

A gecko lizard suns itself in Lower Fourmile Canyon, Henry Mountains complex.

be prohibited in some areas. If pets are allowed, keep them leashed and under control. Keep an eye on children, too! Do not allow them to feed, harass, or attempt to touch wild animals.

PROPERLY DISPOSE OF HUMAN WASTE. Different methods of disposing of human waste apply in different regions. In arid areas of the state, bury your waste in a 6- to 12-inch cathole in organic soil (the darker, moister layer of soil found in vegetated areas) around shrubs or trees, at least 300 feet from water sources. In lightly used areas where discovery by other people is unlikely smear your waste on rocks where the dry desert air will soon reduce it to dust.

The cathole method is also recommended in mountainous regions. Be sure you bury your waste away from trails and at least 300 feet from any water source.

In heavily used canyons, regulations may require you to pack out your waste. The easiest method for storing and carrying waste is to make a poop tube from a 4-inch diameter, 12-inch length of plastic pvc pipe capped at one end and threaded for a screw-on lid at the other end. Simply scoop waste from the ground into a paper bag and stuff it in the tube. Drop in a cotton ball soaked in ammonia to reduce odors and screw on the lid. At trip's end empty the tube at a municipal sewage treatment plant or other site approved by local land managers.

Whatever method best fits your trip, bag and carry out your toilet paper, as well as feminine hygiene products. A cotton ball saturated with ammonia OR a teaspoon of dry bleach (NOT both) in the zip-locked bag will reduce odor.

PACK OUT TRASH. If you pack it in—pack it out! *All* of it! Carry out all trash, yours as well as any you encounter. All backcountry users need to pitch in to properly care for the public lands we hold in common. Trash includes cigarette butts, chewing gum, dental floss, and candy and gum wrappers, as well as food leftovers. Careful meal planning can prevent the last item.

The bottom line is to make your passage through wild country wholly invisible to your successors. Help the land remain pristine.

Archeology and the Law

The law regarding sites and objects of archeological significance is simple: pick up the modern trash, but leave all artifacts in place. Trash more than 50 years old is protected by both state and federal laws prohibiting removal or destruction of archeological and historical resources. Numerous examples of vandalized sites exist to sensitize any hiker to the need for such a hands-off policy.

The ancient peoples who inhabited these lands for centuries before the arrival of the Euro-Americans left a plethora of structures, artifacts, and artwork. Their spirit remains in the alcoves and canyons, lending a magical sense of their eternal presence. As visitors in their homeland we must be proper guests. You don't pocket the silverware when you're a dinner guest; likewise do not remove projectile points, flakes, or potsherds from archeological sites. Such lithic scatter is of immense archeological value.

Even simply visiting sites requires special care. A multitude of footsteps does permanent damage to structures and middens (ancient trash piles). Avoid touching walls and roofs as well as plaster. Rock art, likewise, must not be touched, rubbed, chalked, or traced. Make your camp far from ancient habitation sites to reduce damage to their archeological integrity. These treasures can be easily and permanently destroyed by thoughtless visitors. All fossils found on public land are likewise not to be disturbed or removed.

Report any vandalism you witness to state and federal resource authorities. The Bureau of Land Management Law Enforcement Hotline is 1-800-722-3998.

Rock art north of the Fins, in Behind the Rocks.

Preparedness and Safety

An enjoyable backcountry outing requires preparation. This book and the maps suggested in the hike write-ups are a good start in gaining knowledge about your hiking area. Carry good maps and a compass, and know how to use them. Calculating the time required for a desert or canyon hike defies any formula. Terrain is often rough; extensive detours around boulders, pouroffs, and dropoffs mean longer trips. Distances are never what they appear to be on a map. Plan your excursion conservatively, and always carry the emergency items listed in Appendix A in your pack.

Driving to the trailhead is statistically far more dangerous than hiking. But being far from the nearest 911 service requires knowledge of possible hazards and the proper precautions to avoid them. It is not an oxymoron to say "have fun and be safe." Quite the contrary, if you're not safe, you won't have fun. Know what to expect; at the risk of generating paranoia, we offer the "treacherous thirteen" hazards:

DEHYDRATION—It cannot be overemphasized that plenty of water is necessary for hiking in Utah. Even with minimal exertion, the arid atmosphere dries you out. In areas without reliable water, carry one gallon per person per day in unbreakable screw-top containers. And pause often to drink it. Carry water in your car as well so you'll have water to return to. As a general rule plain water is a better thirst quencher than any of the sports drinks on the market.

GIARDIASIS—Any surface water, with the possible exception of springs flowing directly out of the ground, is apt to contain *Giardia lamblia*, a microorganism that causes stomach cramps and severe diarrhea. Giardiasis can lead to extreme fatigue and rapid dehydration. To keep this pesky parasite out of your digestive tract, use an approved water filter or boil all water for at least five minutes. Chemical treatments, such as iodine drops, may not offer complete protection and often produce their own undesirable side effects.

CHANGEABLE WEATHER—Utah's deserts and plateaus are well known for sudden changes in weather. The temperature can plummet 50 degrees Fahrenheit in less than an hour. Prepare yourself with extra food and clothing, including rain and wind gear. Before leaving on a trip let someone know your exact route, especially if traveling solo, and your estimated time of return. Don't forget to let them know when you get back.

FLASH FLOODS—Dry washes and canyons can become traps for unwary visitors when rainstorms hit. A storm anywhere upstream in the drainage can result in a flash flood in a lower canyon. Never camp in areas that show signs of flooding. Check on regional weather conditions at a ranger station before embarking on your backcountry expedition. In some areas, such as Paria Canyon, you must register before departure for just this reason. When floods do

An early spring snowstorm at a campsite on Hackberry Creek, Grand Staircase wilderness complex.

occur, stay out of the water. Do not cross a flooded wash. Both the depth and the current can be deceiving. Wait for the flood to recede, which usually does not take long.

HEAT-RELATED ILLNESS AND HYPOTHERMIA—Protect yourself from sun and heat with proper clothing. A broad-brimmed hat is mandatory equipment, as are sunglasses. Avoid overexertion during hot weather and drink plenty of water. Even in the cool days of winter, a delightful time in Utah, the sun's rays are intense. Wear sunscreen with a sun-protection factor (SPF) of at least 15.

During spring and summer the Utah traveler should be alert for signs of heatstroke, a potentially fatal condition. Avoid exertion during the hottest part of the day, seek shade, and, again, drink plenty of fluids.

Abrupt chilling is as much a danger as heat stroke. Storms or nightfall can cause temperatures to plunge. Wear layers of clothes, adding or subtracting layers depending on conditions, to avoid overheating or chilling. Even with stable weather, hypothermia can strike after a chilly river crossing in the shadows of a deep canyon. Know the symptoms of hypothermia, and keep an eye on your companions.

VEGETATION—Watch out for spiny desert vegetation, such as yucca and prickly pear. Both poison oak and poison ivy lurk in Utah's shady moist canyons. Be sure you can recognize this dastardly duo before your trip.

RATTLESNAKES, SCORPIONS, TARANTULAS—These desert denizens are easily terrified by unexpected human visitors and they react predictably to being frightened. Do not sit or put your hands into dark recesses, especially during the warmer "snake season" months. Carry and know how to use a snake bite venom extractor kit for emergencies when help is far away. In the event of a snakebite, seek medical assistance immediately. Keep tents zipped and always shake out boots, packs, and clothes before putting them on.

MOUNTAIN LIONS—Sections of Utah are prime mountain lion country. Attacks on humans are very rare, but it's best to always be alert when large predators are around. Avoid hiking at night when lions are often hunting. Instruct your children on appropriate behavior when confronted with a lion: do not run. Keep children in sight while hiking; stay close to them in areas where lions might hide.

MINE HAZARDS—Utah contains thousands of abandoned mines. All of them should be considered hazardous. Stay away from all mines and mine structures. The vast majority of these mines have not been secured or even posted. Keep an eye on young or adventurous members of your group.

HANTA VIRUS—In addition to the mines, there are often deserted old buildings around mine sites. Hanta virus is a deadly disease carried by deer mice and possibly other rodents. Entering any enclosed area increases the chances of breathing the airborne particles that carry this life-threatening virus. As a precaution, do not enter deserted buildings and don't camp where rodent droppings, nests, or burrows are abundant.

LIGHTNING—Especially during summer, lightning is a potential hazard. Stay off ridges and peaks when storms threaten. Shallow overhangs and gullies should also be avoided because electrical current often moves at ground level near a lightning strike. Seek low ground and discard any metal equipment, such as a pack frame or fishing rod.

CANYONEERING—The thrill of exploring a deep winding canyon can end quickly if you move carelessly. In addition to being alert to flash flood conditions, be wary of unstable rocky slopes and slickrock when your soles are damp or sandy. A 50-foot length of woven strap is a handy item for raising and lowering your packs on hazardous slopes or pouroffs. Do not take foolish chances when in remote areas—don't ignore that "uh-oh" instinct.

AVALANCHE—If you are planning any winter or early spring excursions in Utah's high country, learn all you can about avalanches by taking a class, reading, or viewing a video. The USDA Forest Service distributes a useful pamphlet, *Basic Guidelines for Winter Recreation,* that covers avalanche dangers as well as other tips. Knowing how to avoid avalanche conditions will make your trip safer and more fun.

How to Use This Book

Think of this book as a sort of narrative, broad-scale map to be used for initial trip-planning overview. You can sit back and say to yourself, "Now where should I explore this weekend?" or, perhaps, "Which Utah wild area do I want to learn more about?" Start with the statewide locator map to assess the geographic setting, select an area, and then focus in for greater detail. Begin by referring to the "Trips at a Glance" matrix (Appendix B) for a quick overview of all the trips presented, listed by name, location, recreational activities, distance, and difficulty.

The book divides the state into four major regions: Basin and Range, Hot Desert, Colorado Plateau, and Middle Rocky Mountains and Plateaus. Boundaries between regions are imprecise, but each wildland area or complex of areas falls logically into one of the regions based on its topography, plant communities, and geographic location.

Each of the 45 Utah wildlands in this book is a contiguous, unroaded expanse of undeveloped, mostly federal land or a cluster of two or more roadless areas in close proximity, sharing similar physical characteristics. Where a wildland is shared by two or more land management agencies and/or clustered with two or more roadless areas it is referred to as a "complex." Of the 45 wildlands portrayed in *Wild Utah,* only portions of 15 have been formally designated by Congress as wilderness under the 1964 Wilderness Act. A given wildland is managed by one or more of four federal agencies: the National Park Service, U.S. Fish and Wildlife Service, Bureau of Land Management (BLM), and the

USDA Forest Service. Portions of some of the areas also contain tribal, state, and individual or corporate private land. In terms of number of areas and acreage, the BLM is by far the largest administrative force in Utah. These 45 wildlands encompass most of wild Utah, but they do not add up to a comprehensive inventory of Utah's bountiful wildland heritage. Nor do they represent any kind of priority for wilderness designation, even though all of these publicly administered wildlands are suitable for wilderness as defined by Congress in the Wilderness Act. Rather, these individual areas and complexes of areas sample the richness and diversity of wild Utah.

Trip planning information for each wildland is presented as follows:

THE MAPS—The statewide locator map near the beginning of the book shows the 45 wildlands covered in the book. A more detailed map accompanies the information blocks for each wildland. This map distinguishes between wilderness and nonwilderness, shows major trails and access points, and indicates the driving distance from featured trailheads to the nearest highway or town. These maps are an important reference for trip planning, but in the field they are no substitute for the applicable wilderness maps, surface management maps, or travel plan maps listed in the information blocks or for the 1:24,000 scale topographic maps for each wildland listed in Appendix E.

INFORMATION BLOCKS—contain quick facts, including:

1) *Location*—the direction and straight-line distance to that portion of the wildland closest to the largest and/or nearest town. This is intended only to give a general idea as to where the area is in the vast untamed spaces of wild Utah.

2) *Size*—measured as the total contiguous roadless area or complex of areas in acres, regardless of ownership or land status, based on the best available information. The idea here is to avoid the artificial fragmentation of wildlands that all too often occurs when two or more agencies are involved.

3) *Administration*—names of the responsible federal and state offices. See Appendix D for addresses of offices that administer state and federal land in Utah as well as for the individual wildlands portrayed by this book.

4) *Management status*—reveals the area's designation as wilderness, wilderness study area, national park, national recreation area, unprotected nonwilderness roadless area, and so on. Status changes continually, so some idea is given as to whether a portion of the roadless area is slated for future resource development. Readers are encouraged to obtain more detailed information from the managing agency and to then work with the agency, conservation groups (see Appendix C), and Congress toward improved management and protection of our Utah wildlands.

5) *Ecosystems*—based largely on the broad Kuchler classifications used by federal agencies for Ecosystem Management, along with the major potential natural vegetation (PNV) types that would exist if natural plant succession is allowed to occur with minimum human interference. In short, PNV represents site capability. Because of human and natural disturbances PNV may not be the same as the actual vegetation in an area.

6) *Elevation range*—the minimum and maximum elevations above sea level are listed to give an idea of vertical relief. In some cases the location of these low and high points is given for geographical orientation, especially when multi-area complexes are involved. Where several roadless areas are clustered in a complex, these two points will often exist in different roadless areas.

7) *Established trails/routes*—distances are estimated in miles of designated or numbered trails that may or may not be regularly maintained or of road and/ or informal trails suitable for nonmotorized travel. Most of wild Utah is trail-less, with the best route often being a natural corridor, such as a canyon. In many cases the only trails are what the BLM refers to as "vehicle ways." These are sets of tracks created solely by the passage of vehicles, not by construction and regular maintenance. It is important to remember that a "vehicle way" is not a road and its presence does not disqualify lands for wilderness designation. BLM wildlands in particular are often crisscrossed by these primitive ways, which are in fact far better suited for hiking and horseback riding than for vehicular travel. The presence of a "vehicle way" does not detract from the roadlessness of an area.

Constructed roads that penetrate a roadless area are usually excised from the boundary; that is, the boundary is drawn around the roads, making them resemble a cherry stem on a map; hence the term "cherry-stemmed road."

8) *Maximum core to perimeter distance*—the greatest distance (in air miles) that a visitor inside the roadless area can be from the closest road. Exceptions abound, but this figure gives you some idea as to the wildness of the country in terms of fragmentation, remoteness, and solitude. Note that this depth of the wild country estimate is more a function of area shape than of area size. Where two or more areas exist within a complex the figure given is for the area within the complex having the greatest core to perimeter distance.

9) *Activities*—those nonmotorized pursuits for which the area is best suited, from both a legal standpoint in the case of wilderness as well as the physical lay of the land. Hiking is the common denominator activity of every area. Where applicable, hunting is mentioned as one of the activities in a broad sense, but please remember that this book is not a hunting guide, which would be a major book in its own right. Legal hunting in season takes place in most of these wildlands, including designated wilderness, except for those in national parks, certain tribal lands, and specially restricted areas.

10) *Maps*—a listing of the applicable agency travel maps, surface management maps, or recreation access maps, which are usually small-scale, along with the applicable wilderness map on a contour base. The BLM 1:100,000 scale surface management maps and some of the national forest maps are on a topographic base, usually with 50-meter contour intervals.

11) *Overview*—this narrative captures a bit of the "personality" of the country, including its geology, landforms, flora and fauna, prehistory and history, major points of interest, and, in some cases, management history or status. The idea here is to give you a broad mental image of the country.

12) *Recreational uses*—this section expands on suitable activities and seasons, with occasional trip ideas woven into the text. In keeping with the idea of helping to redistribute use, some of the more heavily visited trails and sites are indicated, where applicable. Your route may still include these more popular locations, but at least you'll know ahead of time that your chances for solitude will be reduced.

13) *How to get there*—detailed driving instructions to the trailheads or jumping off points for the suggested trips. To follow these instructions start with the beginning reference point, which might be a nearby town or important road junction. In many cases an unsigned trailhead may be nothing more than a wide spot in the road for parking. Most road distances were measured with our car odometer and are rounded to the nearest mile, and may vary compared to other car odometers.

14) *A suggested trip idea*—One or more trips are suggested within each wildland. Most of these trips describe routes through lightly used locations, to help redistribute recreational use. These suggestions cover a variety of activities, travel modes, and seasons. Many of the sample trips are on cross-country routes or informal trails because that is all that is available in Utah's mostly trailless canyons and peaks. Those who plan to do any of the suggested bushwhacks through trailless terrain must carry and know how to use a compass and topo map. They should also do everything possible to travel lightly in a fragile environment while minimizing disturbance to wildlife and ecologically sensitive sites.

15) *Distance in miles (round trip, loop, or point-to-point total)*—this is provided along with the starting and maximum elevations of the suggested route. In a few instances the minimum rather than maximum elevation is given when the starting elevation is the highest point, such as in a river float trip. Elevations were measured to the nearest 10 feet with an altimeter, adjusted whenever possible at known points of elevation. An added check was made on 7.5-minute, 1:24,000 scale topographic maps with 20- or 40-foot contour intervals.

16) *Difficulty rating*—The rating from "easy" to "strenuous" is subjective, but is based on the authors' first-hand experience on each sample trip. Easy trips present no difficulty to travelers of all abilities. Moderate trips are challenging to inexperienced travelers. Moderately strenuous will tax even the experienced. Strenuous routes are extremely difficult and challenging, even for the most seasoned backcountry adventurers. Distance, elevation gain and loss, route condition, season, and terrain were considered in assigning the difficulty rating. There are, of course, many variables. The easiest hike can be sheer agony if you run out of water in extreme heat—a definite no-no.

17) *Best months*—dates listed are based largely on the moderate temperature months for the particular trip, and are greatly influenced by elevation. Additional consideration is given to seasonal road access in the higher country. The "best months" for the suggested route may not be best for catching wildflowers in full bloom, a phenomenon that is highly localized and dependent on elevation and rainfall.

18) *Topo map*—the detailed 1:24,000 scale (7.5 minute) topographic map(s) covering the suggested route are listed. Because many sample trips involve off-trail route-finding, topo maps are every bit as important as a pair of well-broken-in hiking boots.

19) *Trip narrative*—the suggested trip and key attractions are described in sufficient detail to avoid getting lost, but not in so much detail that it takes away the surprises and hidden discoveries tucked away along or near each route.

An old cabin from an early logging settlement in the High Uintas.

Appendix A presents a comprehensive gear list organized so that you can add, subtract, and vary items according to the season, length, and type of trip. Appendix B, "Trips at a Glance," is an alphabetical listing by region of every trip outlined in the book. This appendix addresses the often-asked questions of type, distance, and difficulty. Appendix C contains the names, addresses, and phone numbers of the state and federal land management agencies in Utah, including those responsible for managing the 45 wildlands and complexes of wildlands featured in *Wild Utah*. Contact the appropriate agency to get on the mailing list for those wildlands you are most concerned about and to receive current information about land status, resource issues, recreation permits, and public access. It is also important to check in with the managing office or closest ranger station before the trip for an update on road access, trails, permits, water, and weather. Keep in mind that the only certainty is change. The Appendix D listing of conservation groups is presented for those of you who want to become more actively involved in advocating the protection of Utah's wildlands.

The last page in the book is a roadless area monitoring form that you are invited to reproduce and use on future trips as a means of keeping track of the wildlands you visit. To help with future updates we would be delighted to receive a copy of any of your visitation records, care of Falcon Publishing, P.O. Box 1718, Helena, Montana 59624. With your permission this information may be shared with the applicable citizen conservation group and/or land management agency.

Introduction

The land west of Interstate 15, one-third of Utah, is often regarded as a vast wasteland. Lacking vast forested mountain slopes, slickrock canyons, and rushing rivers, this area at first glance has none of the charismatic scenery characteristic of the rest of the state. But the West Desert of Utah does have mountains, canyons, and rivers—they are just spread out, with a lot of flat desert between them. The mountain ranges here present similar silhouettes on the flat desert skyline, but closer inspection reveals their unique qualities and secret beauty.

From the Sierras to the Wasatch Range, this region is striped with block-fault mountain ranges created 20 to 60 million years ago by the stretching of the earth's crust. Jutting sharply above the desert floor at angles of 60 degrees or more, the ranges are sloped on their western side and have sharp escarpments on the east, like a series of skateboard jumps facing eastward. The Great Basin of Nevada and western Utah is corrugated with these north-south running ranges. Closer together in Nevada, more spread out in Utah, they feature abrupt canyons and sharp ridges. In addition to the fault action, geologic excitement is also evidenced by remains of volcanic activity. Western Utah is home to craters, cinder cones, and lava flows.

A second chapter in the geologic history occurred more recently, with the end of the Ice Age 10,000 to 12,000 years ago. The huge basin filled with glacial run-off, forming Lake Bonneville, 1,000 feet deep and spread over 20,000 square miles of northwestern Utah. The mountain ranges became islands in this vast inland sea. Eventually the lake shrank, leaving only traces of water behind. Today Utah Lake, Great Salt Lake, and Sevier Lake are vestigial reminders of Lake Bonneville.

Despite the vanishing lake and a drier climate, the mountains are still islands, but now they are in a sea of desert. Unable to relocate due to the surrounding "sea," wildlife and vegetation cling to their isolated niches. Some migrated to the islands on the wind or in bird droppings. Others, such as the Lake Bonneville cutthroat trout in the Deep Creek Range, are left over from the Pleistocene Era; their habitat simply contracted. Such microcosmic ecosystems are of interest to biologists and others concerned with island biogeography because existence here is precarious. The balance can be easily upset, and there is no corridor by which to escape.

Although they may appear naked from a distance, the higher elevations feature a diversity of vegetation in spite of the harsh conditions. Above 8,000 feet, annual precipitation supports Douglas-fir, spruce, subalpine fir, ponderosa pine, limber pine, and aspen. During spring wildflowers coat meadows and basins. Bristlecone pines cling to rocky slopes. At drier, lower elevations, the vegetative cover shifts to pinyon-juniper woodland, gnarly mountain mahogany, and the ubiquitous sagebrush. At the lowest elevations, the sage and shadscale brush community and grasses grow between boulders and rock outcroppings. The arid ecosystem of the basin has been changed by an invader—cheatgrass—that crowds out the native bunchgrasses and shrubs. This intruder has created its own fire regime: fires now sweep the landscape in early and mid-summer while the native perennial grasses are still growing and vulnerable, but the cheatgrass, as an annual, has already dropped its seeds.

These mountain ranges are home to diverse wildlife. Mule deer, mountain lion, coyote, kit fox, skunk, jack rabbit, migratory birds, and waterfowl—all find their niche in the remote mountains. The rocky crags also provide nesting sites for raptors. Bald and golden eagles and peregrine falcons are often sighted soaring on the thermals off the cliffs above the desert, watching for tasty rodents below. Bighorn sheep and pronghorn antelope were eliminated by overgrazing livestock, habitat destruction, and poaching, but these species are being reintroduced. Small herds of wild horses can be found in hidden mountain valleys, such as on King Top and in the Mountain Home Range.

Utahns are, fortunately, showing a heightened interest in the value of maintaining these wilderness areas in their pristine condition. More people are also discovering the areas' untapped recreational opportunities. If you think the Basin is wasteland, exploring its ranges is certain to change your mind.

Silver Island Mountains

Location: 10 miles northeast of Wendover, on the northwestern edge of Utah.
Size: 27,200 acres.
Administration: BLM Salt Lake District, Bear River Resource Area.
Management status: Unprotected BLM roadless.
Ecosystems: Intermountain sagebrush province ecoregion, with potential natural vegetation of pinyon-juniper woodland.
Elevation range: 4,223 to 7,563 feet (Graham Peak).
Established trails/routes: No trails.
Maximum core to perimeter distance: 2 miles.
Activities: Hiking, archeology, and geology.
Maps: BLM 1:100,000 scale surface management/land ownership map (50 meter contour), entitled "Bonneville Salt Flat." See Appendix E for a list of the three topo maps covering the roadless area.

OVERVIEW: At the far western edge of the Great Salt Lake Desert, the Silver Island Range protrudes above the sand dunes, alkali and mud flats, and salt flats of this arid lunar landscape. In prehistoric times, when Lake Bonneville covered the region, the range was a real island instead of a metaphorical one. Although the BLM omitted the 27,200 acres of desert mountains from the wilderness process, the Utah Wilderness Coalition is unwilling to allow these roadless acres to be forgotten and has proposed that the northeastern end of the range be protected as wilderness.

The mining era left its mark on all Basin and Range mountains; the Silvers are no exception, but the residual effects are light. A jeep trail that cuts across the range east of Silver Island Pass marks the area's western boundary, and an unimproved road circles the range, establishing the perimeter. Within these boundaries, the Silvers are largely intact. Three dead-end roads represent only short intrusions of 2 miles or less; even these have faded back into the desert. Such "cherry-stemmed" roads—short, dead-end spurs surrounded by roadless lands—are common in Utah's rugged landscape. The lightly used Silver Island Canyon Road divides Cobb Peak from the main range. This northern 13-square-mile section has been untouched by roads and mining activities. Elsewhere old jeep routes are gradually being reclaimed by natural processes in this

I   SILVER ISLAND MOUNTAINS

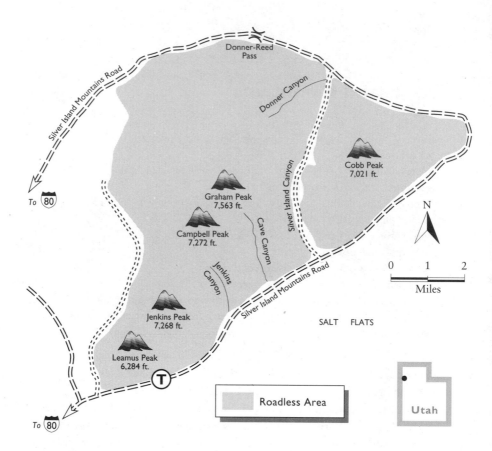

Donner-Reed
Pass

Silver Island Mountains Road

To 80

Donner Canyon

Cobb Peak
7,021 ft.

Silver Island Canyon

Graham Peak
7,563 ft.

Campbell Peak
7,272 ft.

Cave Canyon

Jenkins Canyon

N

Jenkins Peak
7,268 ft.

Silver Island Mountains Road

SALT   FLATS

0   1   2

Miles

Leamus Peak
6,284 ft.

T

To 80

Roadless Area

Utah

harsh desert climate. The wind, rather than vegetation, is largely responsible for this work.

Located just above the famed Bonneville raceway, these eternal mountains have formed the backdrop to many high-tech events focusing on speed. The other human activity in the area involves the military. The Wendover bombing and gunnery range, immediately adjacent to the east and south, was booming during World War II; military use has diminished, but Hill Air Force Base continues to run training flights over the eastern sector.

The mountains represent an island of tranquility in this noisy sea. Surrounded by sand dunes and mud flats, and a perimeter road, the range rises, to over 7,000 feet, with a string of five named peaks punctuating the ridge: Leamus (6,284 feet), Jenkins (7,268 feet), Campbell (7,272 feet), Graham (7,563 feet), and Cobb (7,021 feet). Wave terraces of ancient Lake Bonneville are visible on the lower alluvial slopes of the range. Also of geologic interest are the deposits of tufa—a porous, volcanic rock—in the Cobb Peak unit. The rugged slopes of the range are dotted with numerous caves, especially in the Graham Peak area. Archeological research has been done at nearby Danger Cave, an undeveloped state park below the southwest slope of the range. There, artifacts dating back 10,000 years confirm several waves of prehistoric human presence. It is likely that at least some of the caves in the main range were used by Fremont or Shoshone people. The ill-fated Donner-Reed party traveled across the northern Silver Islands via Donner-Reed Pass on its way to the Sierras. In the last century the pursuit of mineral wealth has brought prospectors to the mountains, with little success. Mine adits, ruins of buildings, and remnants of mining equipment are all that remain.

Little or no precipitation falls here, and the dry Silvers contain only ephemeral streams and no springs. Only sparse desert vegetation can survive here, such as blackbrush, shadscale, rabbitbrush, and sagebrush. The animal population is likewise limited in variety and numbers, with desert rodents and reptiles, and a few migratory raptors pausing for a meal.

The Silvers, drifting like a mirage above the waves of desert heat, are a raw desert range, unique in their untrammeled state.

RECREATIONAL USES: The lack of water limits recreational uses of the Silver Island Range to day hikes. With the perimeter road, accessibility is not a problem for explorations into any parts of the mountains. The only limiting factor is the rugged topography. The cherry-stemmed jeep roads indicated on the topo maps are disappearing due to disuse, so travelers should begin hikes from the main road.

Numerous caves attract visitors interested in both geology and archeology. History and mining buffs are drawn to the mine sites. Here, as elsewhere in Utah, considerable caution is required around old mine sites. Both buildings and mine shafts can be hazardous. It is important to remember, too, that the federal Antiquities Act protects artifacts 50 years old and older, so it is unlawful to remove miners' "trash." Please leave items untouched so others can discover the local history for themselves.

Outings to the high ridges are considered moderate in cool weather. Any activity here is considered strenuous from May through September. Getting to the peaks, however, is well worth the effort—the view is magnificent on a clear western Utah day!

HOW TO GET THERE: From I-80, take Exit 4, about 4 miles east of Wendover on the Nevada-Utah state line. Go north, following the sign to the Bonneville Speedway. At the Y 1.2 miles north of the freeway, go left, following the BLM sign for the Silver Island Mountains. About 1 mile farther turn right at the next Silver Island sign. This improved dirt road passes downwind from the detritus at the town landfill and then bends north along the salt flats with the mountains on the left. Drive north 14 miles. Here the rocky ridges of the mountains drop close to the road. Park on the side of the lightly used road and begin your hike here.

Day hike

Central Silvers Ramble

Distance: 2 to 5 miles.
Starting and maximum elevations: 4,200 feet and 5,500 feet.
Difficulty: Moderate.
Best months: October through April.
Topo map: Graham Peak-UT.

The ragged Silver Island Range is a stereotypical desert range with jagged ridges, talus and scree slopes, wind, and barren land—all the hostile components of impenetrable mountains. But the Silvers also have surprising and delightful features that lure the hiker. In spring, colorful evening primrose, aster, and paintbrush dot the alluvial fans. Deer droppings prove that wildlife does endure here. The varieties of rock and the many formations, including caves, will delight those with a geologic bent. But the crumbly limestone, shaggy rough conglomerates, and fractured metamorphics make hiking in the Silvers a challenge.

Given the difficult terrain, it is advisable to approach the outing described here as a ramble instead of focusing on a destination. From the roadside trailhead, wind your way up the alluvial fan, picking your path carefully as it steepens. It is tough work to get up the loose slopes, but you'll be rewarded with great views as well as fascinating geology at your feet.

Gaining the summit of one of the low ridges is quite a feat in this rough country.

This is a cool-weather hike; no shade exists. The shadscale is dwarfed and sparse. Isolated junipers eke out a living on the range's lower slopes. The textures and stripes of the geologic formations provide an artistic touch that the vegetation lacks. The jagged high ridges are difficult to reach, and most of the Silvers' peaks are guarded by precipices. Graham Peak (7,563 feet) is the most climbable among them, with the best route on its southeastern side. The 6-mile round trip would require a full day as well as two or three full canteens.

Caves large and small dot the Silvers. Most of them sit high on the steep mountain walls beyond the reach of hikers. Also on the slopes are the etched wave benches of Lake Bonneville, a vivid reminder of the vast geologic and ecologic changes that this land has witnessed.

An outing in the Silvers is a trip back to prehistoric times, providing a sharp contrast to the bustling modern world down the road in the Wendover area. The Silvers loom in the distance as travelers approach on I-80 heading west, but they are seldom visited. A close encounter with this range provides greater understanding of the sense of eternity that exists here in the desert.

Cedar Mountains

2

Location: 52 miles southwest of Salt Lake City, in northwestern Utah.
Size: 62,100 acres.
Administration: BLM Salt Lake District, Pony Express Resource Area.
Management status: BLM wilderness study area (50,500 acres); BLM and private roadless lands (11,600 acres).
Ecosystems: Intermountain sagebrush province ecoregion. Potential natural vegetation is juniper-pinyon woodland.
Elevation range: 4,500 to 7,712 feet (Cedar Point).
Established trails/routes: Short spur routes totaling 18 miles of "vehicle ways" in 11 separate canyon access routes; wild horse trails along divide and east side.
Maximum core to perimeter distance: 3 miles.
Activities: Hiking, horseback riding, hunting, photography, and nature study.
Maps: BLM 1:100,000 scale surface management/land ownership maps (50 meter contour intervals) entitled "Tooele" and "Rush Valley." See Appendix E for a listing of the six topo maps covering the roadless area.

OVERVIEW: Encircled by the Great Salt Lake Desert, the wide open Cedar Mountains display the classic signatures of Basin and Range topography: a north-to-south trending range twisted with complex faulting, situated along an asymmetrical axis. A substantial roadless area of more than 60,000 acres occupies the central heart of this semi-arid upthrust, stretching for 20 miles along a main ridgetop from Hastings Pass south to Rydalch Pass. The crest averages well above 6,000 feet with numerous points above 6,800 feet. From mud and alkaline flats on the west side the mountains rise a moderate 2,800 feet over a distance of 4 miles to 7,712-foot Cedar Point.

Steep, rugged cliffs rise and fall intermittently along 8 miles of east-facing slopes. Erosion has uncovered these cliffs as vertical sedimentary formations that adorn both sides of east-to-west trending canyons. Geologists have identified more than 20,000 feet of geologic strata compressed and slanted sideways within a mere 3,200 feet of vertical relief. The southern reaches of the roadless area are distinguished by volcanic flows of andesite along with pyramid-studded columns of colorful basalt on 6,921-foot Tabbys Peak. Elsewhere,

2 **CEDAR MOUNTAINS**

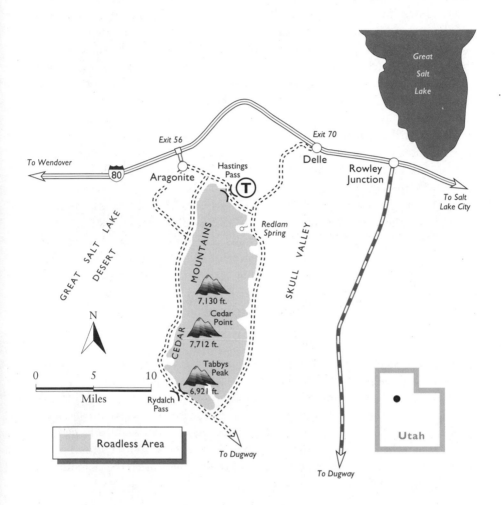

gently rounded hillsides contrast with layers of iron-gray limestone interspersed with rusty, brown bands.

The lower foothills are thinly clad with a mix of salt-tolerant greasewood, shadscale, and horsebrush. Pickleweed and cheatgrass dominate the understory. A transition to juniper occurs about 1 mile above sea level. At first we find big and black sagebrush, rabbitbrush, Mormon tea, bluebunch wheatgrass, and only a few scattered juniper trees. Climbing higher, juniper gradually thickens on the upper slopes. Left to the devices of natural plant succession, the potential vegetation of these mountains would be pinyon-juniper. But you'd be hard-pressed to find a single pinyon pine in the Cedars, which, incidentally, derive their name from the shaggy cedar-like appearance of juniper.

The Cedar Mountains are perhaps best known for their rarely seen population of some 200 wild horses, only about 20 of which live there during summer. Despite the complete lack of perennial streams in these sparsely vegetated mountains, they are home to as many as 137 wildlife species, most of which are birds. Golden eagles soar the thermals year-round and bald eagles are a wintertime migrant. The Cedars are also frequented by a variety of other raptors common to the Great Basin, including ferruginous and Swainson's hawks. A stable mule deer herd of some 300 head browses these barren shrublands, along with a few fleet-footed pronghorn antelope attracted to open alkaline flats on the west side below 5,000 feet. From this elevation the mountains begin to take form, rising to the central ridgetop that is their hallmark.

In the northern reaches cultural surveys have discovered 17 archeological sites, including a petroglyph and numerous scatters of stone tools and pottery shards left by ancient hunter-gatherers on sand dunes in the foothills between 4,700 and 5,400 feet. From the prehistoric to the historic, early travelers and white explorers crossed Hastings Pass, including Frémont's Third Expedition in 1845 and the ill-fated Donner-Reed party a year later. With cultural inventories largely confined to the north end of the roadless area, the potential for finding additional sites is high.

RECREATIONAL USES: The Cedar Range receives light recreational visitation by any measure—fewer than 400 annual visitor days estimated during BLM's wilderness study of nearly 20 years ago. Some off-road vehicle use takes place on 18 miles of jeep trails and doubletrack that touch or enter the edge of the roadless area in 11 separate access routes to all but the north end of the wilderness study area. Although suitable for hiking, most of the tracks are short spur routes in canyon bottoms, the longest of which extends 3 miles up Wild Cat Canyon in the south. Those few intrepid souls who penetrate the interior pursue hiking, horseback riding, geological study, or hunting for the occasional mule deer or the rapid flush of an upland bird, notably chukar.

Lack of water limits extended overnight trips—there are no perennial streams within the roadless area and only two year-round water sources nearby: Redlam Spring and Quincy Spring. Intermittent stream flows are born from ephemeral spring snowmelt and summer thunderstorms. In the past there has been some discussion of a possible crestline trail from White Rocks north to Hastings Pass—a lengthy excursion in the high and the dry of a Great Salt Lake Desert mountain range. Although few hikers trek the main ridge, much of the crest is easily traversed despite the absence of a formal trail. Some wild horse trails exist, but as one ventures northward, ever deeper into the country, evidence of these untamed creatures diminishes.

A prime motivation for traversing the main dividing ridge is an unending vista. The emptiness and vastness of the Great Basin is overpowering—from the Wasatch Front looking east to the Basin and Range country spreading westward and southward to infinity. Only an hour's drive west of Salt Lake City, the Cedars can be readily accessed by way of Interstate 80.

HOW TO GET THERE: From the east on Interstate 80, take Exit 70 for Delle and head south, quickly turning west on a gravel road that parallels the interstate for about 2 miles to a junction with an old sign that reads "Hastings Pass 9 miles, Redlam Spring 12 miles." Turn left and stay on the main improved dirt road, which changes to gravel after about 2 miles. Continue on this main gravel road for about 7 miles to an unsigned junction at the northeast corner of the roadless area. Turn right and head northwest up a rough two-wheel-drive dirt road, reaching Hastings Pass after another 4 miles. Park either at the pass or alongside a jeep track about 0.25 mile south of the pass.

Hastings Pass can also be reached from the west by taking Exit 56 from I-80, driving 2 miles south to the industrial site of Aragonite, and continuing another 4 or 5 miles on a rough unimproved dirt road to the pass. This access is not recommended, however, because the road passes through the middle of an active rock quarry on private land a mile or so below the pass.

Day hike or horseback ride

Cedar Mountain Ridge Ramble

Distance: 6 to 12 miles out and back.
Starting and maximum elevations: 5,780 feet (Hastings Pass) and 6,612 feet.
Difficulty: Easy.
Best months: April through May.
Topo map: Hastings Pass-UT.

From the pass, follow the doubletrack southward, soon intersecting the signed Hastings Cutoff Road—a pioneer route used in the 1840s. Follow a distinct trail visible climbing the hillside to the south. This ridgeline path gains

600 feet in 0.5 mile to a rounded hilltop, opening to expansive vistas of the broad eastern slopes of the Cedar Mountains. A recent fire lends diversity to juniper and grass-clad hills and ridges in these northern reaches of the 62,100-acre Cedar Mountains roadless area. The well-defined trail fades after about 0.6 mile as the divide swings left. No matter—the open crest offers an easy route to follow. The dividing ridge presents an early season snow-free ramble that is especially enjoyable in the spring, when a colorful array of wildflowers decorates the undulating terrain. Red paintbrush, white phlox, and purple vetch are neatly arranged in widely spaced patches. These rolling mountains are a pleasing contrast to their more rugged neighbors—the Stansburys, Deep Creeks, Silver Island Mountains, House Range, and Wah Wahs—all of which can be seen in a continuous 360-degree view along the curving crest of the Cedars.

The weaving, up-and-down divide is punctuated with occasional limestone outcrops and west-side cliffs. Some of the saddles are covered with windblown sand from the desert floor of Skull Valley. Abundant horse sign along the ridge reminds us that as many as 200 wild horses make their home here.

The first prominent point on the divide distinguished by a sheer limestone cliff face makes a scenic turn-around destination for a 6- to 7-mile, half-day round trip. From here the pond of Redlam Spring can be seen below to the southeast. Broad grassy ridges, swales, and southwestern slopes made darker by dense clumps of juniper extend southward toward the 7,712-foot apex of Cedar Point, inviting further exploration. From a practical standpoint, however, the absence of springs along this dry divide limits trip duration by the amount of water that can be carried.

Stansbury Mountains Wilderness Complex 3

Location: 40 miles southwest of Salt Lake City, in northwest Utah.
Size: 80,000 acres.
Administration: USDAFS Wasatch-Cache National Forest, Salt Lake Ranger District; BLM Salt Lake District, Pony Express Resource Area.
Management status: Deseret Peak Wilderness (25,500 acres); national forest roadless land (32,000 acres); North Stansbury Wilderness Study Area (10,480 acres); BLM roadless land (12,020 acres).
Ecosystems: Intermountain sagebrush province ecoregion of pinyon-juniper woodland, with spruce, fir, and Douglas-fir at higher elevations.
Elevation range: 4,200 to 11,031 feet (Deseret Peak).
Established trails/routes: 31 miles in national forest; none in BLM.
Maximum core to perimeter distance: 2.5 miles.
Activities: Hiking, backpacking, hunting, horseback riding, fishing, photography, birdwatching.
Maps: BLM 1:100,000 scale surface management/land ownership maps (50-meter contour interval) entitled "Tooele" and "Rush Valley;" 1994 half-inch/mile map entitled "Wasatch-Cache National Forest—Salt Lake, Kamas, Evanston, and Mount View Ranger Districts" (50 meter contour interval). See Appendix E for a listing of the eight topo maps covering the entire complex.

OVERVIEW: Only an hour west of Salt Lake City, the dramatic Stansbury Mountain Range runs 30 miles north to south with peaks along the jagged ridge jutting to 10,000 feet and higher. The administration of this single eco-logical unit is divided between the BLM and the USDA Forest Service, and is further divided within those agencies between wilderness study area and roadless BLM, and wilderness and roadless national forest, making for a very jumbled map. For Wasatch Front recreationists, the Deseret Peak Wilderness in the center of the complex is a popular destination. To the north and south of the rectangular wilderness lie thousands of acres of roadless national forest. At the northern end of the range, the BLM North Stansbury Wilderness Study Area runs 6 miles along the spine of the mountain range before its gradual descent to the alkali flats of Skull Valley.

The Stansburys are a block-fault range typical of the Basin and Range prov-

3 STANSBURY MTNS WILDERNESS COMPLEX

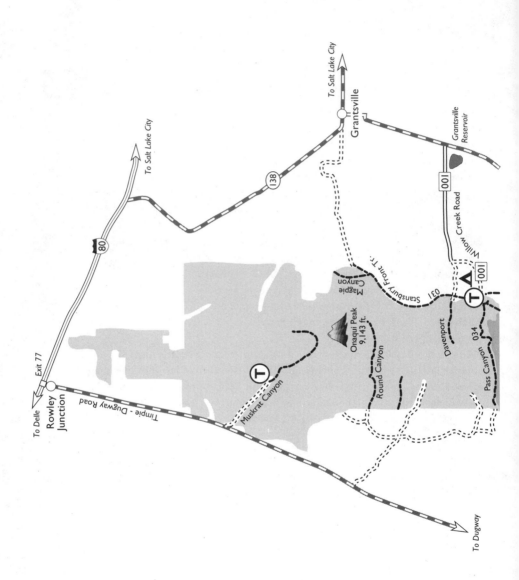

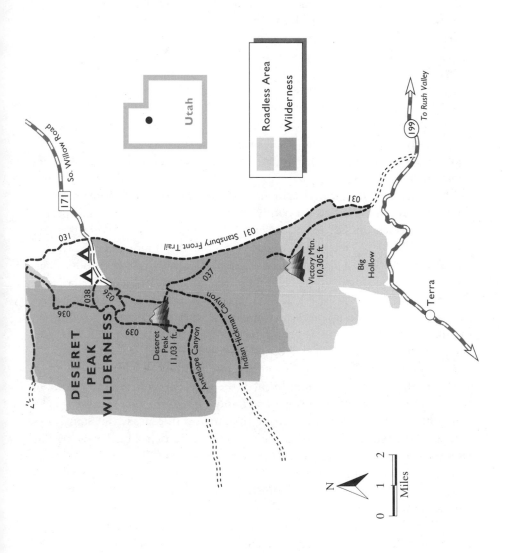

ince, with quartzites and resistant carbonates forming the peaks, ridges, and cliffs, all cut by rugged canyons. To the west is a sharp escarpment, and the eastern side is also steep. Here glaciated cirques are reminders of the Ice Age. Penetrating the Stansburys from the east involves strenuous hiking. Largely of Paleozoic origin, the Stansbury rock types also contain Tertiary volcanics, mostly basalt and latite, as well as some small basalt flows.

The vegetation is typical of island mountains in Utah's west desert. Shrubs, mountain mahogany, and grasses are found above 7,500 feet. Below, Utah juniper and sagebrush dominate, with some aspen. Douglas-fir and white fir can be found on north-facing slopes and in drainage bottoms at higher elevations. Currant, bitterbrush, serviceberry, chokecherry, and mountain snowberry form the understory at middle elevations. The lower foothills and benches support saltbrush and sagebrush. Springtime brings a lush display of wildflowers to the Stansburys' slopes. Annual precipitation is 19 to 30 inches depending on elevation.

Although the Stansburys' streams are only intermittent, and springs are rare, the range supports a broad array of wildlife: more than 50 mammal species, 114 bird species, and 15 reptile species. Mule deer, cougar, and bobcat are numerous. Both golden and bald eagles soar along the mountain walls. Grouse and chukar are the resident gamebirds. The BLM has plans to reintroduce bighorn sheep in the North Stansbury Wilderness Study Area. There is some cattle grazing in the North Stansbury BLM country, but it is limited by steep, poorly vegetated uplands and lack of year-round water. Predator control activities on the northern BLM unit have been aimed at eliminating coyote and cougar. There are no wild horses or burros in the Stansburys.

Cultural sites are rare in the Tooele region south of Great Salt Lake. Only spots of lithic scatter have been located, the rock chip and tool remnants of Archaic hunter-gatherer bands who certainly hunted for deer on these rocky slopes hundreds of years ago. During the nineteenth century the Stansburys witnessed the passage of American pioneers seeking riches further west. The Donner-Reed wagon train passed the northern edge of the range in 1846 on the way to its doom in the Sierras. Captain Howard Stansbury led the first group of white men around the perimeter of the Great Salt Lake in 1849, naming the landmark for later parties. Pony Express riders dashed by the southern flank in their brief heyday, from 1860–1861. It is unlikely that you will encounter artifacts of the mining era. The Monte Carlo Mine, just east of the North Stansbury Wilderness Study Area, was highly productive in its early twentieth-century boom time, but the rest of the range never enticed a flood of prospectors.

RECREATIONAL USES: The Deseret Peak Wilderness, designated by Congress in 1984, provides a popular camping and hiking destination for Salt Lake City residents from May through October. Six small campgrounds, with 36 sites among them, are located along South Willow Canyon Road southwest of Grantsville. All are at 6,000 feet and higher, so they are attractive for summer use. The Deseret Peak Trail takes off at the Loop Campground (7,400 feet) for the 7.5-mile loop hike with vistas of Tooele Valley, the Oquirrh range, Salt Lake, and the Wasatch Front. In winter backcountry powder skiing attracts enthusiasts away from the crowds at the Wasatch Front resorts. The South Willow Canyon area receives the heaviest use in the Deseret Peak Wilderness.

The Stansbury Front Trail runs along the entire eastern edge of the wilderness and on north 5 miles to the Magpie Canyon Trailhead in the national forest; this trail is open to singletrack motorized vehicles. Six roads on the eastern edge of the national forest, beyond the wilderness boundary, are also open to both off-road vehicles and snowmobile use. Consult the Salt Lake City Ranger District Travel Map (1992) for the specifics on motorized traffic. No vehicles, of course, are permitted in the wilderness.

While the outing to Deseret Peak, the range's highest, is spectacular, venturing into the less-traveled areas of the national forest and BLM lands will ensure greater solitude. The small O.P. Miller Campground and trailhead are a good jumping off point for the roadless area north of the wilderness. Or hike into the North Stansburys from the road south of Rowley Junction, walking up Muskrat Canyon to 9,143-foot Onaqui Peak. The view from the summit is magnificent, without the crowds common on the Deseret Peak trip.

For intrepid hikers who don't mind shuttling cars, the cross-country hike 30 miles along the Stansbury divide is an exciting backpack. The ridge from Timpic in the north (right off Interstate 80) provides spectacular panoramas. The drawback is the scarcity of water, but that can be remedied in early spring by melting snow on a cook stove.

In the lower elevations of the South Stansburys, in the Big Hollow BLM unit, horseback riding is popular in the rolling foothills out of the Clover Creek Campground. This is also an attractive area for deer and bird hunters, as is the BLM land on the northern end of the mountains. Just 3 miles north of the Stansbury Range, Timpie Springs Waterfowl Management Area is a mecca for shorebirds, migratory ducks and geese, and wading birds.

HOW TO GET THERE: *Muskrat Canyon:* From Interstate 80 on the southern edge of the Great Salt Lake, take Exit 77 (Rowley/Dugway) south 6 miles along the western side of the Stansbury Range. The arrow-straight road bends slightly to the west. About 0.5 mile after the bend, turn left on an unmarked rough gravel road. At 0.2 mile the road goes left at a power substation and becomes rough unimproved dirt, passable for a two-wheel-drive vehicle. High clearance will make the journey less stressful. Bear right at the Y, 0.5 mile from the pavement. Continue southeast up the alluvial fan, crossing numerous shallow dry washes, heading for the wide mouth of Muskrat Canyon.

Stop and park when the highly eroded jeep track limits further progress. The 5,150-foot contour is about as far as even the most intrepid four-wheel-drive, high-clearance vehicle should venture. This is about 2.5 miles from pavement. Park to the side of the lightly used double track, and begin your hike here.

North Stansbury Ridge: From I-80, on the southern edge of the Great Salt Lake, take Exit 88 (Burmester Road) south 6 miles to Grantsville. Turn right on Main Street. After 1 mile, turn south on West 400 at a Forest Service sign to the Stansbury Mountains trailheads. About 4 miles later turn right at the Forest Service sign to North Willow. This paved road (Forest Road 001) passes Grantsville Reservoir on the left. The road changes to gravel and then becomes an improved dirt, dry-weather road suitable for passenger vehicles. After another 4 miles, turn left at the sign to North Willow and the O.P. Miller Campground, which is 2 miles beyond the turn. The road deteriorates drastically beyond the campground. Only high-clearance, four-wheel-drive vehicles should continue. All others should park at the campground and begin the hike from there.

Day hike

Muskrat Canyon

Distance: 6 miles round trip.
Starting and maximum elevations: 5,150 feet and 7,200 feet.
Difficulty: Moderate.
Best months: April through May; October.
Topo maps: Timpie-UT; Salt Mountain-UT; North Willow Canyon-UT.

This hike into the 10,480-acre wilderness study area in the North Stansbury Range is a true mountain outing. While the area is close to Salt Lake City, it lacks the crowds and the vehicles common elsewhere in the Stansbury mountains. This basic out-and-back hike's low elevation means the route is clear of snow when the rest of the range is still buried.

From your parking spot, hike up the eroded doubletrack. At 0.3 mile you'll have to climb across a stock fence. Rising above Skull Valley, the old doubletrack makes an excellent trail, one you will especially appreciate as it cuts through a gooseberry and serviceberry thicket that would block all bushwhacking. The vegetation of the valley begins with sage and spotty juniper woodlands alternating with grassy meadows. Eventually, above 6,000 feet, Douglas-fir appear. The Muskrat drainage forms a broad valley; only after it angles sharply east at 6,800 feet does it exhibit features of a canyon. There the jagged slopes of 9,143-foot Onaqui Peak rise, coated with the dense green carpet of conifers between the exposed limestone ridges and cliffs.

The eroded track, our trail, reaches the high basin of the Muskrat at 6,800 feet, where it finally ends. Campsites here are used by hunters in the fall, and cattle graze at this elevation during warm summer months. The rusting hulk of an old Ford truck sits amid the boulders of the streambed, demonstrating the folly of trying to drive into this rocky world; its carcass marks the end of the old road. A stock trail continues up the Muskrat drainage, which angles sharply east into a fold on Onaqui's slope. The heavily vegetated bottom is clogged with mountain mahogany. Pinyon pine gives way to the dark green of coniferous forest and bright patches of aspen. Remains of a stock-watering system litter the dry streambed of the upper Muskrat. Every available drop or seep has been harnessed to fill the cows' trough. These efforts appear to be futile; the tank remains dry.

Although no water is visible in the stream, the upper Muskrat is a lush world, tucked away in the Stansburys, 2,000 feet above desolate Skull Valley. The sharply slanted layers of the mountain are tilted like loosely arranged library books. The range appears impenetrable from the valley below, but here in the canyon you can discern a route to the summit ridge. A route up the sloping north wall of the upper Muskrat leads to a 7,805-foot point on the high ridge, which, again with painstaking route-finding and detours, allows you to reach the main ridge at 8,800 feet. From there, Onaqui, which is at the northern edge of the Wasatch-Cache National Forest, lies 0.5 mile to the south. This strenuous trek requires lots of water and a very early start to complete the 10-mile journey during daylight.

For the basic out-and-back canyon excursion, you can retrace your steps, or, for a partial loop, take the high ridge that runs above the Muskrat on the west back down the valley, omitting more than a mile of the hike on the old road. To reach the ridge, stay to the left of the basin as you descend. A well-trod foot path angles up on the left to the flat-topped ridge, littered in the spring with penstemon and biscuit root, as well as traces of an old herders' 'shack. Stay on the right side of the grassy knoll that runs 200 feet above the Muskrat's bottom. Intriguing chunks of granite and quartz are scattered along the ridge, but even without a trail it's easy walking. Here too are enjoyable views of mountains, canyon, and valley, perfect for panoramic photos. Drop back down the ridge (cross country) for the final mile on the doubletrack. For greater comfort, descend from the ridge before you reach the juniper thicket that coats its foot. The return ridge route allows you to view the changing ecosystem, from moist montane to desert sagebrush, in the valley of the Muskrat.

This canyon hike is different from other outings in this mountain range, due not only to its topography but also to its solitude. The western side of the range is lightly visited; here a wilderness experience commences as soon as you get out of sight of your car.

Hiking up the North Fork Willow Creek Trail on the east slope of the Stansbury Mountains.

Day hike

North Willow Loop

Distance: 6 to 8 miles round trip.
Starting and maximum elevations: 6,800 to 8,843 feet.
Difficulty: Strenuous.
Best months: May to October.
Topo map: North Willow Canyon-UT.

This 15,000-acre national forest roadless area in the North Stansburys abuts the popular Deseret Peak Wilderness. Although dropped from wilderness consideration as one of the compromises made to gain passage of the 1984 Utah Wilderness Act, this mountainous roadless unit is the crucial bridge between the wilderness to the south and the BLM North Stansbury Wilderness Study Area on the north. The Stansbury Front Trail, the eastern boundary of the roadless region, is open to bikes and motorcycles, but the mountains themselves are too rugged for wheeled vehicles so they are a *de facto* roadless area. The congressional deal to drop the unit is not binding on citizens or on a future Congress; the North Stansbury area remains primitive and untrammeled, patiently awaiting its wilderness designation.

From the O.P. Miller Campground, which sits astride the Front Trail, hike on up the Forest Service road. About 0.5 mile from the campground, bear right at a Y on the lesser-used road. This lightly used, rough four-wheel-drive road becomes a trail 1.2 miles from the campground trailhead. Stream crossings are relatively easy, even in spring. The trail crosses the stream three times, twice as a road and once, later, as a trail. After the last crossing the trail curves around a ridge north of the stream. It then returns to the north side of the drainage to climb steeply to the summit ridge of the mountain range.

A cross-country route to the summit ridge is possible. At 7,356 feet, before the trail goes south to North Willow Creek, a direct, steep climb to the ridge keeps you out of the shaded creek canyon. In early spring, when the snow is still deep in east-facing forests, this open ridge route will be clear to the summit. Spires of limestone and jagged metamorphic rocks rise like a gothic cathedral above the steep grassy slopes. The dark granite of the mountain core looms above. Intermittent escarpments guard the ridge, but avenues are open to the energetic hiker willing to do some moderate scrambling.

The view from the 8,600-foot windy ridge is spectacular. The Oquirrh Range erupts on the other side of the Tooele Valley to the east. Peeking above it are the peaks of the Wasatch Front. Beyond Skull Valley on the west, the low rolling Cedars are in the foreground, with the vast Great Salt Lake Desert stretching into the distance. A sloping plateau of tundra vegetation makes travel along the ridge easy. Douglas-fir and mountain mahogany grow in thick patches, with broad grassy swales between. Far above the motorized world in the valleys below, the Stansburys are a quiet refuge.

Several options exist for a loop trip, although distance is limited due to lack of water in the high country. One alternative is to continue north on the summit ridge and then descend into Davenport Canyon, which parallels North Willow Canyon 1 mile to the north. The final leg of this 9-mile excursion would be on the Front Trail and might be unpleasant or even hazardous due to vehicle use. For a partial loop, avoiding the Front Trail, hike north on the summit ridge to the high, rounded point (8,760 feet) that stands between North Willow and Davenport canyons. From this point, drop down the precipitous but negotiable eastern edge to the ridge between the two drainages. You can follow the ridge as it curves and drops back to the campground and trailhead. Or, from the first saddle below the summit, you can descend into North Willow via a side drainage, returning to the original route where the doubletrack road vanished in the creek bottom. Dense vegetation in the side canyon makes the latter route challenging for the final 0.2 mile, but the Eden-like quality of this secluded side canyon compensates for your scratched legs.

The motor enthusiasts who visit North Willow do not get into the high backcountry. The Wasatch-Cache forest plan has made them welcome, but their play area is at low elevations. Fortunately, the result is a wilderness experience for hikers just beyond the end of the road.

Deep Creek Mountains

Location: About 80 miles southwest of Tooele and 42 miles south of Wendover, 5 miles east of the Utah-Nevada state line in west-central Utah.
Size: 90,200 acres.
Administration: BLM Salt Lake District, Pony Express Resource Area (north); BLM Richfield District, House Range Resource Area (south).
Management status: BLM wilderness study area (68,910 acres); unprotected BLM, state, and private roadless lands (21,290 acres).
Ecosystems: Intermountain sagebrush province ecoregion containing an unusually diverse mix of juniper-pinyon woodland, western ponderosa forest, Great Basin sagebrush, and saltbrush-greasewood, plus small areas of riparian vegetation along major streams and alpine tundra on the highest peaks.
Elevation range: 5,000 to 12,087 feet (Ibapah Peak).
Established trails/routes: About 5 miles of trails and 20 miles of jeep tracks in the major canyons well suited for hiking and horseback riding.
Maximum core to perimeter distance: 3 miles.
Activities: Hiking, backpacking, mountaineering, rock climbing, horseback riding, cross-country skiing, nature study, photography, hunting, limited fishing.
Maps: BLM 1:100,000 scale surface management/land ownership maps entitled "Wildcat Mountain" and "Fish Springs" (50 meter contour interval). See Appendix E for a listing of the nine topo maps covering the roadless area.

Overview: The isolated and remote Deep Creek Mountain Range is a wildland packed full of surprises. Certainly one would not expect to find glacial cirques, alpine tundra, verdant forests, wet meadows, ferns, and clear-flowing trout streams in the Great Basin of Utah's West Desert, yet these treasures, and many more, are among the hidden discoveries awaiting explorers of the Deep Creek Mountains.

Perhaps most startling is the more than 8,000 feet of vertical relief in only a couple of miles, from a 4,000-foot desert floor to lofty peaks rising suddenly to more than 12,000 feet. This dramatic increase in elevation makes the Deep Creeks Utah's most scenic West Desert range, as well as the most ecologically diverse. The white granite of the high peaks of Ibapah and Haystack contrasts vividly with the brilliantly colored talus adorning Red Mountain, exemplify-

4 DEEP CREEK MOUNTAINS

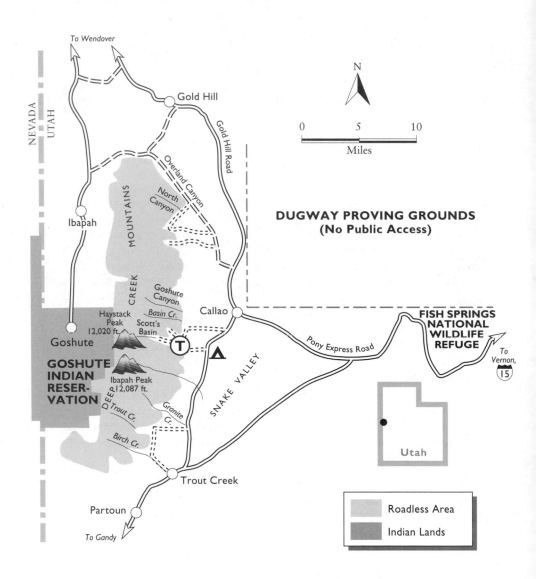

To Wendover

Gold Hill

Gold Hill Road

Overland Canyon

North Canyon

NEVADA

UTAH

Ibapah

DEEP CREEK MOUNTAINS

Goshute Canyon

Basin Cr.

Haystack Peak 12,020 ft.

Scott's Basin

Callao

T

Goshute

GOSHUTE INDIAN RESER-VATION

Ibapah Peak 12,087 ft.

DEEP Trout Cr.

Granite Cr.

SNAKE VALLEY

Birch Cr.

Trout Creek

Partoun

To Gandy

DUGWAY PROVING GROUNDS (No Public Access)

N

0   5   10
Miles

Pony Express Road

FISH SPRINGS NATIONAL WILDLIFE REFUGE

To Vernon, 15

Utah

Roadless Area

Indian Lands

ing unworldly geologic chaos. Glaciers have scoured these peaks, leaving steep, rocky basins that often hold late-summer snowbanks sitting directly above a surrounding sea of desert baked by searing heat in excess of 100 degrees F.

When climbing from lower elevations in the Deeps, hikers move through distinct landscapes, beginning in rolling, light-colored hills with washes, shallow canyons, and sparse vegetation. Above 7,000 feet the juniper-pinyon woodlands become thicker, filling the spaces between rugged rock outcroppings. From 8,000 to over 12,000 feet landforms consists of steep canyons and cliffs, high mountain meadows, and rocky peaks with patches of alpine tundra. The resulting grand tapestry is highlighted by the contrasting colors of green conifers, grasses, wildflowers, and desert shrubs, interspersed with rock forms of every shape, size, and color imaginable.

In a sense, the Deep Creeks defy superlatives by exaggerating typical Basin and Range topographic features. Their main ridge is north-south trending along massive block-faulted planes, soaring to steep, high mountains abruptly without the stairstep effect of foothills. A generous display of rock outcrops and cliff faces are formed of ancient sedimentary rocks, some of which are intruded with the granite known as Ibapah stock. Surrounded by high-angle faults, this stock accounts for much of the rugged grandeur of these mountains. In addition, volcanic dikes are exposed in the northwest portion of the roadless area. Geologic structures reflect the complexity of a land of overturned synclines and tightly folded anticlines.

Don't forget your binoculars—these mountains are near the center of a region estimated by the Environmental Protection Agency to possess the clearest and farthest visibility in the nation. The level expanse of the Great Salt Lake Desert stretches to the north and east. To the south and west, isolated mountain ranges dot the barren landscape to infinity. This is the setting of 30-mile-long, 8,000- to 12,000-foot crest that is the Deep Creek Range.

The Deep Creeks are an unusual mixing zone for plants of widely separated habitats—from the Pine Valley Mountains, 200 miles to the south, to the Wasatch Range and central plateaus, 100 miles to the north and east. Lower slopes are covered with the classic desert shrub communities of sagebrush, shadscale, saltbrush, Mormon tea, snakeweed, and cactus. Upslope, juniper-pinyon woodland dominates more than half of this wildland. The most diverse plant community is the montane forest found at the higher elevations of cooler north- and east-facing aspects. Here we find ponderosa pine, Douglas-fir, white fir, Engelmann spruce, and subalpine fir, as well as limber pine and bristlecone pine high up on windswept ridgelines. Although their annual growth rings have not been counted, the three bristlecone pine stands found here approach the size and appearance of the planet's most ancient living trees in California's Methuselah Grove. With an abundance of young trees, this population is self-perpetuating. Other vegetative wonders among the 431 known plant species here include a 1944 discovery of grapefern growing above 10,000 feet in Indian Farm Canyon—an occurrence most unusual this far south.

Another rare species of special interest is a pure strain of Bonneville cutthroat trout once thought to be extinct. These trout fin the upper reaches of two of the eight perennial streams that flow from the east side—Birch and Trout creeks. These surviving fish are a remnant of the population that lived in ancient Lake Bonneville, a body of freshwater that once covered most of western Utah. Another waterborne rarity is the giant stonefly (up to 2.5 inches long) which, though uncommon in Utah, exists in most of these mountain streams. No less than a dozen plant and animal species native to the Deeps are found nowhere else.

From antelope racing across the lower benchlands to introduced Rocky Mountain bighorn sheep in the high country, 83 species of mammal live here. Elk too have been introduced here recently, by the Goshute Tribe. They aren't native to the Deep Creek Mountains but are expected to thrive in habitat made at least partially secure by virtue of remoteness and ruggedness. Mule deer are the most numerous large mammal, but none of the wide array of species here are considered abundant. Interestingly, this high country harbors more deer winter range than summer range, most of which is in the north end. Blue grouse, chukar, bald and golden eagles, several hawk species, and the federally listed endangered peregrine falcon are among the 185 kinds of bird found here either seasonally or throughout the year.

Cultural surveys in the southeast corner of the roadless area have located several dozen sites, mostly lithic scatters and caves or rock shelters. They tell the tale of semi-permanent occupancy over a span of 8,500 years, from Paleo-Indian cultures to prehistoric Paiute-Shoshone. In 1827 Jedediah Smith became the first white explorer to enter the Deep Creek Mountains. The Pony Express route skirts the northern edge and still provides access for the modern-day explorer.

RECREATIONAL USES: Clear flowing water in the Deep Creek Mountains, a mirage throughout most of the Basin and Range, enhances a wide spectrum of recreational activities. In particular, the availability of water expands the myriad of potential hiking and horseback trips from day use to extended overnighters, making it possible to live in and really get to know the country.

For rugged and challenging hikes or horseback rides take your pick of Basin, Goshute, or Indian Farm creeks. A favorite route for hikers is up Granite Creek or Indian Farm Creek to the rocky pinnacles of Ibapah or Haystack peaks. Granite Creek offers the easiest approach to Ibapah Peak, rooftop of the Deeps. The 12.5-mile round-trip route includes caves along the way and a vertical ascent of 1 mile—a full day in the mountains by anyone's measure. The Granite Creek Trailhead can be reached by four-wheel-drive vehicle about 2 miles above the canyon mouth.

The Basin as seen from the head of Middle Canyon during an early spring snowstorm.

Indian Farm Creek offers a direct but strenuous route to 12,020-foot Haystack Peak, on the crest of the range. Because of its unusual white granite mounds and broken formations it is also well suited for a shorter out-and-back day hike. The turnoff is 4.5 miles south of Callao, next to the BLM's CCC Campground. Turn right (west) at the sign and drive about 2 miles to the parking area and picnic table on the north side of the creek. A four-wheel-drive route crosses the creek, ending after about 0.5 mile. The rugged brushy canyon narrows dramatically 0.5 mile above the end of the jeep trail. A faint and hard-to-find unofficial trail makes this bouldery drainage a wild place for slow ambling rather than fast hiking. To the immediate south of Indian Farm Creek, trailless Red Cedar Canyon is both rugged and pristine.

Several of the lower east slope canyons are accessible by low-standard roads, notably the Middle, Toms, Granite, Trout, and Birch Creek drainages. Unlike most canyons here, Trout Creek offers enjoyable trail hiking. For climbers, the prime season is late June to late October when the routes are mostly snow-free. During summer, however, climbers are well advised to begin their ascents early in the morning before the rising sun beats down unmercifully. The western slope is drier, and public access is more difficult due to travel restrictions on the Goshute Indian Reservation.

Most of the hunters drawn to the Deep Creek Range are in pursuit of mule deer and chukar partridge. There is limited hunting of smaller populations of elk, antelope, and blue grouse. Anglers occasionally wet a line for rainbow trout in the dozen or so miles of fishable streams that drop from mountain meadows into steep-walled canyons. Note that some streams are closed to fishing to protect the rare Snake Valley strain of Bonneville cutthroat. Anglers should carefully return these fish to the stream if they happen to catch them.

Those interested in nature study can have a field day in these mountains observing the amazing variety of flora and fauna.

HOW TO GET THERE: From the east at Callao turn south (left) at the T junction of the graveled Pony Express and Gold Hill roads. Drive past the Callao landfill sign, making a turn to the right (west) after 2 miles, which is just beyond an irrigation ditch and is signed, "Toms Creek, Middle & Goshute Canyon." The improved dirt road leads straight toward the mountains. The first junction is reached after about 2 miles. Continue up the foothills toward the distinctive triangular peak on a road that changes to unimproved dirt as it follows a ridgeline to the southwest. The junction of Middle and Toms Canyon roads is reached after another 2 miles. Turn left (south) and drive 0.5 mile. This is a good place to park. The steep, rocky doubletrack from here on is better suited for hiking and horseback riding. The BLM would do well to close it to vehicles to prevent erosion and to safeguard wildlife habitat.

Day or overnight hiking or horseback riding loop

Scotts Basin Loop

Distance: 12 miles (basic loop).
Starting and maximum elevations: 6,100 feet and 8,515 feet (high point of loop) or 10,748 feet (Rocky Peak).
Difficulty: Moderately strenuous to strenuous (depending on side trip options).
Best months: Mid-May through June; September through October.
Topo maps: Goshute Canyon-UT; Goshute-UT; and Indian Farm Creek-UT.

This varied day-trip loop into the east-slope core of the wild Deep Creeks can readily be extended to several days of explorations into side canyons and nearby peaks. The basic loop starts up Toms Canyon to The Basin, returning by way of Middle Canyon. Rough and rutty four-wheel-drive routes are used for about 8 miles of the 12-mile loop, a fact largely compensated for by the rugged splendor of the canyons. Although these routes show evidence of use, they should be closed to vehicles for resource protection.

From the trailhead the steep, rocky doubletrack climbs across Dell Canyon, reaching a 7,600-foot pass above Toms Creek after about 2 miles. Toms is a wide sweep of open grassy sagebrush slopes with granite boulders and knobs dotting the north side. Stringers of fir and aspen line the brushy stream bottom. Two sets of rustic log cabins separated by about 1 mile sit next to the rushing creek 3 to 4 miles up. The doubletrack continues up the north (right) side of the creek to an 8,515-foot ridgetop pass directly above The Basin. The great curving swale of The Basin is bound by pointed peaks and filled with granite mounds, spires, and columns separated by aspen groves and green carpets of coniferous forest. From the pass drop about 800 feet northward into the lower Basin, recently named Scotts Basin in honor of the late Utah Governor Scott Matheson. The Governor was instrumental in raising critically needed funds for The Nature Conservancy to acquire 3,200 threatened acres in The Basin. A subsequent transfer to the BLM makes possible a more ecologically complete Deep Creek Mountains wilderness as envisioned by Governor Matheson.

If time allows, set up a secluded base camp near the springs in Scotts Basin for an easy climb to the 8,925-foot saddle at the head of Basin Creek along the main divide. From here hike and scramble along the open crest 1.5 miles northward to the summit of 10,748-foot Rocky Peak. Other possible side trips include a visit to the petroglyph site shown on the topo map, which is at 8,000 feet along the north branch of Basin Creek, and exploring the brushy but hikeable North Canyon, which joins Basin Creek about 0.5 mile below the petroglyphs.

To continue the loop from Scotts Basin, angle cross-country to the east on the right (south) side of Basin Creek, picking up a distinct trail above a spring that climbs to a well-defined 8,350-foot gap at the head of Middle Canyon. From the pass a primitive jeep trail drops into Middle Canyon. The pass opens to distant views of isolated mountain ranges and of cinder cones and lava fields far below in Snake Valley. Drop into Middle Canyon on the steep, sandy doubletrack where a major contact zone between white granite rock formations to the south contrasts vividly with metamorphic rock and sandstones on the north. After about 2 miles the primitive road bypasses the most rugged stretch of the canyon and swings right (southeast) across side slopes and ridges. For the final 0.5 mile back to the trailhead at the base of the Toms Creek jeep trail, you may wish to cut straight south in order to avoid the tiresome up-and-down road route.

Dugway Mountains   5

Location: 70 miles southwest of Salt Lake City, in northwestern Utah.
Size: 23,100 acres.
Administration: BLM Salt Lake District, Pony Express Resource Area (north);
BLM Richfield District, House Range Resource Area (south).
Management status: Unprotected BLM roadless.
Ecosystems: Intermountain sagebrush province ecoregion, with pinyon-juniper
woodland as the potential natural vegetation.
Elevation range: 4,590 feet to 6,749 feet (Castle Mountain).
Established trails/routes: No trails. 14 miles of jeep tracks, suitable for hiking.
Maximum core to perimeter distance: 2 miles.
Activities: Hiking, bird watching.
Maps: BLM 1:100,000 scale surface management/land ownership map entitled
"Rush Valley" (50 meter contour interval). See Appendix E for a listing of the four
topo maps covering the roadless area.

OVERVIEW: The Dugways were rejected by the BLM in its inventory of roadless
areas suitable for wilderness. Perhaps the Dugway Mountains should instead
be designated a national historical site because they played a significant part
in the birth of the environmental movement in America. The Dugways, located
immediately south of the U.S. Army's Dugway Proving Ground, gained promi-
nence in 1968 when more than 6,000 sheep on BLM grazing allotments and
nearby ranches died. The army denied any connection between the sheeps'
deaths and activities at the proving ground, but did compensate the ranchers
for their losses. Some months later, the army's decision to cease testing nerve
gas at Dugway was announced; all the remaining canisters of the deadly material were to be shipped by rail to the Atlantic seacoast where they would be
disposed of in the ocean. But those hillsides littered with dead sheep had de-
livered quite a jolt to the American public, and the prospect of shipping this
toxic load through densely populated areas and then casting it into the ocean
created a major uproar. The army reconsidered, and instead the deadly gas was
deactivated at Dugway. The entire scenario served to electrify the nascent environmental movement, and provided clear evidence of the hazards of modern
technology.

5 DUGWAY MOUNTAINS

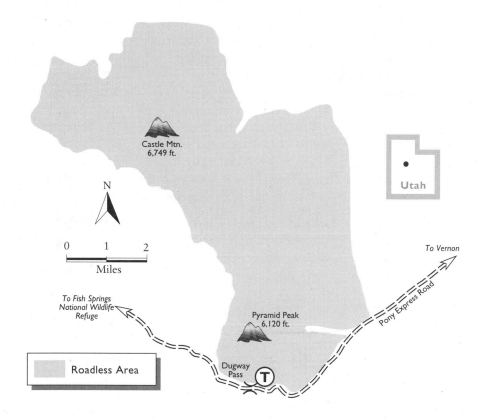

Castle Mtn.
6,749 ft.

N

0   1   2
Miles

To Fish Springs
National Wildlife
Refuge

Pyramid Peak
6,120 ft.

Pony Express Road

To Vernon

Utah

Dugway
Pass

T

Roadless Area

The army still operates Dugway Proving Grounds, testing chemical and biological defense matériel and munitions for the government and corporate manufacturers. The army's glossy promotional literature touts the grounds' reliability, environmental compliance, conservation, and preservation programs, as well as vast monitoring and medical support for the employees. Hikers in the Dugways today are assured of greater longevity than the sheep population and wildlife of 3 decades ago.

Native species have rebounded, for they too were obliterated by the cloud of nerve gas that drifted south in 1968. The Dugways are home to a few coyotes and bobcats, rodents, migratory raptors, and deer who cross the Pony Express Road from the Thomas Range. Juniper and sage dot the higher elevations; the lower slopes of the Dugways support shrubs typical of the Basin and

Range province: blackbrush, shadscale, winterfat, and greasewood. The interior valleys are grassy meadows, traditional sheep pasturage. There is no water.

The wilderness proposed by the Utah Wilderness Coalition excludes the northern end of the range, which has been hammered by mining. Even the BLM in a draft environmental impact statement disdainfully noted this mining damage, describing the scattered debris as "bones after the feast," and speculating that "perhaps the banquet is not yet over." In this case, mining etiquette was clearly not up to banquet standards; a more accurate analogy would be hyenas at a carcass. The southern Dugways, luckily, were spared a BLM-endorsed feeding frenzy, and deserve to be protected as wilderness.

The single ridgeline of the proposed area curves north-northwest 8 miles from the gravel Pony Express Road. Castle Mountain, in the northern section, is the highest peak, at 6,749 feet. The 23,000-acre range is seldom visited.

RECREATIONAL USES: Tucked away in the desert, subject to overflight from the Wendover Gunnery Range, and lacking water, the Dugways might intimidate most recreationists. Their obscurity, on the other hand, assures solitude for the

Hiking north toward Pyramid Peak in the Dugway Range.

intrepid off-trail hiker. Two roads north of the Pony Express provide access to both flanks of the range. From any point, a day trip to the ridge will provide the adventure of discovery, as well as sweeping views of Lake Bonneville Basin stretching in every direction. To the west the Deep Creeks soar to the horizon, and the Wasatch Front is ever-present to the east, Mount Nebo punctuating its southern end. When northern Utah's mountains are snowed in, the Dugways offer terrific hiking.

HOW TO GET THERE: The trailhead at Dugway Pass is on the Pony Express Road, a rough, improved dirt and gravel road, best traveled in dry weather. The BLM is touting the road in its Back Country Byways program, with informational leaflets and historical markers. The 5,410-foot pass is 21 miles east of headquarters at Fish Springs National Wildlife Refuge and 44 miles west of Vernon. At the pass a Pony Express route marker stands by a pullout on the south side of the road. Park here and begin the hike by crossing the road and heading up the slope on the north side.

Day hike

Pyramid Peak

Distance: 5 miles round trip.
Starting and maximum elevations: 5,410 and 6,120 feet (Pyramid Peak).
Difficulty: Moderate.
Best months: March through April.
Topo map: Dugway Pass-UT.

Pyramid Peak stands out as a landmark on the bumpy Pony Express Road as it winds along the southern edge of the vast Great Salt Lake Desert. This hike provides a pleasant leg-stretch to break up the cross-desert journey, and it also gives travelers a glimpse of the quiet, private world wrapped inside desert mountain ranges. The low-rise Dugways catch little moisture; consequently, wildlife and vegetation are sparse. The arid windswept peaks and hummocks are silent, except for the call of the raven. In early spring the yellow, red, and purple hues of wildflowers, along with bright orange lichen, coat the hillsides and valleys. At other times grasses, low sage, and shadscale color the beige desert world with a green carpet. Hardy junipers dot the landscape but give little relief from the sun and wind. Bring plenty of water for this short hike.

From the unsigned trailhead at the pass (also unsigned), go up the hill on the north side of the road. Look ahead to see your destination, slightly west of due north. The best route is via the up-and-down ridges, so continue up the hill to 5,712 feet where the first panorama of the central desert gives you reason to pause. Pyramid Peak is to the left, and on the right is a distinct volcanic cone, even more triangular than the peak. Here too you will discover hidden valleys, typical of basin ranges. These clumps of mountains appear so flat on the desert horizon, but each range contains surprises. The Dugways' gentle green slopes, traditional sheep range, are like a secret desert golf course. The jagged rock outcroppings on the ridge spines and peaks sharpen the contrast with the soft curves of the Dugway valleys.

There is no convenient continuous ridge leading to Pyramid Peak. From your vantage point at 0.4 mile you can select your route to approach the peak from the east or the southeast. Either route involves some moderate hand and foot work up through craggy volcanic formations. Each of the rolling ridges invariably drops to a saddle, or even a valley, making for repeated losses and gains of 150 to 200 feet 3 or 4 times before you reach the slopes of Pyramid itself.

The peak is an abrupt 500-foot ascent over just 0.1 mile. The holey surface provides a ladder of handy footholds. With some route selection you can avoid the treacherous loose fragments on the steep mountainside. The small flat peak of shadscale and juniper is a comfortable location for perching and enjoying the scenery. A couple of huge sheepherders' monuments on the west edge are artifacts of a bygone era and attest to the immense boredom involved in watching sheep. The Dugway Range curves on to the northwest. Castle Mountain (6,749 feet) dominates the view 2 air miles away. With low rolling ridges between Pyramid and Castle, it would be a long, dry, and fairly tedious excursion to continue in that direction. All around the Dugways, mountain ranges erupt from the desert floor. Bring a Utah highway map to help with their identification from the peak.

After enjoying the vastness of the desert, head back to the pass. You might select a different route for the return trip by dropping to the valley between the ridges. An alternative for a longer hike is to swing east and scramble up the volcanic cone (5,783 feet). This side trip would be strenuous—the surface of the sharp peak is loose.

After completing this outing along the desolate Pony Express, you gain new insight into the complexity of the mountain range. This roadless unit is unchanged since Pony Express riders streaked over the pass in 1860 and 1861. None of those young men—and few other people—have ever stopped to venture into the Dugways.

House Range Complex   6

Location: 33 miles west of Delta, in west-central Utah.
Size: 139,400 acres (three roadless units).
Administration: BLM Richfield District, House Range Resource Area.
Management status: Three BLM wilderness study areas (Swasey Mountain, Howell Peak, Notch Peak) totaling 125,430 acres, including 9,000 acres in the Notch Peak area designated an Area of Critical Environmental Concern and National Natural Landmark; plus 13,970 acres of unprotected BLM and state roadless lands.
Ecosystems: Intermountain sagebrush province ecoregion; potential natural vegetation types are juniper-pinyon woodland and saltbrush-greasewood.
Elevation range: 4,500 to 9,669 feet (Swasey Peak).
Established trails/routes: About 38 miles of primitive jeep tracks suitable for hiking and horseback riding. There are no formal trails; most hiking and climbing routes are cross-country.
Maximum core to perimeter distance: 3.5 miles (Notch Peak area).
Activities: Hiking, backpacking, rock climbing, horseback riding, hunting, spelunking, rockhounding and fossil collecting, nature study, photography.
Maps: BLM 1:100,000 scale surface management/land ownership map entitled "Tule Valley" (50 meter contour interval). See Appendix E for a listing of the 11 topo maps covering the roadless area.

OVERVIEW: Rising from the West Desert, massive cliffs of sheer limestone punctuate 50 miles of north-south trending block-faulted mountains known as the House Range. The impressive 2,700-foot precipice of Notch Peak is so distinctive that it is clearly recognized from as far away as 70 miles. Best known for fossils and caves, most of the House Range remains wild and lightly visited. This sizable complex includes three BLM wilderness study areas and contiguous wildland draping both sides of a serpentine mountainous crest. From north to south they are Swasey Mountain (57,000 acres), Howell Peak (25,000 acres), and Notch Peak (57,400 acres). Separated only by rugged canyons and dirt roads, the three roadless areas are actually a single, interconnected ecosystem.

The Cambrian rock formations of the Swasey Mountain country include interbedded Wheeler shale, which holds a rich assortment of half-billion year

6 HOUSE RANGE COMPLEX

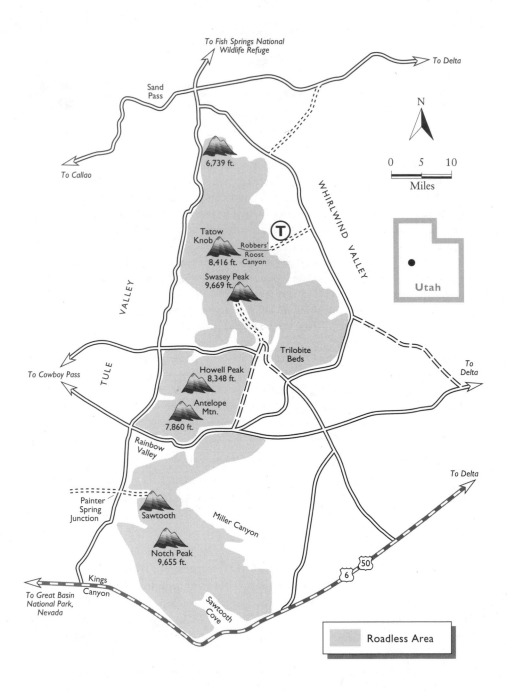

To Fish Springs National
Wildlife Refuge

To Delta

Sand
Pass

N

To Callao

6,739 ft.

0   5   10
Miles

WHIRLWIND VALLEY

Tatow
Knob
8,416 ft.

Robbers'
Roost
Canyon

T

Utah

Swasey Peak
9,669 ft.

VALLEY

Trilobite
Beds

To Delta

To Cowboy Pass

TULE

Howell Peak
8,348 ft.

Antelope
Mtn.
7,860 ft.

Rainbow
Valley

To Delta

Painter
Spring
Junction

Sawtooth

Miller Canyon

Notch Peak
9,655 ft.

50

6

Kings
Canyon

To Great Basin
National Park,
Nevada

Sawtooth
Cove

Roadless Area

old fossils. Most notable are the trilobites, a now extinct beetle-like marine invertebrate. According to the Smithsonian Institution these fossil fields are of national significance, particularly the Antelope Spring Trilobite Bed at the southwest corner. Surface geology here is dominated by limestone; water and calcium carbonate have slowly acted together to form at least seven large caves.

Landforms rise a vertical mile to the apex of the House Range, 9,669-foot Swasey Peak. The country is only moderately steep along its western and eastern edges, becoming much more rugged in the interior. The centrally located Howell Peak roadless area encompasses 7 miles of a 3,000-foot high striated limestone escarpment that rises along a dramatic west face to 8,348-foot Howell Peak. The limestone is riddled with caves, including Council Cave near Antelope Peak. With the largest entrance of any cave in Utah, Council Cave can be seen from more than 50 miles away.

To the south the Notch Peak wildland displays the most spectacular topography in the House Range. Its most dramatic feature is the gigantic west face of Notch Peak, which is one of the highest cliffs in North America, rivaling that of Yosemite's El Capitan. This 9,655-foot massif is the second highest point in the range. The tilted block fault of this stretch of the mountains makes the west face extremely steep. Of the several deep, narrow canyons that cut through the limestone the best known are Hell 'n Maria and Sawtooth.

Most of these roadless lands are mantled with sagebrush and shadscale grading gradually to pinyon-juniper woodland. At higher elevations mountain mahogany and stringers of montane forest mixed with Douglas-fir, white fir, ponderosa pine, limber pine, and aspen add to the ecological and visual landscape. Hardy bristlecone pines, known for their longevity, cling to higher exposed ridges. Several rare and possibly endangered varieties of buckwheat and milkvetch are found in this roadless desert montane island.

A band of about 80 wild horses roam Sawmill Basin northeast of Swasey Peak. These mountains also provide year-round refuge for antelope and mule deer, which are the staple of the few reclusive mountain lions that stalk these remote canyons and benches. The skies are graced by federally listed endangered peregrine falcons and threatened bald eagles as well as golden eagles and prairie falcons. However, with thousands of wintering domestic sheep surrounding these mountains, these and other predators are threatened by government-sponsored poisoning, trapping, and aerial gunning.

Cultural surveys have recorded at least 14 prehistoric sites, mostly caves and rock shelters used by Archaic, Fremont, and Shoshone peoples. More recent sites include a rock cabin in Hermit Canyon within the Howell Peak Wilderness Study Area. The unmistakable face of Notch Peak was a major landmark for those traveling the early trails to Nevada. A colorful history includes tales of horse thieves who once used a rough pack trail north of Swasey Peak near Tatow Knob. Other outlaws may have hidden in Robbers' Roost Cave just southeast and below Tatow Knob.

RECREATIONAL USES: With at least seven springs, the House Range is wetter than most of the West Desert mountain ranges. But at least one water source, Painter Spring, is too saline for human consumption. These widely spaced springs make overnight camping more feasible, but in all cases the water should be treated before using.

Arid conditions allow for a lengthy hiking season up into the higher elevations from April to late November. Most hiking routes are cross-country. The most popular day hikes are climbs of either Swasey Peak (9,669 feet) or Notch Peak (9,655 feet). Swasey Peak can be summited by way of a 4.5-mile, 1,700-foot vertical gain loop route from the Sinbad Overlook road. The best jumping-off point for this off-trail ridge route is from a large meadow about 2 miles southwest of the peak. The topo maps covering this hike are Marjum Pass-UT and Swasey Peak-UT.

The west face of Notch Peak is an astounding 4,450-foot vertical rise, 2,700 feet of which is sheer. The easiest hiking route to this formidable summit is from the east side via Sawtooth Canyon. A privately owned rock cabin in Sawtooth Canyon marks the trailhead for the 9-mile round trip, which includes a 1,700-foot vertical gain. The topos that cover this trip are Notch Peak-UT and Miller Cove-UT. A southern route to the peak can be accessed by way of Hell 'n Maria Canyon. A four-wheel-drive road through Amasa Valley offers a more challenging northern approach. Some of the best granite climbing walls in the intermountain west are located at the west base of Notch Peak's north face. Visitors sometimes hear strange underground drumming noises emitting from fissures along the higher ridges of Notch Peak. One possible explanation is that the sounds are created by trapped air shifting in subterranean caves. The views from the top of both summits are stunning—both within the House Range and gazing outward to the Tule Valley, Deep Creek Mountains, and other ranges far into Nevada.

The popularity of spelunking and fossil collecting in the House Range ranks right up there with hiking and climbing. Most mule deer and chukar hunting takes place on the more moderate western and eastern slopes surrounding the rugged central cores of the three roadless areas that make up the House Range Complex.

HOW TO GET THERE: From the west on U.S. Highway 50/6 drive through Kings Canyon and take the first left-hand (north) road (unsigned gravel), which is just east of mile marker 27. After about 6 miles, stay left (north) at a Y intersection and drive another 3 miles to the Painter Spring junction. A quick trip idea from this point would be to drive 2 miles east to the end of the Painter Spring Road and then hike a short distance up the colorful, rugged canyon directly below Sawtooth Mountain in the 57,400-acre Notch Peak roadless area.

Continuing toward the trailhead, stay left (north) toward Marjum Pass for another 5 miles to the third unsigned road junction. Turn right toward the mountains and Rainbow Valley, which separates the Howell Peak and Notch Peak roadless areas. Watch to the north for the huge opening of Council Cave near the top of Antelope Mountain. The road crosses Marjum Pass after 6 miles. Keep to the right at another road junction 2 miles east of the pass. Turn left after another mile, cross under the powerlines, and continue on the unsigned gravel road about 7 miles to a signed four-way intersection (38 miles from Delta by way of US 50). Trilobites are signed to the left. Go straight on the road marked "Swasey Spring 12 miles." Come to another junction after about 9 miles with a road entering from the right signed "Delta 35 miles." Continue left (north) for about 4 miles to an unsigned junction; stay right (north) on the main road. After about 3 miles turn left onto an unsigned dirt road winding toward the unmistakable block of Tatow Knob visible to the west. The road forks after about 3 miles. Turn left (south) on a rough two-wheel-drive road and continue about 1.5 miles to where the road begins swinging back to the north next to the shallow wash of lower Robbers' Roost Canyon. Pull over and park in one of several sagebrush flats just north of the wash. At this point you've driven a slow 50 miles northeast of US 50, or about 46 miles west of Delta if approaching from the east. Despite seemingly endless miles of dirt and gravel this scenic trailhead route offers a grand auto tour around the edges of all three wild areas within the House Range Complex.

If approaching from the east, drive west on US 50/US 6 from Delta to a major road five miles past Hinckley. The road veers right and runs due west.

The sheer west face of Notch Peak, at right, rises 2,700 feet.

Follow this road 13 miles to the second major road to the right, which heads northwest. Take this road 11 miles to the junction, mentioned above, with the signed Swasey Spring Road. This junction is also signed "Delta—35 miles." Turn right (north) and refer to the above directions to the Robbers' Roost trailhead.

Long day hike loop

Robbers' Roost Canyon–Tatow Knob Loop

Distance: 10 to 12 miles round trip (basic loop).
Starting and maximum elevations: 5,950 feet and 7,900 feet (south of Tatow Knob) or 8,236 feet (north of Tatow Knob).
Difficulty: Moderately strenuous.
Best months: Late April through mid-June; October through November.
Topo map: Swasey Peak-UT.

Both the long and short versions of the Robbers' Roost–Tatow Knob loop penetrate the heart of Swasey Peak—the 57,000-acre northern component of the House Range Complex. Robbers' Roost Canyon provides a direct route to the crest, which can then be hiked for miles in either direction.

From the trailhead, hike past the jeep trail that swings north and head up a doubletrack in the first wash on the left. This lower stretch of Robbers' Roost Canyon is bound by low-lying sagebrush ridges dotted with juniper. The steep-

Sheer limestone walls hundreds of feet high guard the main canyon south of Tatow Knob.

walled mesa of Tatow Knob rises due west and is a major West Desert land-mark visible for at least 100 miles in every direction. The doubletrack winds up the wide sandy wash for about 2.5 miles. As the tracks fade in the narrow-ing canyon, high rims of dark limestone sit atop slopes of pinyon-juniper. Keep a watchful eye out for wild horses—Robbers' Roost is one of their favored hideouts.

At 3 miles the canyon closes in for a short stretch and then opens to a junc-tion. Follow the main left-hand canyon to the source of Robbers' Roost Spring. From the spring, climb the right side of the draw on an unofficial trail for about 0.25 mile to the large alcove overhang of Robbers' Roost. A 50-foot high lip funnels water during springtime. Although eroded from limestone this great gap is not an actual cave. Hikers can, however, reach a small cave opening about 0.25 mile west and above Robbers' Roost by climbing along the steep slope below cliffs to the immediate west.

To attain the main crest of the range, climb cross-country to the southwest, gaining 750 feet in about 0.5 mile, thereby covering a total of about 4 miles from the trailhead to the divide. A dense mantle of pinyon-juniper, shadscale, Mormon tea, and mountain mahogany along the fractured limestone ridge opens every so often to west slope formations resembling wedding cake layers of sheer cliffs, spires, and pinnacles plummeting 4,000 feet to the desert floor. The apex of the range—9,669-foot Swasey Peak—rises 4 miles to the south and can be climbed along the broad pinyon-juniper plateau that defines this por-tion of the divide. The shortest and most direct climbing route, however, takes off from just below Sinbad Spring on a wide south ridge.

As the crest ascends northward toward Tatow Knob it opens to rocky points with breathtaking views of remote valleys guarded by high cliffs. The 8,416-foot butte of Tatow Knob is crowned by cliff walls on all sides. To climb the unnamed 8,236-foot butte to its immediate north, angle around the moderate east slope of Tatow Knob and look for a route on the gentler northeast ridge of Butte 8236. A long loop back to the trailhead, totaling about 14 miles, is possible by way of a rugged cross-country traverse north to the plateau ridge northwest of North Canyon Spring in the head of North Canyon. After a steep descent to the spring follow a double track down North Canyon to its mouth and from there southward 2 to 3 miles to the trailhead.

An equally scenic and somewhat shorter 10- to 12-mile loop involves start-ing the return from a 7,900-foot butte about 0.5 mile southeast of Tatow Knob. From there drop to the main ridge that parallels Robbers' Roost Can-yon to its immediate north. Follow the distinct wild horse trail to the east as it drops into saddles and skirts around the side of several knolls. A varied mosaic of reefs and small interior valleys of high grass harbor wild horses during the spring. The trail becomes faint as it drops the final 0.5 mile across sagebrush flats, but at this point the trailhead is in view. Allow a full day to savor the wild isolation of these northern reaches of the House Range.

King Top

7

Location: 50 miles southwest of Delta, in west-central Utah.
Size: 78,800 acres.
Administration: BLM Richfield District, Warm Springs Resource Area.
Management status: BLM wilderness study area.
Ecosystems: Intermountain sagebrush province ecoregion, with desert shrub and pinyon-juniper woodland, and scattered Douglas-fir.
Elevation range: 4,500 to 8,000 feet (King Top).
Established trails/routes: No trails; 20 miles of jeep tracks suitable for hiking.
Maximum core to perimeter distance: 3.5 miles.
Activities: Hiking, backpacking, fossil hunting, hunting, horseback riding.
Maps: BLM 1:100,000 scale surface management/land ownership maps entitled "Tule Valley" and "Wah Wah Mts. N." (50 meter contour interval). See Appendix E for a listing of the seven topo maps covering the roadless area.

OVERVIEW: In the desert region of west-central Utah, the King Top Wilderness Study Area lies at the southern end of the Confusion Range. It is separated from the House Range Complex by U.S. Highway 50/6, which crosses the mountain range at Kings Canyon. King Top is the largest wilderness study area in the West Desert. It is also unique because, at 84,770 acres, the wilderness study area is larger than the proposed wilderness. Road-impacted sections on its edges have been deleted from the Utah Wilderness Coalition proposal.

The King Top Plateau dominates the wilderness study area. This geologic feature is an anomaly in the Basin and Range province where sharp mountain ranges are common. The plateau rises abruptly from the desert floor and is protected by jagged ridges of exposed Devonian carbonate bedrock; the exterior cliffs are very intimidating as you approach King Top on the highway. This is not gentle country, but it is attractive for hikers who enjoy a scramble. Both the western and the steeper eastern flanks of the triangular King Top formation present formidable barriers. But both sides are cut with steep canyons that allow visitors to penetrate the heart of King Top and see the softer world that lies within.

The predominant vegetation consists of desert shrub and pinyon-juniper woodland. Douglas-fir grows in small areas on the 8,000-foot King Top

7 KING TOP

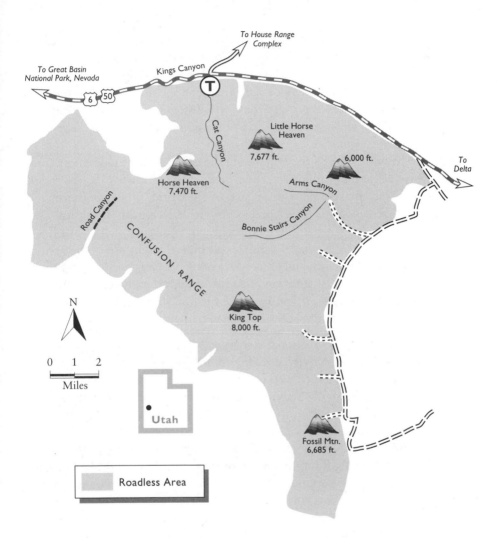

Plateau. Wheatgrass, shadscale, horsebrush, and cheatgrass are the dominant vegetation types in this arid wilderness study area.

There are no springs or live water. With a very low annual precipitation of 8 to 12 inches, King Top is usually accessible to hikers year-round. The present use of this island mountain area is for grazing, largely by sheep, with more than 7,000 animal unit–months* in the wilderness study area. Permittees haul water for their flocks and herds. An active program to eliminate coyotes has been

*An animal unit–month is the amount of forage required to sustain a cow and calf pair for a month.

pursued. A small herd of wild horses travels the flattops, canyons, and valleys. Appropriately named, Little Horse Heaven is an 800-acre interior valley surrounded by rocky peaks. Horse Heaven is above it, on the rocky plateau below King Top.

Lack of water limits wildlife populations. BLM management plans call for establishing nine guzzlers (watering sites for wildlife), though these artificial habitat manipulations would be inappropriate in a wilderness area. Currently King Top hosts small numbers of deer and antelope in addition to the wild horses. Bald eagles and peregrine falcons (both federally listed endangered) and the golden eagle (a sensitive species) enjoy the mid-desert privacy of the seldom-visited King Top pinnacles.

Fossil Mountain (6,685 feet) on the southeast edge of the wilderness study area is a mecca for paleontologists. Here, Lower Ordovician fossils, 450 to 500 million years old, attract visitors from all over the world. While not thoroughly surveyed by archeologists, King Top has not yielded a wealth of cultural sites. The chance discovery of two small lithic sites and one rock shelter by oil and gas exploration and MX missile siting teams indicate light use of the area by nomadic Archaic, Fremont, and Paiute-Shoshone peoples. Certainly other undiscovered sites may exist since small bands of hunter-gatherers roamed this West Desert for centuries. If you have the thrill of discovering any artifacts, leave them in place so your successors can experience the same enjoyment.

RECREATIONAL USES: Recreational activity in King Top is light. Fossil collecting is the most popular activity, focused on Fossil Mountain. This location is reached by a cherry-stemmed jeep track 1 mile east of the Blind Valley Road near the southern apex of the wilderness study area. The uplifted strata of Fossil Mountain reveal a multitude of fossilized marine life forms from the early Paleozoic Era.

Meanwhile, the U.S. Air Force maintains a presence in the sky above. The Utah Test and Training Range lies north of the Confusion Range; low-altitude military overflights are common, although Defense Department budget reductions are making them less so. Off-road vehicle use is presently limited to the 30 miles of oil, gas, and uranium exploration tracks that penetrate the wilderness study area's boundaries along the plateau's foothills. Many of these old routes are fading back into the wild. Beyond, the rugged terrain protects the area from vehicular intrusion.

Lack of water sources limits backcountry travel, but day hikes and short backpack trips are rewarding for their solitude. Cat Canyon runs south into the wilderness study area off U.S. Highway 50 at Kings Canyon for a 10-mile round trip (see below). For a longer hike, a side trip to the hidden valley of Little Horse Heaven at 7,350 feet is an option. The latter destination is also accessible from Blind Valley and Blackham Canyon roads. Any of these adventures would provoke wonderment over BLM's withholding of King Top from wilderness recommendation. Here naturalness, solitude, and primitive unconfined recreation opportunities reign supreme!

HOW TO GET THERE: From the west US 50/6 crosses the Nevada border at the Border Inn, which features the last gas, food, and lodging for 80 miles. Go east to King Canyon. Halfway between mile markers 26 and 27, in the King Canyon narrows, there is an unmarked pullout on the south side of the highway at the mouth of Cat Canyon. A lone ash tree stands across the highway, the only landmark for the trailhead. From the east the turnoff is 62.5 miles west of Delta on US 50/6. The turnoff south of the highway allows you to leave your vehicle about 20 yards from the pavement, at the brown wilderness study area marker. This is the shortest paved access to wildlands in the West Desert, and perhaps in all of Utah.

Day hike

Cat Canyon

Distance: 12 miles round trip.
Starting and maximum elevations: 5,550 feet and 7,480 feet.
Difficulty: Moderate.
Best months: March through May; October.
Topo map: Bullgrass Knoll-UT.

King Top, like most of the desert mountain ranges, holds secrets that are available only to explorers who venture on foot into its interior. Cat Canyon is a spectacular route, not only for its canyon features but for its rather brief pathway to the land of wild horses and mountain lions and its interior rolling meadows. The desert and the highway both seem lightyears away!

From the pullout trailhead, go south into the canyon mouth of dark jagged limestone. The fine gravel of the dry streambed makes an excellent hiking surface. Pinnacles and arches decorate the intricate canyon walls, which are interspersed with broad grassy slopes. About 0.1 mile from the trailhead the canyon turns and the highway vanishes; by 0.2 mile, even the noise of the rare vehicle has disappeared in the silent desert air. Ubiquitous cat scat shows that the canyon was appropriately named, and that the wilderness has begun. In early spring, vetch and paintbrush brighten the canyon bottom with splashes of purple and red, while joyous songbirds' voices echo from the canyon walls. Low sage and grass on the benches above the bottom allow for easy shortcuts across the meanders. Soon horse hoof prints begin to mark the trail.

The canyon narrows 1.7 miles from the trailhead. The walls close to 10 to 12 feet apart in places, and dry pouroffs, easily stepped over, are reminiscent of slickrock canyons. Centuries of water and wind have eroded the limestone walls, creating a ghoulish landscape. Simultaneously the vegetation becomes more lush. Sagebrush, Mormon tea, juniper, pinyon pine, and sawgrass grow in bright profusion, although no water is evident on the surface.

At 2 miles the canyon widens into a broad, grassy, interior valley. Evidence of horse and mountain lion becomes more widespread at your feet. Travel quietly as you hike up the gently sloping valley and you may be rewarded with the view of a band of wary horses. They won't linger long if they spot you.

For a side trip to Little Horse Heaven, take off about halfway up the valley to the ridge rising on your left (east), north of high limestone cliffs. There is a gradual ascent to the 7,015-foot location on the topo map; continue south up the ridge to its high point (7,480 feet). Here you have a terrific view of the Nevada mountains to the west, with Wheeler Peak and Mount Moriah dominating the skyline. The 2,700-foot escarpment of the Notch in the House Range rises to the east. Just below, also to the east, is one of the intimidating exterior cliffs of the King Top unit. The view of the cliff to the east and the meadows below you on the west epitomizes the contrasts of this mountain range.

To get a view of Little Horse Heaven you have to drop into the saddle to the southeast, climb a knoll, cross to a ridge, and then descend the wooded slope to a clearing. With binoculars you may be able to spot a band of the elusive horses in the distance. Little Horse Heaven is a high sage and grass dell, surrounded by dense woodland of pinyon-juniper and Douglas-fir.

For your return journey head west to the crest between Little Horse Heaven and Cat Canyon. Select a ridge route that will take you down to the unused jeep track in the valley below. Drop to the doubletrack and follow it north to the head of the Cat Canyon valley. Continue back down the canyon to the trailhead. Again, travel quietly and you may see the wild residents.

Emerging at the highway, you may need a moment to shake off the Alice in Wonderland sensation. Cat Canyon resembles Alice's rabbit hole, while the interior of King Top is even more spectacular and real than her wonderland.

Wah Wah Mountains Complex   8

Location: 25 miles northwest of Milford, in west-central Utah.
Size: 109,700 acres (two roadless units).
Administration: BLM Richfield District, Warm Springs Resource Area (North);
BLM Cedar City District, Beaver River Resource Area (Central).
Management status: BLM wilderness study area (42,120 acres in North Wah
Wahs, which includes two units totaling 6,610 acres, designated as Research
Natural Areas and Outstanding Natural Areas/Areas of Critical Environmental
Concern), plus unprotected BLM and state roadless lands (67,560 acres).
Ecosystems: Intermountain sagebrush province ecoregion—potential natural
vegetation is juniper-pinyon woodland and saltbrush-greasewood, plus a small
acreage of unusually large bristlecone pines along main ridge.
Elevation range: 5,100 to 9,393 feet.
Established trails/routes: No formal trails; about 11 miles of jeep tracks in
peripheral canyons and benches suitable for hiking or horseback riding.
Maximum core to perimeter distance: 3.5 miles (central Wah Wahs).
Activities: Hiking, rock climbing, photography, nature study, backpacking, hunting.
Maps: BLM 1:100,000 scale surface management/land ownership maps entitled
"Wah Wah Mtns North" and "Wah Wah Mtns South" (50 meter contour interval).
See Appendix E for a listing of the 13 topo maps covering the roadless area.

OVERVIEW: The Paiute Indian name for alkaline seeps is *wah wah*, and these
are certainly found in the lowlands surrounding their namesake mountains.
The Wah Wahs harbor some of the most remote and untouched wildlands in
the West Desert. The western escarpment is an especially dramatic expression
of basin and range block faulting, rising above 9,000 feet in places along a
rugged north-south crest for 32 miles. Separated by Utah Highway 21, the
60,500-acre North Wah Wahs and 49,200-acre Central Wah Wahs comprise
a single wildland complex of 109,700 acres.

On the north end, the prominent snow-white pinnacle of 7,106-foot Crystal Peak is readily identified from great distances. The soft, crumbly white rock
is called Tunnel Springs Tuff, which erupted from volcanoes long before the
formation of the Wah Wah Mountains took place. This relic mound of volcanic ash stands out vividly against the more subdued tans, grays, and greens of
what are mostly barren outcrops of limestone. To the south, collectible fossils

8 WAH WAH MOUNTAINS COMPLEX

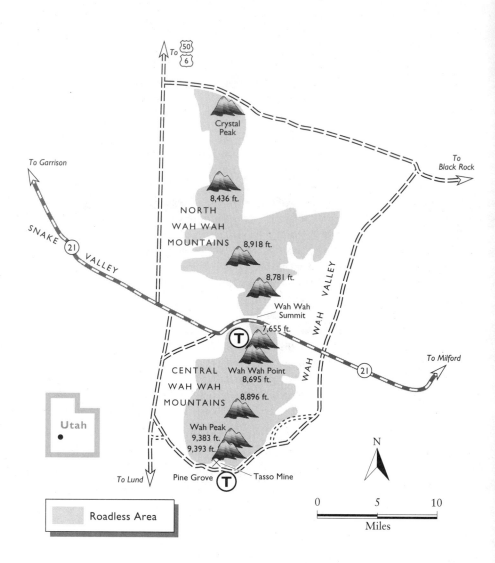

To 50 6

Crystal Peak

8,436 ft.

NORTH WAH WAH MOUNTAINS

8,918 ft.

8,781 ft.

Wah Wah Summit

7,655 ft.

To Garrison

SNAKE VALLEY

21

WAH WAH VALLEY

To Black Rock

To Milford

21

T

Wah Wah Point 8,695 ft.

CENTRAL WAH WAH MOUNTAINS

8,896 ft.

Wah Peak 9,383 ft. 9,393 ft.

Pine Grove

Tasso Mine

T

To Lund

Utah

N

Roadless Area

0   5   10

Miles

are encased within these sedimentary rocks. The Wah Wahs are characterized by cliffs on the west, changing to rugged, rocky topography on the eastern slope. Students of geology are attracted here by the only Jurassic rock in the Great Basin. The main dividing ridge of the Central Wah Wahs runs for 12 rough-hewn miles. Of the 15 peaks dotted along the crest, the high point of Wah Wah Peak rises in the south end to just under 9,400 feet; the highest point in the range is an anonymous peak south of Wah Wah Peak.

This wide open landscape supports a variety of grasses, sagebrush, and shadscale at lower elevations, changing to the scattered pinyon-juniper woodland that covers close to 75 percent of the country. Higher up, pockets of aspen, ponderosa pine, and white fir grow on protected north-facing aspects. Enclosed within this conifer-aspen forest type are a couple hundred acres of exceptionally large bristlecone pine. Some of these big trees surpass 50 feet in height on sheltered sites east of the main central ridge. Surprisingly, they may be much younger than their gnarled, slow-growing counterparts in other higher mountain ranges to the west.

Utah prairie dogs (listed as threatened by the federal government) have been documented on the flats west of the main divide. These and other low benchlands on the periphery of the roadless areas provide a year-round home for a small number of pronghorn antelope and a modest population of mule deer that range up into the higher country. A few mountain lions stalk the remote fastness of deep canyons and steep slopes. Scarcity of water holds down wildlife numbers, but chukar partridge remain widespread over most of the complex. A variety of raptors ride the thermals above high windswept ridges, including peregrine falcon, bald and golden eagles, and several kinds of hawk. As year-round residents of the Wah Wahs, golden eagles likely nest on secure cliff ledges here.

The BLM hasn't inventoried cultural values in the lightly visited Central Wah Wahs. However, three archeological sites have been found near Crystal Peak in the north end of the northern mountains. Surely, many more await discovery.

RECREATIONAL USES: Don't let the name scare you off—these pristine mountains are well worth a visit. The main access is west from Milford on UT 21. On a seasonal basis short overnight backpacks are possible. But these dry desert peaks and canyons are devoid of springs or live water, so most hiking and climbing is best done on day trips. Once in a while equestrians and deer hunters venture into the Wah Wahs on day excursions, but their use is also confined by lack of water and the steep, rugged terrain. Thus, trip possibilities are limited only by time, energy, imagination, and water—carry lots with you.

Most of the light hiking use in the Wah Wahs is associated with geologic sightseeing, botanical study, or fossil collecting. With sheer limestone cliffs and wildly remote canyons, hiking and climbing can be rigorous and challenging. But the scenery alone makes this effort well worthwhile. The main divide offers a humbling, overwhelming perspective on the profound and empty space of the surrounding Great Basin. This off-the-beaten-track stretch of undeveloped mountains lacks the conveniences of formal trails and trailheads. Virtually all hiking and climbing routes are cross-country; a compass and a detailed topo map are indispensable. Some of the short jeep track routes are used by grazing permittees, but they also provide access for hikers and horseback riders into several of the lower canyons.

Hikes in the Central Wah Wahs can begin from points along dirt roads near Wah Wah Summit and Pine Grove. The rugged heart of this central section is especially scenic with superb opportunities for nature study. One suggestion for an enjoyable outing is to begin hiking from the end of a four-wheel-drive road above Pierson Cove on the southwest corner of the northern Wah Wahs (elevation 6,600 feet). Head north about 2 miles up the main canyon that veers left to a broad plateau. Continue climbing northwest about 1 mile to Point 8918 for commanding views of Pine Valley and the vast expanse of Basin and Range country. For a shorter hike, climb distinctive Crystal Peak in the northern edge of the complex. Begin by heading west up the ridge just south of the peak. After wrapping around to the southwest ridge follow it to the summit.

HOW TO GET THERE: *Corral Canyon*: drive west from Milford on Utah 21 to an unsigned, unimproved dirt road that takes off to the left (south) about 1.5 miles west of Wah Wah Summit, close to an arrow sign and mile marker 43 on the highway. This is the first side road west of the summit heading south. Take this high-clearance two-wheel-drive road for about 2 miles and park just before the second crossing of Corral Canyon wash. The bulldozer trail to the right is the return hiking route.

Pine Grove: From UT 21 between mile posts 42 and 41 turn left (southwest) at Lime Point on an improved road marked only with a stop sign. The road is paved at first, changing quickly to gravel. This is also the road to the Mountain Home outing. Proceed about 4 miles and turn left (south) on an improved dirt road. Drive another 5 miles and take an unsigned left-hand road that angles southeast toward Pine Grove. After another 2 miles the improved gravel road passes corrals on the right and signs for "Pine Grove 5 miles" and "UT 21, 9 miles." Continue on toward the lovely grassy bottom of Pine Grove, passing a reservoir and a wire gate next to a cattleguard. The unsigned trailhead and parking area is another 2 miles east of the gate, below and in sight of the old Tasso Mine, which is shown on the topo map. Park just beyond a gravel pit on the left at a point where dirt doubletracks take off in opposite directions from the main road. If car camping, avoid camping on the private

A mid-April snowstorm dumps six inches of wet snow at Wah Wah Summit on the northern end of the Central Wah Wahs.

inholdings in Pine Grove. There are several great campsites in grassy pine parks on nearby public land.

Cross-country day hike or climb

Corral Canyon–Wah Wah Point Loop

Distance: 5 to 6 miles.
Starting and maximum elevations: 6,660 feet and 8,695 feet (Wah Wah Point).
Difficulty: Moderately strenuous.
Best months: Late April through early June; October.
Topo map: Sewing Machine Pass–UT.

This entire cross-country route in the north end of the 49,200-acre Central Wah Wah Mountains roadless area can be seen from the trailhead. Begin the recommended clockwise direction of the loop by climbing the open grassy pin-yon-juniper slope on the left side of the drainage, which leads up to the rocky ridge to the right (south) of Point 7655. Upon reaching this main ridge, con-tinue southward above a series of cliffs about 1.5 miles to the rounded tree-crowned summit of 8,695-foot Wah Wah Point. If time allows, hike out and back for several miles along the lofty main north-south crest of the range.

For the return descent from Wah Wah Point take the main northwest-trending ridge. Cliffs guarding the top can be avoided by skirting around to the right (north) through a pocket of conifer forest. Continue working your way along the up-and-down ridgeline to a distinctive 7,200-foot saddle. From here follow an old bulldozer trail to the north, which drops back to the trailhead after about 1 mile.

Day hike, climb, or extended point-to-point backpack

Pine Grove to Wah Peak, Central Wah Wah Crest

Distance: 7 to 8 miles (loop); 20 to 25 miles (point-to-point backpack).
Starting and maximum elevations: 7,240 feet and 9,393 feet.
Difficulty: Moderately strenuous.
Best months: Late April through early June; October through November.
Topo Map: Lamerdorf Peak-UT (day trip).

The entire route to the 9,393-foot high point of the 49,200-acre Central Wah Wah roadless area can be seen from the trailhead and parking area. Hike straight north on a doubletrack, skirting around to the right (east) of the Tasso Mine, which is on a private inholding. Continue climbing cross-country up the distinctive pinyon-juniper ridge, which changes abruptly on its west side to limestone cliffs towering above North Canyon. As elevation is gained the broken limestone ridge requires route-finding around rocks and brush, but the gradient is steady and moderate. After about 1.5 miles you'll arrive at a prominent 8,900-foot point marked by old survey poles. The view from this commanding perch is sweeping—from hidden pockets of fir and pine directly below to panoramas of desert basins and block-faulted ranges. From this rocky ledge hike eastward another 1.5 miles on an up-and-down ridge of mountain mahogany, fir, and limber pine to the unnamed apex of the Wah Wahs at 9,393 feet. A peak register was placed here in 1988, but a 1997 climb revealed a four-year gap since the most recent recorded visit. The pinnacle named Wah Peak is 10 feet shorter and 0.5 mile to the north. A night-and-day contrast exists between its barren western slopes and densely forested east side.

During April a brief window may exist when lingering snowbanks provide a water source for an extended 20- to 25-mile traverse of the rugged crest and its 15 peaks all the way north to Wah Wah Summit on Utah Highway 21. This strenuous three- to four-day adventure would require dropping along the east side of the divide in search of sheltered campsites flat enough for a tent. The round-trip car shuttle between Pine Grove and Wah Wah Summit isn't much longer than the hiking route.

For the return leg of the day hike loop, from the 9,393-foot southern apex of the Wah Wahs, double back on the west ridge for about 0.75 mile to Point

8898 and then begin bushwhacking due south down the ridge toward the road. The first 800 feet of woodsy vertical descent is choked with thick mountain mahogany, requiring constant ducking and dodging. The remaining 800-foot drop involves more open zigzagging around pinyon-juniper and rock outcrops. Upon reaching the road turn right for the remaining 0.5- to 1-mile walk back down to the trailhead.

Mountain Home Range

Location: 75 miles northwest of Beaver, on the western edge of central Utah.
Size: 19,019 acres.
Administration: BLM Cedar City District, Beaver River Resource Area.
Management status: BLM roadless and state lands.
Ecosystems: Intermountain sagebrush province ecoregion.
Elevation range: 6,220 feet to 9,480 feet (The Needle).
Established trails/routes: None.
Maximum core to perimeter distance: 1.5 miles.
Activities: Hiking, hunting, geology.
Maps: BLM 1:100,000 scale land management/surface ownership maps entitled
"Wah Wah Mtns North" and "Wah Wah Mtns South" (50 meter contour interval).
See Appendix E for a list of the four topo maps covering this roadless area.

OVERVIEW: The Mountain Home Range rises west of the Wah Wah Mountains
near the Nevada border. It forms the northern end of the rambling Indian Peak
Range and doesn't even get its own name on some maps. On other maps, the
Mountain Home area is called the Needle Range for a row of modest hills that
run along its eastern side, rising to 7,000 feet above Pine Valley. To add to the
confusion, the highest peak in the Mountain Homes is a 9,480-foot peak called
The Needle, in spite of the fact that it is actually a plateau edged by cliffs. With
such a degree of anonymity that no one is even sure of its name, the range also
enjoys the privacy of its remote location in the West Desert. Here solitude is
ensured.

This roadless unit of nearly 30 square miles has a backbone plateau, shrinking to a narrow ridge as it goes south. A line of crests over 9,000 feet high
punctuates the skyline, while a limestone escarpment separates the high country from the timbered slopes below. Shallow caves dot the limestone outcropping; they have not been inventoried for their archeological value. The slopes
below the plateau and ridge are especially steep and rough in the northern half,
but descend more gradually above broad Hamlin Valley in the south. A trace
of an old vehicle track intrudes on the summit plateau for a little over 1 mile
south of Cherry Spring, and the privately held section at Cougar Spring is excised, along with its cherry-stemmed access road. Aside from these exceptions,

9 MOUNTAIN HOME RANGE

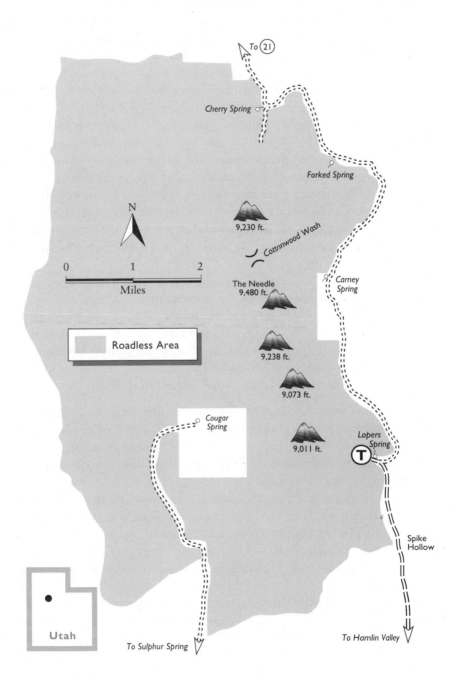

To (21)

Cherry Spring

Forked Spring

N

9,230 ft.

Cottonwood Wash

0   1   2

Miles

The Needle
9,480 ft.

Carney
Spring

Roadless Area

9,238 ft.

9,073 ft.

Cougar
Spring

9,011 ft.

Lopers
Spring

(T)

Spike
Hollow

Utah

To Sulphur Spring

To Hamlin Valley

the Mountain Home Range forms a large block of continuous roadless acres in the highly roaded world of Utah's West Desert.

The range has other unique attributes, the most noticeable being the lack of mineral development. Here there are no old mining roads and no deserted mines. A second striking feature is that there are no grazing allotments in the Mountain Home unit. The rugged terrain is too inhospitable for cows and sheep. Thus the natural botanical world of the desert mountains has not been modified, but remains in its original condition. Ancient bristlecone pines grow on the mountainsides.

Several springs on the lower slopes of the range dot the perimeter roads that define the roadless area's boundary. Above 7,500 feet, however, there is no reliable water. Wildlife somehow copes with this dry situation. A band of wild horses hides out here, as well as herds of elk and deer. In the primitive privacy of these far-away mountains, these grazers and browsers can move from winter range to the mountains in the summer with only the slight barrier of a gravel country road. Predators are also plentiful, from raptors to mountain lions. With no grazing, there has been no official program to eliminate coyotes and mountain lions.

The Mountain Home Range was dropped from the BLM wilderness study list, and was simply overlooked by the Utah Wilderness Coalition. Loyal hikers who have visited the Mountain Home Range, however, support its preservation. An enthusiastic BLM range conservation official called the range "a gem," one of those nifty secrets hidden in the West Desert. Anonymity and remoteness are an asset to the Mountain Homes, for they remain wild and undeveloped, a *de facto* wilderness, untrammeled by people.

RECREATIONAL USES: The lack of water in this dry windy range limits recreation to day trips, but the slender dimensions of the unit mean you can easily access the summit ridge on short excursions. Hiking the Home's ridge with binoculars and camera is rewarding, for you may spot eagles or elk. The skittish wild horses are more secretive.

Southeast of Cherry Spring, the ridge track goes south, rising above 9,000 feet. From here the view of the Needles and the Wah Wahs is unencumbered by vegetation. To the west the ranges and deserts of central Nevada stretch to a hazy infinity. Wheeler Peak (13,083 feet) and the other lofty mountains of Great Basin National Park dominate the northwest horizon although they are 50 miles away.

A rough four-wheel-drive high-clearance road circles around the unit on the northern end. A vehicle way and jeep trail extend from this unmaintained road down the ridge of the range for 2 miles, stopping above Cottonwood Wash; this is not heavily used due to its remote location. Hikes can be launched from the road for explorations of the plateau. Forked Spring and Carney Spring to the east are also good jumping off spots for energetic hikers who wish to climb to the ridge instead of driving up the road to the northeast. The excursion from Lopers Spring (see below) combines a vigorous hike up the mountainside with a shorter drive on the rough road.

HOW TO GET THERE: The 1:100,000 BLM map "Wah Wah Mtns South" is necessary for finding the route in this heavily roaded region. Beaver County road graders have been industrious in the West Desert, resulting in a confusion of roads, few of which are signed.

From Utah Highway 21, 35 miles northwest of Milford, turn left (south) at Lime Point onto the Pine Valley Road (unsigned). This is the same road to the Pine Grove hike in the Wah Wahs, so these two outings can be conveniently paired. The graded dirt road goes south down the valley to the west of the Wah Wah Mountains, then slants to the southwest to pass on the south of Sawtooth Peak, a distinctive landmark. Follow BLM road signs toward Hamlin Valley. About 5 miles after passing Sawtooth, a BLM sign indicates Lopers Spring to the right. Turn here and go north. The actual distance to Lopers Spring (9 miles) is greater than the BLM acknowledges on the sign, so don't be impatient. This road up the east side of the Mountain Homes is an improved dirt dry weather road suitable for passenger vehicles. Beyond the trailhead at Lopers Spring, however, it grows much rougher as it climbs to Mountain Home Pass, so only rugged four-wheel-drive high-clearance vehicles should continue from there.

Resting on the lee side of the Mountain Home Range with rugged limestone cliffs to the north.

The road to Lopers goes through a burned and chained area, the Mountain Home Seeding Area. This 1,000-acre project, begun in 1989, was designed to provide grass for the herds of elk and wild horses. The efforts of the BLM and the Utah Department of Wildlife have been successful, and these herds are thriving. Watch carefully along the juniper on the edges of the clearing for the wary residents. After passing Spike Hollow Spring (signed, on the right) it's another 1.3 miles to the BLM sign to Lopers Cabin. Turn left and go 0.2 mile to road's end at the cabin. There's a spring and watering tank for wildlife just beyond the cabin. For the sake of the thirsty wild critters, do not camp near the spring; there are several suitable sites 0.2 mile back at the turn-off that won't disturb the spring's nocturnal visitors.

Day hike

The Needle

Distance: 9 miles round trip.
Starting and maximum elevations: 7,520 feet (Lopers Cabin) and 9,480 feet (The Needle).
Difficulty: Strenuous.
Best months: April through June; October.
Topo map: Lopers Spring-UT.

This hike to the high ridge at the southern end of the Mountain Home Range and then north to its highest peak traverses wild country visited only by deer, elk, and wild horses. Rare in Utah, no signs of human visitors or off-road vehicle tracks mar the landscape. The route features open hiking up gentle slopes dotted with juniper and desert shrubs. This easy exercise abruptly ends with dense scratchy vegetation—mountain mahogany, shadscale, Mormon tea—necessitating zigzagging upward for the final 1,000 feet to the ridge. Limestone outcroppings also require detours in your route. In addition, a limestone shelf protects each peak along the ridge, and a 200-foot limestone cliff guards the Needle summit on the east. Your efforts are rewarded, however, with both the view and the experience of being in country shared only by wildlife.

From the trailhead at the cabin, cross the spring's streambed north of the cabin, climb the low rise, and hike northwest up the dry, wide drainage. Eventually the going gets too rocky to be fun, so climb along the side of the ridge on your right (north), continuing to angle higher as you head northwest toward the crest of the ridge. Eventually you will reach the hummock (8,240 feet) that stands southeast of the main mountain ridge; from here you can see the sloping ridge to the west, your route to the top. Drop to the saddle and then continue to climb. The vegetation thickens as you go, making travel difficult. Periodically game trails and horse paths appear, making passage somewhat easier. Eventually you will break out at the limestone outcropping that skirts the southern point of the main ridge (9,011 feet). This is the first of the four high plateaus that mark the southern Mountain Home skyline, each one bounded by a larger limestone cliff as you progress northward.

From this southern summit it is another 1.5 miles along the ridge to the destination, the highest peak in the range. The route requires dropping to saddles, losing 100 to 200 feet each time, between the increasingly higher peaks. The most strenuous scramble is after the third one, on the way up to the sweeping plateau of the sloping Needle. Its limestone cliff has several breaks in its south face that permit scrambling to the windy summit.

White fir and bristlecone pine thrive in the brisk wind along the summit ridge. The stretches of plateau are largely barren tundra mixed with fragmented limestone pavement. This surface is a welcome respite after the rugged climb. The view is breathtaking, with a sea of mountain ranges rising like waves in all directions. There is plenty of evidence of elk and deer at this high elevation. The Mountain Home horses are also comfortable in the high country, and they have left their calling cards along the ridge.

The 0.5-mile long plateau of the Needle marks the northern end of the hike. This high point of the range is untouched by vehicles. Directly to the north, a dramatic 300-foot limestone cliff rises, marking the edge of the range's northern plateau. The cliff keeps all vehicular intruders from continuing down the range, preserving the wilderness values here.

To return to the trailhead, retrace your route, or, for the more adventuresome there is a loop option. For the latter, the only way down from the Needle is via the cleft in the cliff face just south of the peak. This descent is rocky and steep, and is further complicated by the usual thorny and thick brush. Persevere, and descend through the shrubbery, dropping sharply to the southeast where a drainage descends to the road, only 0.8 mile (by air) away. The southern hillside of the drainage is less encumbered with bushes and is striped with game trails. It's a steady downhill to finally hit the seldom-used road. From there, it's a little over 2 miles to hike back south to the trailhead. The final mile runs through a portion of the Mountain Home Seeding Area. Aside from Lopers little cabin, this range modification is the only evidence of alteration in the area. The quiet, obscure Mountain Home mountains are home to wilderness, not man.

SOUTHWEST
HOT DESERT

Introduction

The southwestern corner of Utah is a unique area of the state. It is here that the Mojave Desert, the Great Basin Desert, and the Colorado Plateau overlap, creating an interesting hybrid. The hot, dry climate is a product of southern latitude and low elevation. The lowest point in Utah is in Beaver Dam Wash at 2,200 feet. Daytime winter temperatures range in the comfortable upper 50s, although the nights can drop below freezing. Such wide temperature ranges are common in the desert. Summers, of course, see daytime temperatures of over 100 degrees. Annual precipitation in nearby St. George is 10.4 inches. This growing urban area attracts thousands of winter visitors and shares the predicament of Las Vegas and Los Angeles: insatiable thirst and scant available water.

In the natural world, plants and animals have adapted splendidly to this high desert. A plant handbook for the southwest desert is the ideal guide for the resident vegetation. Big sagebrush, rabbitbrush, bitterbrush, and blackbrush are the typical desert shrubs in Utah's Dixie. The yucca and Joshua trees of southern California are right at home. Barrel cactus, cholla, and prickly pear await complacent passers-by with their inhospitable spikes. Desert animals complete the Mojave picture. Smartly decorated chuckwallas, poisonous Gila monsters, California king snakes, desert tortoises, kangaroo rats, and roadrunners live in the low desert areas.

On higher ground, the plants and animals shift to the Great Basin collection. Upland vegetation includes pinyon-juniper woodland, the ubiquitous potential natural vegetation of the island mountains of the basin and range region of western Utah as well as of the Colorado Plateau. Intermixed are live oak and Gambel oak. Mule deer, mountain lion, and coyote are residents of the benchlands and uplands above 4,000 feet.

Stream vegetation is rare, but it does appear in Cougar Canyon–Docs Pass, where mountain streams last through the dry summer months. Cottonwood, willow, tamarisk, and ash crowd the stream bottoms. Migratory birds can often be heard in these garden spots in spring, for this is an important seasonal corridor.

The terrain of the hot desert section is also a combination of features found in the nearby deserts and plateaus. Red rock cliffs and slickrock plateaus of Navajo sandstone are the features of Red Mountain, suggestive of the Colorado Plateau, which is visible from its heights. Here too are the sandy expanses and sand dune topography of the desert in the Beaver Dam Slopes. Cougar Canyon's volcanic cores and lava flows typical of the Great Basin complete the geologic picture.

From early times the delightful winters were an attractive feature for human inhabitants as well as wildlife. Brigham Young established his winter home in St. George and visited here annually until his death in 1877. He sought relief for his rheumatism and arthritis in the dry desert climate. Today, new generations of "snow birds" are attracted by the climate and also by the many recreational opportunities in the area. In addition to the golf courses and the baseball fields of St. George and its suburbs, the wildlands of the hot desert attract visitors with endless hiking opportunities when the rest of Utah's trails are clogged with snow.

Cougar Canyon–Docs Pass Complex   10

Location: 20 miles northwest of Shivwits, and 16 miles southwest of Modena, in southwestern Utah.
Size: 59,400 acres.
Administration: BLM Cedar City District, Dixie Resource Area; USDAFS Dixie National Forest, Pine Valley Ranger District.
Management status: BLM Cougar Canyon Wilderness Study Area (10,000 acres) and Docs Pass unprotected roadless land (19,400 acres); USDAFS unprotected roadless land (30,000 acres).
Ecosystems: Intermountain sagebrush province ecoregion, with pinyon-juniper woodland, sagebrush, and riparian zones.
Elevation range: 5,100 to 7,380 feet.
Established trails/routes: 10 miles of trail in the national forest; in the wilderness study area and BLM roadless area old jeep tracks make excellent hiking routes.
Maximum core to perimeter distance: 2 miles.
Activities: Hiking, camping, rock climbing, fishing, hunting, horseback riding.
Maps: BLM 1:100,000 scale surface management/land ownership maps entitled "Cedar City" and "St. George" (50 meter contour interval); USDAFS 1995 half-inch/mile planimetric map entitled "Dixie National Forest-Pine Valley & Cedar City Ranger Districts." See Appendix E for a listing of the six topo maps covering the roadless area.

OVERVIEW: On the western edge of Utah, 30 miles northwest of St. George, lies an obscure patch of roadless area. A larger section of this unit lies over the border adjacent to Nevada's Beaver Dam State Park. Here in the Utah portion, wrinkled, jagged ridges of granite and lava rise above clear-flowing perennial streams. The cool mountain streams of Beaver Dam Wash provide more than 5 miles of trout fisheries, the only native reproducing fisheries in southwest Utah. Also present in these mountain waters may be the Virgin River spindace, a spring-rayed minnow, a candidate for federal listing as threatened or endangered.

These emerald pools and stream bottoms are also the sites of lush riparian vegetation. Cougar Canyon, Sheep Corral Canyon, Sheep Canyon, Pine Park Canyon, and Headwaters Wash have dense stands of willow and cottonwood. The splash of bright green, the fluttering leaves, and the chattering stream make

10 COUGAR CANYON–DOCS PASS COMPLEX

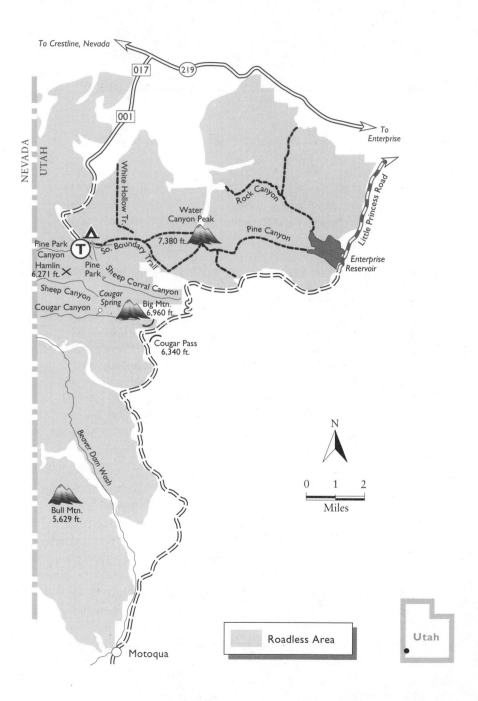

To Crestline, Nevada

017

219

001

To
Enterprise

NEVADA

UTAH

White Hollow Tr.

Rock Canyon

Little Princess Road

Water
Canyon Peak

Pine Canyon

Pine Park
Canyon

So. Boundary Trail

7,380 ft.

Enterprise
Reservoir

Hamlin
6,271 ft.

Pine
Park

Sheep Corral Canyon

Sheep Canyon

Cougar
Spring

Big Mtn.
6,960 ft.

Cougar Canyon

Cougar Pass
6,340 ft.

Beaver Dam Wash

N

0   1   2
Miles

Bull Mtn.
5,629 ft.

Roadless Area

Utah

Motoqua

these spots unique in this otherwise arid region. The remarkable vegetative diversity of pinyon-juniper woodland here includes Utah serviceberry, live oak, Gambel oak, cheatgrass, muttongrass, curly grass, lupine, eriogonum, and penstemon. Ponderosa pine and Douglas-fir flourish in the higher reaches of the national forest. The lower sagebrush community features big sagebrush, rubber rabbitbrush, antelope bitterbrush, squirreltail grass, cheatgrass, and the rare willowseed.

Little archeological research has been done in these canyons. Evidence, however, suggests that Archaic, Fremont, Anasazi, and recent Paiute peoples hunted and fished here, and even engaged raised crops in the damp, wider valley bottoms. During a weekend's ramble, modern-day explorers might come across rock shelters, lithic scatters, or rock art, all of which must be left untouched for later generations.

Nestled between the Meadow Valley Range in Nevada, with Sawmill Mountain rising above it on the west and the Bull Valley Mountains to the east, this rugged remote canyon complex offers primitive recreation opportunities for intrepid off-trail hikers. Visitors may spot mule deer and bobcat, coyote and beaver, as well as the wily mountain lion. Travelers here are unlikely to run into other hikers.

The administration of this area is a patchwork of federal agencies, with both the BLM and USDA Forest Service involved. The wilderness study area covers the northern portion of Sheep Corral Canyon and the head of Beaver Dam Wash. Farther south, the roadless Beaver Dam Wash, Docs Pass Canyon with its dramatic narrows, and Deep Canyon lie in unprotected BLM jurisdiction. In its draft environmental impact statement the BLM deemed these southern areas too rugged for recreational use, so solitude and adventure are assured! To the north, the Dixie National Forest Pine Park area continues the roadless expanse east of the small Pine Park Campground. An additional 30,000 acres of roadless national forest land lies here.

RECREATIONAL USES: There is considerable hunting and fishing activity in Docs Pass–Cougar Canyon; this is a rare resource in extreme southwest Utah. Lack of road access does limit the hunting public to only the most energetic. The terrain is considered too rugged for off-road vehicles and horses.

Pine Park Campground in Dixie National Forest is open from Memorial Day to the end of September. With only 11 spaces and no water, its primitive conditions correspond to the wild qualities of this canyon country. From the campground, hiking trails in White Hollow and Pine Park Canyon swing through the southern portion of Dixie National Forest. Off-trail adventures lie to the south, in the canyons heading toward the Nevada line.

From the south, the rough road up Beaver Dam Wash north of Motoqua gets you to the take-off point for a 10-mile or longer round trip up the wash to explore Deep Canyon, or continue on to Docs Pass Canyon and its narrows.

Just to the east, the road on the ridge above Slaughter Creek swings around the eastern edge of the roadless area, climbing through 6,340-foot Cougar Pass and then continuing north to Sheep Corral Spring before turning east away from the roadless area. This backroad provides limitless trailheads for off-trail adventures, but is accessible only to high-clearance four-wheel-drive vehicles in dry weather.

HOW TO GET THERE: From the junction of Utah Highway 18 and Utah Highway 219 in Enterprise, go west on UT 219. The paved road becomes improved gravel 8 miles west of town. About 5 miles farther UT 219 enters Dixie National Forest. Continue west another 10 miles to turn left on Forest Road 017 at a sign marked "Pine Park 10 miles." Go south 1 mile on the improved gravel road to a Y intersection. Go left on Forest Road 001, which has a sign marked "Pine Park 9 miles." The unimproved dirt road gets better, becoming improved gravel after about 2 miles. This is a two-wheel-drive low-clearance road, though a sign warns of its being a narrow and rough one. Stay on FR 001 to its end at Pine Park Campground and the trailhead, 10 miles from the turnoff at UT 219.

Day hike or backpack

South Boundary Trail

Distance: 10 miles out and back.
Starting and maximum elevations: 5,430 feet and 6,410 feet.
Difficulty: Moderate.
Best months: March through May; September through October.
Topo maps: Pine Park-NV, UT; Water Canyon Peak-UT.

Pine Park Campground is tucked away in a canyon of volcanic tuff on the very western edge of Utah in the southwestern corner of Dixie National Forest. The roadless national forest unit is immediately east of Forest Road 001, which runs to the campground. These 30,000 acres of wildlands abut the BLM's Cougar Canyon Wilderness Study Area, south of the national forest.

These jurisdictional differences are invisible on the ground. The topography is complicated and rugged, with bouldered ridges and volcanic outcroppings dissected by deep canyons with drainages diving to meet them from all directions. From the timbered benches and scattered peaks in Utah, the complex's northern streams and canyons drain westward to Nevada and Beaver Dam Wash. The wash begins in Round Up Flat in the Dixie Forest, north of the campground, as Headquarters Wash, before bending through Nevada and its Beaver Dam Wash State Park and returning to flow south through Utah to Arizona.

Docs Pass Canyon and Deep Canyon in the south originate in the high country of eastern Nevada and drain eastward to join the wash in Utah. These complexities create mapping and hiking difficulties. The contorted landscape and densely vegetated canyon bottoms make off-trail travel difficult, painful, and—in places—impossible. Following the South Boundary Trail is a wilderness experience, requiring topo maps, the Forest Service map, and compass. The trail is lightly signed, with illogical mileages and arrows to nonexistent trails, and marked only intermittently with ancient blazes, tree cuts, and, rarely, cairns. This area is far from the beaten path!

Commencing at Pine Park Campground could create expectations of a tame outing. The campground is a lovely spot. Glistening white mounds of volcanic tuff rise ghostlike above and around the campground; eroded into fanciful cartoon shapes they attract cavorting climbers. There's also a clear spring babbling through the campground to Pine Park Canyon below, while stately ponderosa pines add to the alpine symphony in the mountain breeze. The outhouse, picnic tables, barbecues, and fire pits are the only conveniences. Tracks of off-road vehicles suggest that non-hikers congregate here in spite of the fact that the Dixie Forest travel map labels the area as closed to vehicle use to prevent erosion. But only 100 yards away, where the trail begins, this world is entirely left behind.

Before departing from the campground you will want to take a look at Pine Park Canyon. This section of the canyon is thickly vegetated, and it's a rough mile downstream before Pine Park Canyon's bottom opens up for hiking. To get there it would be easier to drive to Beaver Dam State Park in Nevada and hike up from that end. This Utah section is stunning to look at but is not hospitable to travel.

The trailhead sign at the campground indicates the direction of the South Boundary Trail (east) and the distance (3 miles to Mud Spring). It doesn't tell you where the trail is, nor is it accurate on the mileage. To find the trail, hike up the hill behind the sign for 0.2 mile. You'll encounter a faint path along the foot of the ridge. Turn right. Very quickly the influences of the campground and the off-road vehicle tracks fade and you're on a narrow but clear footpath heading east through the thick pinyon-juniper forest. Views of Pine Park Canyon open below you, and Water Canyon Peak is visible straight east.

About 0.75 mile from the trailhead, the trail runs along a stock fence and drops into a meadow with a spring flowing from a side canyon to the north. Cross the stream and bear left to pick up the trail angling up the rise on your right. From this low point climb high on the north wall of Pine Park Canyon to a magnificent view of the surrounding wooded plateau country, punctuated with jagged, disorganized volcanic outcroppings. The trail is intermittently faint in the heavy pinyon-juniper, but cattle use it, keeping it visible. Above 5,800 feet the trail breaks out of the forest to curve across a high volcanic shelf. From here the ascent continues up the ridge to merge above a side canyon north of the main Pine Park Canyon. This section of the trail is lightly cairned, but dense manzanita patches make trail finding a challenge.

The trail drops across a lava slope marked with cairns, angling northwest toward the head of the stream and a small cemented rock dam. For 0.6 mile the trail goes upstream from the dam, crossing the stream often but spending most of the time on the south bank. When the main stream bends south watch for the trail heading out of the drainage to your left. This faint pathway leads up a low ridge to a sage and juniper flat above Mud Flat. A buff sandstone bluff sits to the north, with bulbous outcroppings looking like browned refrigerator biscuits; to the south of the flat is a low ridge of gray rocks, wrinkled like sleeping elephants. Here you might encounter a very weathered ancient trail sign on the path. Though nearly illegible, it assures you that you're on the trail, even though you'll find the mileages puzzling. The trail arrives at Mud Flat 0.25 mile from the sign, 4 miles from the campground. From here the pack trail continues to become better defined, curving south and back toward the head of Pine Park Canyon. At 5 miles from the campground, you will arrive at the Colie Flat trail junction, above the brushy head of Pine Park Canyon.

From here a moderately strenuous scramble up 7,380-foot Water Canyon Peak, 1 mile to the north, would add several miles to the hike and provide a sweeping view of the region. In early spring, enough water exists in the side canyons to do this as a backpack, establishing a camp in Colie Flat before climbing the peak.

Colie Flat is a good turn-around point for an out-and-back excursion in these western wildlands. For a different route back, you might be tempted to take the White Hollow Trail up to meet FR 001 above the campground. Like so many other sign discrepancies in this area, the White Hollow Trail is longer than indicated (it's 4 miles, not 2), and it emerges from White Hollow farther north than the maps and the Forest Service sign suggest. It comes up from White Hollow in a sagebrush flat in burned over Pine Park, 1.5 miles north of the White Hollow Trail sign on FR 001. These mistakes are understandable, for even the USGS topo maps do not adequately reflect the complexity of this land. With no primary mountain feature to provide focus, the ridges, canyons, and ravines are chaotic.

Consequently, this is an untrammeled region, used mostly by hunters. Fall is the season of heaviest human use. Resident cougars and coyotes hunt year-round, leaving their footprints and scat boldly along the trail as a reminder to visitors of who lives here permanently. Pairs of golden eagles find the remote canyon ideal for aerial acrobatics and hunting. Even mallards can be found in Pine Park's pools, along with quick little rainbow trout.

Hiking back to the ghostly shapes of grainy tuff at the campground, it can be difficult to locate the trail again, but the views westward are terrific; enjoy the pauses while you try to find your path. The contrast of life at the campground is even more noticeable after your expedition in this wilderness wonderland, protected from interlopers by its rough, remote terrain.

Beaver Dam Slopes Wilderness Complex ▪ 11

Location: 8 miles southwest of St. George, in the extreme southwest corner of Utah bordering Nevada and Arizona.
Size: 40,997 acres (Utah portion of complex; additional 30,300 acres in Nevada and Arizona).
Administration: BLM Cedar City District, Dixie Resource Area.
Management status: Beaver Dam Mountains Wilderness (2,597 acres in Utah); Joshua Tree Natural Area/BLM Instant Study Area (1,040 acres); unprotected BLM and state roadless lands (37,360 acres).
Ecosystems: Intermountain sagebrush province ecoregion—ecological transition zone between the Mojave Desert, Great Basin, and Colorado Plateau; potential natural vegetation of juniper-pinyon woodland, along with sagebrush and characteristic hot desert plant species, such as Joshua tree, creosote bush, and barrel cactus.
Elevation range: 2,200 feet (lowest elevation in the state) to 6,784 feet (Joshua Tree unit).
Established trails/routes: There are no formal trails or trailheads. Cross-country routes follow washes, canyon bottoms, and ridgelines. Several miles of four-wheel-drive roadways in the Joshua Tree unit are suitable for hiking and horseback riding.
Maximum core to perimeter distance: 2 miles.
Activities: Hiking, backpacking, horseback riding.
Maps: BLM 1:100,000 scale surface management/land ownership map entitled "St. George" (50 meter contour interval). See Appendix E for a listing of the four topo maps covering the roadless area.

OVERVIEW: Tucked away in the extreme southwest corner of Utah is an obscure three-part wildland within and adjacent to the Beaver Dam Mountains. The 1984 Arizona Strip Wilderness Act set aside the 19,600-acre Beaver Dam Mountains Wilderness, which includes 2,597 acres in Utah along Cedar Wash and the Virgin River. The remaining two unprotected roadless segments of this small but ecologically diverse complex are Beaver Dam Wash (24,900 acres) and Joshua Tree (13,500 acres), which are split by Old U.S. Highway 91.

The hot desert slopes of the Beaver Dam Mountains come together here as the juncture of three distinct life zones: the Great Basin, Colorado Plateau, and Mojave Desert. As such, the lower elevations are unlike any other wildland in

▮▮ BEAVER DAM SLOPES WILDERNESS COMPLEX

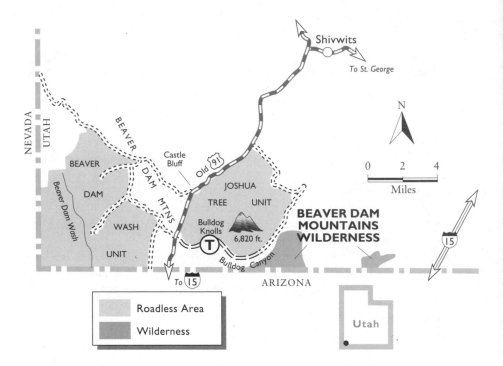

Utah. At only 2,200 feet, the exit from Utah of corrugated Beaver Dam Wash is the state's lowest point. This dry, deeply eroded landscape is overseen by the angular Beaver Dam Mountains. The wash carries intermittent water with some riparian vegetation near sporadic pools. Classic indicators of the Mojave Desert are the creosote bush, known for its longevity through cloning, and the Joshua tree, whose upsweeping branches lead the faithful to the land of Canaan, as interpreted by early-day Mormon pioneers. This bizarre tree-sized yucca attains heights of 30 feet or more and is actually a member of the lily family.

Some of the more than 180 bird species identified by the Brigham Young University Lytle Ranch Research Station occur nowhere else in Utah. Beaver Dam Wash and the Virgin River are important bird migration corridors. The Beaver Dam Mountains appear to block the movements of several avian species, thereby confining their presence in Utah to Beaver Dam Wash. These include the white-winged dove, brown-crested flycatcher, and hooded oriole.

Adding to the uniqueness of fauna are several kinds of reptiles that exist nowhere else in the Beehive State, such as the Mojave and speckled rattlesnakes, desert iguana, and desert night lizard. The elusive Gila monster and the federally listed threatened desert tortoise also rely on the security of this unroaded habitat. Loss of habitat and illegal collecting jeopardize the very existence of these rare and sensitive reptiles. Beavers inhabit the wash, of course, as do mule deer, porcupine, rabbit, fox, bobcat, and several birds of prey, including golden eagles and the federally listed endangered peregrine falcon.

Eastward, the Joshua Tree roadless area drains into Beaver Dam Wash from a jumble of stark peaks and ridges that rise to nearly 7,000 feet. The country contains a rich mosaic of Mojave plants dotting the open slopes of an austere desertscape: cholla and barrel cacti, agave, Spanish bayonet, creosote bush, and, of course, Joshua trees. In fact, the 1,040-acre Joshua Tree Natural Area was established by the BLM some 30 years ago because of its unusual Mojave plant community. The 3,040-acre Woodbury Desert Study Area, within the Joshua Tree unit, harbors near-pristine associations of creosote bushes, Joshua trees, pinyon-juniper woodland, and bursage. Maintenance of this relic community in a natural condition is vital for scientific study. Many of the rare plant and animal species found in Beaver Dam Wash extend their range into the adjacent Joshua Tree roadless area.

The Joshua Tree unit is located in a land rich in Old West history. It was originally on the route of the Old Spanish Trail, used by pack trains between the Los Angeles Basin and Sante Fe back in the 1820s. The road to Bloomington skirting the northeast end of the complex was first traveled by Mormon pioneers en route from settlements in Arizona and Nevada to St. George.

RECREATIONAL USES: Beaver Dam Wash is especially attractive for early season hiking and backpacking. Camping along the wash, using intermittent pools as your water source can be delightful in early spring when wildflowers and cacti are in full bloom. Nature study, especially bird watching, is often exceptional during this time of year. A walk down Beaver Dam Wash south of the Lytle Ranch Research Station makes an enjoyable and easy nature study hike.

The higher country of Joshua Tree is more suitable for day-use horseback riding, backpacking if sufficient water is carried, and more strenuous hiking in the rugged canyons and rough-hewn ridges. Keep in mind that this country is most definitely hot desert. If comfortable backcountry recreation is one of your requirements you will want to avoid the dry, 100+ degree F heat that often bakes the land from June until early fall. Inviting day hikes into the northern reaches of the Joshua Tree unit can be started from old US 91 about 2 miles southwest of Utah Hill Summit, which is identifiable by a large microwave tower. Pull off and hike toward rolling hills and the higher bluffs of Castle Cliff.

HOW TO GET THERE: *From the South:* Take the Littlefield exit (Exit 8) off Interstate 15 and drive north past Beaver Dam, Arizona, on old US 91 (Old Mormon Wagon Road) for about 10 miles, turning east (right) on the improved gravel Bulldog Canyon Road, which is also signed "Woodbury Desert Study Area."

From the North: From the Gunlock Road junction drive 15 miles south on old US 91 and turn left (east) on signed Bulldog Canyon Road. After about 1 mile Bulldog Canyon Road reaches BLM's Joshua Tree Natural Area and the Woodbury Desert Study Area where Drs. Woodbury and Hardy conducted pioneer research on the desert tortoise from 1936 to 1948. The study area was established in 1977. Keep to the right on the main road for another 1.4 miles to a point just past a cattleguard and exit sign for the study area. Turn left (north) onto a rough double track, drive about 0.2 mile, and park at the end of the road next to a concrete water cistern and primitive campsite.

Day hike
Bulldog Knolls–Joshua Tree

Distance: 4 to 8 miles round trip.
Starting and maximum elevations: 3,400 feet and 4,200 feet (below rougher slopes).
Difficulty: Easy to moderate.
Best months: November through April, with the best time being the early spring desert bloom period, which normally occurs between late March and mid April.
Topo map: Jarvis Peak-UT/AZ.

This open desert hike into a small BLM wilderness study area within the 13,500-acre Joshua Tree roadless area begins 0.1 mile below the mouth of a dramatic dark brown volcanic canyon cut deeply through the Bulldog Knolls. A varied Mojave Desert plant community includes Joshua trees, creosote bush, Spanish bayonet, agave, and a host of cacti, including cholla, barrel, hedgehog, and prickly pear. When the plants are in bloom during early spring the alluvial fans glow with the bright flowers of Cooper golden bush and desert lavender. Most impressive are the rich reds, purples, and yellows of cactus flowers. With its Joshua Tree Natural Area the BLM recognizes the unblemished quality of these near relict communities that span three life zones from hot desert near Beaver Dam Wash to Great Basin and Colorado Plateau at higher elevations.

Desert denizens in the vicinity of this route include the Mojave rattlesnake, Gila monster, and desert tortoise, which can live more than 35 years. Its longevity is surely enhanced by sleeping underground during summer and winter.

Once through the canyon (just under 0.5 mile up) the country opens to a wide basin mantled with noticeably larger Joshua trees and barrel cacti. Rolling ridges radiate from rugged cliffs of Precambrian granitic gneiss below the crest of the Beaver Dam Mountains. In the spring the land is alive with mourning doves and other small birds. Golden eagles circle their nests high on the cliff faces.

For panoramic views southward far into the Great Basin of Arizona and Nevada, gradually climb to the right (northeast) to the base of the steeper rock slopes. After gaining about 600 feet to an elevation of 4,200 feet along the base of the steeper and rougher rocks, contour around to the north and drop into the main draw. Another option is to hike straight north about 0.5 mile from the head of the Bulldog Knolls canyon toward a low ridge. This will put you in the main gravelly wash. It turns east (right) and then northeast for about 2 gradual miles. This easy hiking is followed by a steep 1- to 2-mile rock scramble to a 6,000-foot bench, or on up another 0.5 mile to the top at 6,786-foot Scrub Point. An ascent to these higher ridges would be an extremely strenuous scramble on loose rock with no water and precious little shade. A more reasonable hike up the wash to where it noticeably steepens below the cliffs is an excellent 7- to 8-mile round-trip introduction to this hot desert country.

On the way back down, the broad Joshua tree valley funnels directly to the canyon that slices through Bulldog Knolls. Stay on the left side of the wash for easier walking and superb vistas of the surrounding Beaver Dam Mountains. Depending on how far you ascend the main wash above the canyon, the distance of this out-and-back excursion can be expanded or reduced in this lowest, driest, and warmest corner of Utah.

Looking east toward rough volcanic cliffs below the crest of the Beaver Dam Mountains.

Red Mountain   12

Location: 5 miles northwest of St. George, in extreme southwest Utah.
Size: 20,400 acres.
Administration: BLM Cedar City District, Dixie Resource Area; State of Utah.
Management status: BLM wilderness study area (19,035 acres) plus
approximately 1,365 acres of contiguous Snow Canyon State Park.
Ecosystems: Intermountain sagebrush province ecoregion. Potential natural
vegetation is pinyon-juniper woodland.
Elevation range: 3,240 to 5,570 feet.
Established trails/routes: 5 miles of old jeep track that has eroded into a trail;
unofficial trails exist on ridges.
Maximum core to perimeter distance: 2 miles.
Activities: Hiking, backpacking, horseback riding.
Maps: BLM 1:100,000 scale surface management/land ownership map entitled "St.
George" (50 meter contour interval); 1995 USDAFS half-inch/mile planimetric map
entitled "Dixie National Forest-Pine Valley & Cedar City Ranger Districts." See
Appendix E for a listing of the four topo maps covering the roadless area.

OVERVIEW: Red Mountain is aptly named for a massive block of Navajo sandstone bounded by the Santa Clara River and Gunlock Fault on the west and
the Santa Clara River valley and Snow Canyon State Park on the south and
east. This roadless island of some 49 square miles consists mainly of BLM land
along with a couple thousand acres of State of Utah land within the wilderness
study area and at the head of Snow Canyon within the adjacent state park. The
vast tabletop of Red Mountain forms a dramatic sweep of sandstone punctuated by dozens of rock pinnacles and outcrops scattered across this flaming
amber mesa.

The southern and eastern flanks of Red Mountain are guarded by impressive 1,400-foot cliffs that provide a spectacular backdrop to the nearby communities of Ivins and Santa Clara. Here the vibrant colors of Utah's southern
Colorado Plateau meet block-faulted rocks of classic basin and range country.
The lofty expanse of Red Mountain is dotted with pinyon pine, juniper, and
sagebrush. Diverse flora and fauna reflect the variety of conditions found in

12 RED MOUNTAIN

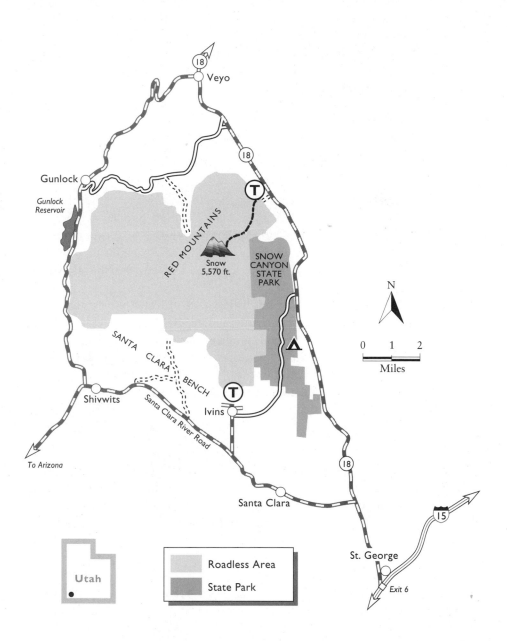

Veyo

18

Gunlock

Gunlock
Reservoir

RED MOUNTAINS

Snow
5,570 ft.

SNOW
CANYON
STATE
PARK

18

T

N

0   1   2
Miles

SANTA CLARA BENCH

Shivwits

Santa Clara River Road

Ivins

T

To Arizona

18

Santa Clara

15

St. George

Exit 6

Utah

Roadless Area

State Park

this transitional mixing of zones between the warm Mojave and cooler Great Basin deserts.

This rugged landscape can easily hide the mountain lion's secretive stalking of mule deer amidst clumps of ponderosa pine, Gambel oak, yucca, and agave. Bald eagles hunt small mammals during winter, but their golden cousins may occasionally be seen riding canyon thermals most anytime of the year. These southern reaches of the Colorado Plateau provide undisturbed habitat for species as rare and diverse as the desert tortoise, Gila monster, Great Basin silverspot butterfly, ferruginous hawk, southern spotted owl, mountain plover, Merriam's kangaroo rat, and Virgin River montane vole.

This is a wildland also rich in archeological history. At least seven prehistoric sites used by Southern Paiute Indians have been documented within the roadless area.

RECREATIONAL USES: Visitors enjoy breathtaking vistas throughout this varied uplift of sandstone slickrock. Day hiking is the most popular activity, followed by horseback riding. Some portions of the roadless area cannot be easily reached on day trips. A small number of visitors backpack for an overnight stay in order to access the more remote southern and western rims above the Santa Clara River.

Extended multi-day trips are precluded by lack of water, which also limits most horse rides to one day. Snow Canyon State Park and the adjacent BLM wilderness study area are a wonderful complement to each other, not only from the standpoint of enhanced wildland values but also in terms of longer and more vigorous hikes. For example, for those seasoned canyon trekkers adept at rock scrambling, a descent from the Red Mountain plateau into one of the steep northern tributaries of Snow Canyon offers a challenging point-to-point adventure if arrangements are made for a car shuttle at the parking area in lower Snow Canyon.

HOW TO GET THERE: Take Utah Highway 18 north from St. George. Mile markers on UT 18 indicate the distance from the Interstate 15 interchange. At 0.3 mile beyond milepost 15 turn left (west) at the Red Mountain sign. Continue west 0.3 mile on a good dirt road that crosses under the powerlines. A maze of dirt roads branch in different directions, but head directly west to a wider parking area at the point where the dirt road becomes a rough trail. The hike starts here.

Car shuttle for point-to-point hike: park your return vehicle on the north edge of Ivins, adjacent to the very southern edge of the Red Mountain escarpment. Your pathway down this steep ridge incline is clearly visible from Ivins. Ivins is reached by way of the Santa Clara River road a few miles northwest of St. George.

Hikers stop at a rock catch basin on Red Mountain in the Red Mountain Wilderness Study Area.

Day hike

Red Mountain Traverse

Distance: 10 miles point-to-point or 10 miles out-and-back.
Starting and maximum elevations: 4,700 feet and 5,070 feet.
Difficulty: Moderately strenuous.
Best months: March through April; October.
Topo maps: Veyo-UT; Santa Clara-UT.

This hiking route follows an ancient jeep track for the first 5.2 miles. The second half of the excursion is a cross-country traverse of the Red Mountain plateau to a rough, unofficial trail down to the community of Ivins. Sweeping panoramas of the Red Mountains to the west, eagle's-eye overlooks down into twisting Snow Canyon, and scenic views of the soaring spires of Zion National Park far to the east make this vigorous all-day exploration both exhilarating and enchanting.

The trail begins at the unmarked parking area, with a sandy doubletrack leading southwest amid pinyon-juniper woodlands, sagebrush, and prickly pear cactus. Despite the nearby booming population center, a sense of solitude will soon envelope you. The increasingly rocky trail winds southwest over a rolling plateau of manzanita, holly, and Spanish bayonet, broken by patches of pinyon pine and juniper. At 1.3 miles the trail tops out on a stunning overlook at just under 5,000 feet elevation with an overpowering view of the black magma of the Pine Valley Mountains to the northeast.

Continuing on to the southwest the trail passes a commanding overlook of the deep abyss of Snow Canyon at 2.4 miles. At 5,570 feet this promontory is the high point of the hiking route; it is a perfect place to pause with binoculars and study the striking contrast of red and white cliffs dropping almost 2,000 feet to the narrow floor of the winding canyon. The trail in the middle and lower reaches of the canyon is heavily used, so you may see a few ant-like dots far below to provide perspective. Sheltered from the wind and nurtured by runoff from the plateau, the sheer cliff walls are decorated by remarkably lush vegetation. Another 0.1 mile along the canyon rim sprawling St. George comes into full view, 10 miles down the canyon. Continue following the track, staying to the left along the canyon rim. The plateau broadens, with redstone amphitheaters separating intermittent pinnacles thrusting 80 to 100 feet above the gently sloping slickrock.

Long portions of the trail consist of sand, providing a beach-like feeling to the place. At around mile 5 the spires of Zion National Park become visible to the east along with the vibrant Red Mountains to the west. At 5.2 miles the sandy track vanishes on the tablerock plateau of Red Mountain. The 5,570-foot apex of the roadless area at Snow Point rises 500 vertical feet to the north but is not readily apparent. If you've not arranged for a car shuttle this is an excellent turn-around spot for a 10.4-mile out-and-back hike and, if time and energy permit, a quick sidetrip to the jumbled red rock top of nearby Snow Point.

The second cross-country half of the point-to-point hike continues southward toward Ivins. The lower expanse of Snow Canyon drops to the east. If you wander in that direction you will be treated to more vistas of the St. George vicinity. Try to avoid stepping on patches of fragile cryptobiotic soil as you work your way down the plateau. In early spring, or after a storm, pools of sparkling water fill countless shallow basins on the red slickrock surface, but otherwise this is a long, dry hike. The wide open, windswept mesa is a perfect place for flying your favorite kite, for those so inclined.

With topo map in hand, head for the most southern point of the plateau, from which the drop is made to Ivins. If you get too far to the east or west the canyon rim will lead you around to the correct point of descent. Directly north of the downhill user-created trail are two of the higher points of the southern edge of the plateau; these will also help guide you. A noticeable but unofficial trail winds steeply down the shale slope to a handy cut in the cliff, enabling you to safely reach your awaiting vehicle far below, in Ivins, an exciting grand finale to a wide roaming traverse—so remote yet so close to St. George.

SOUTHEAST
COLORADO PLATEAU

Introduction

From the Greater Dinosaur on the northeast to Greater Zion on the southwest, the vast Colorado Plateau is a complex jumble of mesas covering nearly half of Utah in its eastern and southern sections. A misleading impression of gently rolling terrain is gained from distant views across its surface. But once out on the land, travelers discover a remarkable slickrock world of sculptured canyons, buttes, spires, mesas, arches, and badlands within countless wild tributaries of the serpentine Green, Colorado, and San Juan rivers.

A chaotic sequence of uplifts and folds produced the monumental scale of the Book Cliffs, San Rafael Swell, Waterpocket Fold, Circle Cliffs, and Grand Staircase. Igneous rock, later uncovered by erosion, is brilliantly displayed by the rounded peaks of the La Sal, Henry, and Abajo ranges, which float like apparitions on a surrounding sea of elevated plateaus. Exposed layers of increasing age vary from black volcanics in the north to Pink Cliffs (Wasatch Formation), Gray Cliffs (Mancos shale), White Cliffs (Navajo sandstone), and Vermilion Cliffs (Chinle and Wingate formations) toward the south.

Most of these wildlands lie within the Upper Sonoran Life Zone at 3,500 to 5,500 feet, with much of the remaining higher country grading to the Transition Life Zone up to 8,000 feet. Sagebrush is the dominant shrub along with shadscale, Mormon tea, and grasses. Salt flats host greasewood and salt grasses, whereas blackbrush prefers nonalkaline soils. Higher plateaus pick up enough moisture to support a dense woodland of pinyon-juniper. This is a favored niche of reptiles, along with scattered populations of mule deer, pronghorn antelope, and desert bighorn sheep.

In the higher transition zone ponderosa pine and Douglas-fir mix with a chaparral association of scrub oak, mountain mahogany, and sagebrush. Coyotes and red foxes rely on the abundance of rabbits and other small mammals.

Despite a geologic wonder of wild country unmatched on Earth, only three national forest roadless areas here and part of one BLM wildland (which is mostly in Arizona) are formally protected as wilderness under the 1964 Wilderness Act. The overwhelming majority of the 24 Colorado Plateau wildlands featured in the following pages remain as *de facto* wilderness. Despite their unofficial status these uncluttered expanses of wild Utah provide an irreplaceable source of inspiration and recreation.

Cottonwood Canyon 13

Location: 3 miles northeast of St. George, in southwestern Utah.
Size: 22,400 acres.
Administration: BLM Cedar City District, Dixie Resource Area; Dixie National Forest, Pine Valley Ranger District.
Management status: BLM wilderness study area (11,330 acres); BLM roadless land (170 acres); USDAFS roadless land (6,700 acres); roadless state land (4,200 acres).
Ecosystems: Transition zone between Intermountain sagebrush province ecoregion on the west and Colorado Plateau province ecoregion on the east. Potential natural vegetation type is pinyon-juniper woodland.
Elevation range: 3,200 to 4,870 feet.
Established trails/routes: 6 miles.
Maximum core to perimeter distance: 1.5 miles.
Activities: Hiking, backpacking, canyoneering, photography, nature study.
Maps: BLM 1:100,000 scale surface management/land ownership map entitled "St. George" (50 meter contour interval); USDAFS 1995 half-inch/mile planimetric map entitled "Dixie National Forest-Pine Valley & Cedar City Ranger Districts." See Appendix E for a listing of the two topo maps covering the roadless area.

OVERVIEW: The Cottonwood Canyon roadless land is a 7-mile-long by 3-mile-wide rectangle located in Utah's fast-growing Dixie region in the southwest corner of the state. With short mild winters, the St. George area is a magnet for "snow birds" and other winter visitors. On the main route to Zion National Park and Las Vegas, the booming town draws a wide spectrum of tourists all year long. The roadless wilderness lies just minutes north of the hubbub of St. George.

From the BLM's Red Cliffs Recreation site, adjacent to Interstate 15 on the eastern edge of the wilderness study area, Cottonwood Canyon's roadless acres stretch westward along the lower ridges of the Pine Valley Mountains to the north. Cottonwood's red Navajo sandstone ridges stand out against the jagged black outcroppings of granite and basalt in the Pine Valleys. These grainy textured Triassic and Jurassic sediments have been sculpted into the usual sinuous curves, ridges, mushrooms, alcoves, and canyons found to the east on the Colorado Plateau. Some Quaternary basalt is exposed along the ridges below the northern mountains, echoing the mountains' igneous origins.

13 COTTONWOOD CANYON

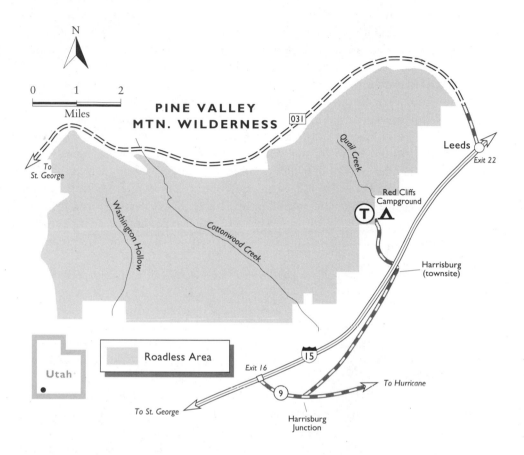

According to the BLM survey, nearly 80 percent of the Cottonwood Canyon Wilderness Study Area is rock outcrop, stony colluvial land, and badland. Vegetation is sparse. Pinyon-juniper woodlands are scattered at elevations above 4,000 feet. On the northern lands of the Dixie National Forest, low mountain slopes are home to big sagebrush, antelope bitterbrush, Utah serviceberry, and mountain mahogany. But large expanses of slickrock limit such vegetation to less than five percent of the land surface.

At lower elevations, blackbrush desert shrub vegetation, with intermittent bursage, Mormon tea, and desert bitterbrush, is the dominant type. Here too plant life is restricted by slickrock and rock outcrops that comprise nearly 90 percent of the surface.

Riparian zones vary greatly in their vegetation density and moisture. Fremont cottonwood, velvet and singleleaf ash, and screwbean mesquite grow along the intermittent streams—Mill Creek, Quail Creek, and Heath Wash. Tilting downward to the north beneath the wilderness study area is the Navajo sandstone aquifer that supplies the municipal water for burgeoning St. George and nearby Washington. Proposed water development and nearby urban growth pose serious threats to this wildland.

Straddling the boundary between Basin and Range and Colorado Plateau, this transition zone provides habitat for a diversity of wildlife. The lower desert elevations are significant habitat for desert tortoise. In the higher reaches, mule deer use the northern portion as winter range; cougar, bobcat, and coyote are also found here, although the predators are less numerous. Birders may find eagles and falcons swooping along cliffs on the northern boundary, especially in winter. Both bald and golden eagles use the area for winter hunting. Several sightings of peregrine falcons and prairie falcons have been reported near St. George and along the northern cliffs, respectively. Among other bird species are Gambel's quail, mourning doves, and red-tailed, Cooper's, and sharp-shinned hawks.

Gila monsters and chuckwallas enjoy the nooks of Cottonwood's lower rocky terrain; observant hikers may see these and other reptiles. If you are lucky enough to catch a glimpse of the shy desert tortoise, show respect by steering a wide berth.

The babbling brook and the low protected canyon of Quail Creek provided a home for prehistoric peoples. Rock shelters and pictographs date to a few hundred years ago. Tragically these sites have been heavily vandalized by modern boors who defaced the rock art by adding their own names and messages. Elsewhere in the roadless area, undiscovered sites may exist. If you visit them, leave them in their pristine condition for later explorers to enjoy.

This convenient roadless area is a gem in light of the blossoming urban and suburban growth in southwestern Utah. Future generations will appreciate its wilderness values probably even more than do the residents of today.

RECREATIONAL USES: Naturalness and solitude survive in the hinterlands of roadless Cottonwood Canyon. The heaviest recreational use, according to a BLM survey, is by sightseers and photographers who never even enter the area; they see it from Interstate 15 as they travel past the eastern end. The second area of heavy use is the Quail Creek area, just off the interstate. Here the BLM operates the Red Cliffs Recreation Site Campground. Tent and trailer sites are located amid cottonwoods along the seasonal stream in the valley. The campground closes at 10 P.M. to discourage nocturnal festivities by the younger set from nearby towns. Several short hiking trails begin at the campground and are shown on a large map at the campground entrance.

While there are no designated trails outside of the Red Cliffs Recreation Area, opportunities for solitude and exploration abound in the Mill Creek and Washington Hollow drainages at the southwestern end of the wilderness study area. The Cottonwood–Heath Canyon complex and the wild upper region of Quail Canyon can be reached from Forest Road 031 on the northern boundary of the roadless area. Cottonwood Canyon is seldom used by hunters since other areas nearby have both more game and easier road access.

Most, if not all, of Cottonwood Canyon has been designated critical habitat for the desert tortoise, listed as endangered by the federal government. Visitors are strongly urged not to pick up, take home, or harass the tortoises in any way. This is a fragile place made more so by the booming sprawl of St. George and surrounding communities. Visitors to this wildland need to show respect and restraint.

HOW TO GET THERE: From St. George drive 7 miles north on I-15 to Exit 16 (the Harrisburg exit). Go east 0.75 mile and turn left on Old Highway 91. Continue north on this frontage road 4.3 miles to a Red Cliffs Campground sign. Turn left (west) and go 1.75 miles on the paved road to the campground. This access road may present a challenge to oversize vehicles. The freeway underpass has an 11-foot height limit (and narrow opening), and sharply angled stream crossings may cause longer vehicles to drag their rear bumpers.

Day hike

Quail Creek

Distance: 2 miles out and back; additional mileage for exploring.
Starting and maximum elevations: 3,240 and 3,450 feet (upper pool).
Difficulty: Easy to the first pool in 0.3 mile; moderately strenuous to strenuous for additional exploration.
Best months: Year-round.
Topo map: Harrisburg Junction-UT.

This short hike is very popular, and for good reasons. It features a seasonal stream (dry by late summer and into the fall), waterfalls and deep pools, a slotted canyon, and a pictograph alcove surrounded by steep red-rock cliffs and canyon walls. The trail from the campground winds along a nature trail above the cottonwood and willow thickets in the bottom of Quail Creek and through the canyon of Navajo sandstone.

A stunning waterfall and pool appear at 0.3 mile, providing respite and a possible turn-around point for less energetic hikers. Otherwise, return to the trail above the falls and hop across the stream. The trail steepens and arrives at an overlook above the lower trail. Here you have entered a slightly higher

Falls and pools grace Quail Creek on the northeastern edge of the Cottonwood Canyon Wilderness Study Area.

world with another pool and a slickrock slot canyon with alcoves and grottos. High on the slope above the willowed bottom is one of the heavily vandalized archeological sites. Its archeological integrity has been destroyed and it cannot be dated, but enough of the original pictographs exist to evoke a sense of the ancient inhabitants of this enchanting spot. High on the sandy talus slope, beneath the enormous rock overhang, Paleo-Indians enjoyed security, nearby water and fuel, and a sweeping view down the canyon. This is the turn-around for the basic short hike.

To continue on the more strenuous portion of the hike, drop to the stream, and with skillful footwork bypass the pool to the left, leap across the stream's narrow spot, and continue up the slot canyon via the ancient step-holes in the steep rock to the right of the cascading stream. At 0.1 mile above the steps, the canyon splits. The main canyon runs to the right. Immediately, a steep slanted rock must be negotiated above a pool on the right. After that the canyon wash is clear for some distance and can be easily explored.

A possible 0.5-mile strenuous side loop begins at the canyon junction above the rock steps. Climb steeply to the north, gaining 450 feet as you cross the slanted layered rock to the top ridge. Drop down to the right (east) with the main canyon bottom directly below. Turn right to proceed down canyon, by-passing several pouroffs by angling left, ending up just below a large pictograph alcove close to Quail Creek.

Another side trip is to head up a well-used foot trail heading southwest (left) about 0.25 mile along the main trail from the campground. After 0.25 mile on this trail, a narrow slotted canyon can be bypassed by climbing up and to the left. Some tricky footwork may be required to climb a large, dead tree trunk leaning like a ladder in the slot. Then you must wedge your way up a chimney to the ridgetop. After reaching the ridge, work around to the left for a route back down to the campground. From this height you will enjoy views of Zion's pinnacles to the northeast. In the foreground lies vast Quail Creek Reservoir above the Virgin River. Route finding is moderately challenging as you find yourself cliffed out on three sides. Persist, and head for the high point of the ridge above the cliffs. Drop down that ridge to the northeast through an expanse of large mushroom-shaped rocks to a side canyon that leads straight east to the campground. This outing provides the excitement of route finding without the possibility of getting lost since the campground is intermittently visible below.

Pine Valley Mountains
Wilderness Complex   14

Location: 10 miles north of St. George, in southwest Utah.
Size: 111,395 acres.
Administration: USDAFS Dixie National Forest, Pine Valley Ranger District.
Management status: USDAFS wilderness (50,000 acres); unprotected USDAFS roadless land (61,395 acres).
Ecosystems: Colorado Plateau province ecoregion, with pinyon-juniper woodland (potential natural vegetation), to ponderosa pine and Gambel oak, to spruce-fir at high elevations.
Elevation range: 4,500 to 10,360 feet (Signal Peak).
Established trails/routes: More than 120 miles of trails in the national forest.
Maximum core to perimeter distance: 3 miles.
Activities: Hiking, backpacking, rock climbing, horseback riding, photography, hunting, cross-country skiing, snowshoeing.
Maps: BLM 1:100,000 scale surface management/land ownership maps entitled "Cedar City" and "St. George" (50 meter interval contour); 1995 USDAFS half-inch/mile map entitled "Dixie National Forest, Pine Valley and Cedar City Ranger Districts" (50 meter contour intervals). See Appendix E for a listing of the five topo maps that cover the roadless area.

OVERVIEW: The swiftly growing towns and subdivisions of Utah's Dixie wrap around three sides of the Pine Valley Mountain Wilderness Complex. The mountain range is a laccolith, created by a massive igneous intrusion, as were, other ranges on the Colorado Plateau—the Henrys, the Abajos, and the La Sals. Here on the western edge of the Colorado Plateau, the naked dark pinnacles of the Pine Valleys rise to 10,000 feet, towering above the communities that cluster in the broad valleys 6,000 feet below. The Chinle formation that covered the region was deformed and subsequently eroded, leaving the monzonite cores exposed. This black rock of the steep mountain slopes stands in sharp contrast to the reds of the Navajo sandstone elsewhere; the Red Mountains, 8 miles to the west, are strikingly different in color, texture, and contour.

The rough-grained quartz monzonite of the Pine Valleys provides a tempting surface for rock climbers. The freeze-thaw cycle, especially on the sunny southern exposure, has created fissures and fractures in the granite monolith. These forces have also expelled gargantuan boulders from the mountain core; they rest miles below the peaks amid ponderosa pines on the lower slopes.

From pinyon-juniper woodlands on the lower slopes, the mountain vegetation progresses to Gambel oak, mountain mahogany, and serviceberry amid ponderosa pine and aspen. High elevations support subalpine and Douglas-fir, Engelmann spruce, ancient bristlecone pine, and the wind-sculpted limber pine. Lower reaches of the mountains were heavily logged beginning in 1856, when St. George was first settled. Protected as wilderness since the 1984 Utah Wilderness Act, the virgin stands on the steep slopes of the high mountain core are safe from logging.

Seven units of roadless national forest spreading beyond the wilderness boundaries comprise an additional 61,395 acres of roadless wildlands. Looping out from the wilderness like lace on the doily around a Valentine heart, these presently unroaded lands provide essential winter range for wildlife. The Cottonwood–Yankee Doodle Hollow unit south of the wilderness area connects the Pine Valleys to the Cottonwood Canyon Wilderness. The Maple Hollow and Sandy Creek units on the east protect the wilderness core from encroaching development. Growth along the adjacent Interstate-15 corridor poses a hazard to unprotected wild country. In this arid region, annual rainfall in the valleys totals only 10 inches, while the mountains get twice that much precipitation each year. The water resources of the Pine Valleys and especially the aquifer below are eyed covetously by nearby communities and developers.

The Pine Valley range supports a large mule deer herd. An equally healthy population of mountain lions moves invisibly across forested slopes, peering over ledges, and padding silently through the canyons. Hikers can also watch for droppings and tracks of black bears on trails. Beaver are also here, leaving their signatures, on pointed willow stumps along streams. Chipmunks and marmots squeal and scurry amid talus. Peregrine falcons and golden eagles perch their nests high on rocky outcroppings, watching for these tasty little critters; the raptors are a common sight, soaring on the thermals created by the interaction of sharp mountains and the warm valleys below. Enticing anglers, mountain streams provide habitat for brook, rainbow, cutthroat, and brown trout.

Paleo-Indian use of the forested range was apparently slight. Nomadic hunters sought game, but no evidence of permanent residence has been found. Lithic scatters indicate a transitory presence one thousand years ago.

In historical times people's focus was first on timber. Then, from the 1870s to the early 1900s, silver mining brought prospectors to these steep mountainsides. The Silver Reef historical site in Leeds, immediately to the south, and the Leeds Creek Kiln in the national forest, are artifacts of the

14 PINE VALLEY MOUNTAINS WILDERNESS COMPLEX

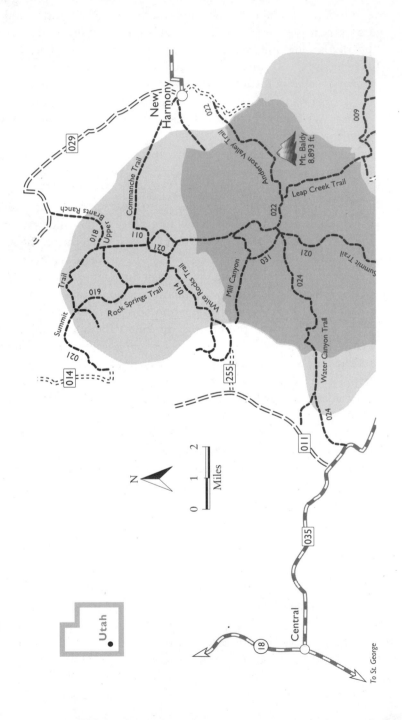

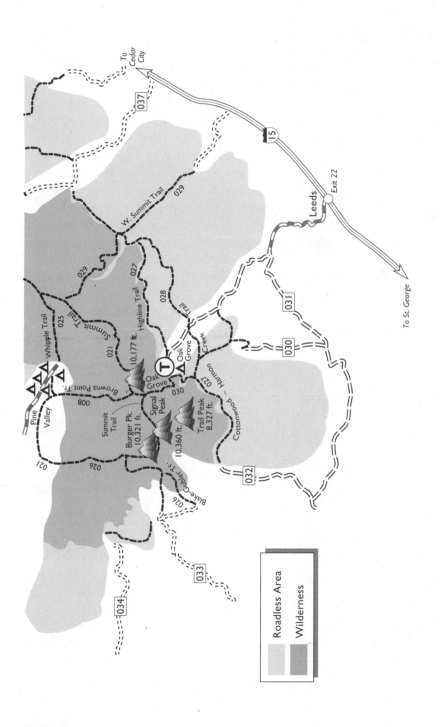

silver era. The role of the Pine Valleys today is as a recreational area for residents and tourists alike. Tourism has become the leading industry in Utah's Dixie; this handy wilderness complex is a non-depreciating asset.

RECREATIONAL USES: The Pine Valley Recreational Area on the northwest side of the mountains is a complex of campgrounds and an equestrian center. There are a total of 77 campsites here. At this 6,800-foot elevation the season runs from May 28 to the end of September. During summer, all spaces are usually filled. Reservations can be made with MISTIX (800-283-CAMP). A small primitive campground is across the mountains to the south at Oak Grove. It too is open from the end of May to the end of September. The roads and trails on the southern side, however, are usually snow-free before those on the north, permitting access for early hikers combating cabin fever.

Hiking opportunities are limitless. Trailheads from both campground areas provide a wide variety of routes. Trails to the summit ridge are all quite steep, gaining 4,000 feet in 2 or 3 miles. Several lengthy loop trips are popular from the Pine Valley trailheads. Three trails—Forsyth, Brown's Point, and Whipple —follow steep routes to the Summit Trail, enabling backpackers to enjoy an entire route of discovery with no car shuttle. The Water Canyon Trail out of Grass Valley leads to the northern end of the Summit Trail. From there, the trail along the ridgeline south to Burger Peak winds through alpine meadows and hidden valleys, with awe-inspiring vistas of the Red Mountains and the peaks of Zion National Park. Forsyth Trail drops back into the Pine Valley complex. A 2-mile car shuttle or other creative transportation is necessary to return to the Grass Valley Trailhead to complete this 27-mile journey. With water available throughout the summer, long backpacks are possible in the Pine Valleys. Hiking the crest trail from Big Pine Spring to New Harmony, or, for a longer trek, to Pinto Spring on the northwest, is an exhilarating seven-day trip.

Other trails loop along the edge of the wilderness. The Cottonwood–Harmon Creek and Highland trails on the southern border of the wilderness area weave along the contours and provide outstanding views of the valley below and the towers of Zion in the distance. These lower trails, especially on the south, become passable early in the spring. Trailheads at Pinto Spring, Upper Grants Ranch, New Harmony, and Mill Canyon provide access into the roadless northern unit around Rancher Peak. Hikes up Sandy Creek or from the gauging station on Mill Creek take you into the lightly used areas just west of I-15.

Lower areas of the mountains are utilized by backcountry horsemen. In the fall, heavy use by hunters dictates that hunters and hikers alike wear neon orange. If you hike with your dog, make sure it too is properly attired.

HOW TO GET THERE: From St. George drive 12 miles northeast on Interstate 15 to Exit 22 (for Leeds/Silver Reef). Go northwest on Silver Reef Road to the national forest boundary. When the pavement ends at 1.6 miles, bear right on the gravel road and drive 8 more miles to Oak Grove Campground. The sign in the center of the campground indicates Trail 030 to the summit ridge.

Day hike

Oak Grove Trail

Distance: 7 miles round trip.
Starting and maximum elevations: 6,800 feet (campground) and 9,922 feet (crest).
Difficulty: Strenuous.
Best months: April or May (depending on snow conditions) through September.
Topo map: Signal Peak-UT.

This steep climb up the southern face of the Pine Valley Mountains provides magnificent views of the St. George region and Zion National Park. The well-marked trail is clear of snow earlier than those out of shadier, chillier Pine Valley Recreation Area on the northern side of the range, although you can plan on deep crusty snow for at least the last 1,000 vertical feet to the top. The panorama that awaits you is definitely worth the effort.

The summit of the Oak Grove Trail.

The dramatic gain in altitude is spread evenly along the trail. From the campground, Trail 030 rises 500 feet by the time it reaches the wilderness boundary, after about 0.75 mile. The transitions from Gambel oak to ponderosa pine to Douglas-fir mark the increase in altitude. At 1.5 miles the trail intersects a ridge with a promontory jutting above the valley below and a majestic view of the mountain's southeast-facing cliffs.

Protected by huge monzonite boulders, a suitable campsite is nestled in this 8,100-foot aerie. There is, however, no water available here so you'll have to carry some if you intend to stay the night.

From this resting spot the trail continues to ascend through the fir-pine forest, with occasional mountain mahogany and scrub oak vegetation. Just west of the switchbacking trail tower sharp cliffs of quartz monzonite with dramatic vertical fractures, framed by large, picturesque, fire-scarred snags. The final section to the summit probably just seems steeper than it is, coming at the end of the hike up. Gaining more than 3,000 feet in about 3 miles requires considerable effort. The granite spires of Signal Peak (10,360 feet) and Trail Peak rise above the ridgeline. The dense spruce-fir forest seems squatty compared to the towering snags left by an ancient fire; this is a rare stand of virgin timber, with the snags as evidence of how large these trees can become. The sweeping views of the Leeds Valley and the pinnacles of Zion are a sensational reward for your effort.

After pausing at the overlook to enjoy the view, drop to Deer Flat at the summit trail junction. As time and energy permit, exploring the Summit Trail to the south 1.5 miles to Burger Peak (10,321 feet) would add another adventure to your outing. For another variation, Brown's Point Trail (008) drops down from the Summit Trail due north of the Oak Grove Trail, ending at the Upper Pines Campground in Pine Valley. For a point-to-point, trans-mountain hike, arrange to exchange car keys with friends who have parked at the Upper Pines Campground as you traverse the summit to enjoy a 9-mile hike without a lengthy car shuttle.

For the out-and-back trip, drop back down Oak Grove Trail, enjoying the panorama as you descend. You too may be skeptical of the "Summit Trail 3 miles" message on the USDA Forest Service sign at the Oak Grove Trailhead by the time you return.

Greater Zion Complex

Location: 23 miles northeast of St. George, in southwestern Utah.
Size: 253,395 acres.
Administration: BLM Cedar City District, Dixie and Kanab resource areas; Zion National Park.
Management status: BLM wilderness study areas (61,540 acres in six areas) and unprotected roadless land (71,235 acres); NPS roadless land recommended as wilderness (120,620 acres).
Ecosystems: Colorado Plateau province ecoregion featuring ponderosa pine and mountain shrub at higher elevation and on north-facing slopes; pinyon-juniper woodland (potential natural vegetation), sagebrush, and scattered riparian vegetation, with barren slickrock.
Elevation range: 3,666 feet (Coalpits Wash) to 8,726 feet (Horse Ranch Mountain).
Established trails/routes: More than 100 miles of trails within the park; many more miles of old jeep track in adjacent BLM areas.
Maximum core to perimeter distance: 3.5 miles.
Activities: Hiking, backpacking, horseback riding, rock climbing, canyoneering, photography, wildlife viewing.
Maps: BLM 1:100,000 scale surface management/land ownership maps entitled "Panguitch" and "Kanab" (50 meter contour interval). See Appendix E for a listing of the 14 topo maps covering the roadless area.

OVERVIEW: The rectilinear borders of Zion National Park are clear evidence that the federal legislation setting aside this first Utah national park did not acknowledge terrain, drainages, or ecosystems. These serious omissions are rectified in the Greater Zion Wilderness Complex. Some of these additions around the edges of the park are fragmentary BLM holdings as small as 35 and 40 acres. Others, such as Orderville Canyon (home of the North Fork of the Virgin River) and Parunuweap ("Roaring Water") Canyon are extensions of the canyons of Zion. Canaan Mountain, south of Zion's main entrance, has vast cliffs, canyons, and a sculpted plateau on par with Zion. A physiographic map of the region, with all political and administrative boundaries omitted, would reveal that all of these areas are one ecological unit.

In 1974 the National Park Service recommended that 120,620 of Zion's

15   GREATER ZION COMPLEX

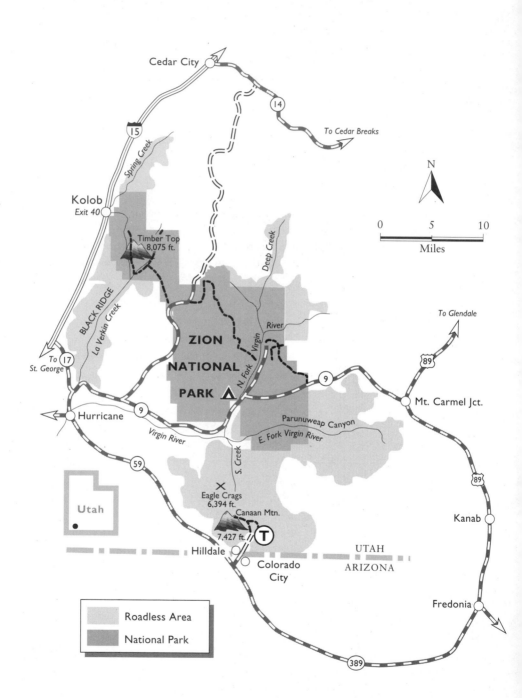

Cedar City

To Cedar Breaks

14

15

Spring Creek

N

Kolob
Exit 40

0   5   10
Miles

Timber Top
8,075 ft.

Deep Creek

To Glendale

BLACK RIDGE

La Verkin Creek

River

Virgin

ZION

89

NATIONAL

N. Fork

To
St. George

17

PARK

9

Mt. Carmel Jct.

Hurricane

9

Parunuweap Canyon

Virgin River

E. Fork Virgin River

S. Creek

59

89

Utah

Eagle Crags
6,394 ft.

Canaan Mtn.

Kanab

7,427 ft.

T

UTAH

Hilldale

ARIZONA

Colorado
City

Fredonia

Roadless Area

National Park

389

147,000 acres be designated as wilderness by Congress. Except for the entrance road in the Kolob area, the Little Creek Road that cuts through the narrow neck, and the developed corridor from the south entrance to the Temple of Sinawava, nearly the entire park would be managed as wilderness. During the BLM wilderness inventory process, the Park Service recommended that the adjacent BLM roadless areas be designated wilderness and be managed accordingly. Zion administration was concerned about the future of the park's "viewshed," as well as preservation of the flow of the Virgin River, the forks of which originate outside the park. Reducing the flow in the Virgin would significantly disturb wildlife and vegetation. Endangered and threatened fish species would suffer from reduced habitat, and Zion's famous hanging gardens would wither. The place of peace and refuge, which is the connotation of the park's name, would be destroyed.

The most spectacular attributes of Zion country are definitely the spires, cliffs, canyons, and monoliths created by centuries of moving water. Vegetation is also a spectacular feature. Four vegetation zones occur in the Zion area, due to its varied altitude and its location at the junction of the Mojave Desert, the Great Basin, and the Colorado Plateau.

At low elevation, away from water, prickly pear and cholla cacti, creosote bush, honey mesquite, and purple sage enjoy the arid land and the warm to hot temperatures reminiscent of the Mojave Desert. At higher elevations, pinyon pine and Utah juniper, with live oak and mountain mahogany, are reminders of the Great Basin island mountains. Higher plateaus and cooler, wetter canyons support patchy forests of ponderosa pine, white and Douglas-fir, and aspen. Along permanent streams and at the springs, lush stands of cottonwood, box elder, willow, and ferns stun the visitor with the accompanying symphony of babbling water. Keep an eye out for poison ivy, an unwelcome interloper in this garden of Eden. In hidden canyon hollows, where springs leak their moisture down the sandstone walls, exotic hanging gardens flourish, with tenacious ferns and mosses dangling from their vertical beds.

Both in Zion and its neighboring canyons and plateaus, a plethora of wildlife flourishes. Elk, mountain lion, and black bear top the mammal species list. Mule deer and desert bighorn sheep move in small groups along the benchlands and canyon rims. Smaller mammals include porcupines, jackrabbits, rock squirrels, and cliff chipmunks. In the dark, bats swoop though cliff passages collecting insects, returning to their nooks and alcoves by dawn. Birders have counted more than 270 species in and around Zion. The cliff swallows are exhilarating in their canyon acrobatics. Raptors such as the peregrine falcon keep the rodent population in proper balance.

This region, a botanical crossroads, was also a cultural junction in ancient times. Traces of small Anasazi villages have been found in the Virgin River bottoms. For one thousand years, these early agriculturalists existed with their small plots of cultivated land surrounded by the towering cliffs. By 1200 A.D. they had left, to be replaced by the southern Paiutes, primarily hunter-gatherers, who used the area seasonally until the Europeans arrived. John Wesley Powell's 1872 visit spread the word of Zion's wonders, leading to national monument status in 1909 and then designation as a national park in 1919. Powell's exploration of the area was not exhaustive, however, for he would have been impressed with the surrounding plateaus and canyons also.

Nearly 90 archeological sites have been identified in the Zion Park portion of the canyon. The roadless wilderness study area outside of the park has pre-historic secrets yet to be discovered.

Canaan Mountain, with 52,000 acres, is the largest BLM unit in the com-plex. Akin to the biblical promised land for which it was named, this is a slickrock paradise. A high plateau surrounded by 1,000-foot escarpments of the Vermilion Cliffs, Canaan Mountain is a dominant sentinel on the park's southern horizon. The Navajo sandstone cliffs have been sculpted into ram-parts, hollows, buttresses, alcoves, and gargoyles. Water Creek, Squirrel Creek, and others have cut plunging canyons, providing dramatic topographic relief as well as strips of lush riparian vegetation amid the barren slickrock. Even the dour BLM confesses that Canaan Mountain is similar in character to Zion National Park. The southern extension of this awesome stretch of the Vermil-ion Cliffs lies in Arizona; that state's BLM office supported its designation as the Cottonwood Point Wilderness.

The lower portion of Parunuweap Canyon impressed Major Powell when he came through in 1872. Upstream, beyond the park boundaries, the Parunuweap continues to stun visitors with spectacular narrows, soaring and looming canyon walls, and hanging gardens. The canyon is a ferocious water chute in flood, with the East Fork of the Virgin rising 40 feet on occasion. Such immense and erratic water volume tempts dam builders.

The small Watchman Wilderness Study Area (600 acres) stands at the very gates of Zion, on the west slope of the famous Watchman formation. As with the North Fork (1,040 acres) and Orderville Canyon (6,500 acres) units, this piece of the BLM puzzle is a logical and necessary extension of Zion's very limited, straight boundaries.

Six additional BLM units lie to the north of Zion, on the Kolob Terrace. Totalling 27,646 acres, these lands are contiguous to the park and a logical extension of the watershed, wildlife habitat, and viewshed of the park. South of the Kolob addition to Zion, Red Butte soars to 7,410 feet, and, also outside the park, the dramatic igneous faults of Black Ridge rise above the red Navajo sandstone. These features, along with the plunging canyons of LaVerkin and Taylor creeks, which begin their descent within the park, are continuations of the features of Zion. The central wilderness core of Zion has been set aside for future generations; the same protection needs to be extended to these unpro-tected BLM lands.

The view from the Timber Creek trail.

RECREATIONAL USES: Hiking and camping opportunities in Zion National Park are vast. Hiking trails, from a modest 0.5 mile to a 26.6-mile marathon, provide spectacular trips with stunning views. Check at the visitor center for regulations and weather conditions; backcountry camping permits are required in the park.

The BLM units are lightly visited, with two exceptions. The famous hike through the Narrows of the Virgin River begins in the Orderville Canyon BLM unit. Likewise, park visitors exploring Parunuweap Canyon in Zion may be unaware that they've hiked onto BLM land as they explore the East Fork's spectacular beauty.

Outings elsewhere in the Greater Zion Wilderness are sure to provide solitude and the thrill of discovery. Immediately at the park's south entrance, the Watchman unit, across the North Fork of the Virgin, invites explorers to climb the Watchman (6,555 feet) or Johnson Mountain (6,153 feet). Canyoneering, climbing, and fishing are available in the proposed wilderness additions along LaVerkin Creek, Taylor Creek, Spring Creek, Beartrap Canyon, and Black Ridge.

Canaan Mountain offers spectacular hiking, rock climbing, and canyoneering opportunities far from the crowds of Zion. The sandstone plateau and the miles of surrounding cliffs are accessible via Horse Valley Wash south of Rockville and also by the spray of roads that heads up the canyons north of Hilldale.

Zion typifies the wonders of the Colorado Plateau better than any other park. Its easy accessibility via Interstate 15 makes it a popular destination. These contiguous BLM roadless areas more than double Zion's wilderness, adding more wild lands to explore.

HOW TO GET THERE: From Kanab drive 7 miles south on U.S. Highway 89 to Fredonia, Arizona. Turn right and continue 30 miles on Arizona Highway 389, curving through the Kaibab Indian Reservation to Colorado City, Arizona. Bear right on the signed Colorado City turnoff (Arizona Highway 377, or Central Street). Drive north through Colorado City toward Hilldale, immediately north of the state line. Above the road are the abrupt cliffs of Canaan Mountain.

Northeast of Hilldale is the mouth of Squirrel and Water canyons and the trailhead. Use the break in the cliffs as your landmark, and head for the road up into the canyon. Or, if you prefer more precise instructions: Go north on Central to University. Turn right. At Hilldale Street, turn left. Hilldale Street winds and crosses the dry wash of Short Creek, entering the town of Hilldale. Turn right on Utah Avenue, which soon bends north at the edge of town and becomes Canyon Street. Canyon Street goes to the trailhead. It changes from pavement to an improved dirt road, but it has sticky spots when wet. Bear right at the major Y intersection after the pavement ends, and go 1 mile into the canyon to the turnoff on the right for the short spur road to the BLM Squirrel Canyon trailhead. If you miss this unmarked turn and continue straight you will end up at the town reservoir 0.6 mile farther up Canyon. This is the exit for the hike, but you should leave your vehicle at the official BLM trailhead parking area.

From the west, take Utah Highway 59 about 22 miles southeast from Hurricane to Hilldale and follow the directions above to the BLM Squirrel Canyon trailhead.

Day hike or backpack

Squirrel Canyon–Water Canyon Loop

Distance: 10 to 12 miles for loop; longer for backpacking explorations.
Starting and maximum elevations: 5,100 and 6,800 feet.
Difficulty: Moderately strenuous.
Best months: March through May; October.
Topo map: Hilldale-UT-AZ.

This is a spectacular combination of canyon and mountain, featuring the intimacy and adventure of travel in a tight canyon and the sweeping panoramas of southeastern Utah from the top of Canaan Mountain. The fractured faults in the Vermilion Cliffs of Canaan Mountain have been slotted by streams, creating narrow plunging canyons. This is a Zion experience without the crowds and regulations of the park. And yet the drive through town on the way to the trailhead provides a different kind of scenery. You can't miss the town dump, glistening in the sun down the wash below the trailhead. Up Short Creek visitors encounter a bizarre riprap configuration of cabled tires. This is a land of contrasts.

The outing can be done as a full day hike, or as a base camp backpack in early spring when the headwaters of Water and Squirrel creeks are flowing. At other times, surface potholes on Canaan Mountain may hold rainwater, possibly, permitting you a longer trip, but counting on this could be risky. In either case, take plenty of film with you.

The loop hike from the trailhead goes up Squirrel and comes down Water Canyon. From the parking area, head east through the gate at the BLM Squirrel Canyon sign. After crossing the wash the trail runs adjacent to a dirt driveway for 0.25 mile before dropping to Short Creek and going north into the canyon. About 1.25 miles from the trailhead the trail forks. The all-terrain-vehicle way goes to the right. Bear left into the notch that is Squirrel Canyon.

The grassy canyon floor, clear spring, and gentle stream of the first 0.5 mile in the canyon immediately erase the memory of burgeoning development in the valley below. Here, nature— especially the wind—rules, as the downed old cottonwoods will attest. After a gradual ascent in the second 0.5 mile, the trail climbs steeply 600 feet up the east canyon wall of sandstone, popping out on the top just below the sweeping slopes of The Beehive (6,476 feet). At this spot, while pausing for breath, you're sure to be awed by the contrast of the jagged surface of the Vermilion Cliffs' peaks, the sharply vertical walls of the canyon, and the sensuous curves of the looming Beehive. From here the cairned trail continues to climb, though more gradually, through pinyon, juniper, manzanita, holly, and ponderosa pine.

From the top, at 5,880 feet, pick up the old pack trail that bears to the northwest along the headwaters of Spring Creek. Here, at the top of the mountain and deep within the wilderness study area, you'll be struck by the incongruous sight of all-terrain-vehicle tracks everywhere. An old jeep track up Broad Hollow provides access for these vehicles, which then run amuck on the rolling mountain top, carving tire tracks into the soft earth. The country is still magnificent despite this mayhem, but you may be inspired to drop a note to the district ranger in Cedar City informing him or her of this vehicle abuse in the wilderness study area.

To the north of Spring Creek rises a massive mound of sloping sandstone covered with a multitude of beehive mounds of wind-eroded sandstone. Large expanses of slickrock cover the rolling top of Canaan Mountain, making route finding challenging. The old pack trail follows the south side of the Spring Creek drainage in its ponderosa-lined slickrock runway, climbing to the low divide where it enters the Water Canyon drainage.

As the trail rises toward this divide you'll begin to see Water Canyon opening below. It is worth the 1-mile side trip to drop down along the eastern ridge above Water Canyon to any of the several beehive promontories that dot the area. Numerous faults have opened to crevices, capturing water and providing an opportunity for ponderosa pines to take root. From the lookout you have a falcon's view of the larger faults in the Vermilion Cliffs that have developed into this canyon. Across the canyon on its west wall is a multi-tiered ribbon waterfall, plunging from the plateau to the cave-like slot 200 feet below. As you enjoy this view, consider the fact that the trail down Water Canyon goes down that same wall, just south of the falls. You may spot the lower section of the trail on the bench below the fall, but the switchbacked trail that will get you to that point is invisible on the vertical canyon wall.

After enjoying the view, continue your hike above Water Canyon. The pack trail intermittently appears in sandy patches between the slickrock, continuing to rise along the slickrock runway. When the sandstone hill on the north has subsided to a more gentle grade, take another side trip up over that rise. The view is amazing. The canyon of South Creek dives through the Vermilion Cliffs below, while Zion National Park's towering skyline rises beyond the Virgin River valley. The Eagle Crags jut from the northern side of Canaan Mountain with the dark Pine Valley Mountains on the western horizon. This is a photographer's paradise.

When you've exhausted your film supply, head back to the pack trail to locate the Water Canyon footpath. Continue on the pack trail west of Water Canyon as it continues to rise on the sandy soil. Within 0.1 mile of where the side trip to the north took off, the faint footpath departs to the south. The landmark for locating the trail is a low earthen ridge about 100 yards long parallelling the trail to the south. It is covered with wind-dwarfed Gambel oak and sage. There is a slight dip in the middle of the ridge. The faint Water Canyon Trail heads south through this gap. If you were to continue on the pack trail another 0.1 mile you would come to a set of wind-eroded sandstone mounds nestled in a ponderosa grove just to the right of the trail. This would mean you've missed the footpath. Another way to find the path is to skirt around the head of Water Canyon on its slickrock apron, watching for the depression of a trail in the sandy ridge to the west.

The faint footpath follows a ridge above the canyon's slotted gorge, aiming directly toward the large point (6,850 feet) that towers above the west wall. It takes a sharp eye to keep on the trail. Sawn-off stubs on pines along the upper trail will reassure you that you're on track. The trail follows the crestline of the sandy ridge, then drops sharply to the stream that feeds the waterfall, about 0.5 mile from the packtrail.

Cross the stream above the uppermost waterfall in a series of small stair-step falls. Watch for a cairn on the steep south bank. The trail angles up the slope heading east, toward the canyon, and out of this side valley, still heading for that high point on the west canyon wall. In less than 0.5 mile of climbing the trail reaches the top of the bluff below the high point. Cairns and the worn footpath will lead you along the rim before the trail drops, descending in switchbacks through Douglas-fir and ponderosa pine, down that canyon wall you saw earlier.

The journey through Water Canyon follows an exciting trail down the gorge. It shoots straight down faults, drops through narrows, and wedges down through slotted chimneys. Staying on the west wall above the streambed you get to enjoy the variety of waterfalls and hanging gardens. There's even an arch, high on the canyon's east wall, near the mouth. It is especially striking in the evening light. Water Canyon is well named. It's a symphony of water falling. Numerous springs emerge throughout its course. The broadening path takes you from the canyon down to the reservoir. From there it is a short (0.6 mile) walk down the improved dirt road to the trailhead.

For a backpack, traversing the mountain is an option, which requires a car shuttle to the Eagle Crags Trailhead (see *Hiking Utah,* Falcon Publishing, 1995). A loop trip, with a campsite in upper Water Canyon, would enable you to explore Eagle Crags on a day trip. An old windlass and a sawmill left from the 1920s are along the west rim pack trail on the way to the Crags. The mountain provides endless opportunities for exploring, with incredible views. An advantage of the loop outing is the dramatic descent in Water Canyon, but this journey could be tricky with a heavy pack.

Moquith Mountain   16

Location: 1 mile west of Kanab, in southwest Utah.
Size: 26,500 acres.
Administration: BLM Cedar City District, Kanab Resource Area.
Management status: BLM wilderness study area (14,830 acres, which includes 225 acres in the Water Canyon–South Fork Indian Canyon Area of Critical Environmental Concern), plus unprotected BLM and state roadless lands (11,670 acres). The roadless area is also included within BLM's Moquith Mountain Special Recreation Management Area.
Ecosystems: Colorado Plateau province ecoregion of juniper-pinyon woodland potential natural vegetation.
Elevation range: 5,000 to 7,050 feet.
Established trails/routes: The South Fork Indian Canyon Pictograph Trail (0.5 mile) is the only formal trail in the roadless area. 11 miles of primitive doubletracks used by off-road vehicles also provide access for hiking and horseback riding.
Maximum core to perimeter distance: 1.5 miles.
Activities: Hiking, backpacking, canyoneering, horseback riding, hunting, photography, nature study.
Maps: BLM 1:100,000 scale surface management/land ownership map entitled "Kanab" (50 meter contour intervals). See Appendix E for a listing of the two topo maps covering the roadless area.

OVERVIEW: At first and last light the famed Vermilion Cliffs hug the Arizona border with a blazing intensity that hushes the moment and captivates the eye. Sandwiched between Coral Pink Sand Dunes State Park and the town of Kanab, Moquith Mountain is an ecologically varied extension of the fiery Vermilion Cliffs. This wildland is a rich mosaic of diverse terrain and vegetation—from the top of Moquith Mountain to the bottom of deep canyons.

Most distinctive are the green, long-needled ponderosa pine trees growing out of pink sand dunes—but this is only the beginning. The western edge of Moquith Mountain is marked by a series of cliffs cut by short, steep canyons abutting the pink sand dunes. This escarpment is the product of up and down movements along the north-trending Sevier Fault. Across the broad plateau of Moquith Mountain rock outcrops abound, most of which have come from the Jurassic Navajo formation. The summit consists of a series of alternating sandy

16 MOQUITH MOUNTAIN

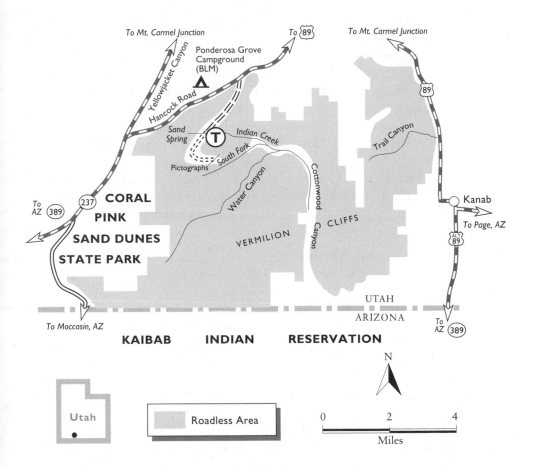

ridges and shallow ravines lined with rocky breaks and sandstone formations. Although not far from Kanab and U.S. Highway 89, solitude can be complete in rugged canyons and in the broken, densely vegetated terrain atop Moquith Mountain.

Pinyon-juniper woodland covers most of the roadless area, along with big sagebrush and a sparse assortment of upper Sonoran Desert plants such as mountain mahogany, Gambel oak, cliffrose, serviceberry, snakeweed, and rabbitbrush. A federally listed threatened species of milkvetch maintains a tenuous foothold here.

Slickrock mesas, flowing perennial streams, aspen trembling at the heads of Art and Cougar canyons, and hanging gardens clinging to cliffs in the South Fork of Indian Canyon are among the hidden treasures of Moquith Mountain. Cool, north-facing ledges in upper Water Canyon harbor relic groves of Douglas-fir. These relic plant communities are guarded by cliffs and by the special BLM designation of Area of Critical Environmental Concern.

Thick pinyon-juniper woodlands and dissected terrain hide mule deer, offering places for wide-antlered bucks to elude both mountain lions and hunters. At least three rare and sensitive bird species live on and around Moquith Mountain: fox sparrow, Lewis's woodpecker, and roadrunner. An abundance of cottontail rabbits lures a variety of raptors, including an occasional bald eagle or peregrine falcon. Mourning dove are especially common from May to September.

Three archeological sites have been recorded near the northern and eastern edges of the roadless area. They consist of one lithic scatter site and two pictograph sites, the most notable of which is in the South Fork of Indian Canyon.

RECREATIONAL USES: Hiking, backpacking, nature study, and photography top the list of varied activities. Scenic destinations include 1,500 acres of ponderosa pine-studded sand dunes, vibrant red and orange cliffs, unusual pockets of aspen and Douglas-fir, and the South Fork of Indian Canyon Pictograph Site. Hikes are many and varied, with possible routes in every canyon and across the plateau of Moquith Mountain. The best routes for horseback riding are on Moquith Mountain and in lower Water Canyon. To minimize impact, all visitors should follow existing routes wherever possible, taking care to avoid the cryptobiotic soil that is slowly reclaiming some of the scars of past off-road-vehicle use.

The 3,700-acre Coral Pink Sand Dunes State Park touches the western boundary of Moquith Mountain and includes a campground and picnic area. Heavy off-road-vehicle use on the dunes peaks in May, and is carefully controlled by the park. These ever-shifting dunes rise several hundred feet over an area of about 2,000 acres. The BLM maintains the semi-primitive Ponderosa Grove Campground (no water, no fee) on the northwest edge of the roadless area adjacent to the dunes. Several other undeveloped camping sites provide jumping-off points for beyond-the-road excursions. The most sought-after experiences are enjoying vistas from the top of Moquith Mountain and traveling into the South Fork of Indian Creek with its strange display of prehistoric rock art.

Fall brings fairly heavy deer hunting pressure, although deer numbers are not particularly high. Dove hunting takes place south and east of the Vermilion Cliffs where the speedy little game birds find food, water, and shelter in the lush riparian bottom of Cottonwood Canyon. Flowing southward, the main,

Cottonwood drainage bisects the roadless area, providing access to wildlands on either side of the canyon.

The 7,000-foot plateau of Moquith Mountain offers panoramic views of the pink sand dunes, northward to white and pink cliffs, and of distant reefs and mesas far to the eastern horizon. Once on the summit plateau, take time to walk along and above the rims of canyons and cliffs to savor such color contrasts as the intense green of manzanita shrubs against a backdrop of red Navajo sandstone.

HOW TO GET THERE: From the west 3 miles south of Colorado City, Arizona, on Arizona Highway 389, turn left (east) on unsigned County Road 237. Continue 4.5 miles east on this improved dirt road, at which point the road makes a sharp turn to the left (north). Drive several more miles into Utah where the road becomes paved. After a few more miles the road passes Coral Pink Sand Dunes State Park on the right. Proceed a few more miles to the signed Hancock Road junction, which is 20 miles from AZ 389. Turn right onto Hancock Road, passing the BLM Ponderosa Grove Campground. About 1 mile past the campground make a sharp right turn to the southwest on the Sand Spring dirt road, which is marked with a stop sign. A nearby sign on Hancock Road reads "Coral Pink Sand Dunes 7 miles." Drive 2 miles on the sandy dirt road to the Sand Spring primitive campsite (fires prohibited), which is nestled in a lovely

Pictographs in South Fork Indian Canyon. Only the Indians who lived in this alcove around 1200 A.D. knew the meaning of this rock art.

ponderosa pine grove next to a set of old corrals. The last 0.25 mile of this road is rough and may require four-wheel-drive. From Kanab on the east side of the roadless area, head 7.25 miles north on U.S. Highway 89 and turn left on the unsigned but paved Hancock Road. Continue southwest for about 6 miles and turn left onto Sand Spring Road, which leads 2 miles beyond to the Sand Spring trailhead, parking area, and campground.

Day hike

Indian, South Fork, and Water Canyon Rim Ramble/Loop

Distance: 10 to 12 miles.
Starting and minimum elevations: 6,220 and 5,960 feet (South Fork Pictograph).
Difficulty: Moderate.
Best months: Mid-March through May; October through November.
Topo map: Yellowjacket Canyon-UT/AZ.

This long day trip is a rambling rim excursion into the northwest end of BLM's Moquith Mountain Wilderness Study Area, which is encompassed within a larger 26,500-acre roadless area immediately west of Kanab. For the most part the walking is pleasurable with good footing on compacted sand. Anywhere on the broad plateau top of Moquith Mountain, the country takes on a sense of timelessness and unlimited space—from the blue haze of the Arizona Strip north to Boulder Mountain and the Sevier Plateau. Absent is any worry about how to get in or out of cliffed-out canyons. This is a high rim ramble where the wilderness wanderer can experience the sheer joy of exploration without being tied to a specific destination.

If there is any structure at all to this trip it is to simply drop into the head of one or two canyons, follow their rims, and then gradually loop around cross-country back to the trailhead. Following is a general description of one such ramble.

From the Sand Spring Trailhead follow an off-road-vehicle track north about 0.25 mile into the shallow head of Indian Canyon. Sandy benches of dense pinyon-juniper and ponderosa pine sprinkled with manzanita, sagebrush, and blackbrush grade into the steep-walled canyon. Drop eastward about 0.5 mile to a 40-foot pouroff and spring development overseen by high cliff walls on the north side. Double back up the canyon and climb to its south rim. For a point of reference, a northern extension of the coral pink sand dunes dotted with ponderosa pine forms the western horizon next to the Sand Spring Road.

Hike about 1 mile east above the south rim of Indian Canyon at elevations between 6,000 and 6,200 feet to where the ridge forms a point above the canyon. Scan the horizon for high-flying golden eagles and early Indian granaries tucked away in alcoves below the north wall of Indian Canyon. Continue around the rim by heading southwest above the densely forested South Fork Indian Canyon. Gradually angle downslope and cross the upper reaches of the northern tributary to South Fork Canyon at an elevation of about 6,000 feet. This is a short distance above a breathtaking 100-foot pouroff, which opens to a grand vista of the lower canyon. From the lip of the pouroff climb south to the rim and angle southeast to the end of the South Fork Pictograph Trail Road. Here a 0.5-mile constructed switchback trail drops some 300 feet into the northern tributary to the South Fork, ending at the South Fork Indian Canyon pictographs.

The strange faces and animal shapes depicted here were inscribed by an early Indian culture around 1200 A.D.; this is the finest example of prehistoric rock art in the region. Sadly, mindless vandalism has forced the BLM to fence off the gallery, but it can still be viewed from the end of the trail.

Continuing the rim loop, climb back to the South Fork Pictograph Trailhead and walk to the southwest below and parallel to the cherry-stemmed four-wheel-drive road along small sand dunes, shelf rock, and deer trails. This is a land of big desert muleys, where both deer and mountain lion sign is abundant. After about 1 mile, drop south to grassy parks with stately ponderosa pine in the shallow upper wash of the South Fork. Angle around to the southeast and climb about 200 feet to the 6,400-foot ridge dividing the upper forks of Water Canyon. The panoramic view into the upper canyon is of a completely natural relict plant community of hanging gardens, Douglas-fir forest, oak, and maple guarded by formidable cliffs.

Depending on time and energy the hike can be continued southward in and out of upper canyon washes for another 2 to 3 miles to the Vermilion Cliffs of Art Canyon. A shorter, more direct return route is to head cross-country about 2 miles northwest to the South Fork Pictograph Trail Road near its intersection with Sand Spring Road. From there, hike to the trailhead on a 2-mile trek northward through a dense cover of pinyon-juniper and oak. If time is short, hike the well-traveled Sand Spring Road to the northeast at a fast pace for the remaining 1.5 to 2 miles back to the trailhead. By the time the sand dunes meet the road, you're there.

Upper Kanab Creek

17

Location: 7 miles north of Kanab, in south-central Utah.
Size: 42,200 acres.
Administration: BLM Cedar City District, Kanab Resource Area.
Management status: Unprotected BLM roadless.
Ecosystems: Colorado Plateau province ecoregion. Potential natural vegetation is pinyon-juniper woodland, with sagebrush, sandsage, and rabbitbrush at lower elevations.
Elevation range: 5,200 to 7,174 feet.
Established trails/routes: 2.5 miles.
Maximum core to perimeter distance: 1.5 miles.
Activities: Hiking, rock climbing, canyoneering, photography, wildlife study.
Maps: BLM 1:100,000 scale surface management/land ownership map entitled "Kanab" (50 meter contour interval). See Appendix E for a listing of the five topo maps covering the roadless area.

OVERVIEW: The area north of the southern Utah town of Kanab has been used to film hundreds of movies and TV westerns, so you may experience that eerie *deja vu* sensation as you gaze out on the rugged cliffs, complex canyons, and sandstone washes. Depending upon your cinematic knowledge, you may recognize some of Hollywood's backdrops here and be able to play "name that film." One old movie set is just east of the main route to Upper Kanab Creek, a couple of miles off U.S. Highway 89.

Kanab Creek begins high on the Paunsaugunt Plateau, some 45 miles north of this unit, the Upper Kanab Creek unit. The stream continues south 70 miles to join the Colorado River in the Grand Canyon. The creek and its tributaries drain a vast area of south-central Utah; as a result the water has done a spectacular job over the centuries of eroding the massive White Cliffs here. An example of the stream's power was provided for early Mormon settlers attempting to farm along its banks. During a massive flood in 1883, the raging Kanab cut a new bed 40 feet below its former course. The Mormon pioneers moved to a more hospitable location. The Kanab is a powerful creek.

The canyons along the White Cliffs in the Upper Kanab valley are intricately and sharply incised, providing endless opportunities for exploration. The

17 UPPER KANAB CREEK

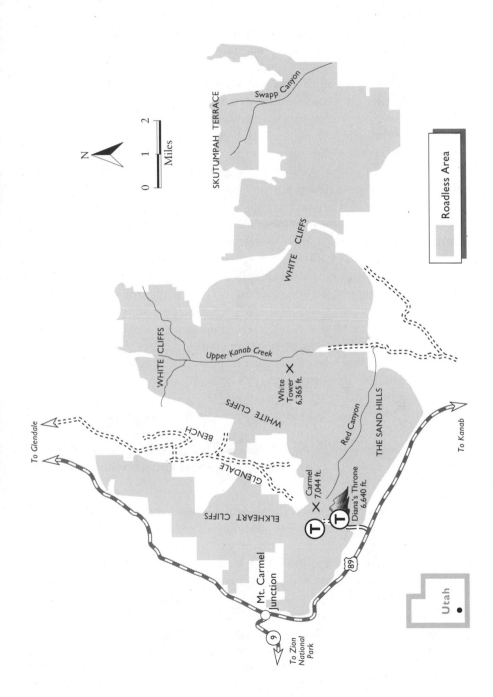

rims of the White Cliffs rise more than 1,000 feet above Kanab's canyon floor, which ranges from 5,200 feet to 5,700 feet in elevation. Numerous pinnacles, islands of the White Cliffs formation left standing, soar above the creek bed. White Tower rises a sudden 450 feet and sits more than a mile from the cliff face. Many other spires in Kanab's canyon are equally imposing, along with buttresses and peninsulas of cliff that jut out from the main cliff face.

These White Cliffs, a light sandstone of the Navajo formation, represent a southern outcropping of the High Plateau section of the Colorado Plateau. Geologically they are a southwestern extension of the Grand Staircase, a series of 6 brightly colored cliff formations with appropriate names: Chocolate, Vermilion, White, Gray, Pink, and Black. At 15 miles across, the Upper Kanab roadless area covers a wide swath of the White Cliffs where they drop 1,000 feet and more from the Skutumpah Terrace to Wygaret Terrace, which lies above the Vermilion Cliffs along the Arizona border.

Erosion in Kanab Canyon has exposed lava flows on the valley floor. Ancient volcanoes far to the north sent the lava down the sloping Colorado Plateau. Here it appears as a finely grained igneous version of slickrock.

The name *kanab* is Paiute for "place of the willows," which grow densely along the creek's bottom. The lower valley features sagebrush and grasses amid the slickrock and sand. The benches are covered with pinyon-juniper vegetation, while the higher reaches of the White Cliffs support ponderosa pine forests atop the brilliant white Navajo sandstone faces. The Kanab is a very colorful spot in the beige world of southern Utah.

Small herds of mule deer make their home on the benches of Kanab Creek. The cliffs' rocky ledges provide perfect nesting sites for bald eagles and peregrine falcons, both of which enjoy the rodent population. The cry of the coyote can be heard echoing through the canyons on quiet evenings in Upper Kanab.

Off the beaten track, Upper Kanab ensures the solitude of a wilderness. There are no guide books or road signs to attract visitors. Only the wonders of the White Cliffs.

RECREATIONAL USES: Upper Kanab's south-facing exposure and the presence of water make this an outstanding destination for hiking year-round. Here, as with everywhere in Utah, it is mandatory to treat the water, but its reliability makes backpacking here a more lightweight experience than in many other canyons. The intricate folds of the White Cliffs, the shadows, and the colors all combine to make this a prime location for photographic excursions. Rock climbers find Upper Kanab has limitless vertical adventures.

The wildland unit is relatively convenient, but the combination of difficult road access and private holdings makes it almost remote. A multitude of jeep roads swarm up John R. Canyon and John R. Flat south of Upper Kanab. Many of these routes travel through deep sand and are suitable only for four-wheel-drive vehicles. Caution is also necessary in wet weather when the unimproved dirt road east of the creek becomes impassable. The southwestern corner of the complex is the most accessible section of the Upper Kanab unit.

From above, the rough road east out of Glendale skirts the northern boundary of the roadless area. Both Glendale Bench and Skutumpah Terrace have patchwork private lands and some rustic roads, but these are wildlands worth exploring. Wandering the sand dunes on the cliff benches, winding through the dramatic white sandstone buttresses below the cliffs, and exploring Upper Kanab Creek itself provide a spectacular wilderness outing only 7 miles from Kanab.

HOW TO GET THERE: From U.S. Highway 89, about 7 miles south of Mount Carmel Junction and 10 miles north of Kanab, turn north on the improved dirt road toward the White Cliffs. This turn is just south of milepost 77. The improved dirt road crosses old Highway 89 at 0.1 mile and changes to an unimproved sand and dirt road. Low-clearance vehicles can make the trip with ease. Continue north 0.5 mile and turn right toward Diana's Throne, where the road ends in 0.2 mile. For the Kanab cliff hike, continue past the turn, straight north, 1 mile to road's end.

Day hike

Diana's Throne

Distance: 0.75 mile round trip.
Starting and maximum elevations: 6,320 feet and 6,640 feet.
Difficulty: Moderate.
Best months: March through April; October.
Topo map: Mount Carmel-UT.

The ascent to Diana's Throne is a short peak climb providing sweeping vistas of the White Cliffs and the region around Kanab. Close to U.S. Highway 89, the trailhead is readily accessible to ordinary passenger vehicles. Rising 700 feet above the road, hikers leave the bustle and hum of traffic and enter the quiet realm of this wilderness where bald eagles soar.

From the end-of-the-road trailhead, hike toward the hill just below the Throne's saddle. Climb up and angle along the serrated surface of the grainy white sandstone. The sandy gap between the Throne and the main cliffs provides angled routes that easily get you to the saddle. Here you have a 20-foot hand scramble up a sloped serrated outcropping to gain the top.

Rumor has it that Diana threw herself from this lofty spot in despair over unrequited love. She must have been an athletic woman. It is surprising that her endorphins didn't kick in during the climb to cheer her up. The tragedy must have occurred on a cloudy day, for the view from the summit is uplifting. It also reveals why this area is recommended for wilderness designation by the Utah Wilderness Coalition.

The main White Cliffs soar another 250 feet above the Throne. Their crumbling sandstone and angled face makes them inaccessible from the Throne. Below lie the Sand Hills and the Kanab Creek valley with its winding sandy washes and juniper-studded flats. In the western distance, the Pine Valleys jut darkly beyond Zion's ethereal white towers. Far to the southeast the north rim of the Grand Canyon stands out, especially if it is coated with snow. To the east the variegated 600-foot escarpment of the White Cliffs continues its abrupt march across the southern Colorado Plateau.

The jaunt up the Throne is a great leg stretcher with immediate gratification. It also provides a good aerial geography orientation of the region, before or after exploring southern Utah.

Day hike

Upper Kanab Cliff Climb and Rim Tour

Distance: 4 to 6 miles round trip.
Starting and maximum elevations: 6,360 feet and 7,147 feet.
Difficulty: Strenuous.
Best months: March through April; October.
Topo maps: Mount Carmel-UT; White Tower-UT.

The White Cliffs are an imposing sight from U.S. Highway 89. Rising above Long Valley they appear to be impenetrable and remote. This ascent to a jutting section of the cliffs allows an inside look at this world, revealing the cliffs' complexities. Plus the hike is entirely on public land, and begins only 1 mile from the paved road. This hike is not a technical climb, but because it involves rock scrambling on steep, loose sandstone we recommend it only for experienced hikers. Route-finding skills and mountaineering agility are prerequisites.

From the end-of-the-road trailhead go up the ridge just north of the road. From this vantage point you can view the hidden world of the unnamed canyon nestled in this southern extension of the White Cliffs. Moving west down the ridge, drop to the golden sand promontory above the canyon bottom. From here you can see up into the box canyon and can visualize your route to the top of the cliffs. It lies northwest of your lookout point, at the southern tip of the White Cliffs across the canyon. Here the talus slope creates an avenue up the cliffs.

The box canyon in the bottom is entirely cliffed in but offers a worthy side trip. Your climb begins back down the canyon where the slanted wall will enable you to climb to the tree-studded slope. The unstable rock above the lower pink walls requires careful travel. After angling left up the rock slope, follow the edge of the trees right to a safe break in the cliff. Then head left below the jagged, buff-colored formation that rings the promontory. At the south point of the cliff you can climb above the buff ring to the plateau.

This route up is also your route down—the steep cliffs prevent all other exits. From the plateau you can wander on this island set apart from the main Glendale Bench on the adjacent White Cliff formation. The bench, like most of the higher land on the cliffs, is privately owned. Several high points dot this small winding plateau of public land. Carmel (7,044 feet) is not the highest point, but it is the most prominent, being at the southern tip. Plan on a 3-mile round trip on top, to incorporate Carmel in your hike.

This outing in the cliffs demonstrates the variety of this region. Far from monochromatic, this hidden, anonymous canyon was painted from a stunning palette: rose-hued sandstone with angled fracture lines, golden sandstone swirled into tiny layered lines, massive white sandstone with both swirls and vertical fractures, and a stripe of jagged buff running horizontally near the top. All the elements have been swirled by wind and water. The bright greens of pinyon-juniper and ponderosa dot the slopes.

The hard work of getting to the plateau is rewarded with an incredible view of the southern Colorado Plateau. Only 1 air mile from a main highway, you have a sense of the primitive wildland of Upper Kanab.

Looking northwest to White Cliffs from Diana's Throne.

Grand Staircase Wilderness Complex 18

Location: 20 miles southeast of Panguitch (north end) and about 28 miles east of Kanab (south end); in southwest Utah.

Size: 341,697 acres.

Administration: USDAFS Dixie National Forest, Escalante Ranger District; BLM Cedar City District, Kanab Resource Area; NPS Bryce Canyon National Park.

Management status: Paria Canyon–Vermilion Cliffs Wilderness (Utah portion is about 20,000 acres); Grand Staircase–Escalante National Monument; BLM wilderness study area (4 units totaling 203,407 acres; Paria-Hackberry Wilderness Study Area includes the 2,000-acre No Man's Mesa Area of Critical Environmental Concern); unprotected BLM and state roadless lands (65,223 acres); unprotected national forest roadless land (29,400 acres); and Bryce Canyon National Park roadless land (23,667 acres).

Ecosystems: Colorado Plateau province ecoregion, potential natural vegetation of juniper-pinyon woodland and saltbrush-greasewood.

Elevation range: 4,150 feet (exit of Paria River from Utah) to 10,188 feet (Powell Point on Table Cliff Plateau).

Established trails/routes: At least 41 miles of primitive jeep tracks within BLM roadless units suitable for hiking and horseback riding; 61 miles of trails in Bryce Canyon National Park; about 5 miles of USDA Forest Service trails.

Maximum core to perimeter distance: 4 miles (Paria-Hackberry).

Activities: Hiking, backpacking, canyoneering, rock climbing, horseback riding, hunting, cross-country skiing, snowshoeing, photography, nature study (botanical and geological), rockhounding, fossil collecting, mountain biking (on peripheral roads cherry-stemmed within roadless units).

Maps: USDAFS 1995 Dixie National Forest Map (Powell, Escalante, and Teasdale ranger districts), half-inch/mile, 50 meter contour interval, (includes Bryce Canyon National Park); BLM 1:100,000 scale surface management/land ownership maps entitled "Panguitch," "Escalante," "Kanab," and "Smokey Mtn" (50 meter contour interval). Refer to Appendix E for a listing of the 26 topo maps covering the complex.

OVERVIEW: The uplift of the Colorado Plateau began somewhere around 16 million years ago. Deep, uneven pressures forced the soft silty limestone surface, once an ancient lakebed known as the Claron formation, to split along fault lines into a set of smaller plateaus at different levels, forming the "Grand Staircase." This monumental series of mesas and cliffs climbs an astounding 8,000 feet from the depths of the Grand Canyon to over 10,000 feet on Table Cliff Plateau. The steps of this biologically diverse masterpiece span six major life zones, from the lower Colorado (Sonoran) desert to alpine forest.

Climbing the stairs, colorful Chocolate, Vermilion, White, Gray, and Pink Cliffs represent four billion years of geologic time along with a fossilized record of life on Earth. In the Utah portion of the Staircase, the first step is found in the Navajo sandstone formations of the Paria Canyon–Vermilion Cliffs Wilderness (20,000 acres in Utah). Then comes the Cockscomb roadless area (10,300 acres) split by 3 miles of the Paria River and the serrated ridge of The Cockscomb—a striking southern continuation of the East Kaibab monocline west of the river. East of the Paria the benches and flat tops of The Rimrocks are sliced by small canyons draining to the river.

Two steps in the Staircase are in the Paria-Hackberry Wilderness Study Area, which, at 158,700 acres, is one of the largest unroaded expanses in Utah. The lower 8 of the 25 miles of the Paria River that flow through this central portion of the complex are bounded by Vermilion Cliffs of dark red sandstone atop a base of color-banded Chinle badlands. The upstream segment of the shallow, silt-laden river is confined by White Cliffs of Navajo sandstone and by Carmel formation mesas on the north and west borders. Clear water flows year-round in the deep and often narrow chasms of Sheep Creek and Hackberry Canyon. Benchlands above the Paria and its larger side canyons are dotted with knobs, domes, and aprons of white Navajo sandstone separated by sand dunes. Deposits of petrified wood lie in Hackberry Canyon. The better known of the many natural arches eroded from the sandstone are Sam Pollock Arch, near the head of a tributary to Hackberry Canyon, and Starlight Arch, on the western boundary of No Man's Mesa.

The moderately incised Mud Spring Canyon gives its name to 55,100 acres of BLM wildland that reaches northward from blue-gray shale badlands to 8,000-foot mountainous terrain near Canaan Peak. The double row of steeply pitched, knife-edge fins known as The Cockscomb begins in the center of the roadless area and continues south almost to Arizona.

Some 35,300 acres of BLM and Forest Service roadless lands in Squaw and Willis creeks, East of Bryce, and Box Canyon, unfold eastward below Bryce's high cliffs. This is the scenic foreground below the rim and the location of several hiking and horse routes that climb up into the national park. The Squaw and Willis creeks wildland is separated from the Paria-Hackberry Wilderness Study Area by a dirt road that runs between Alton and Connonville. The red beds of the Carmel formation cover most of the benches and drainages, with Navajo sandstone exposed in upper Bull Valley Gorge. To the north the cliffs of the Box Canyon and East of Bryce roadless areas rise 500 feet.

18 GRAND STAIRCASE WILDERNESS COMPLEX

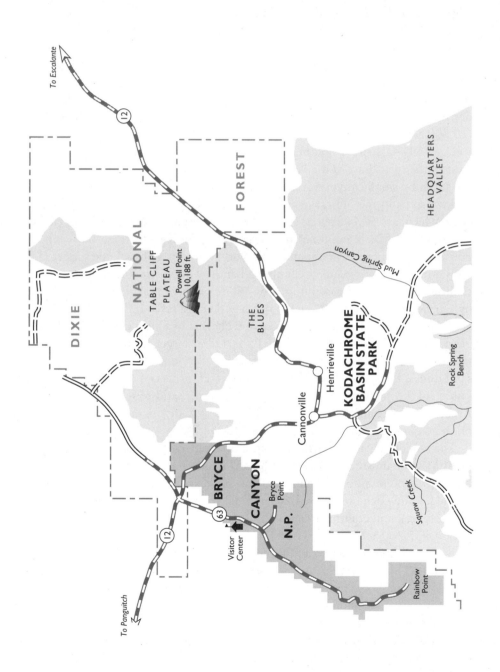

To Escalante

12

FOREST

NATIONAL

TABLE CLIFF PLATEAU

Powell Point 10,188 ft.

DIXIE

THE BLUES

HEADQUARTERS VALLEY

Mud Spring Canyon

KODACHROME BASIN STATE PARK

Henrieville

Rock Spring Bench

Cannonville

BRYCE

CANYON

N.P.

Bryce Point

Squaw Creek

63

Visitor Center

12

Rainbow Point

To Panguitch

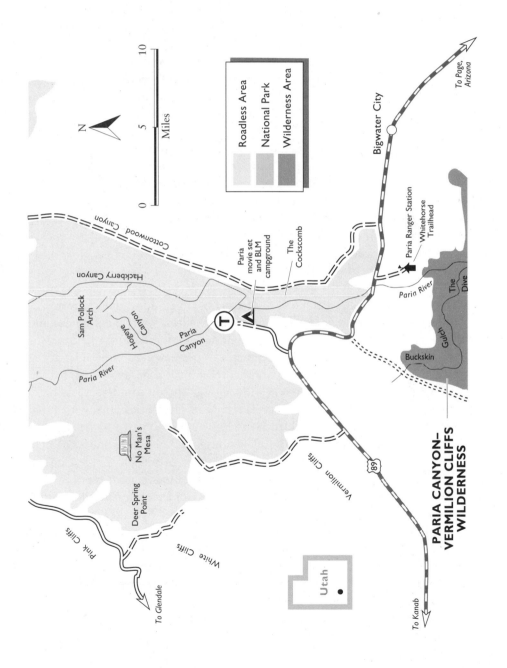

Bryce Canyon National Park is a wonderland of rock spires beneath the lofty cliffs of the Paunsaugunt Plateau. This intricate labyrinth is eroded from soft limestone that glows with changing light and shadow in shades of reds, yellows, oranges, pinks, purples, and creams. Bryce Canyon is not a canyon at all but rather several huge amphitheaters cut into the Pink Cliffs. Colored by iron and manganese, these cliffs harbor a whimsical fairyland of hoodoo formations.

Northeast of the park, the Blues is a 38,600-acre stretch of BLM and Forest Service roadless land that ascends more than 3,000 feet from rugged shale badlands to pink cliffs below 10,188-foot Powell Point on Table Cliff Plateau. The lower west side is a land of deeply dissected sandstone canyons draining to the south.

The Table Cliff Plateau roadless area (Dixie National Forest) is adorned with a montane forest mix of ponderosa pine, Douglas-fir, white fir, aspen, and open parks. Similar elevations at Bryce also support conifers, including a few venerable bristlecone pine trees high along the rim. Forest edges are marked with a dense growth of manzanita, juniper, snowberry, chokecherry, and bunchgrasses. In contrast, the hotter, drier benches far below are mostly pinyon-juniper woodland along with a few scattered ponderosa pines and a sparse understory of shrubs.

No Man's Mesa in the Paria-Hackberry Wilderness Study Area is a remote 2,000-acre plateau guarded by 1,000-foot cliffs on all sides. Unlike most BLM land it has never been grazed by cattle. The resulting relict plant community of pinyon-juniper, sagebrush, waist-high native grasses, and thick mats of cryptobiotic soil is one of the last remnants of pre-grazing southern Utah vegetation. A sheer waterfall protects another relict plant community in upper Dry Valley Creek Canyon within the Muddy Spring Canyon country. A few hardy pinyon pine trees grow on the rocky backbone of The Cockscomb, with a typical mix of desert shrubs sprinkled below.

This wide range of topography, elevations, and habitats produces a corresponding diversity of wild denizens. The higher country in Bryce Canyon, Table Cliff Plateau, and the upper reaches of the Blues is frequented by mule deer and seldom-seen cougars and black bears. Golden eagles hunt for cottontails. Each level of the Staircase is occasionally visited by bald eagles and federally listed endangered peregrine falcons. Other sensitive birds include western bluebird and Lewis's woodpecker. Gambel's quail, bandtailed pigeons, and mourning doves inhabit lower elevations near the riparian bottoms of Paria, Hackberry, and Cottonwood canyons. Lower stretches of the Paria are also relied upon by antelope for springtime fawning.

The Paria-Hackberry has a greater density of known archeological sites than that of the surrounding stairs, with at least 41 recorded locations. These vestiges of prehistory include rock shelters, lithic scatters, and a pit house.

Pictograph panels are located in Deer Creek Canyon and petroglyphs are found in the canyon of Snake Creek. At least one of these sites is from the Anasazi culture. Of more recent historic interest are the old Hattie Green copper mine diggings on the crest of The Cockscomb.

The Paiute Indians called the silty river *Paria,* meaning "muddy water." From its headwaters in Bryce to its mouth on the Colorado, this south-flowing sluice of muddy water is the lifeline of an undeveloped watershed that is still a single, integrated wilderness. The Paria River remains as the unsevered biological corridor of a rugged canyonland basin that is wild from head to foot. The Paria is the thread that ties Bryce Canyon together with the Grand Canyon in a staircase that makes the adjective "grand" seem inadequate.

In recognition of this ecological whole, President Clinton set aside most of the Grand Staircase Wilderness Complex as the western portion of the new 1.7 million-acre Grand Staircase–Escalante National Monument. This September 1996 declaration withdrew the monument from new mineral entry, thereby protecting the surface from proposed industrial coal mining. Although every other national monument is administered by the National Park Service, the executive order provides for most traditional land uses and continued BLM administration. Refer to the "Overview" section of the Kaiparowits Plateau chapter (19) for a more detailed assessment of the Grand Staircase–Escalante National Monument. This important designation is consistent with an earlier recommendation by the National Park Service that the entire length of the Paria River be considered for National Wild and Scenic River status.

RECREATIONAL USES: With 61 miles of signed, well-graded trails, Bryce Canyon National Park is a three-season hiking paradise and a good winter destination for those on skis or snowshoes. There are two major backpacking trails, but day-hiking trails provide the best views of cross-bedded sandstones and differential weathering of Bryce's famous Claron formations. The strenuous 5- to 7-mile Peekaboo Loop is the only day-use trail in the park open to horses. Another possibility is to hike the lightly used 3.8-mile round-trip trail to the Hat Shop. Gird your loins for the steep uphill return to the Bryce Point Trailhead. For unmatched scenery take off from Sunset Point on a 2.8-mile round trip combining the Queen's Garden and Navajo Loop trails. The 8-mile Fairyland Loop is a strenuous hike from Sunrise Point, providing views of the Chinese Wall, Tower Bridge, Boat Mesa, and bristlecone pines.

To really get up close and personal with the backcountry of Bryce get your free use permit from the visitor center and slip into your backpack. Here are a few ideas. For starters consider the strenuous up-and-down, 22.5-mile, point-to-point backpack from Bryce Point south to Yovimpa Point (apex of the park at 9,100 feet) on the Under-the-Rim Trail (see Hike 57 in *Hiking Utah* from Falcon Publishing for a detailed route description). There are a number of ways to lengthen or shorten the distance with connecting trails, such as the 9.3-mile trek from Bryce Point to Sheep Creek. Midway camping destinations at Sheep Creek and Swamp Creek invite exploration of nearby side washes leading up toward the cliffs. Another enjoyable choice for an overnighter is the 8- to 9-mile Riggs Spring Loop Trail that begins from Yovimpa Point and descends gradually to a valley below the cliffs at the south end of the park.

During winter cross-country skiers and snowshoers can camp at five designated campsites accessed by the Under-the-Rim, Fairyland Loop, and Yovimpa Pass trails. There is a limit of three days at any one campsite.

To reach the Bryce Canyon cliffs from the east, hike from low benches to canyon bottoms on up to the high country through the Squaw and Willis Creek wildland. Easier day hikes and horseback rides are possible on game trails and old jeep tracks, such as the one in Willis Creek. Along the northeast edge of the park, hikers can explore Box Canyon just off Utah Highway 12 north of the town of Tropic.

Next door, the Paria-Hackberry Wilderness Study Area contains prime hiking and backpacking routes in Sheep Creek, Bull Valley Gorge, and Hackberry canyons and along the Paria River. With persistence and route-finding know-how, loops are possible from one canyon to another by crossing benches between drainages. Refer to Hike 58 in *Hiking Utah* for a description of an 18-mile, point-to-point overnighter down Hackberry Canyon. Along the way check out side trips into Round Valley Draw, Stone Donkey Canyon, and Sam Pollock Arch.

The BLM has produced an excellent mile-by-mile hiking brochure for the designated wilderness section of the Paria Canyon narrows. It details the 36.3 river miles from the White House Trailhead downstream and southeast to Lees Ferry on the Colorado River. See also Hike 59 in *Hiking Utah*. Due to the danger of flash floods hikers must register with the BLM (Paria Canyon Ranger Station or BLM office in Kanab) within 24 hours before taking this popular 4- to 6-day backpack trip. A shorter, more rugged choice is to traverse Buckskin Gulch to its confluence with the Paria River from the Buckskin Trailhead (16.3 miles) or from the Wire Pass Trailhead (13 miles). Not surprisingly, these magnificent narrows have attracted ever increasing numbers of visitors— 10,000 people in 1996 alone! In 1997 the BLM initiated a reservation permit system limiting the number of daily entries into the wilderness to protect its physical and sociological values. Contact the BLM's Kanab Resource Area office for permit application procedures.

Varied hiking and backpacking trips are waiting to be enjoyed northeast of Paria in the Blues–Table Cliff Plateau. One good bet is to head up Henderson Canyon on a jeep track, changing to a pack trail, all the way up to Table Cliff Plateau west of Powell Point. Fat tire enthusiasts can mountain bike an advanced 21-mile round-trip route all the way to Powell Point. The route involves roads, doubletracks, and a singletrack trail for the final mile. See Ride 38 in *Mountain Biking Utah* (Falcon Publishing) for a detailed description. Whether reached by foot, horse, or mountain bike, the truncated table of Powell Point is a throne from which to witness the grand stairs dropping southward.

The best rock climbing occurs on Wahweap or Straight Cliffs sandstone walls above Henrieville Creek, the east wall of lower Pardner Canyon, and on the 7,950-foot monolith east of Pasture Canyon. Those seeking adventure with solitude can explore a maze of rough and confusing terrain in the upper reaches of Pardner, Jimmie, and Pasture canyons.

In the Mud Spring roadless area to the south, equestrians will find their best riding in Little Creek, upper Mud Spring Canyon, Wiggler Wash, and the intervening benchlands. The most popular use here is big game hunting, with lesser opportunities for upland game bird hunting. The country is big and diverse enough for quality hiking and backpacking excursions. Key hiking attractions include The Cockscomb, the forested head of Mud Spring Canyon, and the waterfall and relict plant community in Dry Valley Creek Canyon.

HOW TO GET THERE: From U.S. Highway 89 between mile posts 30 and 31, about 10 miles west of the Paria Ranger Station and about 35 miles east of Kanab, turn north on an improved gravel road signed "Paria Movie Set 5 miles." The gravel ends after about 3 miles. The remaining 2 miles of improved

Wading the Paria River at the mouth of Hogeye Creek.

dirt road to the movie set and adjacent BLM campground may become impassable when wet on the steep hills dropping down to the movie set. The campground is a good parking area and trailhead for this three- to four-day backpack. If the extended forecast calls for dry weather you may wish to drive another 1.5 miles to the Paria River on a road signed "Old Pahreah Townsite—four-wheel-drive only," which passes the old cemetery. Actually, two-wheel-drive vehicles can easily negotiate this clay road when dry; if wet, even four-wheel-drive won't get you there or back. Pull over and park before crossing the river. The stone and dugout remains of the townsite are just downstream on the opposite bank.

Backpack loop

Paria Canyon–Hackberry Canyon–Hogeye Canyon

Distance: About 25 miles.
Starting and maximum elevations: 4,750 feet and 5,800 feet.
Difficulty: Most of the route is moderate to moderately strenuous with several short strenuous sections.
Best months: April through May; October through November.
Topo maps: Calico Peak-UT; Fivemile Valley-UT.

At 158,700 acres the Paria-Hackberry roadless area is one of the largest expanses of undesignated wild country in Utah; most of it is contained within a BLM wilderness study area. Trips that begin as loops in these canyons often end at vertical cliffs and pouroffs, forcing an unexpected out-and-back route. Knowing ahead of time that this loop can be accomplished with a bit of route finding and rock scrambling, combined with a traverse across remote, rarely visited terrain, makes it all the more special.

From either suggested trailhead cross the shallow, silt-laden Paria River and head upstream (north) across broad sagebrush flats overlooked on the east side by the lofty red cliffs of the Kayenta and Moenave formations atop color-banded Chinle badlands. Expect numerous but easy river crossings along mud flats and off-road-vehicle routes during the first 2 miles, at which point the first major side canyon enters from the right. This is also where the colorful shale badlands give way to red rock talus slopes dotted with pinyon-juniper beneath towering broken red walls. A distinct jeep track makes a clear, solid trail, passing through an old stock fence at mile 2.5.

After about 5 miles Hogeye Creek enters as the fourth major side canyon from the right (east) side of the river above the trailhead. These first 5 miles are excellent for horseback riding, but from this point on the loop is suitable for hikers only. A cottonwood grove provides welcome shade near the mouth of Hogeye, with the river narrowing noticeably upstream. Turn right and head up Hogeye Creek to where the canyon is blocked by large boulders 0.75 mile up. A faint trail to the right is marked by occasional cairns. The first of two springs begins another mile up, in a short slot canyon below shelf rock. The red-rock Hogeye Creek Canyon is a natural wind tunnel, as evidenced by wind-blown cottonwood and box elder branches strewn along the bottom. Several small, intimate campsites can be found near the two short stretches of year-round water in the canyon. These watercourses are brushy, but the dry washes in between are open, with easily climbed stair-stepped waterfalls. Campers should make room for wildlife by camping out of sight and several hundred feet from water sources.

Plan on camping the first night near one of the springs, allowing time to explore up to the rim. About 2.5 miles up Hogeye Creek Canyon, just past the second spring, a giant spike-topped ponderosa pine in the bottom and a large rock column on the right mark the spot on the left side where an easy scramble to the rim is possible. The top is a picturesque blend of white- and buff-colored formations atop red sandstone tablets.

On the second day continue up Hogeye. About 4 miles up red-layered walls open to white Navajo sandstone. The main canyon turns sharply to the right (southeast), bound by a high buff-colored wall on the right. Continue up this main, right-hand canyon for about 0.3 mile to a left-hand fork that quickly climbs bare white sandstone. The main canyon to the right ends after 0.5 mile in a steep, impassable rocky notch. Take the smaller left fork, climbing up slanted rock and sandy slopes left of a huge mound of Navajo sandstone capped with a buff-colored crown. Wrap around to the right behind the mound toward the head of the Hogeye Canyon bottom out of which you have just climbed. Continue along the base of a white rock wall, heading southeast across the broad sloping pinyon-juniper mesa that separates the Paria River drainage from Hackberry Canyon, which is also known as Lower Death Valley. For visual reference, follow a southeast compass bearing toward one of the distant white buttes to make certain you don't veer too far south toward the Paria River. After about 1.5 miles you'll enter one of the upper draws leading into the major tributary to Hackberry Canyon. It contains the sizable Sam Pollock Arch in its upper reaches. A pouroff blocking the canyon 1.2 miles below the arch can be bypassed on the left (north) side.

Make the second night's camp along the stream in Hackberry Canyon, and plan a possible layover on day three for up-canyon exploration. In 1987, a rockfall created a temporary lake about 1.5 miles above the mouth of Sam Pollock Canyon and just above the mouth of a wild, rarely visited side canyon that joins Hackberry from the west. This side canyon is blocked by a series of 60- to 100-foot pouroffs. It is possible to climb out of the canyon on its left side about 0.2 mile above its mouth.

Continuing the loop down Hackberry, look for the remains of a sturdy log cabin built around 1920. The cabin sits on a west side bench about 0.25 mile below the mouth of Sam Pollock Canyon. Wet-foot hiking is easy through most of Hackberry Canyon. The stream is especially impressive where it cuts through The Cockscomb in deep narrows of Navajo sandstone for about 2 miles all the way down to its mouth. During and soon after storms the sheer walls literally weep with flowing water and plunging waterfalls. Following the narrows, Hackberry Canyon joins Cottonwood Creek, which has a dirt road and powerline on the other side. To complete the loop, turn right and walk down Cottonwood Creek where it parallels the rugged rock face of The Cockscomb for about 2 miles to its intersection with the Paria River.

Turn right again and hike upriver through the dramatic narrows of the "Paria Box"—where some of the best is saved for the last. A deeply recessed twin alcove sits near river level about halfway through The Box. After another mile and several river crossings, the valley opens to the old Pahreah townsite (right side) and the movie set and campground, which are reached by angling across the flat to the foot of the ridge on the left.

And there you have it—a vigorous and varied 25-mile loop through the heart of the Paria-Hackberry Wilderness Study Area. In so doing, you have climbed two giant steps in the Grand Staircase—from Vermilion Cliffs of dark red Moenave sandstone up to White Cliffs of Navajo sandstone.

Kaiparowits Plateau Complex

Location: 2 miles south of Escalante, in south-central Utah.
Size: 667,280 acres.
Administration: BLM Cedar City District, Escalante Resource Area; NPS Glen Canyon National Recreation Area.
Management status: BLM unprotected roadless (198,826 acres) and wilderness study areas (five units, totaling 451,674 acres) in Grand Staircase–Escalante Canyon National Monument, under BLM management; national recreation area roadless land (167,380 acres).
Ecosystems: Colorado Plateau province ecoregion. Potential natural vegetation type is pinyon-juniper woodland, interspersed with desert shrub and sagebrush.
Elevation range: 3,800 to 7,828 feet (Death Ridge).
Established trails/routes: No official trails, but miles of deserted jeep tracks and open canyon bottoms make excellent hiking routes.
Maximum core to perimeter distance: 4 miles.
Activities: Hiking, backpacking, canyoneering, geology study.
Maps: BLM 1:100,000 scale surface management/land ownership maps entitled "Escalante" and "Smoky Mountain" (50 meter contour interval). See Appendix E for a listing of the 32 topo maps covering the roadless area.

OVERVIEW: The vast wild country of the Kaiparowits Plateau is a land of extremes. With contrasting names like Death Ridge and Paradise, Warm Creek and Burning Hills, the Kaiparowits also represents both the heartland of the wild Colorado Plateau and the potential for industrialization, specifically coal mining. In September 1996 this latter image was set aside when President Clinton signed a proclamation creating the 1.7 million-acre Grand Staircase–Escalante National Monument. Although its name was omitted from the title, the Kaiparowits Plateau lies at the center of the new monument. Its coal reserves are now off-limits, except for pre-existing leases. Grazing, hunting, off-road vehicles, and mountain biking are allowed in the monument, which is under BLM jurisdiction but remains officially part of the National Park System.

Designation as a national monument is achieved by the stroke of the executive pen—but it doesn't carry the security of national park status or the permanence of wilderness protection. What can be created so easily can also be modified or ended in the same fashion. Other national monuments have had their boundaries adjusted or their restrictions altered; Joshua Tree, before it became a national park, is an example of shifting boundaries. Monument status is therefore only a reprieve from coal development, pipelines, and strip mines. A visit to the Kaiparowits will provide evidence of the wilderness values here, worthy of enduring preservation.

From Cottonwood Canyon Road and the Cockscomb Formation on the west to Hole-in-the-Rock Road and the Straight Cliffs on the east, the Kaiparowits Plateau forms an equilateral triangle with the town of Escalante at the apex and Lake Powell as the base. Surrounded by name-brand tourist destinations—Bryce Canyon, Capitol Reef, and Glen Canyon—the Kaiparowits is raw wild country. From the captive waters of Glen Canyon to shady wash and canyon bottoms, to the arid windy ridges, benchlands, and badlands, the Kaiparowits epitomizes all that is both spectacular and inhospitable in Colorado Plateau wilderness.

Although bisected by the rough Smokey Mountain Road, most of the Kaiparowits is remote. Access is difficult at best. Like varicose veins, a scramble of old four-wheel-drive roads cuts the Kaiparowits into pieces. These remnants of the century-old search for minerals and fuel (uranium first, then coal) follow ridges and benches. But the land is so vast their impact is negligible. Solitude is everywhere.

The rough, arid plateau hosts ancient pinyon-juniper woodlands. On Fourmile Bench in the Wahweap area some trees are estimated to be 1,400 years old. Desert shrub vegetation and sagebrush dot the lower benches. Riparian vegetation is rare, appearing in Wahweap's intermittent stream bottoms. There are isolated communities of oak and ponderosa pine in the higher elevations of Death Ridge on the northwest edge of the plateau. In the adjacent patch of Dixie National Forest, Canaan Peak at the southern end of the Escalante Mountains rises to 9,196 feet; this is the high point of the geologic unit of the plateau. It is also the origin of the Paiute name; *Kaiparowits* means "the mountain's son." Oil field exploration and development in the Canaan Peak area eliminates it from inclusion in the roadless area.

Kaiparowits' remoteness protects wildlife, which is remarkably diverse and plentiful for such an arid location. Mule deer, pronghorn antelope, cougar, desert bighorn, and cottontail rabbits enjoy the freedom of life on the plateau. Hunting pressure is minimal due to inaccessibility and rough country. By BLM reckoning nearly 60 mammal species make their home here, as well as 47 species of reptile that relish their privacy. About 200 species of birds either live here or migrate through the area. Nearly two dozen different raptors soar from the cliffs and cruise the quiet canyons of the Kaiparowits.

19 KAIPAROWITS PLATEAU COMPLEX

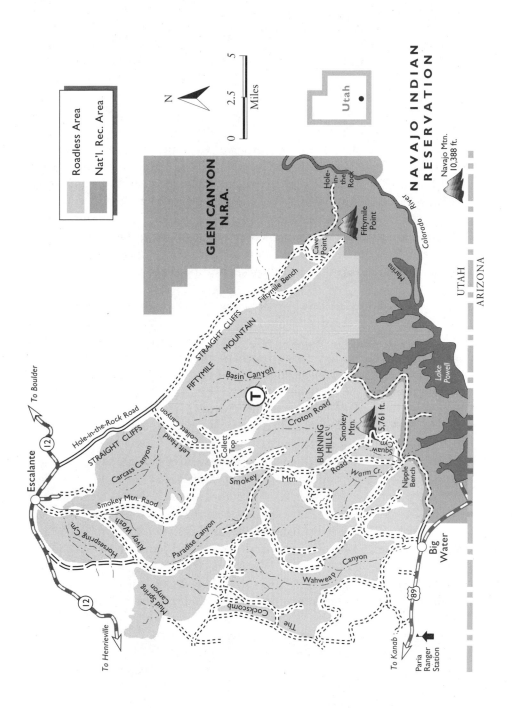

The location of the Kaiparowits puts it at the junction of several prehistoric cultures. The hunter-gatherers from the forested region to the northwest and the agricultural groups to the south overlapped here. Archeological sites span eight thousand years of human presence, from Archaic to Fremont and Anasazi, to southern Paiute and Navajo. Sites are small, as were the bands of these early nomads. Lithic scatters and hunting camps represent the Archaic and southern Paiute cultures. Rock shelters with storage cisterns or caches, granaries, masonry rooms, and rock art are the traces left by small agricultural settlements of Fremont and Anasazi bands. The temporary hunter sites are usually atop the plateau, while the more permanent agricultural sites are located on canyon sides and bottoms where shelter and water are available. An exception to the pattern is on the Straight Cliffs side of the plateau. Masonry structures can be found on mesa tops, looking over sagebrush meadows that surely were fields in wetter times. Although no thorough inventory has been conducted, estimates suggest that the Kaiparowits could hold four thousand sites. Most of these are in pristine condition due to low visitation and inaccessibility. If you come across a site, please leave it untouched. Pocketing even small artifacts destroys the archeological integrity of a site. It is also against the law.

The units of the Kaiparowits represent a variety of plateau terrain. Carcass Canyon, in the northeast, is adjacent to the town of Escalante. Here the 7,133-foot Escalante Rim marks the northern end of the Straight Cliff formation, rising abruptly 1,300 feet above the town. The drainages in Right Hand and Left Hand Collett canyons have cut 700-foot divots into the plateau. Views from the rim over the Escalante canyons to Waterpocket Fold are magnificent. Even close to Escalante, these canyons provide perfect solitude. Fossils of invertebrates and vertebrates can be found in the shale and sandstone of this northern extension of the Straight Cliffs.

Death Ridge, immediately to the southwest, rises to nearly 8,000 feet as it abuts the foothills of Canaan Peak in the nearby Dixie National Forest. Here, too, sharp canyons have been cut by centuries of erosion. Even the intermittent (and highly alkaline) Last Chance Creek chewed through the bench, creating Paradise and Little Escalante canyons. This stream picks up arsenic, sulfate, and dissolved solids, and is undrinkable for man or beast, even when treated.

The Burning Hills unit lies to the south along Last Chance Creek. Here the undulating plateau is marked by red and pink hilltops, discolored by centuries of smoldering subterranean coal fires. Ignited by lightning strikes these mysterious fires must have provoked wonder in prehistoric times. The 800-foot cliff of well-named Smokey Mountain rises above Last Chance where it joins the former Colorado River in Glen Canyon. The Last Chance drainage boasts some of the most rugged badland topography of the Kaiparowits.

To the west of the Burning Hills, the Warm Creek unit, split by roaded Nipple Bench, has evanescent springs in the heads of Nipple and Tibbet canyons. Here patches of cottonwood and tamarisk suddenly appear in the hostile Kaiparowits environment. Predictably these are sites of archeological evidence. In addition, Cretaceous Wahweap formation at Nipple Bench contains fossilized vertebrates.

Wahweap–Paradise Canyon is the largest unit of the Kaiparowits with 228 thousand contiguous roadless acres. On the southwest corner of the Kaiparowits triangle, it lies adjacent to the Grand Staircase complex at The Cockscomb. Here a staircase of formations steps down from Death Ridge, to the delight of anyone with an interest in geology. Over 100 million years of strata are exposed, from the Jurassic through the Cretaceous period. The mid-Cretaceous Wahweap formation contains fossils. Wahweap Canyon, with its numerous side canyons, runs more than a dozen miles, parallelling The Cockscomb and matching its Cads Crotch for vertical relief. The bench lands of Wahweap are heavy with pinyon pine and Utah juniper, rising to ponderosa pine. Wahweap's arid badlands and high desert, once targeted by the BLM for motorcycle film settings, are contrasted with wash bottom thickets of serviceberry, snowberry, holly grape, and buffalo berry. Riparian patches along Wahweap and Tommy Smith creeks provide startling patches of greenery in this otherwise beige world.

The most majestic piece of the Kaiparowits jigsaw puzzle is Fiftymile Mountain, running all along the eastern side of the plateau. Around 7,200 feet high at its slightly undulating eastern edge on the Straight Cliffs, the mountain slopes slightly southwest, where it is sharply cut by canyons draining toward Lake Powell. The Straight Cliffs form the sharp 3,000-foot edge of this enormous uplifted Cretaceous sea bed. The yellow-gray sandstone, mudstone, and shale escarpment drops to Fiftymile Bench, a late Jurassic Morrison formation. In addition to coal, the bench also contains fossilized bones of reptiles.

Fiftymile Point juts out from the mountain wall at the southern end, like the dot of a huge exclamation mark. This dot is 7,561 feet high. Further on to the south is Navajo Point, overlooking flooded Glen Canyon and the Navajo Reservation to the south.

RECREATIONAL USES: Its central location in southern canyon country makes the views from the Kaiparowits magnificent. The incised canyons, steep benches and ridges make for rough going, but guarantee solitude since few venture into Kaiparowits country.

This is an arid plateau, so any outing requires an adequate supply of water to weigh down your pack. There are only a few patches of trails, but aged jeep tracks are especially plentiful on the ridges. These afford excellent hiking routes into the backcountry. You are only limited by water, time, and energy.

Day hikers in the Carcass Canyon unit find easy access on Hole-in-the-Rock Road or through Alvey Wash out of Escalante. Devil's Garden Outstanding Natural Area, 17 miles southeast of Escalante, also provides a jumping off point for Carcass Canyon hikes. Also near Escalante, the Horse Springs Canyon area has several twisting, narrow canyons on the lower slopes of Canaan Peak. These canyons—Mitchell, Willow Spring, and Horse Spring—drain to the northeast and provide excellent day hikes.

Up on Death Ridge, both Little Escalante and Paradise canyons are gently sloping canyon hikes good for day trips. Or, for a longer backpack, hikers can loop over Paradise Bench. Down by Lake Powell, ambitious hikers can explore north of Glen Canyon City Road to Nipple Bench. Or take the Tibbet Canyon Road to the top of the bench overlook and explore from there.

In Wahweap–Paradise hiking opportunities are numerous. Wahweap Creek and Tommy Smith Creek run intermittently, as do streams in Fourmile Canyon and Long Canyon. On the west, from Cottonwood Creek Road, the Grosvenor Arch turnoff provides access to Long Flat. From the springs at the trailhead, a nearly 20-mile loop trip takes you down Wahweap to the junction with Tommy Smith Creek Canyon, which leads back north. At the confluence of Tommy Smith and Halfmile canyons, find an exit on the west and climb to the old jeep track that cuts across Long Flat back to the trailhead in Wahweap Creek. The trip can be cut in half by taking Long Canyon just west of Long Flat for the return route to the jeep track.

The most inspiring outings, of course, are to climb to the top of Fiftymile Mountain. From Hole-in-the-Rock Road, the escarpment can be climbed just south of Sooner Slide, about 50 miles south of Escalante. This too is a dry hike.

HOW TO GET THERE: It is a long, four-wheel-drive, high-clearance journey to get to this Kaiparowits hike, but the trip to the trailhead gives you a broad view of the diversity of the Kaiparowits region. In Escalante, where there are as yet no signs indicating that the national monument is nearby, turn south from Main Street onto 500 West. The pavement ends in 1 mile, changing to an un-improved dirt, dry-weather road named Smokey Mountain Road. The road follows Alvey Wash between white stair-step cliffs. About 9 miles south of Escalante, bear left toward Big Sage Junction (23 miles farther). Stay on the main road, disregarding side roads, as it rises to Camp Flat, where you will be surrounded by acres of chained pinyon-juniper carcasses. Smokey Mountain Road swings to head southeast, paralleling the ridge of Fiftymile Mountain, 20 miles to the east. About 32 miles south of Escalante, at the intersection where Smokey Mountain Road goes right (south), continue straight (east) on the unimproved dirt road. A major corral and a windmill mark this junction.

Go east along a fenceline marking a state section. At 1.5 miles you arrive at signed Collett Top junction. Bear right on Croton Road. Stay on the main road, disregarding the many side roads cut through the sage and juniper. About 9 miles from the Collett Top junction you come to a three-way intersection. The Croton Canyon Road to Big Water goes right. Take the road signed "Dead Ends" that goes just to the right of straight ahead. The Kane County bulldozer has been busy in this area, so road conditions may change and new roads may appear. With the BLM Escalante Resource Area map and the topo maps you can locate the trailhead by using topographical landmarks despite the confusing maze of roads.

After 1.5 miles on the Dead End Road, turn left. A mile farther bear left at the head of Surprise Canyon. Another 0.5 mile from the Y, bear left again on the road heading east and dropping off the ridge toward Willow Gulch and Rogers Canyon. This is a rocky, unimproved dirt road suitable only for four-wheel-drive, high-clearance vehicles. Road conditions may change due to the county road programs and Conoco's drilling on state-owned sections here on the plateau.

This road winds and dips for 2 miles, seemingly forever, until you see it stretching straight ahead across the sage flat toward the canyon, directly east. Here, 12 miles from the Collett Top junction, a washout ends your journey east. Turn left (north) on a hook-shaped road running north across the sage flat to a clump of junipers. You can park and camp among the trees on the site of an old cowboy camp, with an outstanding view of the canyon country and early morning sun. The road curls around to the left of the junipers and drops to its end in 0.1 mile. In windy conditions camping down in the draw may be preferable to the juniper site. The trail begins where the road deteriorates in a rock-strewn washout to become a cowpath down into the canyon.

To reach the trailhead from the south, from U.S. Highway 89 in Big Water City, just 0.5 mile east of milepost 8, go north on Ethan Allen Road. Follow the main road when it bends right to Glen Canyon National Recreation Area. Graveled at first, the road becomes improved dirt, suitable for dry weather only. This is a four-wheel-drive, high-clearance trip in spite of its benign beginning. About 16 miles from US 89 turn left on Smokey Mountain Road, where the sign indicates Escalante is 58 miles away, to climb the steep, twisting route up Smokey Mountain. Continue north on the main road, disregarding turns to Smoky Hollow and Heads of Creek. Some 32 miles from its origin in the national recreation area the road comes to a T intersection with a corral and windmill. Here you leave Smokey Mountain Road. Turn right and follow the directions to the trailhead starting in the second paragraph of this section for the remainder of the trip.

Day hike or base camp backpack

Rogers and Basin Canyons

Distance: 12 to 14 miles.
Starting and minimum elevations: 5,720 feet and 5,100 feet.
Difficulty: Moderately strenuous.
Best months: March through April.
Topo maps: Basin Canyon-UT; East of Navajo-UT.

The plateau label is quite deceptive for the Kaiparowits. This huge region has mountains, hills, ridges, and miles of canyon systems, many without names. It certainly isn't the flat tableland that grade school geography texts associate with the term plateau. Your trip along Smokey Mountain Road provides eye-popping evidence that this is no ordinary plateau.

This exploratory journey into the complex land of the Kaiparowits can be done as a long day hike, but for more leisurely and lengthy hiking it is advisable to establish a base camp 1.5 miles down Rogers Canyon from the trailhead. There a spring provides reliable water to pump, and cottonwood benches have suitable campsites above the tamarisk and willow infested bottom.

After the long drive through the roaded and chained plateau, the remote canyons of the east Kaiparowits are a welcome refuge from development. Here, on the west side of Fiftymile Mountain, only the grazing in Rogers Canyon provides evidence of mankind's presence. Basin Canyon, where a rockfall has blocked access for cattle, is preserved in its primitive state and provides miles of hiking opportunities. Alas, it has no water. But with prior planning, or the cooperation of devoted friends, it is possible to cache water for a point-to-point hike on up Basin Canyon to Wits Peak (7,319 feet) on Fiftymile Mountain. From the summit, you can hike down Fiftymile Bench via the pack trail to Coyote Hole. For additional information see *Hiking Utah* (Falcon Publishing). This trip would take three days and involve carrying water, and is only for adventurous, well-conditioned hikers.

The out-and-back hike into Basin Canyon, deep within the wilderness study area, is more than adequate to savor the wildness of this land. From your parking spot continue to follow the totally deteriorated road (now only a footpath) north of the trailhead, dropping 400 feet as it zigzags down the gully to the floor of Rogers Canyon 0.75 mile from the trailhead. Note well the topographical features of this canyon junction for your return trip.

Rogers is broad bottomed, with eroded alluvial deposits creating benches 10 to 15 feet above the dry streambed. Amphitheatrical sandstone cliffs, with eroded Swiss-cheese holes, feature rows of junipers lining the stair steps that climb 400 feet above the canyon floor. Head down Rogers to the southeast, following the gravel streambed or any of the several cowpaths. Above the sage you can spot cottonwood trees 0.25 mile down Rogers, announcing the presence of the spring. Here dense tamarisk, willow, and cottonwood groves cover the valley floor. The usually reliable spring emerges about 0.1 mile into this thicket. The clear water flows for about 0.1 mile, then vanishes. The volume of cow use here dictates both pumping and boiling the water to be safe. Possible campsites are up on the cottonwood benches at the south end of the water zone. Since this spot is less than 2 miles from the trailhead it isn't a total disaster if the stream is dry and you have to turn this into a day hike.

The vista down Rogers, with sections of tamarisk clogging the bottom and more patches of cottonwoods showing, confirms that more springs lie ahead. This upper one has the most vigorous flow, however, and better campsites. Hiking on down Rogers for 3.5 miles you'll encounter intermittent springs and dense tamarisk stands where groundwater supports them. There is heavy cattle use around these watering spots, and fortunately the bovines have created paths through the streambottom thickets. In spring the songs of warblers indicate that others are also delighted with the water in this arid country.

A narrow side canyon joins Rogers from the north just below the first spring. Its narrow brushy floor rises sharply toward Fiftymile Mountain. This side canyon's two forks and multiple heads cover more than 18 square miles, yet it is unnamed. As President Clinton mentioned in his dedication of the national monument, this country was the last part of the continental United States to be mapped. There is no sign of water in this rugged side canyon, but its wildness invites exploration. Or continue on down the winding bottom of Rogers. The main canyon narrows and zigzags sharply to the east. Selective erosion of the sandstone walls has produced fanciful holes that decorate the cliff faces.

The wild majesty of Rogers Canyon is scarred by heavy-handed grazing practices. It is startling to encounter sagebrush benches that have been denuded by the chainsaw. Other sagebrush benches have been burned, and an entire stretch of tamarisk has likewise been torched. The remoteness of the area contributes to such abusive range management. The destruction along Smokey Mountain Road was disturbing; here it is shocking. Concerned citizens can help the BLM in its task to manage the only national monument it has ever had in its jurisdiction. Notify the BLM Cedar City District office of inappropriate activities in the new monument. The BLM management planning process for the monument is not due to be completed until 1999, so your input is important.

About 4 miles down winding Rogers Canyon, Basin Canyon enters from the north; at this point Rogers has just completed a narrow east-west zigzag course through honeycombed narrows of sandstone. Turn left into Basin Canyon. At the junction (5,100 feet), Basin Canyon's bottom is narrow, but the open gravelly streambed makes a firm path. While usually dry, the canyon has several huge water chutes, like luge runs, in the sandstone walls where it bends sharply, evidence of seasonal torrents. Sculpted sandstone formations, slotted narrows on the slickrock floor, and diminished evidence of cattle combine to create a more intimate canyon experience here.

About 0.75 mile north of the entrance some moderate bouldering is necessary. Through this narrow section the several pouroffs and blockages can be negotiated by hikers but not by cattle; from here on up the canyon is pristine and primitive. There are no trails or footpaths, no cairns, and no footprints. Basin is a delightful exploratory journey. After the narrows, its mostly grassy bottom alternates with gravel and occasional slickrock pavement. In the latter, catchbasins may hold pools of water left by the early spring snowmelt, but you can't count on the availability of water here. Periodic boulder barricades create moderate challenges.

The canyon winds more than 8 miles into and up Fiftymile Mountain, growing narrow and rugged as it climbs toward Wits Point. An out-and-back hike into Basin makes for a long day trip, but it's not easy to decide where to turn around. The variety in the canyon entices you onward, to round the next bend, to discover the secrets of this remote canyon. About 2.5 miles from its mouth, Basin's bottom broadens, a side canyon comes from the north, and the 600-foot cliffs step back to form an enormous amphitheater. Here, at 5,750 feet, is a good spot to pause and enjoy the space and solitude of the Kaiparowits. It's also a good turn-around point. When you return to the trailhead you'll be able to distinguish this amphitheater in the rugged topography of the plateau.

After sauntering back down Basin Canyon you can't help being struck by the contrast between Basin and Rogers. Basin is a real gem, appreciated by the bald eagles soaring above as well as by the hikers below. The odds are that you will see more of the former than the latter on your outing here. Upon returning to the trailhead be sure to take a moment to gaze east over the razor-edge rim of the Straight Cliffs. Thick vegetation coats the land with dense pinyon-juniper forests covering large areas. Even Douglas-fir flourish here, at elevations of less than 6,000 feet. The remote Kaiparowits is unique in many ways.

Escalante Canyons Wilderness Complex 20

Location: 8 miles southeast of Loa (north end) and 1 mile east of Escalante (west end), in south-central Utah.

Size: 1,085,640 acres.

Administration: USDAFS Dixie National Forest, Teasdale and Escalante ranger districts; BLM Cedar City District, Escalante Resource Area; NPS Capitol Reef National Park and Glen Canyon National Recreation Area.

Management status: Much of the complex is included within the east half of the Grand Staircase–Escalante National Monument. Within and adjacent to the monument are the Box–Death Hollow Wilderness (USDAFS 26,000 acres); Glen Canyon National Recreation Area roadless land (304,350 acres); Capitol Reef National Park roadless land (about 104,000 acres); BLM wilderness study areas (five units totaling 221,023 acres, including five Outstanding Natural Areas totaling 44,370 acres plus 425 acres in the Calf Creek Recreation Area and the 2,213-acre Wolverine Petrified Wood Natural Area); unprotected BLM and state roadless lands (156,417 acres); unprotected national forest roadless land (about 200,000 acres).

Ecosystems: Middle Rocky Mountain province, potential natural vegetation of Douglas-fir forest and western spruce-fir forest; Colorado Plateau province, potential natural vegetation of pinyon-juniper woodland, galleta-threeawn shrub steppe, saltbush-greasewood, and blackbrush.

Elevation range: 3,700 feet (Lake Powell high water mark) to 10,886 feet (Trail Point).

Established trails/routes: Capitol Reef National Park contains 12 developed trails totaling 20.6 miles; there are more than 150 miles of trails and primitive routes along the Escalante River and side canyons, with most routes being cross-country. An additional 50 miles of trails cross national forest roadless areas.

Maximum core to perimeter distance: 10 miles (Upper Stevens Canyon in Glen Canyon National Recreation Area).

Activities: Hiking, backpacking, canyoneering, rock climbing, horseback riding, cross-country skiing, snowshoeing, floatboating, photography, nature and cultural study.

Maps: BLM 1:100,000 scale surface management/land ownership maps entitled "Loa," "Escalante," "Hite Crossing," "Smokey Mtn," and "Navajo Mtn"; USDAFS 1995 half-inch/mile map for the Dixie National Forest, Escalante and Teasdale ranger districts (50 meter contour interval). See Appendix E for a listing of the 41 topo maps covering the complex.

20 ESCALANTE CANYONS WILDERNESS COMPLEX

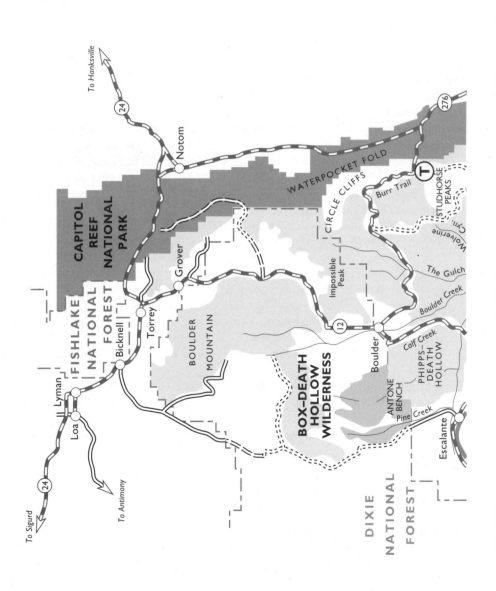

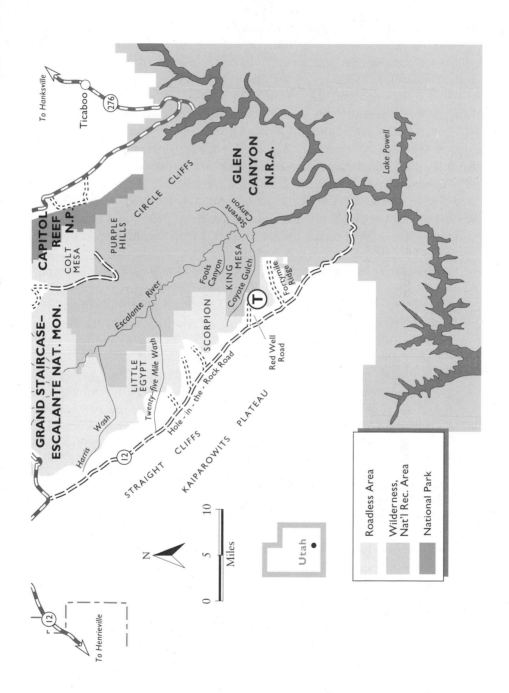

OVERVIEW: The Escalante River begins its 125-mile journey to Glen Canyon from the lake-studded meadows and forests of the Aquarius Plateau. The river drops more than 6,000 feet through glades of aspen, spruce, and ponderosa pine into a 1,000-mile maze of narrow, twisting canyons feeding into an expansive basin floor of bare rock. The 1 million acres of wildlands within Escalante Basin are bordered by the Aquarius Plateau on the north, the Circle Cliffs and Waterpocket Fold to the east, and by the Straight Cliffs of the Kaiparowits Plateau on the west. Massive uplifting caused by shifting and buckling of the earth, followed by stream erosion, exposed a great cross-section of geological formations deposited much earlier during alternating periods of inland seas, lakes, and deserts. Some of the formations are a storehouse of fossilized dinosaur bones, sea shells, land and marine animals, and petrified wood from ancient forests. The stunning result we see today is an elaborate jumble of volcanic boulder fields, uplifted plateaus, domes and buttes, deep canyons, sheer cliffs, pedestals and balanced rocks, arches and natural bridges, water pockets, and ironstone concretions.

On the north end of the Aquarius Plateau the 11,000-foot top of Boulder Mountain is the highest plateau in Utah, and, with 50,000 acres of rolling terrain, it is also one of the largest landforms in the state. On the northeast side of Boulder Mountain the BLM's 19,400-acre Fremont Gorge roadless area encloses deep chasms of limestone and sandstone bordering national park wildlands, including 6 fast-flowing miles of the Fremont River. This high-elevation desert stream is a refuge for such rare birds as bald eagles and peregrine falcons. Boulder Mountain drains south into 34,400 acres of BLM wildlands surrounding Steep Creek, which links the headwaters of the Escalante to its wild canyon country. The centerpiece is The Gulch, which leads up into the Circle Cliffs where large specimens of petrified wood are preserved in the ancient Chinle and Morrison formations.

Also to the south of Aquarius Plateau, Death Hollow is the main artery of one of the nation's finest slickrock wildernesses. Pine Creek flows through the narrow canyon of The Box, lined with 1,500-foot walls, wild rose, Douglas-fir, and ponderosa pine. Both Pine Creek and Death Hollow contain native fish. Elk, deer, and antelope winter on the higher benches. BLM's 43,500-acre Phipps–Death Hollow wildland is a continuation of the wilderness, with 40 miles of perennial streams winding south to the Escalante. Hanging gardens adorn desert varnished walls of golden Navajo sandstone. Antone Flat is an especially important wildlife winter range wedged between Death Hollow and the river.

These and other northern headwater streams have each carved a distinctive slot through white Navajo sandstone. Within these 144 thousand acres of wild northern Escalante canyons are intricately carved alcoves, natural bridges, and arches bound by slickrock walls and riparian plant communities. The higher mesas and benches support a scattering of desert shrubs and pinyon-juniper. Mule deer, elk, and mountain lions roam secluded highlands and secret upper canyons. Perhaps the most impressive slot canyons in the basin are tucked away in BLM's 38,100-acre Scorpion roadless area some 25 miles southeast of Escalante, as exemplified by a dramatic pouroff at the start of Scorpion Gulch. Slickrock benches serve as vantage points into the canyons and eastward to the cliffs and spires of Waterpocket Fold, where countless tiny pools of water are trapped in the tilted strata.

The Studhorse Peaks (19,500 acres) and Colt Mesa units (23,500 acres) provide a southwest buttress to Capitol Reef National Park of high mesas and sandstone cliffs. Canyon gorges fan out from 7,243-foot Deer Point, a lonely and lofty slickrock sentinel of the Waterpocket Fold. Across the Fold to the east, 28,300 acres of colorful badlands, slot canyons, and eastern flanks of Waterpocket Fold complement the adjacent national park and national recreation area. One of many notable features here is a 600-foot-deep cut into Entrada sandstone known as Long Canyon.

For several centuries before and after 1200 A.D., Kayenta and Fremont agricultural peoples lived in the basin. Somewhere around 1275 A.D. a large Kayenta Anasazi village was abandoned at the present townsite of Boulder. Hopi peoples hunted in the region for several centuries. Beginning four and five hundred years ago Southern Paiutes occupied the country into historical times. Sites include rock art, campsites, granaries, and shelters.

Adding to its wild mystique, the Escalante River is widely regarded to be the last major river discovered by white people in the lower 48 states. In 1866 Captain James Andrus led his troops east from Kanab through the basin in pursuit of Paiute Indians. In 1879 the Hole-in-the-Rock Expedition of 236 Mormon pioneers left Escalante to settle the untamed San Juan region. They quickly built the first 50 miles of the Hole-in-the-Rock Road. Progress was slowed across the following 6 miles of slickrock to the cliff notch of Hole-in-the-Rock. The determined settlers blasted a road up and down the cliffs bordering the Colorado River. Six months later the exhausted party made it to the present-day site of Bluff on the San Juan River.

RECREATIONAL USES: From its snowy top to its muddy bottom, the Escalante tops the wild Utah list in its range of wildland recreational pursuits. And of all the ways in which people can experience wild nature here, extended backpacking ranks number one in popularity, length of season, and number of choices. So while the big draw is exploring the country for several days or more on foot, one can also pedal, paddle, fish, photograph, rockhound, climb, and ski into absolute ecstasy.

In the Boulder Mountain country on the Dixie National Forest Utah Highway 12 provides winter access for cross-country skiers. One of many day trip options for skiers is to head south from 9,500-foot Point Lookout on a high ridge out-and-back, or north into the heads of Steep Creek, Deer Creek, and nearby mountain lakes. From late spring to late fall hiking and horse riding opportunities abound on trails in the remaining high lake roadless country of the Aquarius Plateau. Northeast of Boulder Mountain, hikers and anglers can walk along the Fremont River when water levels are low, from UT 12 through the gorge all the way down to the Capitol Reef visitor center. Easier trails into the forks of Sulphur Creek start at the visitor center. While you're in the neighborhood, Grand Wash presents a short, easy, trailless hike. The trailhead is about 5 miles east of the visitor center on Utah Highway 24. Navajo sandstone walls soar 800 feet above a narrow 20-foot-wide canyon. Grand Wash is one of only five canyons slicing completely through Capitol Reef.

Floatboating is one of the more surprising activities in this arid land of desert mesas and ephemeral streams. In years of at least normal runoff the Escalante River is floatable during peak snowmelt from the Aquarius Plateau, which usually lasts two to three weeks sometime between early April and late May. Kayaks or small inflatable rafts work best for tricky maneuvering in the shallow, rock-strewn water. Escalante Canyon begins just below Escalante and runs south for about 85 miles to Lake Powell. The only bridge crossing is on UT 12 about 15 miles below Escalante, which is the usual put-in spot for the 70-mile, five- to seven-day float. The first 2 miles of the Escalante below the bridge are privately owned with no camping allowed. Some people are able to talk a friend into picking them up by boat from Bullfrog or Halls Crossing marinas. Those less fortunate usually take out at Crack in Wall below Coyote Gulch and carry their boats and gear for nearly 3 miles with a 1,000-foot gain to the Fortymile Ridge Trailhead. The takeout trailhead is about 43 miles south of UT 12 by way of the Hole-in-the-Rock Road and a short four-wheel-drive road at the end.

River floaters and all other backcountry campers need to obtain a free backcountry permit at the Escalante Interagency Visitor Center or at one of several trailhead locations. Maximum party size is 12 with a voluntary limit of eight. For horse parties the maximum number of stock is also 12. There are many canyons and interconnecting mesas suitable for both hiking and horseback riding, and some, such as Death Hollow and Calf Creek, have the added attraction of trout fishing.

One of the classic "narrows" hikes is an extremely arduous 30-mile, four- to five-day descent of steep-walled Death Hollow from Hells Backbone south to the Escalante River. From the mouth of Death Hollow the route can end either upstream at Escalante or downriver at the UT 12 bridge. The contrast is amazing between the first 11 miles of dry walking, followed by continuous wading for the remainder of the journey. To the southeast, a one- or two-day hike in Little Death Hollow is another exciting "narrows" trip. A less strenuous choice is to spend two days hiking downriver from Escalante 15 miles to the UT 12 bridge, with side explorations of Death Hollow and Sand Creek.

Rock scrambling, steep climbing, and brushy bottoms make for a moderately strenuous three- to five-day, 27-mile, point-to-point trip from The Gulch down to the Escalante River and then upriver to the UT 12 bridge. Another popular but somewhat difficult trip is a 4- to 6-day, 37-mile, point-to-point backpack down the river from the bridge to Harris Wash, which is reached from the Hole-in-the-Rock Road a few miles south of UT 12. Boulder Creek, The Gulch, Horse Canyon, and Silver Falls Canyon are among the many choices for short or extended side trips. A shorter option is a two- to three-day, 20-mile loop from the Egypt Trailhead, which is 26 road miles from Escalante. Begin by following Fence Canyon to the river, then go downriver 6 miles to 25 Mile Wash. Head back up 25 Mile Wash, ending the loop with a cross-country hike to the trailhead. An extended trip would be to take an 82-mile, nine- to ten-day backpack from the UT 12 bridge downriver to the Red Well or Hurricane Wash trailheads. The latter trailhead is on the Hole-in-the-Rock Road, 33 miles south of UT 12. For a short, educational day hike the Calf Creek Falls Trailhead and campground is only about 1.5 miles north of the bridge. The BLM has established a 5.5-mile round-trip interpretative trail through the deep canyon to the 126-foot Lower Calf Creek Falls—a refreshing respite on a hot summer day. The upper falls can be reached only by a demanding 1-mile hike over slickrock from UT 12, about 5.5 miles north of the campground.

Moody Creek Road south of Burr Trail Road provides hiking access to secluded Deer Point—one of the highest features on the 100-mile-long Waterpocket Fold. Deer Point is a little known promontory reachable by a long adventurous hike up Middle Moody Canyon. See Hike 64 in *Hiking Utah* (Falcon Publishing) for directions to the Moody Creek Trailhead.

Mountain bikes are not allowed off designated roadways throughout most of the Escalante backcountry, particularly in BLM wilderness study areas and National Park Service lands, but bikers have an incredible range of choices for combination bike/hikes. Muscle-powered cyclists can gain access to side hikes into northern Escalante canyons by taking the 36-mile Wolverine Road loop (see Ride 54 in *Mountain Biking Utah,* Falcon Publishing). The loop passes Horse Canyon, Wolverine Creek, Little Death Hollow, Moody Creek, and many other prime hiking destinations. In the southern Escalante the final 19 miles of the Hole-in-the-Rock Road is an ideal mountain bike route, passing several canyons well suited for short leg-stretchers, such as Willow Gulch for a 4- to 5-mile round trip to Broken Bow Arch. Refer to Ride 56 in *Mountain Biking Utah* for details.

HOW TO GET THERE: *Fools Canyon–Coyote Gulch Loop:* From the town of Escalante drive 5 miles southeast on Utah Highway 12 to the signed Hole-in-the-Rock Road. Turn right (south) and follow the graded dirt road 31 miles to the Red Well Road turnoff. Take a left (west) and drive 1.5 miles to the Red Well Trailhead at road's end.

Studhorse Peaks Scramble: From the paved Burr Trail (County Route 1668), about 0.5 mile south of the "ref 45" green marker post, and about 29 miles east of the UT 12-Burr Trail Road junction, turn west on an unsigned, unimproved two-wheel-drive dirt road that parallels the southeast side of a sandstone ridge connecting the Studhorse Peaks. After passing some old dugouts drive about 1 mile and park along side the road. The unmarked trailhead is the first place where the road comes close to the Studhorse Peaks ridge with huge boulders nearby.

Four- to eight-day backpack

Fools Canyon–Coyote Gulch Loop

Distance: 35 miles (basic loop).
Starting and maximum elevations: 4,420 feet and 5,020 feet (King Mesa).
Difficulty: Moderately strenuous.
Best months: April through May; September through November.
Topo maps: King Mesa-UT; Stevens Canyon South-UT.

This challenging, mostly off-trail loop is a wonderful sampler of Escalante Canyon country with open high desert hiking and canyoneering in deep, narrow chasms. The terrain varies from high slickrock mesas to the Escalante River bottom 1,000 feet below. Most of the route is within Glen Canyon National Recreation Area, with about 0.5 mile of Coyote Gulch passing through a small BLM wilderness study area. The basic 35-mile loop descends Coyote Gulch a few miles, then heads north over King Mesa to Fools Canyon, then down Fools Canyon to the Escalante River, continuing downstream to Coyote Gulch, which is then followed back up to the trailhead. The loop can be rushed in three or four long days, but seven to eight days is highly recommended to accommodate side trips and a more relaxed pace. Water is available in each of the canyons but should be boiled or filtered before using. In fact, much of the route is *in* water, so bring sturdy wading shoes. Practice minimum impact camping—use a backpack stove and refrain from building campfires.

From the trailhead follow the wash down a few hundred yards to the confluence of Big Hollow Wash and Coyote Gulch. Continue eastward down Coyote Gulch about 4.5 miles to a cattle fence with a hiker's gate. Another 0.5 mile brings you to the mouth of "Sleepy Hollow" (not named on the map), which enters from the left (north). The hollow can be hiked for a couple of miles. It also offers a way out of Coyote Gulch for the 5-mile cross-country traverse to Fools Canyon. About 0.4 mile up Sleepy Hollow, the east (right) wall slopes back into a bowl that can be climbed to King Mesa—a high expanse of slickrock knobs and buttes. From the rim above Sleepy Hollow continue northeast along the right side of a small drainage 2 to 3 miles to a major pass along the crest of King Mesa (shown as Point 5,020 on the topo map). The pass can't be seen until you're in it. From the pass follow the drainage northeast another 1.5 to 2 miles to the high rim of Fools Canyon. Hike east along the rim for about 0.75 mile to a prominent point between the main canyon and a short, deep canyon to the south. Drop down the end of the point to an old stock trail, which turns west and drops steeply into Fools Canyon. The most challenging obstacle in the loop is a pouroff and plunge pool about 0.75 mile down Fools Canyon. To get around this narrow chute climb 20 to 30 feet up to the right using small footholds in the slickrock. A 25-foot rope or webbing is needed to pull packs up, around, and below the plunge pool. The brushy bottom of Fools is slow going with tempting side canyons that can make the trip even longer.

From the mouth of Fools Canyon 9 to 10 miles down to Coyote Gulch the Escalante River flows through a narrows of alternating deep water and fast current. You'll soon lose count of the number of stream crossings so use a stick to probe the reddish-brown water for the safest fords. Sheep Canyon enters from the left about 2 miles below Fools Canyon. This 4-mile canyon, a refuge for bighorn sheep, is well worth a full day of exploration. Stay high on the right side to avoid large boulders in the first 0.5 mile.

Another 6 miles downriver the mouth of Stevens Canyon presents a stunning view of Stevens Arch. Grottos, arches, alcoves, sheer cliff walls, and plunge pools make Stevens ideal for several layover days of exploration. Four miles up canyon, high cliffs and pouroffs necessitate scrambling steeply on the right side. Be on the lookout for poison ivy in this stretch. After another 0.5 mile, climb the left slope to a high, broad bench that invites miles of wandering to the northeast.

Continuing the loop, about 0.5 mile below the mouth of Stevens Canyon look for a primitive bypass trail to Coyote Gulch in order to avoid a slow, muddy stretch of the river caused by the backup of Lake Powell. The trail heads up the second short draw on the west (right) side of the river below Stevens Canyon. Upon reaching Coyote Gulch drop back down to the river for a quick side trip. A pouroff in Coyote Gulch about 0.5 mile above the river requires steep sidehilling on the south (left) side. To complete the loop follow Coyote Gulch all the way up to the Red Well Trailhead. Along the way take time to savor Cliff Arch, Coyote Natural Bridge with nearby Anasazi ruins, and Jacob Hamblin Arch. This stretch of Coyote Gulch is popular with weekend day hikers. In contrast, the outer edges of the loop offer wilderness solitude in a rugged region that is close to the maximum distance from a road within the entire vast complex.

The entire Circle Cliffs amphitheater can be seen from the top of Studhorse Peaks.

Short off-trail day hike

Studhorse Peaks

Distance: 1 mile round trip.
Starting and maximum elevations: 6,900 feet and 7,160 feet.
Difficulty: Moderate.
Best months: March through October.
Topo map: Wagon Box Mesa-UT.

While driving the Burr Trail Road to or from Capitol Reef National Park consider a quick scramble up one of the Studhorse Peaks for an incredible vista of the Circle Cliffs amphitheater and of much of the Escalante Complex—from Boulder Mountain to the southern tip of Fiftymile Mountain. Car campsites abound along the short Studhorse Peaks Road, so if possible make the 20-to 30-minute, 0.5-mile climb during early morning for the best photographic light.

The Studhorse Peaks are a ridge of red Moenkopi buttes capped with white Shinarump conglomerate on the east-central edge of an unprotected 19,500-acre BLM roadless area. From the pullout along the road head northwest toward exposed 50-foot white cliffs above a pinyon-juniper woodland interspersed with rock outcroppings. Moderate bouldering and slithering between great slabs of sandstone provides a canyoneering effect. After climbing to the right toward a low point on the ridge, angle left up white table rock to the summit of this centrally located butte on the Studhorse Peaks ridge. The rims of White Canyon can be seen winding westward through the heart of the roadless area. From this point you can easily envision a long point-to-point, 12- to 15-mile day hike or overnighter from an upper southern tributary to White Canyon all the way down to the canyon mouth, ending up on the Wolverine Road about 4 miles south of the Burr Trail Road.

Henry Mountains Complex

21

Location: 12 miles southwest of Hanksville and 4 miles north of Bullfrog, in south-central Utah.

Size: 353,400 acres.

Administration: BLM Moab District, Henry Mountain Resource Area; Glen Canyon National Recreation Area.

Management status: BLM wilderness study areas (four units totaling 189,646 acres) and unprotected roadless areas (159,654 acres); national recreation area roadless land (4,100 acres).

Ecosystems: Colorado Plateau province ecoregion; pinyon-juniper woodland is the potential natural vegetation, with ponderosa, spruce, and fir at higher elevations and sagebrush shrub community at lower elevations.

Elevation range: 3,720 feet (lower Bullfrog Creek) to 11,615 feet (Mount Ellen).

Established trails/routes: No trails, but countless miles of old jeep tracks suitable for hiking or horseback riding.

Maximum core to perimeter distance: 2.5 miles.

Activities: Hiking, backpacking, canyoneering, photography, wildlife study.

Maps: BLM 1:100,000 scale surface management/land ownership maps entitled "Loa," "Hanksville," "Escalante," and "Hite Crossing" (50 meter contour interval). See Appendix E for a listing of the 20 topo maps covering the roadless area.

OVERVIEW: The purple domes of the Henry Mountains dominate the horizon in south-central Utah. Mount Ellen (11,615 feet), Mount Pennell (11,371 feet), and Mount Hillers (10,723 feet) erupt from the Colorado Plateau, surrounded by mesas and deeply dissected badlands. The Henry Mountain wilderness of which they form the core is a rough arrowhead aiming south at the Bullfrog Marina on Lake Powell. Utah Highway 24 and Hanksville are on the north, with Capitol Reef National Park and Waterpocket Fold on the west. Utah highways 95 and 276 run along the eastern side of this 45-mile-long wilderness region.

A striking anomaly on the Colorado Plateau, the Henrys are the volcanic cores of igneous laccoliths, exposed by eons of erosion. The nineteenth-century geologist G.K. Gilbert coined the term laccolith in his study of the Henrys. The rugged badlands that surround the peaks are on par with those in South

Dakota. These mesas, ridges, and benches radiate from the domes of purple granite, making hiking a challenge.

Their abrupt altitude, 5,000 feet above the plateau, creates a mini-climate that is less arid than the surrounding country. Below the naked igneous domes the mountain slopes are clad with the usual pinyon-juniper woodland. You can also discover ponderosa pine, spruce, fir, and aspen, as well as ancient bristlecone pine. The lower elevations feature barren rock outcroppings with patches of sagebrush and desert shrubbery.

Mule deer, pronghorn antelope, bobcat, and mountain lion inhabit the wild canyons and mesas, along with small mammals and numerous raptors. A unique fixture of the wildlife of the Henrys is a small herd of bison, offspring of animals reintroduced in 1941. These 500 head are the only unrestricted group of bison in the nation. The large Henry Mountain complex assures adequate winter and summer range for the species, which requires diverse habitat for survival.

No thorough inventory of archeological sites has been conducted in the Henry Mountains. Usage by Paleo-Indians was limited to temporary sites, as bands of hunter-gatherers passed through in pursuit of migratory game. Areas with lithic scatter are the only clues to their presence many hundreds of years ago.

The Henrys were sighted by the Powell expedition down the Colorado in 1869. Powell named the range for Professor Joseph Henry of the Smithsonian Institute, a supporter of his explorations in the West. The extremely rugged terrain made for light visitation by Americans. Rumors of a lost Spanish gold mine in the Henrys sparked some interest but produced only disappointment. In more recent times ranchers and herders left their primitive dwellings on mesas. These remote remnants of the ranching era suggest a life of hardship and solitude.

In this century the Henrys have been the scene of uranium, gold, oil and gas, and coal exploration, as well as cattle grazing and some logging. Their wild beauty is not diminished by the jeep tracks winding down the rough mesas, or even by the BLM's past chaining program "to improve wildlife habitat." Left on its own, this wild country can reclaim itself. Tracks disappear from sandy mesas; shrubbery eventually covers the scars, rewilding the land.

The Henry complex consists of six roadless units. The Mount Ellen–Blue Hills unit (116,900 acres), one of the largest roadless areas in Utah, lies at the north end of the complex. The complicated Blue Hills badlands, with three large mesas sprinkled like islands between the deep ravines, stretch northwest of towering Mount Ellen. The view of south-central Utah's wild country is magnificent: Capitol Reef, the Escalante River, San Rafael Swell, and the Dirty Devil Wilderness stretch out below.

21 HENRY MOUNTAINS COMPLEX

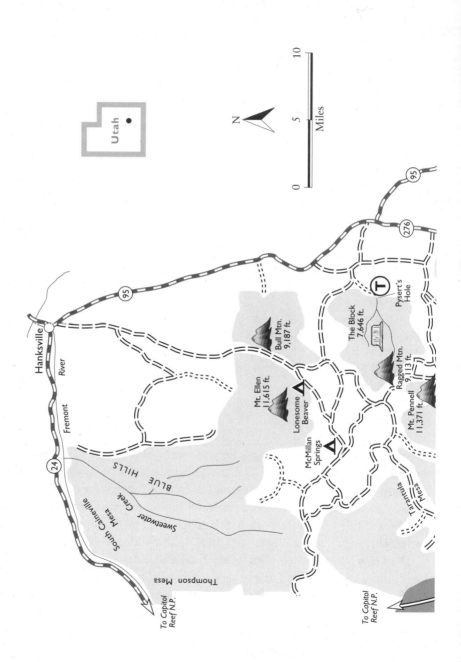

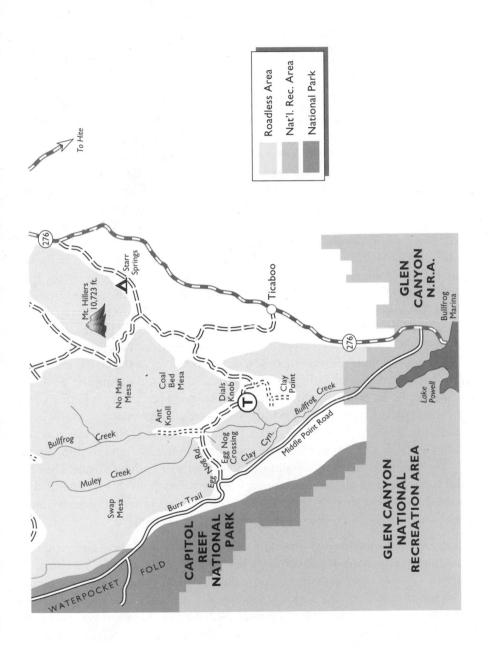

To Hite

Roadless Area
Nat'l. Rec. Area
National Park

276
Starr Springs
Mt. Hillers 10,723 ft.
Ticaboo
276
GLEN CANYON N.R.A.
Bullfrog Marina
No Man Mesa
Coal Bed Mesa
Dials Knob
Clay Point
Ant Knoll
Bullfrog Creek
Lake Powell
Bullfrog Creek
Clay Cyn.
Egg Nog Crossing
Middle Point Road
Muley Creek
Egg Nog Rd.
Swap Mesa
Burr Trail
CAPITOL REEF NATIONAL PARK
GLEN CANYON NATIONAL RECREATION AREA
WATERPOCKET FOLD

The Bull Mountain unit, separated by a gravel road out of South Hanksville, is adjacent to Mount Ellen on the east. Bull Mountain (9,187 feet) is the lowest of the Henrys. Not to be overlooked due to its lesser stature, this peak is an oddity in the range because it is a bysmalith instead of a laccolith. As Bull's igneous intrusion rose through the earth's crust, the overlying layers fractured and faulted instead of folding. The result is a more abrupt, steeper mountainside. Little Ragged Mountain, just to the south, is a smaller bysmalith with faulted sides.

The Mount Pennell unit (141,200 acres) spans the width of the wilderness area as it nears the southern tip of the arrowhead. Some 12 miles across at its widest point and 14 miles long, it is broken by only three incursions: a cherry-stemmed road by Ant Knoll on the south, roaded and mined Tarantula Mesa on the north, and a short road on upper Bullfrog Creek. Swap, Cave Flat, No Man, and Coal Bed mesas consist of intricate badland formations, sweeping up to the dominant igneous core of 11,371-foot Mount Pennell.

To the east of Mount Pennell is Mount Hillers, the last of the string of laccoliths we see before the Little Rockies Range along Glen Canyon. The igneous ridges of 10,723-foot Mount Hillers rise in concentric incised layers above the radiating ridges. Pink cliffs of tilted Navajo sandstone demonstrate the enormous force of the igneous upthrust through the earth's crust. A mesa called Black Table sits to the northeast. This subsidiary intrusion of porphyry stock rises 600 feet. As with little Cass Peak, also next to Mount Hillers, this is a laccolith that petered out before dislodging the sedimentary layers overhead.

The southernmost Bullfrog Creek unit forms the tip of the arrow aimed at flooded Glen Canyon. Bullfrog Creek flows 30 miles, draining the western slopes of the Henrys through its dramatic canyon. The canyon is both a geologic and artistic wonderland. Sandstones, muds, conglomerates, clays, and shales are all revealed in shades of red, brown, beige, pink, white, and gray. A Jurassic-age petrified forest is located on Clay Point in the center of the unit.

The Henrys form the mountainous hub of southern Utah wildlands. They're the landmark and the reference point for any journeys in this section of the state. Rather than driving around them, explore their canyons, plateaus, and peaks on foot to gain a better appreciation for wild country.

RECREATIONAL USES: The Henrys provide a complete outdoor playground for the outdoors person. Rock climbers have many destinations. The Horn, a smooth diorite outcrop northeast of Mount Pennell, is a challenging ascent. The solid surface of the Henrys' igneous peaks contrasts with the sandy Navajo formations more common on the Colorado Plateau. Photographers can enjoy endless mountain top panoramas, or the precise intricacies of the badlands. Hikers and backpackers can explore for miles up the canyons, across mesas, and on to the beckoning heights of the brooding granite giants. The streams and springs assure campers of the availability of water (which must be filtered or boiled, of course). The scenery is fantastic, both from the peaks and of the peaks.

The main BLM campground is at Starr Springs below Mount Hillers. Numerous hiking routes follow old mining roads that lace the benches. The canyons and badlands are an untrammeled universe. With map and compass, as well as the usual hiking supplies (see Appendix A), the Henrys offer limitless opportunities to explore.

HOW TO GET THERE: Pyserts Hole Hikes: from Utah Highway 95, about 26 miles south of Hanksville, turn west just north of the UT 276/95 junction at milepost 26 onto an improved dirt road. This unsigned road becomes paved for a brief stretch when it coincides with a former landing strip, but it quickly returns to improved dirt. About 3 miles from UT 95 bear right at the T junction on the main well-traveled road. 1 mile farther (4 miles from UT 95), turn left at a major road junction, following the sign to Eagle Benches. 0.5 mile from this turn, bear left at the Y on an unsigned, unimproved dirt road. With careful navigation a two-wheel-drive, low-clearance vehicle can make this trip. The road travels southwest along North Wash. It passes through the remnants of an old homestead. You will notice a sturdy old shed built into the hillside to the right of the road. The cherry-stemmed road then bends west into the Ragged Mountain unit along the South Fork Wash. A total of 9 miles from UT 95 the road ends on the eroded bank of South Fork Wash in Pyserts Hole. There is space for several vehicles to turn around and park, and campers can find sites along the dry South Fork.

Bullfrog Canyons: drive south of Hanksville 26 miles on UT 95 to UT 276. Go south on UT 276 toward Bullfrog Marina. Just south of milepost 17 turn right on the improved dirt road to Starr Springs Campground. Drive past the campground, continuing southwest 15 miles to the trailhead at the head of Fourmile Canyon. Use the Clay Point-UT topo map to pinpoint the spot where the western feeder canyon of Fourmile touches the road. The unmarked trailhead is directly south of a prominent badland point, and south-southwest of the feature called Dials Knob. The head of the canyon is also conspicuous because it comes right to the south edge of the road, just after the road bends sharply northwest. The wet-tire Bullfrog Crossing at Eggnog is 5 miles farther down the road. Park along the lightly traveled road and begin your hike by heading south on the east side of the canyon. From the west, take the improved Egg Nog Road east from the Middle Point Road toward Starr Springs Campground. At 4.5 miles the road drops into Bullfrog Creek at the Egg Nog Crossing. Under normal conditions, a two-wheel-drive, low-clearance vehicle can cross the creek. Go a total of 9.5 miles on Egg Nog Road, crossing Saleratus Wash, to the first head of Fourmile Canyon on the right. Look for Dials Knob and the salient promontory of badlands in the rugged terrain to the north of the trailhead. Park parallel on the lightly traveled road's edge, and hike south along the canyon's east rim.

Day hikes

Pyserts Hole Hikes

Distance: 9 miles round trip (North Canyon); 2 miles round trip (The Whale); 5 miles round trip (The Block); 10 miles round trip (Raggy Canyon).
Starting and maximum elevations: 5,640 feet to 6,840 feet (North Canyon); 6,340 feet (The Whale); 7,646 feet (The Block); 7,000 feet (Raggy Canyon).
Difficulty: Moderate (the canyons), to moderately strenuous (The Whale), to strenuous (The Block).
Best months: March through May; September through October.
Topo map: Raggy Canyon-UT.

Pyserts Hole is a dramatic entry into this 23,300-acre wilderness on the eastern side of the Henry Mountains. Though the BLM roadless inventory omitted the Ragged Mountain complex, the Utah Wilderness Coalition has proposed to include it in the greater Henry Mountain wilderness. The Cooper Creek and Slate Creek drainages and the bysmalith Ragged Mountain create varied topography and scenic vistas on the eastern side of the Henrys. But the diminutive laccolith called The Block (7,646 feet), which rises at the center of the unit, best typifies the unique volcanic origins of this mountain range. Around the igneous upthrusting Block, concentric ridges of tilted and eroded sedimentary layers stand as testimony to the powerful forces within the Earth. Deep canyons curve around the Block, corresponding to the strata punctured and distorted by the laccolith's force. Pyserts Hole is the gateway where several Block canyons merge at the South Fork, which pierced this outer ring of the ridge complex. From this trailhead you can choose to venture into canyons north or south of the Block, ascend the massive remnant of Navajo sandstone northeast of the Block, or climb the Block itself.

NORTH CANYON: From road's end, turn right and hike up the dry gravelly rocky wash northwest, taking the left fork at each junction, to head for the north side of the Block. A second approach, if you don't object to a sage scramble, is to bypass the curving wash and cut across the rising sagebrush benches of the Hole. Your route should aim between the large pink whale rising on the left and the low Navajo outcropping, like a herd of pink elephants, on the right. There is a faint jeep track through the sagebrush that you might encounter heading your way. About 1 mile from the trailhead you will meet the wash in a flat canyon bottom. This is the first wash north of the Block. Bear left and follow it into the notch of the canyon.

This anonymous canyon is narrow and intimate. Its deep, dark walls create a cave-like atmosphere. The sharp cliffs of the Block tower on the left as you make your way up the canyon. The sun hits the narrow floor of the gorge for only a brief moment during the day, but there is a breathtaking selection of huge Douglas-fir perched along the intermittent stream, lending an alpine air to this low-elevation hike. High in the canyon, gargantuan trunks of downed giants, some more than 3 feet in diameter, lie caught by boulders where they tumbled from the steep walls. Holly and manzanita flourish wherever they find enough soil, but they do not make hiking the narrow canyon difficult. Sections of slots and narrows are dramatic but negotiable, until you arrive at a series of pouroffs about 3 miles up the canyon. In early spring you'll find a stream here in the canyon's upper reaches. The hike's turn-around point is a 20-foot pouroff.

Geologically exciting, North Canyon is fresh and dynamic. Boulder falls, crumbling banks, and scarred cliffs show the earth at work. The varieties of metamorphic, igneous, and sedimentary rocks are fascinating as you pick your way around and over these minor obstacles. Numerous fossilized brachiopods are displayed in chunks on the canyon floor. Returning to the canyon mouth after hours in this cool dark rift in the Henry Mountains you'll be startled by the brightness of the sage flat. This unnamed obscure canyon suggests the wonders that lie hidden in the Henry Mountains.

THE WHALE: The perfect sequel to the North Canyon outing is a climb to the Block overlook formed by the curvaceous remains of Navajo sandstone jutting prominently northeast of the Block. From either the Pyserts Hole Trailhead or directly from North Canyon you can pick a route up the sloping grainy surface. Some of the pitches are quite steep, especially as you near the summit, but it is possible to walk up the whale's tail and keep going right up the back.

The summit provides a great view of the Block's unique topography. You can see the pieces of ringed ridges spreading from the laccolith center like concentric ripples in a pool of water. Also sweeping around you are the prominent landmarks of the Colorado Plateau: the Book Cliffs, the San Rafael Swell, the pinnacles of the La Sals, the buttes of the Dirty Devil, and the Abajos. If you intend to climb to the Block, there is no route from this overlook, but you can survey the terrain from here and plan your ascent.

THE BLOCK: From the saddle just below the forehead of the Whale, the Block's northeast ridge provides the best access to its pinyon-juniper top. To reach the saddle from the Pyserts Hole Trailhead cross the South Fork wash and head southwest on the sage bench between two low mounds of barren sandstone. Drop to the drainage that curves to the right toward the saddle. The rough rocky drainage climbs sharply. After about a mile cut right to angle up to the ridge. From here, continue to climb above the escarpments to the Block's northern flank. It will take some route-finding skills to get to the top of this massive landmark.

On the Block you are at the epicenter of the intrusion that caused the upheaval in the earth's surface. The top of the Block is also botanically special because it has escaped the influence of grazing. Enjoy your visit, and descend by the same route.

RAGGY CANYON: This canyon swings around to embrace the Block from the south. From the Pyserts Hole Trailhead head south across the wash and pick up a former jeep track, now merely a footpath. Follow the intermittent old miner's track leading south, then southwest. It temporarily disappears as you drop into the wash of Raggy Canyon, but you may discern traces of it up the canyon. The track is being rehabilitated by nature, and it makes a good hiking trail.

The canyon mouth is a sharp V between two steep rock cliffs. After this narrow beginning Raggy opens up. The south wall remains steep, while the north side is more open and sloping. Dislocation by the Block has created a topography similar to the block faulting of Basin and Range geology. About a mile up the canyon the wide valley features sunny spots of cottonwood, pinyon, juniper, and Gambel oak above a seasonal, clear-flowing stream. About 0.5 mile farther this broader floodplain ends and tamarisk and willow thickets

Looking west to the 7,646-foot summit of the Block, at left; the Whale is in the center.

crowd the narrow bottom. Scramble up the bank to get past the vegetation and continue to a major canyon fork. Winding Raggy Canyon goes to the left, curving south.

As the going in the bottom grows more congested, interesting side trip become tempting. The steep rugged canyon to the right rises toward the Block and invites exploration. Or you may want to get above the canyon system. Some of the sedimentary rocks are crumbly, but the sloping wall of the canyon will entice climbers eager to gain a panorama of the country. At the canyon junction look for a small hanging canyon just up the sloping rock north of the fork. Here a quick scramble provides a hawk's view of these endless concentric circles. This is wild and rugged country. The canyon continues with its challenging brushy bottom, providing a full day's adventure for the intrepid hiker.

Day hike or backpack

Bullfrog Canyons

Distance: 10 to 14 miles out and back.
Starting and minimum elevations: 4,660 feet to 4,120 feet.
Difficulty: Moderate.
Best months: March through April; October.
Topo map: Clay Point-UT.

In southern Utah, the name Bullfrog is most readily associated with the Bullfrog Marina on Lake Powell, featuring a motel, restaurants, houseboats, and air strip. There's another Bullfrog—the real one. This Bullfrog is the stream that begins on the north slope of Mount Pennell and flows through the Henry badlands south, winding though a stunning canyon to arrive at Lake Powell. This is a different world, one of the raven, deer, cougar, and coyote. At the southern extension of the Henry Mountain Complex, the creek forms the common thread of the 36,900-acre Bullfrog Creek Unit of BLM roadless land. The BLM dropped it from the wilderness process, but the Utah Wilderness Coalition has included Bullfrog's remote canyons and mesas in its proposal. A trip to the interior of the real Bullfrog verifies that this area has the wilderness characteristics of remoteness and solitude, recreational opportunities, and breathtaking beauty.

This excursion ventures into three canyons: the main Bullfrog Canyon and two tributaries, Fourmile and Clay. The trip can be done as a long day hike, or as a backpack with a base camp at the mouth of Fourmile Canyon, three miles from the trailhead. A third option, requiring a car shuttle, is a point-to-point, three-day backpack down Bullfrog Creek to the Middle Point Road crossing in Glen Canyon National Recreation Area. This would be a moderate 15- to 20-mile trip. Water is available in Bullfrog Creek, but its silt content might clog a filter, so that extensive boiling or settling (before filtering) might be necessary.

The Egg Nog Crossing area, just upstream and up the road from the trailhead, is a magnet for off-road vehicles and four-wheelers. By starting the hike via Fourmile Canyon, all the noise, tumult, and vehicle tracks are omitted. This is a quiet world with only an occasional cow to suggest that humanity has ever ventured here.

From your parking spot along the road, walk along the eastern rim of the canyon to a mining claim post on your right, at the canyon's rocky edge. From here it is an easy 150-foot drop into the canyon on the sloping dirt wall. At the bottom continue downhill in the open valley. Colorful mounds of shale badlands appear along the route, interspersed with sandstone, conglomerate, and mudstone outcroppings. The shallow canyon has slots and narrows here near its head, harbingers of what lies ahead.

About a mile from the trailhead, a 15-foot pouroff causes only momentary delay. Skirt it to the right; the detour will lead you to the main Fourmile Canyon floor. Note this spot for your return trip so you will exit at the same place. Continuing down Fourmile the canyon deepens, narrows, and becomes more dramatic with slots, boulders, and narrows. At 1.5 miles a spring emerges beneath the south cliff wall, creating a rich riparian zone of grasses, willow, tamarisk, and rushes. By 2 miles this rivulet has developed into a clear babbling brook, dropping over rocky ledges to produce the magical tinkling of a desert waterfall. Muddy footprints of coyotes and small felines are proof that Fourmile is an attractive home for wildlife. Zigzagging along the watery course are huge cottonwoods, standing high on the alluvial benches above the stream. The meandering watercourse is gnawing away at these earthen platforms, toppling these old trees along the bank and causing younger ones to claw tenaciously with their roots as they slide inexorably further down the steep banks with each spring freshet. From 2.5 to 3 miles backpackers can find possible campsites along Fourmile down to its confluence with Bullfrog in the broad, flat valley. Fourmile's clear water makes this a prime choice for a base camp from which to explore Bullfrog and Clay canyons.

Fourmile Canyon is only 3 miles long, but it is about 4 miles from its mouth north to Egg Nog Crossing. The motorized crowd doesn't usually venture this far south, so the Bullfrog Creek you see here is remote and quiet. The canyon walls rise 800 feet above the stream bottom. These awesome cliffs feature a wide variety of sedimentary layers stair-stepping above a solid foundation of ruddy sandstone that has been carved into huge alcoves by the widely swinging creek. Although silty, the creek is usually easy to hop across using the conveniently spaced stones. The broad Bullfrog bottom features easy walking in dry weather with low sparse sagebrush and blackbrush. The cacophony of the marina, to the south, and Egg Nog Crossing, to the north, is far away.

Two miles below Fourmile, Clay Canyon joins Bullfrog on the west. The beach at its mouth is a good lunch spot for a day hike, or a campsite for a longer canyon outing. A side trip up Clay completes this canyon trio. Clay is a striking contrast to both Fourmile and Bullfrog. Its cliffs sit wide apart, like Bullfrog's, but its bottom is full of mudstone and sandstone, cut into a winding maze by the seasonal stream. This shaley lower level is topped with a loose clay and boulder mix, more than 20 feet thick, sitting like lumpy frosting on a layer cake. Then, rising 1,000 feet above, are the hard maroon and beige sedimentary layers. This is Bullfrog's stratigraphy turned upside down. If you approached your hike from the south via the Middle Point Road, you may have seen Clay Canyon from above, but you'll still be astonished by its diversity of texture and color. Sage and Mormon tea flourish in the dry sandy bottom. Vetch and paintbrush bloom merrily in March. Cottonwood and tamarisk dot the streambed in the S-curves of the bottom. You can explore Clay Canyon for about 3 miles to its head, then return to Bullfrog.

Reemerging into Bullfrog you'll be struck by the spacious quality of this canyon. These neighboring canyons are completely different, and each is enchanting in its own way. The return to the trailhead up Fourmile completes the picture. Its golden sandstones seem to glow in the mudstone and shale world of the Henry badlands.

Upper Glen Canyon Complex

22

Location: 25 miles southeast of Hanksville (north end) and 4 miles east of Bullfrog
Marina (south end), in southeastern Utah.
Size: 313,170 acres.
Administration: BLM Richfield District, Henry Mountain Resource Area (north
end); Moab District, San Juan Resource Area (south end); NPS Glen Canyon
National Recreation Area.
Management status: BLM wilderness study areas (two units totaling 90,140
acres; the 38,700-acre Little Rockies Wilderness Study Area is also a BLM National
Natural Landmark); unprotected BLM and state roadless lands (78,560 acres); two
units of national recreation area roadless land (144,470 acres).
Ecosystems: Colorado Plateau province ecoregion, potential natural vegetation of
blackbrush and juniper-pinyon woodland.
Elevation range: 3,700 feet (Lake Powell high water mark) to 8,235 feet (Mount
Ellsworth).
Established trails/routes: The complex has no formal trails, but there are more
than 60 miles of trailless hiking routes in the Little Rockies–Glen Canyon National
Recreation Area (north end), along with 25 miles of closed, rehabilitated mining
exploration roads in the Mancos Mesa area suitable for hiking and horseback riding.
Maximum core to perimeter distance: 7 miles (Mancos Mesa).
Activities: Hiking, backpacking, canyoneering, rock climbing, horseback riding,
limited deer hunting, photography, nature study (geology).
Maps: BLM 1:100,000 scale surface management/land ownership maps entitled
"Hite Crossing" and "Navajo Mountain" (50 meter contour interval). Refer to
Appendix E for a listing of the 17 topo maps covering the complex.

OVERVIEW: "So we have a curious ensemble of wonderful features—carved
walls, royal arches, glens, alcove gulches, mounds, and monuments. From
which of these features shall we select a name? We decide to call it Glen Canyon." So wrote John Wesley Powell on August 3, 1869, during his epic journey down the Colorado. With the completion of Glen Canyon Dam on the
river in 1963, one of the world's most delightful canyons was submerged, for
at least the next few hundred years, in a watery tomb named, ironically, after
the man who was so captivated by its wild charm.

22 UPPER GLEN CANYON COMPLEX

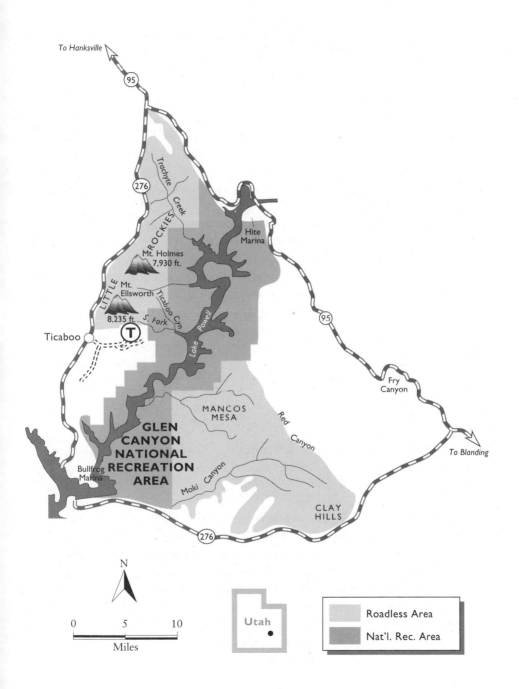

To Hanksville

95

276

Trachyte Creek

LITTLE ROCKIES

Mt. Holmes
7,930 ft.

Mt. Ellsworth
8,235 ft.

S. Fork

Ticaboo Cyn.

Ticaboo

T

Lake Powell

Hite Marina

95

Fry Canyon

To Blanding

MANCOS MESA

Red Canyon

GLEN CANYON NATIONAL RECREATION AREA

Bullfrog Marina

Moki Canyon

CLAY HILLS

276

N

0   5   10
Miles

Utah

Roadless Area

Nat'l. Rec. Area

The good news is that the rugged shores of Lake Powell are flanked by some of the wildest country remaining on the Colorado Plateau—95,000 acres in the Little Rockies to the northwest and, across the lake, another 150,400 unroaded acres on Mancos Mesa stretching far to the southeast.

The extremely rugged Little Rockies are a southeastern extension of the Henry Mountains, but unlike their taller neighbors to the north their overlying sedimentary rocks have not completely eroded away. As with the Henrys, the Little Rockies were formed by tremendous pressures from intrusive volcanic magma, known as a laccolith, which forced up layers of rock thousands of feet. This subrange basically consists of two peaks, 8,235-foot Mount Ellsworth and 7,930-foot Mount Holmes. Their slopes descend to high narrow plateaus separating deep slickrock canyons. The only perennial stream, Trachyte Creek, drains southward in the north end of the roadless area. Volcanic dikes radiate from the peaks, the source of light-colored granite boulders lining the streambeds far below.

To the south, Mancos Mesa is southern Utah's largest isolated slickrock mesa, bound on all sides by cliffs at least 1,000 feet high. Wingate sandstone is exposed in the deep inner recesses of Cedar, Steer Pasture, and Moki canyons. Kayenta sandstone overlies the Wingate, forming benches and steep-ledged slopes. Navajo sandstone rests above the Kayenta, creating vast expanses of slickrock and sand dunes. Draining westward into Lake Powell, twisting canyons are lined by sheer 800-foot sandstone cliffs broken every so often by steep, rocky talus slopes from rim to canyon bottom.

The inaccessibility of Mancos Mesa protects a relict plant community of perennial grasses and shrubs representative of the northern limit of the upper Sonoran life zone. The higher country in the east supports juniper and pinyon pine, changing to blackbrush, yucca, and Mormon tea at lower elevations. Several springs nurture cottonwood, ash, willow, and watercress, in stark contrast to expanses of barren desert bordering the lake. The same species live more sparsely in the Little Rockies due to a predominance of steep mountain slopes and slickrock. Cooler north-facing aspects high on Mount Ellsworth support a few ponderosa pines.

Desert bighorn sheep range year-round in the northern three-quarters of Mancos Mesa. The Utah Division of Wildlife Resources has reintroduced desert bighorns in the Little Rockies, where an abundance of quality sheep habitat exists. This is also good mule deer country although the population is spread thinly over a wide area. A diverse predator population includes mountain lions, bobcats, foxes, coyotes, and golden eagles. Reptiles abound, including chuckwalla lizards on Mancos Mesa, a species rarely found in Utah.

Of the more than 30 archeological sites recorded on the BLM portion of the complex, six are Anasazi rock shelters. Most of the other prehistoric sites on

Looking eastward to Mount Holmes in the Little Rockies.

the mesa and in the Little Rockies are lithic scatters, with four other cultures represented. The Park Service has documented dozens of Anasazi sites in lower Moki Canyon. In the Little Rockies one of the sites is a series of steps carved in the slickrock of a small canyon. Most of the cultural sites found here are on mesas or in small drainages near springs.

RECREATIONAL USES: Lake Powell is Utah's most popular developed recreation tourist attraction. Nonetheless, it's amazing how quickly visitors can achieve total solitude in deep, serpentine canyons—so close to the maddening crowd and yet so far. In terms of difficulty of access and roadless depth, Mancos Mesa harbors the most remote and least visited wildland in the complex. The mesa offers a myriad of challenging day hikes and backpacks, although most routes are out-and-back due to the steep walls that guard even upper stretches of canyons. With arduous climbs just to get up to the mesa the more secluded inner canyons are lightly visited. Occasionally, boaters take day hikes up side canyons from the lake. The Mancos Mesa roadless area is reached by way of a dirt road down Red Canyon taking off from Utah Highway 276 and from the highway between Clay Hills and Halls Crossing. In a few places windblown sand allows hiker access into canyons, such as the "sandslide" in Moki Canyon. An impassable jeep track built for uranium exploration in 1976 is suitable for hiking in and out of Moki Canyon from the top of Mancos Mesa.

Better opportunities for extended backpack loops are found in the sizable slickrock canyon system just east of the Little Rockies peaks and also by hiking down Trachyte Creek. The western boundary of the roadless area is adjacent to UT 276, which also provides good jumping off points into the backcountry. An example is Hike 61 in *Hiking Utah* (Falcon Publishing). This 15-mile round trip down Swett Canyon to the lake and back takes off directly from the highway, penetrating the wild core of the Little Rockies a few miles north of the peaks. It would be possible to extend this route into a longer point-to-point trip by crossing over into Trachyte Creek and hiking north up the canyon. The narrow Maidenwater and Woodruff canyons are more intimate, with the added challenge of climbing around pouroffs. On the north end a small spring at the head of Hog Canyon is easily accessible from UT 95.

HOW TO GET THERE: From Hanksville drive 26 miles south on Utah Highway 95 to its junction with UT 276. Turn right (south) on UT 276 toward Bullfrog/Halls Crossing and a sign that reads "Ticaboo 28 miles." Shortly after passing the Little Rockies and milepost 25 turn left (east) on an improved but rough dirt road marked only with a stop sign. Drive about 3.5 miles past two road junctions, staying left (east) each time on what appears to be the main road. At this point the road becomes unimproved and rougher but still suitable for two-wheel-drive, high-clearance vehicles. Continue left at the third junction after another 2 miles. A mile beyond, the road crests at a hill and then drops down to the mesa toward distant canyons. At the bottom of the hill turn left (north) toward Mount Ellsworth and the south rim of the Ticaboo Canyon complex and drive the downhill road about 0.3 mile to where it ends at a turnaround and large water storage tank below Ticaboo Shelf Spring. To reach this unmarked trailhead and parking area you have driven 8 very slow miles from the highway.

Four- to seven-day backpack

Ticaboo Canyon–Peshliki Canyon

Distance: 30 to 50 miles.
Starting and minimum elevations: 4,800 feet and 3,700 feet (Lake Powell).
Difficulty: Moderately strenuous.
Best months: April through May; October through November.
Topo maps: Mount Holmes-UT; Ticaboo Mesa-UT.

This extended excursion into the intricate Ticaboo Canyon–Peshliki Canyon system starts and ends in BLM's Little Rockies Wilderness Study Area, with most of the trip taking place within the contiguous Glen Canyon National Recreation Area west of Lake Powell. The rugged laccolith of Mount Ellsworth

The Nebo Creek drainage in autumn.

The Blue Valley Benches and the Henry Mountains, seen from the Fremont River.

Slickrock at sunrise in Waring Canyon, near the Colorado River.

Factory Butte and Mancos shale badlands, part of the proposed Muddy Creek BLM wilderness.

Lower Calf Creek Falls in the Grand Staircase–Escalante National Monument.

Anasazi structures in a sandstone alcove at Cedar Mesa, in the White Canyon–Natural Bridges complex.

Sandstone above Gray Canyon on the Green River, part of the proposed Book Cliffs–Desolation Canyon Wilderness.

Indian paintbrush below Mount Timpanogos, in the wilderness named for the mountain.

A creek in Arch Canyon in the BLM's proposed San Juan–Anasazi Wilderness.

A paddler enjoys sunset in Labyrinth Canyon along the Green River.

Exposed root of ancient bristlecone pine in the Ashdown Gorge.

and its exposed, radiating igneous dikes contrasts vividly with white Navajo sandstone outcrops from which domes, fins, canyons, and pouroffs have eroded. The backpack begins in South Fork Ticaboo Canyon with out-and-back explorations of the North Fork Ticaboo Canyon to Fourmile Canyon and Peshliki Canyon. A strenuous loop route might be possible between the main upper forks, but carrying a full pack around the rugged eastern base of Mount Ellsworth would be painfully slow and difficult. The basic recommended trip is to hike down the South Fork of Ticaboo about 6 miles to its confluence with the North Fork just above Lake Powell, and to then explore up-canyon for at least 7 or 8 miles to the unobstructed head of the North Fork.

An incredible complexity of side canyons cut deeply into the Navajo sandstone makes the use of topo maps a necessity, especially if you want to differentiate between main and side branches of these southeast-flowing canyons. Early season water and secluded base campsites abound for varied out-and-back canyoneering that could easily occupy a full week or more. Plan on four days for the bare minimum.

From the trailhead angle down and to the right past the water trough to a distinct old cattle trail marked with cairns. The rocky trail loses 540 feet as it switchbacks 0.5 mile to the bottom of the main southern tributary to the South Fork. A large cairn marks this spot for returning to the trailhead. Turning left up this side canyon will take you through a deep set of narrows below a headwall about 2 miles up. For the main route turn right and head down a wide sandy draw dotted with junipers and desert shrubs. Continue past alcoves to the main South Fork, where a rock wall displays graffiti dating back some 80 years. High red cliffs overlook a riparian bottom of cottonwood, ash, and willow.

The first early season spring water likely to be found is in the main South Fork about 2 miles below the trailhead and 0.5 mile below its junction with its southern tributary. A one- or two-night camp in lower South Fork Ticaboo would allow ample time to visit alcoves and a large cave once occupied by early Fremont Indians, along with two short side canyons entering from the more remote north side. Subsequent camps can be established in the middle and upper reaches of the labyrinthine maze that forms the North Fork of Ticaboo Canyon. The Middle Fork joins the North Fork about 5 miles up and can be explored in its lower end but soon becomes steep, rough, and blocked by pouroffs. The main North Fork can be climbed as it arcs around from the northeast to the southwest near its origin on the jagged northeast buttress of Mount Ellsworth. More feasible is an earlier exit from its shallow upper reaches for a day hike into the head of nearby Fourmile Canyon to the north. Hikers can readily traverse the upper narrows of Fourmile to a much wider valley below.

On the east end of the labyrinth, Peshliki Canyon can be explored as either a full day side trip or for one or two days from a base camp above a set of deep narrows and a pouroff about 2 miles above and north of Lake Powell. The spectacular lower Peshliki Canyon can be accessed by climbing steeply above Lake Powell on the bench separating Ticaboo from Peshliki or by walking around the shore of the lake at low water to the canyon mouth. From the higher bench, hike above the narrows on a mid-level shelf along the west side of the lower canyon. After a couple of miles look for a route to the canyon floor with fairly easy going for several more miles into the upper tributaries.

After establishing several base camps for side explorations in the main South and North forks of Ticaboo, retrace your route back up the South Fork to the trailhead. The round-trip hiking distance in just these two main forks approaches 30 miles. And this is only the beginning.

San Juan–Anasazi Complex

23

Location: 5 miles west of Bluff (east end) and 7 miles south of Bullfrog Marina (west end), in southeastern Utah.
Size: 551,040 acres.
Administration: BLM Moab District, San Juan Resource Area; NPS Glen Canyon National Recreation Area; Manti–La Sal National Forest, Monticello Ranger District.
Management status: BLM wilderness study areas (four units totaling 210,190 acres, which includes the 37,580 acre Grand Gulch Primitive Area); unprotected BLM and state roadless lands (185,610 acres); unprotected national forest roadless land (16,000 acres); two units of national recreation area roadless land (139,240 acres).
Ecosystems: Colorado Plateau province ecoregion—potential natural vegetation is blackbrush, juniper-pinyon woodland, and pine–Douglas-fir forest.
Elevation range: 3,700 feet (high water mark of Lake Powell) to 8,399 feet (Arch Canyon Overlook).
Established trails/routes: About 100 miles of trails in Grand Gulch, upper Slickhorn Gulch, and Cedar Mesa, plus several miles of primitive jeep tracks in other BLM roadless areas suitable for hiking and horseback riding.
Maximum core to perimeter distance: 4 miles (Grand Gulch).
Activities: River floating, hiking, backpacking, canyoneering, rock climbing, horseback riding, nature and archeological study, photography, hunting.
Maps: BLM 1:100,000 scale surface management/land ownership maps entitled "Blanding," "Navajo Mtn.," and "Bluff" (50 meter contour interval); USDAFS 1989 Manti-LaSal National Forest, Monticello Ranger District, half-inch/mile planimetric. See Appendix E for a listing of the 33 topos covering the complex.

OVERVIEW: From Comb Ridge 70 miles west to what was once the confluence of the Colorado and San Juan rivers, the San Juan River forms the serpentine southern boundary of a vast and varied expanse of wild country—more than half a million acres north of the river known as the San Juan–Anasazi. Still more wild canyons, mesas, and monuments continue south of the river deep into the Navajo Indian Reservation. The San Juan River drops more steeply than does the Colorado through the Grand Canyon. High gradient and heavy sediment loads combine to produce the strange phenomena of 3- to 6-foot high sand waves unexpectedly breaking upstream against the current.

23 SAN JUAN–ANASAZI COMPLEX

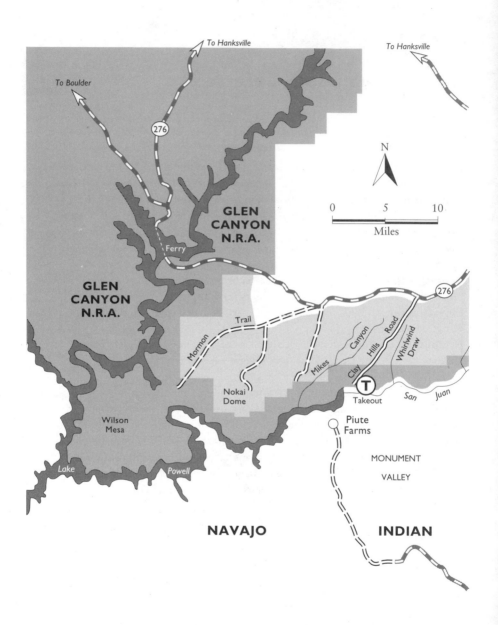

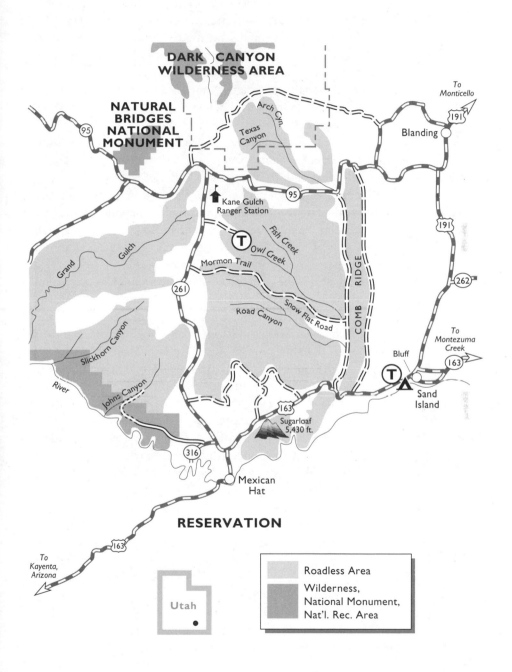

DARK CANYON WILDERNESS AREA

NATURAL BRIDGES NATIONAL MONUMENT

Arch Cyn.

Texas Canyon

To Monticello

191

Blanding

95

Kane Gulch Ranger Station

95

(T) Owl Creek

Fish Creek

Mormon Trail

191

Grand Gulch

261

Koad Canyon

Snow Flat Road

COMB RIDGE

262

Slickhorn Canyon

To Montezuma Creek

Bluff

163

River

Johns Canyon

(T)

Sand Island

163

Sugarloaf 5,430 ft.

316

Mexican Hat

RESERVATION

To Kayenta, Arizona

163

Utah

Roadless Area

Wilderness, National Monument, Nat'l. Rec. Area

Pine-clad highlands drop into deep, geologically young canyons sculpted by intermittent streams that feed into the sandy San Juan. Comb Wash, Grand Gulch, Slickhorn Canyon, Mikes Canyon, Whirlwind Draw, and so many more unnamed chasms are lavishly decorated with arches, buttes, knobs, rincons, sharp pinnacles, and palisades—from the cinnamon-hued Cedar Mesa sandstone on down to deep red shales and sandstone overlooking the San Juan River. The relatively ancient Cedar Mesa formation is older than the more typical canyon country Navajo and Moenkopi regime.

On the west end of the complex Nokai Dome–Wilson Mesa is in one of Utah's wildest and least-explored regions. Huge mesas of slickrock and wind-blown sand slope gently to Lake Powell. Mikes Canyon, Castle Creek, and Lake Canyon host rare spring-fed streams bounded by cliffs cut into the sandstone. The lonely mesa of Nokai Dome provides an overwhelming panorama from the Waterpocket Fold south to Monument Valley.

Pinyon and juniper grow on high plateaus, but the predominant plants are blackbrush and other desert shrubs. Grassy parks dot the Clay Hills, and skinny stringers of riparian habitat hug the bottoms of major canyons, lush enough for beavers to find a niche. A rare peregrine falcon may circle above, while small bands of desert bighorn sheep live here year-round.

Moving east, Grand Gulch is the centerpiece of a "subcomplex" that encompasses 152,870 acres and hundreds of miles of canyons, from Utah Highway 95 south to the San Juan River. The major canyons of John's, Slickhorn, and Grand Gulch are cut into Cedar Mesa sandstone, exposing older rocks in their lower stretches. Anasazi dwellings are sheltered in overhangs and alcoves notched into the protected sides of sheer canyon walls. Broad upland benches span elevations of more than 2,500 feet. Juniper-pinyon woodlands are thicker in these highlands, grading down to desert shrubs in the drier, low southwest corner. Cottonwoods and willows shade the mostly year-round streams in Grand Gulch, John's, and Slickhorn canyons. A few mule deer live in these canyons throughout the year, with some of the country providing important deer winter range. A few bighorn sheep also live here, as do bald eagles during winter.

The southernmost edge of the complex is formed by the 13,100-acre Sugarloaf roadless area bordering the San Juan River just above Mexican Hat. The river has cut through ancient sedimentary rocks of sheer 800-foot walls formed by anticlines. The commanding top of 5,535-foot Sugarloaf Butte rises above an abandoned river channel. Downriver the unmistakable sandstone sombrero of Mexican Hat adorns the north shore.

Occasional cottonwoods, box elders, and the ubiquitous non-native tamarisk line the river bank. Above the river the higher mesas sprout a sparse cover of desert shrubs. Channel catfish are among the fish species found in these thick reddish-brown waters. The adjacent wildland supports a full complement of foxes, coyotes, bighorn sheep, mountain lions, reptiles, and bird life.

To the immediate east rises a dramatic 15-mile unroaded section of the 90-mile-long Comb Ridge escarpment. This north-south ridge is a 600-foot sandstone monocline with a gentle east slope, dropping to west-facing cliffs. The east slope is dissected by short, narrow, secluded canyons. A few pinyon pine, juniper, and desert shrubs dot the eastern slopes and ridgeline. Mule deer and raptors are the most commonly seen residents of this linear wildland.

Back to the west in the south-central part of the complex are 60,100 acres of unroaded land surrounding the narrow slickrock of bottoms of Road Canyon and Lime Creek. The southern edge of Cedar Mesa bisects the area, dropping as much as 1,000 feet in places. The top of the mesa is cut by tight, twisting chasms of stair-stepped sandstone 600 to 800 feet deep. These canyons drain southward through brittle, deep red to purple shale before reaching the Valley of the Gods. The upper mesa is densely carpeted with velvety green pinyon and juniper, breaking to desert shrubs in canyons and lower desert. Mule deer, a few reclusive mountain lions, and migrant bald eagles find their homes here.

To the north and separated only by the primitive doubletrack of the Mormon Trail are 59,000 acres of wild country enveloping Fish and Owl creeks. Both of these steep canyons support unusually diverse riparian vegetation while cutting deeply into the southeast-dipping Cedar Mesa sandstone. Slickrock walls up to 800 feet high have eroded to form huge arches. Mesa tops between canyons are made up of a pleasing blend of dense pinyon-juniper, sagebrush parks, and smooth slickrock. A similar mix of fauna as is found in Road Canyon extends throughout this remote expanse of southeastern Cedar Mesa.

The sandstone fins, spires, alcoves, and arches of Arch Canyon highlight the 31,300-acre northeast corner of the complex. Several of the arches pocket thin ridgelines high above the 1,000-foot deep canyon gorge. Upper Arch Canyon is managed for primitive recreation by the USDA Forest Service, but the BLM allows off-road vehicles to impact the lower canyon. The North and main forks of Mule Canyon to the southwest are bounded by red and white sandstone cliffs. Cottonwoods, aspen, and other water-loving plants thrive near canyon mouths. Old-growth Douglas-fir and ponderosa pine are perched along canyon rims approaching 7,500 feet elevation, with lower mesas and benches supporting a mix of pinyon-juniper, Gambel oak, and sagebrush. Wildflowers that contrast vividly with red, sandy soil reach their peak in mid-to-late spring. Mule deer move through the country during spring and fall migrations. Cougar, bobcat, ring-tailed cat, and coyote make a living in this remote land of high rims, deep canyons, and windblown plateaus.

The Anasazi lived here for more than one thousand years but disappeared about seven hundred years ago. Their artifacts remain, richly displayed in the recesses of Grand Gulch, Slickhorn, Fish, Owl, Arch, and Mule canyons, and in so many more. Stone towers, broken pottery, dried out corn cobs, circular kivas, and the strange spiritually motivated rock art of pictographs are among the legacy they left behind. This concentration of archeological sites may be unsurpassed anywhere in the United States.

The benchlands of Nokai Dome contain the camp and stone chipping sites of Anasazi as well as Archaic and Basketmaker cultures. Lower canyons harbor dwellings and storage structures. The Grand Gulch subcomplex holds about six hundred documented prehistoric sites, with thousands more unrecorded. To the east, the Anasazi cut stair steps into Comb Ridge. Across Comb Wash in Road Canyon surveys indicate that the area may contain more than six thousand Anasazi and Basketmaker sites, many of which are well preserved from canyon bottom to mesa top. The Fish and Owl Creek canyon systems harbor one of the greatest densities of cultural sites to be found anywhere—a treasure trove of Anasazi kivas, cliff dwellings, and burial and chipping sites. High on the red-rock walls of Arch and Mule canyons are found near-perfect ancient dwellings and granaries, along with multi-level structures on south-facing alcoves.

Of historic interest is the Hole-in-the-Rock Trail used by Mormon pioneers in 1879 on their arduous trek from Escalante to settle the town of Bluff. John's Canyon holds the remains of early 1900s oil drilling and ranching.

RECREATIONAL USES: The most popular and perhaps only way to traverse this rugged wild swath across southeastern Utah is to let the river do the work by floating the San Juan from Bluff, 88 river miles down to Clay Hills Crossing on Lake Powell.

For the most part, backcountry enthusiasts can find more solitude in the remote western end of the complex surrounding Nokai Dome and in Lake Powell canyons than in more heavily visited Cedar Mesa. But with a little effort and willingness to climb higher into narrow side canyons, quality wilderness experiences are available throughout San Juan–Anasazi North.

As the star attraction and one of southern Utah's most sought-after, beyond-the-road destinations, Grand Gulch is a spectacular blend of wilderness and two thousand years of Anasazi history. Trips can vary from short day hikes to extended two-week backpack loops and out-and-back round trips of 100 miles or more. The main Kane Gulch Ranger Station and trailhead is reached from Utah Highway 261 a few miles south of UT 95. Visitors must register at the ranger station or at whichever trailhead is used. Two-thirds of visitors to Grand Gulch come during March, April, and May, and most people hike in and out for one or two days. Other popular excursions include a 23-mile point-to-point backpack from Kane Gulch to the Bullet Canyon trailhead and a 36-mile trip from Kane Gulch to the Collins Spring trailhead. Few hike the entire 52 miles from Kane Gulch to the San Juan (not counting irresistible side canyons), but venturing up Grand Gulch a ways is popular with river floaters. For more information see Hike 69 in *Hiking Utah* (Falcon Publishing).

The four forks of Slickhorn Canyon help distribute hikers, and each is well worth exploring. The least-used major canyon is John's, which offers isolated short hikes in its upper reaches. The lower canyon is accessible from the river and a county road west of UT 261. To avoid the crowds visitors should plan trips in the late fall or into outlying canyons to the west of Grand Gulch, such as Whirlwind Draw and Steer Gulch.

To the southeast Road Canyon is far less visited than neighboring Grand Gulch and Fish and Owl creeks. Both Road and Lime creeks can be hiked all the way through, but a 50-foot pouroff in lower Lime Creek necessitates finding a route through a rock tunnel. Lime Creek is crossed by a 16.5-mile dirt road through the Valley of the Gods, which is described as the northern leg of a 27-mile mountain bike loop in Ride 79 of *Mountain Biking Utah* (Falcon Publishing). Riders can stash their bikes near a spring and hike up the canyon a couple of miles to the pouroff and beyond with a bit of rock climbing.

In some instances priceless archeological sites have been vandalized. But damage also stems from innocent hiker impacts. A vital part of no-trace camping is ethical backcountry archaeology, which is mostly a matter of common sense. Never camp within ruins or any type of cultural site. When in a site strive for zero impact.

Relatively obscure Arch and Mule canyons each offer varied hiking and horse trips. Snow runoff from their Abajo Mountains headwaters is usually available along with easy access from UT 95, great campsites, and Anasazi ruins. The two main canyons offer more than 20 miles of explorable terrain, and backpackers can easily spend a week or more. See hikes 71 and 72 in *Hiking Utah* for descriptions of both canyons. An exciting loop of 12 to 15 miles is possible in the contiguous Arch Canyon national forest roadless area by taking the West Rim Texas Canyon Trail (003) into Texas Canyon and then following the canyon about 6 miles down to its junction with Arch Canyon. Turn left up Arch Canyon on primitive Trail 002 and climb above 8,000 feet to Forest Road 092, which can then be hiked back a couple of miles southwest to the turnoff for the Texas Canyon Trailhead. With a car shuttle, a point-to-point hike of about 13 miles from the head of Arch Canyon to its lower canyon entrance would sample rich geologic and botanical diversity during a descent of more than 3,000 feet.

The 93,400-acre Nokai Dome roadless area occupies the western end of the complex just north of Lake Powell in one of the most remote regions of wild Utah. Intense wilderness solitude can be experienced in Mikes Canyon—

a lengthy serpentine chasm up to 800 feet deep with a rare spring-fed stream. Upper canyon tributaries can be accessed directly by hiking south from UT 276. Route-finding and rock climbing skills are needed to find one of the few steep but non-rappelling routes into the upper canyon along its northwest side.

HOW TO GET THERE: *Owl and Fish Creek Canyons:* From Utah Highway 95 west of Blanding drive south on UT 261, passing Kane Gulch Ranger Station. Continue about 1 more mile and turn left (east) onto a 5-mile improved dirt road that ends at the trailhead and register box next to an old drill site.

San Juan River Float: From Bluff drive 3 miles west on US 163 and turn left (south) to the signed Sand Island Recreation Site on the north shore of the river. The site includes a fee campground, but floaters with permits are exempt from paying the fee for the night immediately before their launch date. The north shore takeout at Clay Hills Crossing is at the end of the Clay Hills Road 11 miles southwest of UT 276. The turnoff from UT 276 is 23 miles east of Halls Crossing and 19 miles southwest of the junction of UT 276 and UT 95. Plan on five hours for the 180-mile round-trip car shuttle between Sand Island and Clay Hills Crossing. A waterfall has formed on the river above the former takeout at Paiute Farms, so Clay Hill is now the only feasible takeout below Mexican Hat.

Four- to seven-day backpack loop

Owl and Fish Creek Canyons

Distance: 15 miles (basic loop) to 30 miles (with side trips).
Starting and minimum elevations: 6,200 feet and 4,790 feet (confluence of Owl and Fish creeks).
Difficulty: Moderately strenuous.
Best months: Mid-March through May; October through November.
Topo maps: Snow Flat Spring Cave-UT; Bluff NW-UT.

Years ago the BLM began publicizing the 15-mile Owl Creek–Fish Creek loop to help redistribute the overflow of hikers from Grand Gulch, which is immediately across the highway to the west. The BLM hands out a two-page information sheet on this route, which is also written up as Hike 70 in *Hiking Utah*. The strategy worked, with the Owl–Fish Creek loop becoming one of the most popular extended backpacking treks in Utah canyon country. Although solitude may be tough to come by, depending on season, this exceptional trip is featured here because of its spellbinding beauty, available water, well-preserved archeological sites, and remote penetration into the interior of an outstanding 59,000-acre roadless expanse on the southeastern corner of Cedar Mesa. Side trips into the major forks of Fish Creek can lengthen the loop by dozens of fascinating miles. Because the route includes several steep rock pitches with exposure, this is a trip for experienced hikers only. The loop can be rushed in three days but the better course is to establish two or three base camps along the route, with a full week for respectful visits to Anasazi ruins and side explorations of more lightly visited places, such as McCloyd Canyon and the north branch of Fish Creek.

The main canyons contain water to within a couple of miles of their confluence as well as abundant small to large campsites on sandy benches beneath cottonwoods and overhangs. They vary from broad valley bottoms of sandy gravel to narrow slickrock chutes only a couple of feet wide. Soaring 500-foot high walls rise above hanging gardens and deep spring-fed pools teeming with tiny fish, toads, and frogs.

Most people hike the loop clockwise from Owl to Fish Creek because it is a lot easier to get out of Fish Creek than into it, and because the trailhead is adjacent to the head of Owl Creek. From the trailhead drop into the nearby wash and follow it to the right to the rim of Owl Creek. Look for cairns leading to a slickrock chute left of a pouroff, passing an Anasazi cliff dwelling in an alcove to the right. Cairns mark a ledge rock route left of a second pouroff, quickly dropping to the canyon floor. A well-worn hiker's trail winds down Owl Creek for about 2 miles to a third pouroff or waterfall, which is bypassed by hiking up a side canyon to the left (north). For the next few miles a series of waterfalls and deep pools grace the canyon bottom down to the impressive Nevill's Arch, which eroded high on a jutting fin of Cedar Mesa sandstone.

The wide junction of Owl and Fish creeks is marked with a desert shrub flat dotted with a few cottonwood trees. Turn left (north) and head up the more narrow Fish Creek canyon. Red Cedar Mesa walls towering hundreds of feet harbor nearly intact Anasazi kivas and cliff dwellings nestled below virtually inaccessible overhangs. Slickrock ledges bordering glistening pools lend a mystical quality to this delightful canyon, which is unobstructed for the first 5 or 6 miles. Gaze into the pools for glimpses of tiny killfish, shiners, suckers, and chubs, along with toads and frogs.

Natural Arch is carved high on the left rim of Fish Creek about 5 miles up and is visible only from directly below. The major upper branches of Fish Creek are reached another 2 or 3 miles beyond. The last camp of the trip can be made near this junction for exploration of the rugged north (right) fork. To exit Fish Creek en route to the trailhead hike up the west (left) branch for about 0.5 mile, climbing on the left side above a pouroff. A large cairn marks where the route climbs 800 feet straight up the talus slope to several spots below the rim that allow a safe exit. Follow a well-traveled path with cairns that leads southwest for the final 1.5 miles to the trailhead.

Six- to nine-day river float with side hikes

San Juan River from Bluff to Clay Hills Crossing

Distance: 84-river-mile float plus variable side hikes.
Starting and minimum elevations: 4,160 feet and 3,700 feet.
Difficulty: Moderate, but occasional rapids require that some of the party be experienced river runners.
Best months: Usually floatable throughout the year, but the most pleasant time for floating and hiking is normally April, May, and October.
Topo maps: From upstream to downstream: Bluff-UT; White Rock Point-UT; San Juan Hill-UT; Mexican Hat-UT; The Goosenecks-UT; Goulding NE-UT; Slickhorn Canyon East-UT; Slickhorn West-UT; Whirlwind Draw-UT; Mikes Mesa-UT.

For some people the "triple Ps" of permits, payments, and popularity on the San Juan might detract from an otherwise quality wilderness float. The voyage is presented as a sample trip because there is simply no better way to experience so much of the wild splendor of the complex, provided ample time is allowed for savoring the river gorge and a few of its remote side canyons. The average party takes six days to float from Sand Island to Clay Hills, but on one leisurely eight-day trip we all wished that it had been longer. The choices are to takeout at Mexican Hat 26.5 miles downstream or, preferably, to continue on for another 57 miles to Clay Hills, which is a remote takeout with no facilities. The river is equally suitable for rafts, kayaks, and canoes, depending on number of people, amount of gear, and river running experience.

When planning a San Juan River float latch onto a permit and information packet from the BLM and then get a hold of *San Juan Canyons, A River Runner's Guide* by Baars and Stevenson, which has a detailed river log and maps. Permits are issued only through advance reservation to applicants at least 18 years old. Contact BLM, San Juan Resource Area, Box 7 (435 N. Main), Monticello, UT 84535, or call 801-587-2144 between 8 A.M. and 12 noon Mountain time, Monday through Friday.

A launch reservation during the main season of April 1 through October 31 can be obtained by: (1) pre-season drawing (the best way to go); (2) post-drawing telephone reservation; or (3) post-drawing waiting list. The entire fee payment of $13 per person for floating Sand Island to Clay Hills must be received by the San Juan Resource Area at least 30 days before the launch date. Permits are also required for the non-fee season of November 1 through March 31 and are processed in the order of submission starting the first business day of the calendar year. The same limits and stipulations are in effect, some of which include no camping at the Butler Wash Petroglyph Site (mile 4.2), no trespassing on 1.7 miles of private land between the petroglyph panel and the River House Ruin, one-night camping limit at the five Slickhorn campsites and single Grand Gulch site, and no pets on river trips between Mexican Hat and Clay

Hills. Remember also that the left side from the middle of the river south is on the Navajo Indian Reservation and that alcoholic beverages are prohibited. In order to hike and camp on the reservation apply for a permit at least three weeks in advance to: Navajo Parks and Recreation Dept., Box 9000, Window Rock, AZ 86515, 520-871-6647, fax 520-871-6637.

Now, with permits firmly in hand, an equipment check at Sand Island by BLM, at least a week to let the world go by, and a thirst for adventure, you're ready to launch. Following is a bit of background and a few highlights to enhance your journey.

The enchanting San Juan winds its twisting, deeply eroded path from southern Colorado's lofty San Juan Mountains, through New Mexico, where it pauses behind the Navajo Dam, and then rolls into Utah near Four Corners before ending at Lake Powell. Some of the river's strangest features are 3- to 8-foot high sand waves that suddenly break the surface and roll upstream during high water in the spring. These harmless but entertaining waves are caused by fast currents on the sandy bottom. Downstream from Bluff the river cuts dramatically through ancient sedimentary rocks and anticlines with walls up to 800 feet high.

The first class III rapid (with 4-foot waves) is encountered at mile 11.5, followed by a rapid with 8-foot waves at mile 17.0 in the Narrows. This upper stretch parallels the 13,200-acre Sugarloaf roadless area on the north bank from Comb Wash to Mexican Hat. The country is distinguished by a huge river meander crowned by monumental 5,535-foot Sugarloaf Butte, which can be climbed southward from Utah Highway 163 for rarely seen vistas downriver.

Mexican Hat is reached at mile 26.5, the last supply point during the next nearly 60 miles of wilderness waterway to Clay Hills. The famed gorge of the Goosenecks begins at mile 38 below the Second Narrows. The 139,800-acre Grand Gulch roadless area joins Glen Canyon National Recreation Area wildlands bordering the north shore from above John's Canyon all the way down to Clay Hills Crossing. Ross Rapids break the surface at mile 52.5. These and other rocky San Juan rapids are easy to negotiate by alert floaters, but having dumped a canoe on the San Juan we can attest that they are potentially hazardous.

John's Canyon is bound by Cutler formation sandstone walls up to 1,000 feet high and can easily be hiked from its mouth. Don't miss the spellbinding multi-hued beauty of Slickhorn Canyon (mile 66.3 on the right). Slickhorn is extremely rugged, with Garden of Eden pools and waterfalls. The deepest canyon in Slickhorn is closest to the river. The 52-mile Grand Gulch enters below at mile 70.1 (on the right) with its treasure trove of intriguing side canyons, rock art, and Indian ruins. Although most people float the distance it is possible to hike the 4 miles along the river between Slickhorn and Grand Gulch. The San Juan drops an amazing 11.6 feet per mile through this part of the gorge compared with 8 feet per mile in the Grand Canyon. Sheer sedimentary walls are a cemented blend of sand, mud, and fossils.

Crowded conditions in Grand Gulch can be reduced by hiking during the edge of the season in March or November. Lesser known side canyons also offer quality solitude, such as Steer Gulch and Whirlwind Draw (north shore) only a few miles upriver from the Clay Hills takeout. These lightly visited canyons toward the end prove the old adage that it ain't over till it's over.

White Canyon–Natural Bridges Complex 24

Location: 28 miles west of Blanding, in southeast Utah.
Size: 90,340 acres.
Administration: BLM Moab District, San Juan Resource Area; NPS Natural Bridges National Monument.
Management status: BLM wilderness study area (15,460 acres); unprotected BLM roadless land (69,540 acres); national monument roadless land (5,340 acres).
Ecosystems: Colorado Plateau province ecoregion, with pinyon-juniper woodland (potential natural vegetation), desert shrub, and limited riparian vegetation along canyon bottoms.
Elevation range: 4,100 feet (at Glen Canyon National Recreation Area boundary) to 8,200 feet (upper Cheesebox Canyon).
Established trails/routes: 12.8 miles of trails within the national monument; old jeep tracks and canyon bottoms provide hiking routes in BLM areas.
Maximum core to perimeter distance: 2.5 miles.
Activities: Hiking, backpacking, canyoneering, horseback riding, photography, hunting, geology study.
Maps: BLM 1:100,000 scale surface management/land ownership maps entitled "Hite Crossing" and "Blanding" (50 meter contour interval). See Appendix E for a listing of the six topo maps covering the roadless area.

OVERVIEW: The White Canyon–Natural Bridges National Monument Wilderness complex covers a 33-mile swath of canyons. These drainages plunge through varied layers of sandstone, creating a world of color. The bony fingers of White Canyon's tributaries—Fortknocker, Long, Gravel, Cheesebox, and Hideout—extend from the northeast, while the main channel of White Canyon flows northwest to the upper end of Lake Powell.

White Canyon drains off the southwest side of the Abajo Mountains in the Manti–La Sal National Forest. In spite of the name, this canyon is not associated with Utah's White River, which lies 160 miles to the north. In White Canyon the intermittent stream is more than 40 miles long. Its seasonal waters have created a deep, white-rimmed gorge with fantastic eroded formations. Three natural bridges span the river in the national monument. In 1883 Cass Hite, a prospector, was the first Euro-American to report on these natural wonders, the spans of which stretch to 200 feet and more. A 1904 article in *National Geographic* brought the area to national attention. Responding to the enthusiastic response, President Teddy Roosevelt designated the rectilinear national monument in 1908. The monument included the three bridges (which thereupon regained their Hopi names: Kachina, Sipapu, and Owachomo) and the immediate tributaries that created them.

The remainder of the serpentine White Canyon and its extensive tributaries are equally creative in carving immense canyons. A raucous melody of colors greets the eye here. The dark red of Moenkopi and Chinle slickrock on mesas and upper slopes contrasts with the white sandstone chasm created by flowing waters.

The National Park Service has recommended the entire length of the White for Wild and Scenic River designation from the monument down to Glen Canyon National Recreation Area. This status would protect only the flow of the water, not the land on either side. In 1979 the Park Service recommended acquiring 30,000 acres around the monument from the BLM to protect the monument's viewshed. In its 1995 Wilderness Suitability Study, the Park Service recommended 72 percent of the monument for wilderness, and expressed concern again about the adjacent BLM lands with identical wild characteristics.

These roadless BLM lands possess intrinsic wilderness value beyond their role as a "DMZ" for the monument. The pinyon–juniper-clad slopes and mesas are home to mule deer, mountain lions, and bobcats. The remote upper canyons are crucial reproductive habitat for desert bighorn sheep. In spite of uranium exploration holes, miles of seismic roads, and acres of chaining, the White Canyon complex retains its wildness. The canyon bottoms and ephemeral streams provide a hospitable environment for cottonwoods and willow. Hanging gardens are tucked away at seeps along the canyon walls, delighting the passing hiker with both color and texture in this rocky world. The rocky uplands support Douglas-fir and ponderosa pine forests. Between these two extremes vast barren slickrock of fine-grained Cedar Mesa sandstone brightens this high plateau world.

The three natural bridges of the monument brought national recognition and monument status. In addition to these scenic treasures the monument's canyons and mesas were home to the Anasazi for one thousand years; their pithouses, pottery shards, arrowheads, and masonry dwellings remain since their departure from the region around 1270 A.D. Early hunter-gatherer bands also left rock art, evidently of religious significance, as they sought the wily bighorn sheep. Later, larger and more sedentary clans lived in the area, growing beans and corn in larger canyons bottoms and on mesas; their rock art also served a ceremonial purpose, reflecting agricultural themes. The monument's

24 WHITE CANYON–NATURAL BRIDGES COMPLEX

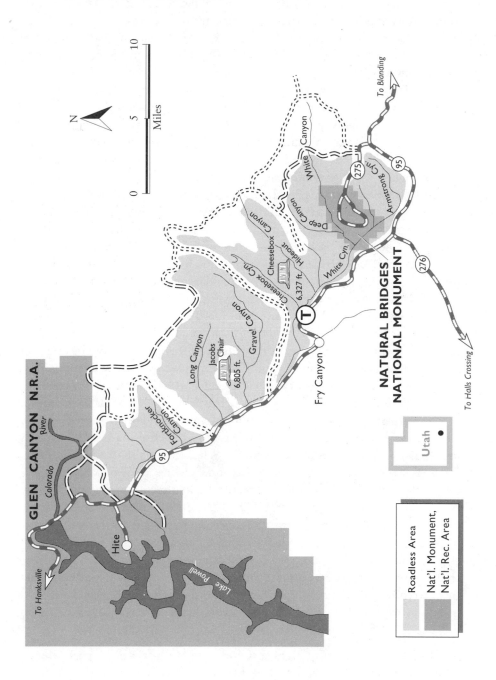

visitor center provides information about the archeological sites in its small corner of the vast White Canyon complex. Beyond the borders of National Park Service jurisdiction, the rugged terrain of the White Canyon unit has fortunately served to protect archeological sites from intruders. Although no general archeological inventory has been done outside of the national monument, the BLM estimates that several hundred sites probably exist in the area. These include cliff dwellings, habitation sites, and granaries. Numerous Basketmaker and Pueblo sites are reported to be in the Harmony Flat area.

Harmony Flat (9,100 acres) is south of the national monument and its entrance via Utah Highway 275. Tuwa and Armstrong canyons begin here and continue on through the monument where they join the White. Lower than the other units of White Canyon country, Harmony Flats offers important deer winter range, as well as winter eagle nesting sites.

The Cheesebox Canyon unit (28,500 acres) includes 15,460 acres of wilderness study area. Deer Flat and Pinon Point have been excluded from this roadless unit because they have roads, private lands, and landing strips. Nevertheless, Cheesebox includes Deer Canyon, Hideout Canyon, Cheesebox Canyon, the Cheesebox itself, and both Butch and White canyons, which sweep around the monument's eastern boundary to UT 275. The highest point in the complex is in the upper end of Cheesebox Canyon. The topography is identical in Gravel and Long canyons (35,000 acres), the two nearly parallel canyons just to the north of Cheesebox, separated only by a gravel road. The odd rock formation of Jacobs Chair sits atop the mesa between Long and Gravel; this roaded and mined peninsula is excluded from the wilderness. The BLM designated this stretch of White Canyon an Area of Critical Environmental Concern for its scenic value for people traveling on UT 95 just to the south.

The northernmost section of the White Canyon wilderness is Fortknocker Canyon (12,400 acres). Short Canyon Mesa is a finger of roads and mine sites that splits Fortknocker from the rest of the White Canyon roadless lands. Here, White Canyon zigzags in a frenzy before it debouches at Glen Canyon, where it completes the trip with a bang. The Black Hole section of White Canyon, between mileposts 55 and 57 on UT 95, is reputed by many to be one of the most challenging hike-and-swim canyoneering outings in the state.

The wild character of the White Canyon Complex has been under constant siege for the past one hundred years. First came white settlers with their hordes of livestock. In the middle part of the century it was uranium prospectors. And most recently multi-national energy companies looking for oil and gas have targeted this area for development. Conservationists must keep a watchful eye on this chunk of the Colorado Plateau.

RECREATIONAL USES: The highways and roads that travel the perimeter of White Canyon country do not even hint at the excitement of the plunging

Looking down White Canyon from the top of the primitive trail.

canyons within the wild country. UT 95 runs along the southwestern boundary; the canyon world lies far below.

From the loop road within the monument the short trail hikes leading to the three bridges can be continued on down or up the canyons. Watch for archeological sites as you travel. Maps and other information are available at the visitor center. Except for the small 13-site campground just west of the visitor center, the park service does not permit camping within the monument. Since the BLM has no such restrictions, a backpacking excursion that leads beyond the monument boundary can provide an extended journey spanning a couple of days. For example, at the south end of the monument, the most ancient of the three bridges, Owachomo, soars across the junction of Tuwa and Armstrong canyons. Following northern Tuwar Canyon, it crosses the monument boundary about 1 mile east of the bridge. Continue 4.5 miles east in the winding canyon. When it peters out, emerge on Harmony Flat. Hike east-southeast to meet Armstrong Canyon for the return leg of a 10-mile loop. It is recommended that you carry water because canyon sources are unreliable.

The canyons north of the monument provide unlimited adventure hiking opportunities for serious, well-prepared canyon enthusiasts. Rock climbing, photography, geology study, or just wandering—these canyons wind for miles. Out-and-back trips, unfortunately, are more common than loop trips due to lack of water, cliffed-out canyon walls, and distances between canyon heads. Stay out of these canyons if there is a danger of flash flooding from heavy rain up the drainage. The deep, dark Black Hole of White Canyon contains a large pool usually more than 200 yards long that requires a cold water swim between walls that narrow to only 1.5 feet where the canyon makes a 90-degree turn. Most Black Hole hikers park at milepost 57 along UT 95 and enter White Canyon by way of a short side canyon. The moderate 7.5-mile route then continues downstream to the Hole and beyond, exiting on a steep rocky trail to milepost 55. A longer trip is feasible by dropping into White Canyon at milepost 61 and continuing on down White Canyon through the Hole to Lake Powell, where you can hop a boat if arrangements are made for a pickup below Copper Point. Or hike 2 miles back up the steep gravel road to UT 95.

You're only limited by your imagination—and by time, water, and energy!

HOW TO GET THERE: On Utah Highway 95 just south of Hite Crossing at Lake Powell, drive to milepost 75 and turn northeast toward the rim of White Canyon on a short, dirt jeep track. After about 0.2 mile pull off and park at the unmarked end-of-the-road trailhead. This turnoff from the paved highway is about 3 miles east of Fry Canyon, where a motel and cafe provide the only services between Blanding and Hite Crossing, making it the most remote desert lodge in Utah.

Off-trail day hike, canyoneering

Cheesebox Canyon–Hideout Canyon Rim Loop

Distance: 7 to 8 miles out and back or a 9- to 10-mile partial loop.
Starting, minimum, and maximum elevations: 5,620 feet, 5,300 feet, and 5,960 feet.
Difficulty: Moderately strenuous.
Best months: Mid-March through May; October through November.
Topo map: The Cheesebox-UT.

This adventurous out-and-back or partial loop in Cheesebox Canyon can be enjoyed as a day hike or extended into an overnighter, sampling slotted canyons and broad mesas in a 28,500-acre roadless area in the center of the complex. The prominent 6,327-foot butte of The Cheesebox, 1.5 miles to the east across steep-walled White Canyon, serves as a pivotal landmark for the trip.

Begin by following a primitive trail marked with cairns that switchbacks along cliff ledges to the floor of White Canyon 300 feet below. Expect one or two tricky hard-to-find spots requiring route finding, rock scrambling, and perhaps a rope for lowering packs. The primitive trail reaches the bottom near the brushy mouth of Cheesebox Canyon directly across White Canyon and only about 0.5 mile from the trailhead.

Venturing into Cheesebox, you'll be immediately met by a plunge pool and pouroff in the lower canyon. Bypass these obstacles by climbing up a crack in a 10-foot rock wall on the right side to a higher ledge that provides an easy route above a dramatically narrow, deep, slot canyon. Great bulging mushroom-shaped lips of overhanging rock faces streaked with desert varnish and topped with balancing boulders line both sides of the riparian bottom of Cheesebox Canyon. One mile up, a large manzanita grove nestles beneath alcoves and pools carved into white Cedar Mesa sandstone. Just as the canyon seems to open up with backsloping sides, vertical cliffs soar on one side or the other.

Nearly halfway up, at around 3 miles, the canyon narrows a second time with slotted walls and deep pools. Hike on a ledge on the right to a cliff wall at the upper end of the slots. At this point the choices are to retrace your route for a 7- to 8-mile round trip in lower Cheesebox Canyon, or climb southward to the rim and either proceed northeast directly above the canyon toward its head or venture cross-country toward the even more rugged Hideout Canyon.

For this latter trip careful route finding and a 450-foot gain in elevation will get you to the white table rock of the plateau. Continue south toward an obvious gap between The Cheesebox and Lone Butte, which displays diggings from past uranium mining. This is a striking landscape of gradually ascending white sandstone tables surrounded by lofty red mesas sprouting pinyon-juniper. Walk southward about 2 miles to the head of the main side canyon immediately southeast of The Cheesebox, and follow it along the right (west) side to the high cliff rim above aptly named Hideout Canyon. A cliff ledge wraps around the cliff to the right for a bird's eye view of the plunging, narrow canyon all the way down to its mouth in White Canyon. Cliff walls, narrows, pools, and pouroffs guard these lower and middle reaches of Hideout.

A Cheesebox–Hideout loop might be tempting, but the more feasible course is to backtrack to the gap east of The Cheesebox, continuing northwest into a side wash that drains to Cheesebox Canyon. Angle to the left (south) of this deepening side canyon, working around several impassable pouroffs before finding cracks and stair-step rocks for a moderate descent to the canyon floor near its junction with Cheesebox Canyon. Turn left (downstream) and retrace the final 2.5 miles to the trailhead.

For those willing to raise and lower packs with ropes in two or three places, a remote early season backpack camp can be established 2 or 3 miles up Cheesebox Canyon, using a nearby catch basin for a water source. By all means treat the water and avoid being caught by a flash flood in canyon narrows if there is threat of rain anywhere in the drainage.

Dark Canyon Wilderness Complex   25

Location: 23 miles west of Monticello, in southeastern Utah.
Size: 219,260 acres.
Administration: USDAFS Manti-La Sal National Forest; BLM Moab District, San Juan Resource Area; NPS Glen Canyon National Recreation Area.
Management status: USDAFS Dark Canyon Wilderness (46,000 acres) and unprotected roadless land (10,240 acres); BLM wilderness study area (68,030 acres) and unprotected roadless land (62,170 acres); and NPS proposed wilderness (32,820 acres).
Ecosystems: Colorado Plateau province ecoregion, ranging from ponderosa pine forest in the national forest, to sparse pinyon-juniper woodland (potential natural vegetation) and desert shrubs on the benchlands and mesas, to riparian vegetation. Large expanses of cryptobiotic soils throughout the plateau country.
Elevation range: 3,700 feet (Colorado River) to 8,648 (North Long Point).
Established trails/routes: 75 miles of trail; extensive canyons provide additional miles of hiking routes.
Maximum core to perimeter distance: 4 miles.
Activities: Hiking, backpacking, canyoneering, nature study, photography.
Maps: BLM 1:100,000 scale surface management/land ownership maps entitled "Hite Crossing" and "Blanding" (50 meter contour interval); and USDAFS 1989 half-inch/mile planimetric map entitled "Manti–LaSal National Forest—Moab and Monticello Ranger Districts." See Appendix E for a listing of the eight topo maps covering the roadless area.

OVERVIEW: The Dark Canyon complex has attracted visitors for centuries. Bands of Anasazi were drawn to its moist canyon bottoms, thick forests, and protective soaring cliffs. Remnants of their extended presence dot the canyons and basins in the northeast section of the roadless area. Butler Wash, Ruin Park, and Beef Basin contain stone structures, granaries, and towers of these Paleo-Indian farmers. Curious hikers can explore canyon alcoves seeking archeological evidence, but please leave all artifacts undisturbed for later visitors.

From Zane Grey novels to rave reviews in BLM hiking guides, the Dark Canyon network has gotten top marks as a region of geologic wonder. In 1970 the BLM recognized the rare features of its Dark Canyon unit by designating it a primitive area, one of the first in the nation. In 1974 the National Park Service placed the contiguous land in the Glen Canyon National Recreation

25 DARK CANYON WILDERNESS COMPLEX

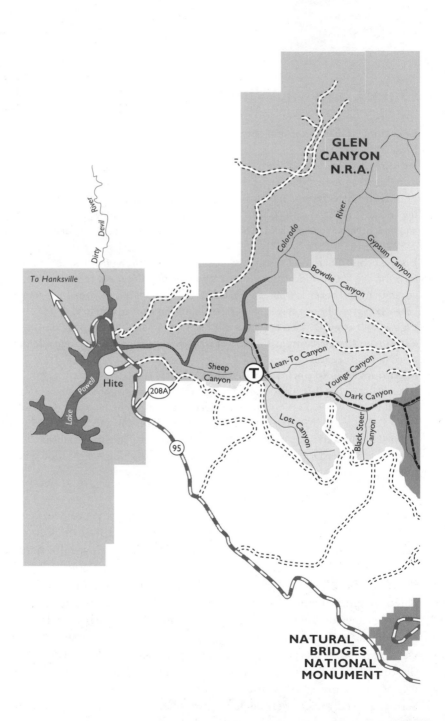

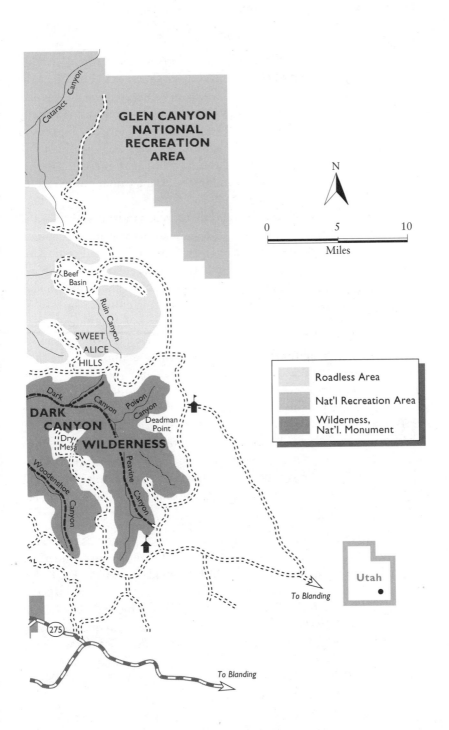

Area, including the last 3 miles of the canyon itself, on its suggested wilderness list. And the USDA Forest Service recommended its upper reaches of Dark Canyon to be set aside as wilderness; this last is the only unit that has actually gained such protection, when President Reagan signed Utah's national forest Wilderness Act in 1984.

This patchwork of different federal jurisdictions forms one geologic and ecologic canyon system, from Elk Ridge on the east down to the banks of the old Colorado River. Falling 5,000 feet from head to mouth, Dark Canyon's deep gorge runs 30 miles. It twists and turns north and west, as other equally dramatic canyons dive from the plateau to join it: Peavine Canyon, Poison Canyon, Woodenshoe Canyon, Black Steer and Youngs canyons, Lost and Lean-To canyons. To the north, Gypsum and Bowdie canyons create another maze of drainages from the Dark Canyon Plateau to the canyon of the Colorado.

Canyon walls up to 2,000 feet high expose layers of sandstone, shales, and limestone laid down up to 300 million years ago. Seasonal streams and numerous springs flow in the tributaries; lower Dark Canyon has a clear-flowing stream, with waterfalls and emerald pools. This miniature Grand Canyon is a damp wonderland of hanging gardens, cottonwoods, and other riparian vegetation, adding color below the sandstone of the soaring cliffs.

From floor to rim, the Dark Canyon region progresses from these riparian gardens to sparse desert shrub and pinyon-juniper patches, to ponderosa pine on the high plateau in the national forest. More than 60 mammals make their home in this varied habitat that provides both summer and winter range. From the charismatic megafauna to rodents, they include mountain lions, black bears, mule deer, bighorn sheep, porcupines, and shrews. Abundant water makes Dark Canyon unique.

Canyon bottoms start in the higher plateau country as wide swales harboring ponderosa pine. They descend and rapidly change to narrow, dark, cliff-walled gorges. Sandy and gravel bottoms make attractive hiking routes, but periodic pouroffs will challenge hikers. Fully exploring Dark Canyon is an activity that would take weeks!

RECREATIONAL USES: Hiking and backpacking outings are best taken in the spring when water is plentiful, or in the fall when temperatures are moderate. In the national forest wilderness area, hiking trails wind down from Elk Ridge Road into the fingers of the canyon system. Woodenshoe, Peavine, and Kigalia canyons in the south have trails that will take you down to the main Dark Canyon. Trailheads for Drift Trail Canyon, Horse Pasture Canyon, and Trail Canyon off of North Point provide other options to enter the canyon world below the ridge. The trailhead at the Notch is the furthest extension of Dark Canyon to the east. With a car shuttle or a bicycle left at a terminal trailhead, any of these canyon hikes could become a loop trip.

A stream at high water in Dark Canyon.

On BLM land, access to the canyons is not difficult. Rough BLM roads can take you near the heads of Black Steer and Youngs canyons. The Sundance Trail goes north of Browns Rim Road, winding down into Dark Canyon just within the Glen Canyon National Recreation Area boundary. The trail drops 1,200 feet, so save some energy for the trip up. See the hike described below.

A point-to-point backpack trip is a great way to enjoy the mysteries of Dark Canyon and its side canyons. From within the wilderness the trip into the deeper and darker depths of Dark Canyon is a 30-mile adventure. Allow plenty of time to explore the side canyons. This is an exhilarating trip, despite the sinister connotations of the name.

HOW TO GET THERE: From the north, on Utah Highway 95 just south of the Colorado River bridge, turn left on the first improved dirt road on the left (east) side of the highway, 1.2 miles south of the bridge, at milepost 49. This turn is just south of the Hite Marina turnoff, which is on the west side of UT 95. Go 5 miles east on the county road to a Y intersection.

From the south, turn right on the improved dirt road just north of milepost 54 onto San Juan County Road 208A. Go 5 miles to a Y intersection.

At the Y intersection continue east, staying on the main road and disregarding all others; 9 miles from UT 95 bear right at a second Y intersection. The road on the left takes you to the same destination, but the road on the right is in better condition. There may be a sign posted at this intersection indicating a "Trail" with an arrow, but it has recently fallen into disrepair. 2.5 miles farther the winding road swings north around a prominent butte formation, Squaw and Papoose, on the right. Opposite this natural statue turn left on an unimproved dirt road and go 0.2 mile to the BLM trailhead for the Sundance Trail. A low-clearance, two-wheel-drive vehicle can make this trip.

The Trails Illustrated map "Canyonlands Maze District, Northeast Glen Canyon" covers the access as well as the canyons of the lower Dark Canyon complex. The Indian Head Pass-UT topo map shows an old trailhead, which requires a longer drive on a rougher road and includes a very tedious hike along an old jeep road for an extra 2 miles. Avoid this! Take the turn at Squaw and Papoose rock (on the topo) and you'll find the new trailhead at the end of the road.

Base camp backpack

Dark Canyon Ramble

Distance: 6 to 20 miles, depending on your degree of exploration.
Starting and minimum elevations: 5,490 feet and 4,100 feet.
Difficulty: Moderately strenuous.
Best months: March through April; September through October.
Topo map: Indian Head Pass-UT.

The BLM has developed the Sundance Trailhead with an information board and a trip register. From the parking area, head east by northeast on the Sundance Trail, descending intermittently and gradually for 2 miles to the rim of Dark Canyon. This easy stretch of trail is well marked by rock cairns and offers grand views east up into Dark Canyon. At the rim the trail assumes a more primitive character. Watch for cairns as the trail goes out on a ridge to the east. Follow the trail when it drops to the left side of this ridge, instead of to the right where the canyon is. This left trail curls around the ridge; its descent into the canyon is steep, but more gradual than the one to the right, which plunges down a 50-degree boulder-strewn slope in kamikaze fashion. In either case, you lose 1,120 vertical feet in less than 1 mile. Here again, enjoy spectacular scenery looking up the canyon, and try to avoid thinking about the hike back up this brutal stretch.

Once down, the trail continues along the floor of Dark Canyon. Spots to pitch a tent are numerous in the area between Lost and Lean-To canyons but almost non-existent in Dark Canyon above its confluence with Lost Canyon to the east, and below its confluence with Lean-To Canyon to the northeast. There's no water on the Sundance Trail until you reach the bottom of Dark Canyon. Water in the main canyon flows year-round but is heavily silted during spring run-off. Boiling and/or filtering is always necessary, but filtering with the sediment is impossible. If your trip is in early spring, carry enough water from the trailhead to satisfy your needs until you can reach Lost or Lean-To canyons to resupply. Don't forget the insect repellent. Mosquitoes hatch early here, although the bats try to keep their numbers down. The bats' evening acrobatic show is entertaining.

From an established camp in Dark Canyon you can take day hikes up Dark Canyon, into Lost Canyon or Lean-To Canyon, or down Dark Canyon:

Up Dark Canyon: Heading up Dark Canyon, a good trail winds along the bottom, criss-crossing the stream. The water level usually enables you to hop across on rocks. Upstream are stands of cottonwood and alder, and higher up, pinyon-juniper. Signs of wildlife are abundant. Mule deer, desert bighorn sheep, and coyotes all reside here. Look skyward for golden eagles, goshawks, red-tailed hawks, or even the federally listed endangered peregrine falcon. Farther up the canyon the trail becomes somewhat more difficult to follow, as the canyon walls grow more sheer, and hikers are forced to the south (right) side of the drainage. Cairns mark the way but picking them out of the rock-strewn landscape requires a sharp eye. Incredible geologic formations dominate this entire hike, treating hikers to marvelous examples of all that Utah canyon country has to offer.

Look for water in catch basins after storms, or at a pure spring about 2 miles up the canyon. Carry a day's supply from your base camp in case these other sources aren't available.

Lost Canyon: From your Dark Canyon base camp, hike up the main drainage about 0.75 mile. At this point Lost Canyon runs into Dark Canyon from the south (right). From the mouth, head straight up the bottom, following the streambed. Gray limestone in the lower section of the canyon gives way to more rugged and sheer red and white Cedar Mesa sandstone. Beautiful spires, buttes, pinnacles, and alcoves stand as impressive testimony to the erosive powers of wind, water, and time. Progress is eventually stymied as the vertical walls converge and a boulder blocks the way, but the spectacular nature of this canyon makes the hike well worth your time. Water can occasionally be found in catch basins after storms, but hedge your bets and carry plenty with you.

Lean-To Canyon: A steep but climbable pouroff guards the mouth of this tributary entering Dark Canyon from the east. Once this initial hurdle is cleared the streambed route of boulders, sand, and slickrock will seem a snap, allowing you to concentrate on the scenic splendor of the canyon itself. Sheer walls, rising 1,500 feet above the floor, boast an incredible medley of colors. Beige, red, and white sandstone and gray limestone combine to make this a rockhound's paradise. In the spring, wildflowers, especially vetch, are numerous, along with the usual canyon flora. Desert bighorn sheep use the area but are elusive when human visitors are in the neighborhood. About 1.5 miles up the canyon look for water in catch basins on the slickrock canyon floor after spring run-off or summer rainstorms. Listen for the sound of dripping water at 1.75 miles and you'll locate a spring on the canyon's south wall. This is a fairly reliable source of clear water when the rest of Dark Canyon's water is too silty to pump. Leave your container under the drip while you explore, and it will be full when you return. At 2 miles an immense 300-foot pouroff prohibits further progress for all but the most inveterate canyon scramblers.

Down Dark Canyon: Below Lean-To Canyon the walls of Dark Canyon grow markedly narrower and more sheer, rising above the canyon floor to a height of more than 1,400 feet. After spring run-off a low-water trail can be negotiated down the length of Dark Canyon to the upper reaches of Lake Powell to the north. During peak water flows in the spring access down the canyon is limited. The shaggy walls of Dark Canyon are spectacular as the gorge narrows and squeezes the stream into its narrow bed. Lake Powell, backed up about 2 miles from Lean-To, is a good turn-around spot.

After a couple of days in Dark Canyon it's time to climb the Sundance Trail. Be sure you've lightened your load and eaten all your food before you exit. Again, take plenty of water for the trip. The Sundance Trail is steep, sunny, and hot.

Bryn Cunningham

Dirty Devil Complex 　　26

Location: 5 miles west of Hanksville, in southeastern Utah.
Size: 297,090 acres.
Administration: BLM Richfield District, Henry Mountain Resource Area; NPS Glen Canyon National Recreation Area.
Management status: BLM wilderness study areas (159,100 acres) and unprotected roadless area (104,500 acres), including some state roadless land; national recreation area roadless land (33,490 acres).
Ecosystems: Colorado Plateau province ecoregion, with pinyon-juniper woodland (potential natural vegetation), sagebrush shrub, and riparian zones.
Elevation range: 3,700 feet (high water mark of Lake Powell) to 6,805 feet (The Block).
Established trails/routes: Only 2 miles of official trails, but countless miles of deteriorated jeep track, plus canyon bottoms and stream beds, for hiking routes.
Maximum core to perimeter distance: 4.5 miles.
Activities: Hiking, river floating, backpacking, canyoneering, horseback riding, photography.
Maps: BLM 1:100,000 scale surface management/land ownership maps entitled "Hanksville" and "Hite Crossing" (50 meter contour interval). See Appendix E for a listing of the 14 topo maps of the roadless area.

OVERVIEW: The Dirty Devil River begins just north of Hanksville where the Fremont River from Boulder Mountain meets Muddy Creek coming in from the San Rafael Swell. The Dirty Devil flows south-southeast 37 air miles to an arm of Lake Powell in Glen Canyon National Recreation Area. In actual river miles the distance is closer to 100 miles due to the river's contortions. The lovely river got its unfortunate name from a member of the 1869 Powell expedition disgusted with the silty river's lack of fish.

The Dirty Devil Wilderness Complex incorporates the vast canyon system that drains into the Dirty Devil, as well as three canyons below Cedar Point on the southwest that drain to North Wash. The complex resembles an irregular projectile point aiming at Hite Crossing on Lake Powell. Utah Highway 95 south of Hanksville bounds the roadless area on the west. On the east side a series of mining and oil and gas roads mark the edge of wilderness along the

26 DIRTY DEVIL COMPLEX

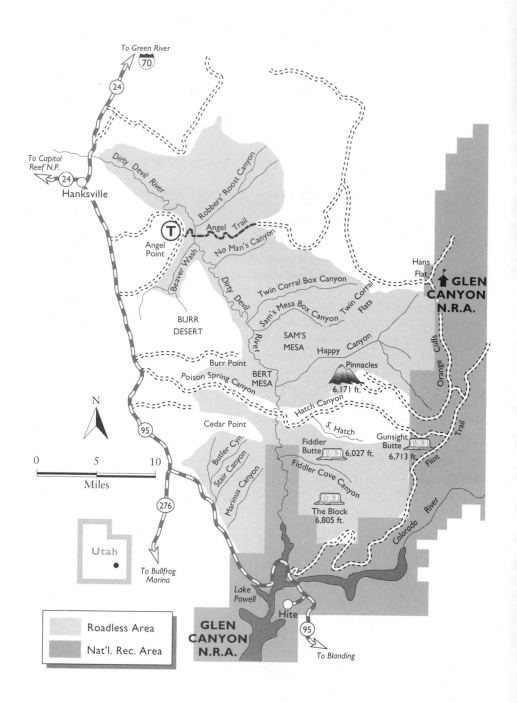

To Green River
70
24
To Capitol Reef N.P.
24
Hanksville

Dirty Devil River
Robbers' Roost Canyon
Angel Trail
T
Angel Point
No Man's Canyon
Beaver Wash
Dirty Devil River
Twin Corral Box Canyon
Sam's Mesa Box Canyon
Twin Corral Flats
BURR DESERT
SAM'S MESA
Happy Canyon
Hans Flat
GLEN CANYON N.R.A.
Orange Cliffs
Burr Point
Poison Spring Canyon
BERT MESA
Pinnacles
6,171 ft.
Hatch Canyon
Cedar Point
S. Hatch
Fiddler Butte 6,027 ft.
Gunsight Butte 6,713 ft.
Flint Trail
Butler Cyn.
Stair Canyon
Marinus Canyon
Fiddler Cove Canyon
The Block 6,805 ft.
Colorado River

N

0   5   10
Miles

95

276

Utah

To Bullfrog Marina

Lake Powell
Hite
95
To Blanding

GLEN CANYON N.R.A.

Roadless Area

Nat'l. Rec. Area

Orange Cliffs. The Poison Spring Canyon–North Hatch Canyon Road, though barely passable even in a jeep, cuts through the Dirty Devil at the Big Ridge.

With the Henry Mountains rising to the west, and the mesas of Canyonlands National Park to the east, the eroded depths of the Dirty Devil canyons might seem pale by comparison. The vast miles of slickrock cut by sharp canyons plunging 1,000 feet and more to streambeds and canyon bottoms below are a private world, with a low profile and no visitor center. Numerous canyons, split by mesas and ridges, feature complex topography and miles of canyoneering adventures. Dramatic scenery abounds in the lower world of the Dirty Devil, inspiring hyperactivity in many a hiker or photographer. Imaginative sculptures have been wrought by centuries of weathering, demonstrating the power of water and wind in this arid land.

While much of the region is barren rock, small patches of pinyon-juniper flourish where soil permits. Riparian zones exist along the Dirty Devil, a perennial stream, as well as near numerous springs and seeps. Patches of blackbrush provide cover for rodents and birds. Wildlife of the Dirty Devil Complex includes mule deer, desert bighorn sheep (reintroduced), antelope, and even beaver. Raptors enjoy nesting sites on the cliffs above the rivers.

As with most of the Colorado Plateau country, the Dirty Devil region has witnessed heavy use in pre-historic times. A projected density of 24 sites per square mile means you can anticipate discovering middens, lithic sites, rock shelters, campsites, and petroglyphs as you explore the canyon bottoms and mesas. Leave all artifacts where you found them, so the next hiker can enjoy them too.

The sub-regions of the complex form a contiguous ecological whole in spite of fragmentation by gravel roads. In the north, below Hanksville, the Dirty Devil begins its frenzied path to the southeast. Sandstone outcroppings and barren badlands spread in all directions. In the canyons—Robbers' Roost, No Man's, Larry, Twin Corral, and Sam's Mesa Box—small riparian vegetation zones and even hanging gardens are found along stream channels, in wash bottoms, and on moist cliffs and crannies. Numerous seeps and sub-surface springs are not mapped in the side canyons that feed the Dirty Devil. Do not count on such erratic sources of water for your exploration; always carry plenty with you!

The area 20 miles east of Hanksville is best known for the Wild Bunch, Butch Cassidy's gang, which used Robbers' Roost Canyon to avoid the law and rest up between escapades. Remains of a cabin used by various fugitives from 1875 to 1905 has been nominated to the National Register of Historic Places. The gnarly former residents would have a hearty guffaw, and the marshals that pursued them would no doubt be horrified at this development.

In the central section of the complex, where it is 20 miles wide, the tributaries of Happy Canyon cut deep, 1,000-foot gorges as they descend from the

Orange Cliffs in the Glen Canyon National Recreation Area to the east. This towering escarpment rises to 6,657 feet within the roadless area above Happy Canyon's forks, and reaches 7,000 feet beyond the perimeter road. Such dramatic relief is enjoyed by the golden eagles and peregrine falcons that swoop from their nesting sites on the cliff face and soar through the canyons. Chuck-wallas, shrews, bats, and salamanders reside in the cool narrows of the canyons. There is little vegetation in this slickrock canyon country. The few spots of soil produce sparse pinyon-juniper patches, desert grass, and blackbrush shrubs. Solitude is ensured for the backcountry user. The BLM survey in the 1970s calculated fewer than two dozen visitor days per year.

The Fiddler Butte area is at the southern end of the Dirty Devil Complex where it joins the roadless area in the Glen Canyon National Recreation Area above Hite Crossing. Here at its southern end the canyon of the Dirty Devil is 2,000 feet deep. On the benchland above the gorge, a mesa of Navajo sandstone, named The Block but shaped like a butterfly, rises 2,000 feet. The lowest point of the complex and the highest are located within 5 miles of each other, but the journey between them would be a long one, via Hatch Canyon. The 4,200-acre mesa atop The Block has not been grazed for nearly one hundred years. Consequently the vegetation there, a pinyon-juniper-sagebrush-grassland community, has rebounded to near relict quality.

The terrain in this southern end of the complex echoes the Needles region of Canyonlands, located just beyond the neck of Glen Canyon to the east. It is a complicated world of abrupt spires, pinnacles, canyons, and gorges. In spite of decades of intrusions by uranium, oil, and gas explorations, this area in the heart of the Colorado Plateau remains wild.

RECREATIONAL USES: The entire Dirty Devil is lightly used. Day hiking is limited due to restricted access points and steep canyon walls and blockages that prevent loop trips. Backpacking outings, especially in the spring when water is plentiful, are possible in this complex region. Contact the BLM office in Hanksville about river conditions; when running full the Dirty Devil is hazardous to cross. With a moderate water level, establishing a base camp at a clear water source and exploring the nearby canyons with a daypack provides the flexibility that makes canyoneering fun. Hiking the length of the river, from Hanksville to Hite, takes at least a week, although additional time would be desirable to explore side canyons.

From Utah Highway 95, explorers can do short outings in Marinus, Stair, and Butler canyons north of Hite. Farther up UT 95 a dirt road leads east to Burr Point, with a view of the heart of Dirty Devil country. From Burr Point, hike southeast across Bert Mesa for a view of the river gorge.

River running on the Dirty Devil is a seasonal possibility. From April to June there is usually enough water; at other times the river is a mere trickle.

Contact the BLM office in Hanksville for up-to-date information on river volume. The Dirty Devil from UT 24 near Hanksville to Lake Powell has been proposed for Wild and Scenic River status but has not achieved this designation yet. The river's twisting course provides magnificent photo opportunities for capturing wildlife and geology on film. Only from the river can you hike into many of the remote canyons, for they are inaccessible from above.

HOW TO GET THERE: A county road loops off Utah Highway 95 south of Hanksville. It curves to the east to the short spur road that goes to the Angel Point Trailhead.

From the north: There are several sandy spots, but otherwise the route is accessible for a low-clearance, two-wheel-drive vehicle. From UT 95, south of Hanksville, turn east on the improved, unsigned dirt road about 0.2 mile south of milepost 5. The road is unsigned, but it does have a stop sign. Follow this main road, disregarding several lesser roads. The only main intersection is a Y about 3 miles from UT 95. Bear left here. The spur to the trailhead is about 10 miles from UT 95, leading southeast 0.3 mile to dead end at the signed Angel Point Trailhead.

From the south: The southern end of the loop road leaves UT 95 at milepost 10. This too is an improved dirt road with a stop sign. Sandy spots are fewer, but they can occur in windy conditions. About 3 miles from UT 95 bear left at the Y intersection. At a second Y, 0.2 mile farther, also stay left, continuing north-northeast. About 10 miles from UT 95 the 0.3-mile, improved dirt road to the trailhead turns to the right, where it deadends at the signed Angel Point Trail.

Day hike or backpack

Beaver Wash Canyon

Distance: 6 miles round trip; longer for exploratory backpack.
Starting and minimum elevations: 4,920 feet and 4,120 feet.
Difficulty: Moderate.
Best months: March through May; September through October.
Topo map: Angel Cove-UT (for longer trips across the river, also Angels Point-UT).

Beaver Wash Canyon, on the west side of the Dirty Devil, is unique in this famed region of winding canyons, not for its geology but for its rare inhabitants. Beavers have created a set of dams and winding ponds that continue up the canyon bottom, creating a lush riparian environment in the barren world of the Dirty Devil. The BLM designated this canyon an Area of Critical Environmental Concern and included it in the Dirty Devil Wilderness Study Area.

This moderate day hike could also be done as a leisurely overnight backpack

A large overhang frames the valley and benches of middle Beaver Canyon.

or extended into a canyon outing of several days. The spring at Angel Cove, along the Dirty Devil just north of the foot of the Angel Point Trail, provides clear water and a campsite necessary for a comfortable base camp from which to explore the canyons of the Dirty Devil Wilderness Study Area. With normal river conditions it is easy to cross the river; first check with the BLM in Hanksville, especially in the spring when the river can rise.

The Angel Point Trail heads east from the parking area, dropping 800 feet in 1.5 miles. The highest portion of the trail is a well-worn footpath. This route was first used by outlaws one hundred years ago as they fled to hideouts in Robbers' Roost across the river. The trail quickly drops to the frozen dune formations of Navajo sandstone. Here conspicuous cairns mark the best route across and down the sloping slickrock. Without these markers it would be easy to elude a posse. It also must have been tough for horses to run on this surface. The trail curves across the slickrock in an arc southward, then arrives at the river right below the trailhead. You can negotiate the steeper pitches by angling across the fall line. The trail affords views of the expansive Dirty Devil drainage with miles of eroded sandstone bluffs carved into fanciful shapes by water and wind.

Beaver Wash Canyon lies immediately to the south of where the trail arrives at the riverbank. The canyon has soaring Navajo sandstone walls, rising sharply above the deep alluvial bottom of the canyon. The perennial stream, modified into ponds and falls by the resident engineers, has cut its way 10 to 20 feet below the brushy alluvial floor. Pouroffs from the benches high above have cut deep gullies in the canyon bottom, creating a miniature badlands topography. The stream is not an inviting walking area with its squishy bottom of settled sediment and its 2- to 3-foot deep pools. Instead, the intrepid hiker has to seek a pathway along the sage benches, through thickets of Gambel oak. A primitive, informal trail leads along the north side of the stream.

About 0.25 mile up the valley a fresh side canyon runs down from the north. The huge blocks of toppled sandstone are reminders of the powerful geologic forces at work here. The fresh edges of the boulders are evidence that Beaver is a growing canyon. At 0.5 mile up the main canyon a huge alcove on the north wall has lost its floor due to furious seasonal water shooting from the slot fall in the overhanging cliff. The beaver aren't the only ones changing the topography of the canyon. This is one gully you can bypass because a path leads around the top of the alcove wall to continue up the valley. Another 0.25 mile brings you to yet another gorge cut in the sandy alluvial bottom. This one you can't avoid. Slide 30 feet down the sandy slope, skirt along the stream edge, and climb to the next sage bench. This up-and-down pattern continues the length of the canyon.

The hallmark of Beaver Canyon, of course, is its unique population. The shy beaver have created a riparian paradise without the benefit of willows, their favorite material, weaving the available reeds and grasses into sturdy water-saving dams. What a varied world is the result: from the rushes and reeds that jam the bottom, to the dry brushy benches above the sand and gumbo banks, to the sheer sandstone half domes that soar 800 feet above. The contrast extends beyond the canyon, as the dry, barren windswept sandstone world of the Dirty Devil surrounds the beavers' waterworld. When you have ventured as far as energy and time permit, return to the trailhead by the same route.

A hike up Beaver Canyon can be part of a longer outing to the more traditional sandstone canyons on the east side of the river. Usually the Dirty Devil is wadeable, so Robbers' Roost, just to the north of Angel Cove spring, or No Man's Canyon and Larry Canyon to the south are exciting targets for exploration. These are cut in the Navajo sandstone, Kayenta formation, and Wingate sandstone, and lack the broad alluvial bottom of Beaver Canyon. The Dirty Devil is a wild area of endless variety.

San Rafael Swell–
Caineville Desert Complex

27

Location: 13 miles west of Green River (north end) and 1 mile north of Hanksville (south end), in east-central Utah.

Size: 902,690 acres.

Administration: BLM Richfield District, Sevier and Henry Mountain Resource Areas; Moab District, San Rafael and Price River Resource Areas; USDAFS Fishlake National Forest; NPS Capitol Reef National Park.

Management status: BLM wilderness study areas (six units totaling 266,085 acres); unprotected BLM and state roadless lands (466,815 acres); unprotected national forest roadless land (four units totaling 71,790 acres); Capitol Reef National Park roadless land (98,000 acres).

Ecosystems: Middle Rocky Mountain province—potential natural vegetation is Douglas-fir forest and western spruce-fir forest; Colorado Plateau province ecoregion potential natural vegetation is pinyon-juniper woodland, saltbush-greasewood, and galleta-threeawn.

Elevation range: 4,255 feet (mouth of Muddy Creek) to 11,306 feet (Thousand Lake Mountain).

Established trails/routes: About 35 miles of national forest system trails; some 60 miles of primitive jeep tracks on BLM land suitable for hiking and horseback riding; about 30 miles of primitive unmaintained hiking routes in Capitol Reef National Park; numerous canyon bottom game trails suitable for hiking that are periodically washed out.

Maximum core to perimeter distance: 3.5 miles (Sids Mountain).

Activities: Hiking, backpacking, float boating, cross-country skiing, snowshoeing, horseback riding, canyoneering, rock climbing, nature study, photography, fishing, hunting.

Maps: BLM 1:100,000 scale surface management/land ownership maps entitled "Manti," "Huntington," "Salina," "San Rafael Desert," "Loa," and "Hanksville" (50 meter contour interval). See Appendix E for a listing of the 45 topo maps covering the complex.

OVERVIEW: The San Rafael Swell is a vast but nonetheless scaled-down version of the Colorado Plateau. This monumental dome of uplifted sedimentary rock covers a 50-by-30-mile basin ringed by upland buttes and mesas, cut by silt-laden desert streams, and pocketed with intricate canyons. The Swell rises

27 SAN RAFAEL SWELL–
CAINEVILLE DESERT COMPLEX

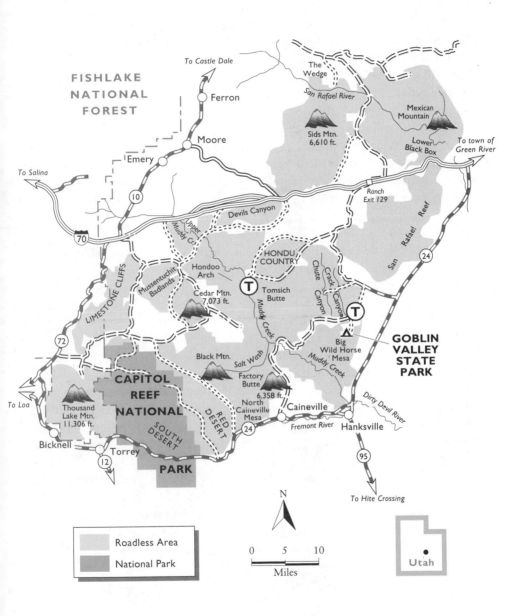

FISHLAKE
NATIONAL
FOREST

To Castle Dale

The
Wedge

San Rafael River

Mexican
Mountain

Ferron

Sids Mtn.
6,610 ft.

Lower
Black Box

To town of
Green River

Moore

Emery

To Salina

Ranch
Exit 129

San Rafael Reef

10

Devils Canyon

70

HONDU
COUNTRY

24

Upper Muddy Creek

Hondoo
Arch

Mussentuchit
Badlands

Cedar Mtn.
7,073 ft.

Ⓣ Tomsich
Butte

Crack Canyon

Chute Canyon

LIMESTONE CLIFFS

Muddy Creek

Ⓣ

△

72

Black Mtn.

Salt Wash

Big
Wild Horse
Mesa

Muddy Creek

**GOBLIN
VALLEY
STATE
PARK**

CAPITOL
REEF
NATIONAL

Factory
Butte

6,358 ft.
North
Caineville
Mesa

Caineville

Dirty Devil River

RED DESERT

Thousand
Lake Mtn.
11,306 ft.

To Loa

SOUTH
DESERT

24

Fremont River

Hanksville

Bicknell

Torrey

PARK

12

95

To Hite Crossing

N

	Roadless Area
	National Park

0   5   10
Miles

Utah

1,500 feet above the surrounding desert in a geologic wonderland of slot canyons, cliffs, domes, and towers. The north-trending uplift began 40 to 60 million years ago, causing the existing formations to bulge into the kidney-shaped San Rafael Swell. Wind and (mostly) water erosion then shaped the Swell with the signatures of deep-cut canyons and rugged terrain. With the greatest uplift and erosion in the interior, the center of the Swell exposes the oldest rocks. Rings of younger formations radiate outward. Perennial streams in narrow canyons cut deeply into this ancient sandstone heartland of almost impenetrable cliffs. Above these older layers lies the light gray to brown Kaibab limestone. Next comes the buff, orange, and brown cross-bedded sandstone of the Wingate formation lining the cliff faces. Red cross-bedded Kayenta sandstone overlies the Wingate at higher elevations. These uplands are also colored by tan, gray, orange, and yellow petrified dunes, arches, caves, and buttes of Navajo sandstone. The Swell is bounded on the east by the more resistant and steeply dipping hogback of the San Rafael Reef.

The vibrant orange cliffs and towers of Cathedral Valley and the Red Desert spread beyond the Swell. On the upper, western end the dark, lava-capped plateaus of Thousand Lake Mountain, Lookout Peak, and Wayne Wonderland send radiating dikes and fins of black basalt down to an elaborately painted desert of agate, chert, geodes, and dinosaur bones. To the south and east of the Swell are blue-gray hills of Mancos shale where fossilized sharks teeth, clams, and gem quality agates are found.

From the lofty volcanic heights of Thousand Lake Mountain stretching far to the northeast past the San Rafael River to Mexican Mountain, the complex encompasses almost a million acres of wildlands in 20 roadless units divided among three federal agencies. The Swell is the breathtaking centerpiece of this multi-jurisdictional jigsaw puzzle. But there is the added dimension of subalpine forests draining east to the north end of Capitol Reef National Park. Beyond lies the Caineville Desert and a maze of mesas and canyons surrounding the Swell.

On the south the Red Desert links the park with the greater San Rafael complex. Banded badlands ringed by Entrada sandstone cliffs combine limitless open space with a deepened sense of solitude. To the north the misnamed Limestone Cliffs, actually made up of sandstone, guard seasonal migration corridors for elk, mule deer, and antelope as they move from ponderosa pine forests through pinyon-juniper woodlands to sagebrush flats.

Next door to the east, the dazzling and highly erodible Mussentuchit Badlands of maroon and cream-colored hills cut by volcanic dikes are a jumble of draws and ravines. Between these badlands and those of Muddy Creek, 7,073-foot Cedar Mountain rises more than 1,000 feet in the midst of igneous intrusions with angular shapes and isolated pinnacles that seem oddly out of place in slickrock country.

Muddy Creek flows through three roadless areas, separated only by dirt roads, heading southeast for 70 miles from Interstate 70 to Hanksville. In its upper reaches Muddy Creek twists through color-banded badlands and cliff-forming sandstones on the western slope of the Swell. The grandeur of these upper 10 miles are accentuated by volcanic fins up to 6 miles long. As the second largest expanse of undeveloped BLM land in Utah, the central Muddy Creek unit displays every landform found in the complex: slickrock domes and canyons, open desert, impenetrable reefs, black walls, and steep-sided mesas. From the junction of lower Muddy Creek Gorge and the slot canyon mouth of the Segers Hole basin, Wingate and Navajo sandstone cliffs run north and east along San Rafael Reef, defining the south and west limits of the Swell. Small twisting side canyons harbor inner gorges of ancient slickrock. A stunted pinyon-juniper forest mantles much of the higher country. Hebes Mountain hosts a square mile of ungrazed relict tall grasses, shadscale, and juniper. Muddy Creek runs for 30 miles through the barren badlands of Wild Horse Mesa. This is a lunarscape of coal black pinnacles and "goblins" deeply incised by occasional canyons.

Eastward, the hidden chasms, benches, and steeply dipping cliffs of San Rafael Reef form the imposing southeastern edge of the Swell. The Reef is cut by many short canyons along with a myriad of fins, arches, caves, and buttes eroded from Navajo sandstone at higher elevations. Grape agate, an extremely rare gem, is found here. Straight Wash exposes the oldest rock formations in the Swell, with other sandstones, almost as old, lining narrow slot canyons. Desert bighorn sheep live throughout most of the Reef, along with mule deer, coyotes, bobcats, badgers, foxes, reptiles, and birds, including golden eagles.

Northward, an obscure blank spot on the map known as Hondu Country provides living space for bighorn sheep and wild horses. Ridges and 400-foot-deep canyons twist and cut through Kaibab limestone into slickrock sandstone. Just south of I-70, Devils Canyon heads up in the pinyon-juniper-clad heart of the Swell, draining west to Salt Wash with its sparse cover of grasses and desert shrubs. This serpentine canyon slices 1,000 feet into the crest of the Swell, exposing sheer walls of ancient formations.

On the north side of I-70 rises the broad mesa of Sids Mountain. These butte-studded sandstone uplands drop into an intricate maze of deep canyons bound by cliffs of Wingate sandstone. The canyons are separated by rolling grassy parks. Sixteen miles of the San Rafael River cuts through the north end of the Sids Mountain roadless area, forming the rugged gorge of the Little Grand Canyon. A sizable herd of bighorn sheep roams throughout the country along with mule deer and a rare mountain lion or two.

Unusual landforms continue east into the Mexican Mountain country where sedimentary rocks have been eroded into black cliffs, cuestas, alcoves, dunes, pinnacles, and buttes. A 1,000-foot cliff of Wingate sandstone parallels 20

miles of the San Rafael River, encompassing the Black Box and Lower Black
Box gorges. Windowblind Peak, one of the world's tallest free-standing monoliths, rises 1,200 feet about 1.5 miles southwest of the river. An astonishing
vertical mile of uplifted strata is displayed in this eastern buttress of the Swell.
Bighorn sheep continue their range into this country along with a full complement of other desert denizens.

This vast array of wildlands is a storehouse of cultural values, most of which
are unrecorded and undiscovered. Most notable are rock art pictographs and
petroglyphs from the Fremont culture near the San Rafael River and in side
drainages, such as Black Dragon Canyon. Remnants of the Old Railroad Grade
and of the Old Spanish Trail pass through the northern reaches of the complex.
Swasey's Leap is a narrow overhang above Black Box Gorge where Sid Swasey
reportedly jumped a horse across the canyon.

RECREATIONAL USES: Perhaps most surprising in this barren desertscape are the
exceptional opportunities for challenging float boating and lazy tubing on the
San Rafael River and Muddy Creek during spring runoff. Depending on the
year, floatable flows in the San Rafael may occur for two to four weeks, normally during May or June. Given the intimate, twisting nature of these watercourses the only way to go is with small craft, such as kayaks or small
inflatables, or in some cases, innertubes. The one- to two-day, 18-mile float
down the San Rafael River from Fuller Bottom to the Buckhorn Wash Bridge
descends colorful Little Grand Canyon. When the water subsides by early to
midsummer the river bottom and side canyons offer a variety of hiking, backpacking, and equestrian routes.

Downstream the San Rafael winds for 34 miles through the Mexican Mountain country. Technical floating is needed to negotiate the obstacles, rapids, and
narrow canyons of the upper and lower Black Boxes. Flat water stretches of
2 to 5 miles above, below, and between the Black Boxes are floatable at moderate to high water levels. Enough water for tubing sometimes lasts well into
July. The Black Boxes are popular for hiking when water levels have dropped,
as are the many side canyons. Creative route finding is needed to find passages
out of most upper canyons, but all of the north side canyons are interconnected
to the north, providing endless variations for loop hikes among the Navajo
sandstone buttes and domes. Scenic horse trails cut across the hummocky surface north of the river and in Nates Canyon.

Hike 50 in *Hiking Utah* (Falcon Publishing) describes a 12.5-mile, point-to-
point wet day hike or overnighter on the San Rafael River, 5 miles of which
involve hiking and wading through the Lower Black Box during low water.
Hike 51 in the same book details a hiking/floating route through the Upper
Black Box from Lockhart Box down to Mexican Bend. Scrambling boulder
fields with some wading, even during low flows, adds a bit of adventure to this
13-mile, point-to-point trip. Numerous climbing routes are also available in the

Black Boxes, ranging in difficulty from moderate rock scrambles to technical climbs.

Easily accessible yet lightly used, Devils Canyon can be visited on a short out-and-back hike or a longer point-to-point trip of about 15 miles from its upper end to Kimball Wash. A jeep trail drops into upper Devils Canyon from Justensen Flats just south of I-70 about 20 miles southeast of Ferron. Highway noise may filter into the canyon for a couple of miles where it comes close to the interstate, but after a few miles quiet canyon solitude settles in.

HOW TO GET THERE: *Muddy Creek Trailhead:* From the town of Green River drive 31 miles west on I-70 to Exit 129. Go south (left) on the improved dirt road for 10 miles to the first signed road junction. Take a right toward Reds Canyon and Tan Seep. The second signed junction is another 4 miles. Take another right toward Reds Canyon and McKay Flat. After another mile turn left toward McKay Flat at the third signed junction. Continue another 9 miles to the fourth signed road junction and turn right toward Reds Canyon (6 miles). After 5 more downhill miles take a left at the fifth signed junction toward Hondoo Arch. The road becomes more primitive but passable for two-wheel-drive vehicles in dry weather. After passing active mine adits at the base of the stunning escarpment of Tomsich Butte during the next 0.5 mile, turn left onto a dirt doubletrack leading another 0.4 mile to the unsigned parking area and trailhead on Muddy Creek.

Crack Canyon Trailhead: From Utah Highway 24 at milepost 137, about 22 miles north of Hanksville and 29 miles south of I-70, turn west on the signed Goblin Valley State Park Road. Continue 5 miles on this paved road to an improved dirt road signed "I-70, Goblin Valley, Temple Mtn." Turn left (south) and drive 5 miles to the crest of a small hill where an unimproved dirt road drops down a ridge to the right toward Wild Horse Creek. Turn onto this road and drive about 0.4 mile, pulling off to the right and parking along the east bank above the stream bottom.

Out-and-back day hike or overnighter

Muddy Creek–Poor Canyon

Distance: 12 miles round trip.
Starting and maximum elevations: 5,050 feet and 5,650 feet (upper Poor Canyon).
Difficulty: Moderate.
Best months: March through May; October through November.
Topo map: Tomsich Butte-UT.

The remote trailhead/parking area/car campsite along the east bank of Muddy Creek is bounded by great cliff walls, domes, and the tepee-shaped

Hondoo Arch to the west and isolated buttes and low-lying benches on the east. Old cow camps and uranium adits lie at the base of Tomsich Butte. Heed the BLM warning signs: stay away from old abandoned mines that may contain explosives and deadly radon gas. From the trailhead hike northward up the wide, flat valley through a cottonwood grove, past the remains of a 1940s cow camp, intersecting with a low-standard road that dead-ends after another 0.5 mile near Muddy Creek below Tomsich Butte. At this first of six crossings of Muddy Creek leading to the mouth of Poor Canyon (12 crossings round trip) both sides of the drainage are marked by massive sheer cliffs of Wingate and Navajo sandstone. A walking stick is needed to probe for shallow gravel bottoms in aptly named Muddy Creek. Depending on water levels, crossings are at or below knee level. The horizon here is wide and varied enough for a three-dimensional effect, yet intimate enough for hidden discoveries. The wilderness study area/vehicle closure sign is reached after another mile as the route enters the northeast edge of BLM's Muddy Creek Wilderness Study Area. Lower benches dotted with black volcanic "bombs" are overshadowed by multi-tiered red and buff cliffs streaked with black desert varnish.

A soft, sandy path well-beaten by cows and wild horses winds across benches from one side of the creek to the other. At 2.5 miles a rincon tower dubbed "The Merry Go Round" appears on the left in the midst of a dry meander. Cross the stream and continue along the rocky remnants of an old mining road for another 0.5 mile to the mouth of Poor Canyon on the right. This spectacular canyon begins in a wide sandy bottom with intermittent springs, junipers, Spanish bayonet, and gnarled old cottonwood. Deeply honeycombed walls wrap around in great sweeping arcs with huge caves and alcoves, some of which harbor Anasazi sites. An extensive pinyon-juniper woodland with a few Douglas-fir trees fills the valley about one mile up. At 1.5 miles the canyon narrows with slotted 30- to 50-foot walls overseen by cliffs soaring upward 600 to 1,000 feet. About 2 miles up, this canyon within a canyon opens up to a secluded pasture frequented by wild horses. The first major junction is another 0.5 mile up. The left fork contains a spring 0.2 mile up near its box canyon head. Stair-step shale paves the floor of the right fork. After about 0.75 mile the canyon narrows and steepens with bouldering and moderate rock climbing required for the next mile to the canyon head. This is a good turnaround point. Backpackers will find flat sandy campsites in both Muddy Creek and lower Poor Canyon.

From the trailhead Muddy Creek can also be explored downstream (southward) at low water through The Chute to the Hidden Splendor Mine. The creek cuts through the colorful Moenkopi formation, Sinbad limestone, and finally the ancient Coconino sandstone. These 15 miles can be traversed as a long, strenuous day hike or as a more moderate overnighter, but there is no place to camp in the narrow chute of Muddy Creek. Logs are jammed into the canyon walls 25 feet overhead in the narrowest stretch of the Chute—a place you don't want to be in if there is a chance of heavy rain in the upper drainage.

Out-and-back canyoneering day hike

Crack Canyon

Distance: 10 miles round trip.
Starting and maximum elevations: 4,870 feet and 5,440 feet.
Difficulty: Moderately strenuous.
Best months: October through April (depending on snow conditions).
Topo maps: Temple Mountain-UT; Goblin Valley-UT.

This sweep of the San Rafael Reef appears as reddish low benches leading to rounded white buttes and knobs on the middle horizon. Cross Wild Horse Creek and head slightly north of west toward a prominent three-pronged, buff-colored butte. The main wash of Crack Canyon is reached after hiking about 0.5 mile cross-country across rolling benches. Turn right up the wide sandy wash and continue another 0.25 mile to BLM's Crack Canyon Wilderness Study Area/vehicle closure sign. A well-traveled path with firmer footing cuts across alternating flats between canyon bends. Low Moenkopi red walls streaked with thin, brittle white plates line the wash. After another mile the canyon is blocked by a 30-foot cliff wall. Double back 0.1 mile and look for an unofficial trail on the north side that climbs about 100 feet up a steep rocky slope to the canyon rim. From a short distance back down the wash another faint trail climbs through a narrow notch directly above the canyon bottom cliff, saving about 0.25 mile of walking in the wash.

Continue north to northwest up the main (widest) wash, which is rimmed by low, deeply pocketed slopes and rippled rock. The wash is open, sparsely vegetated, and best avoided during the heat of the day. The first of five distinct narrow slot canyons appears after another mile, opening to great mounds of bulbous, swirling white, cross-bedded sandstone. The "crack" of Crack Canyon becomes more impressive in each successive slot canyon. The middle "canyon within a canyon" is the deepest, with sheer walls towering hundreds of feet. Moderate rock climbing and lifting up tight 8- to 10-foot-high chutes is required at four points within and between the upper slot canyon sections. A rope or webbing is useful for raising and lowering day packs. The top of the fourth rock ledge is marked by a wider but still deep canyon dotted with pinyon pine. The head of Crack Canyon is bound by massive walls, domes, and spires, as well as a wilderness study area/vehicle closure sign at the end of a primitive jeep track. This is an inspiring vista as well as good turn-around point for the out-and-back exploration of Crack Canyon.

A loop is possible by hiking up the jeep track to an improved dirt road that drops into Chute Canyon, the middle section of which is roadless. This loop is not recommended, however, because roads and off-road vehicle use in this stretch of Chute Canyon detract from the wildness experienced in Crack Canyon. The trip back down Crack Canyon opens vistas of color-banded cliffs and domes. On the way down you'll discover that Crack Canyon is much more than it's cracked up to be.

Labyrinth Canyon Complex 　　　28

Location: 17 miles south of Green River (north end) and 22 miles east of Hanksville, in southeastern Utah.
Size: 185,700 acres.
Administration: BLM Moab District, San Rafael Resource Area (north); Richfield District, Henry Mountain Resource Area (south); NPS Canyonlands National Park and Glen Canyon National Recreation Area.
Management status: BLM wilderness study areas (two units totaling 59,300 acres); unprotected BLM and state roadless lands (112,400 acres); national park roadless land (2,500 acres); national recreation area roadless land (11,500 acres).
Ecosystems: Colorado Plateau province ecoregion, potential natural vegetation of galleta-threeawn shrubsteppe, blackbrush, and juniper-pinyon woodland.
Elevation range: 3,900 feet (Green River) to 6,560 feet (Hans Flat in the Upper Horseshoe Canyon roadless area).
Established trails/routes: Except for about 4 miles of trails in the detached Horseshoe Canyon unit of Canyonlands National Park, there are no formal trails in the complex. There are about 60 miles of informal user-created trails in the vicinity of Labyrinth Canyon and 23 miles of mostly rehabilitated doubletracks on benches above Horseshoe Canyon that are suitable for hiking and horseback riding.
Maximum core to perimeter distance: 4.5 miles (Upper Horseshoe Canyon area).
Activities: River floating, hiking, backpacking, cultural exploration, horseback riding, canyoneering, rock climbing, photography, nature study, and mountain biking.
Maps: BLM 1:100,000 scale surface management/land ownership maps entitled "San Rafael Desert" and "Hanksville" (50 meter contour interval). See Appendix E for a listing of the 11 topo maps covering the complex.

OVERVIEW: In July 1869 John Wesley Powell made his amazing journey of discovery down the Green River, writing that "there is an exquisite charm in our ride down this beautiful canyon...the walls are symmetrically curved and grandly arched, of a beautiful color, and reflected in the quiet waters.... We name this Labyrinth Canyon." This fabled river canyon and the wildlands on both sides begin at the mouth of Three Canyon next to Trin-Alcove Bend, 30 miles below the Green River State Park boat launch. Powell wrote that "three side canyons enter at the same point. These are very tortuous, almost closed

28 LABYRINTH CANYON COMPLEX

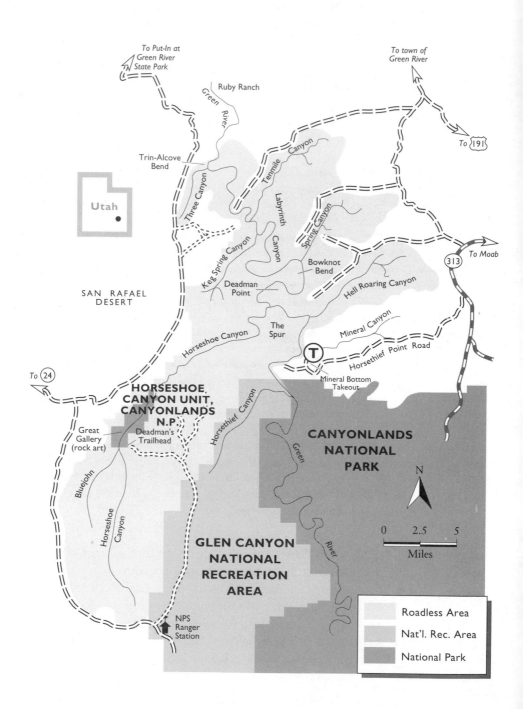

To Put-In at
Green River
State Park

Ruby Ranch

To town of
Green River

Green River

To (191)

Trin-Alcove
Bend

Tenmile Canyon

Utah

Three Canyon

Labyrinth Canyon

Spring Canyon

313

To Moab

Keg Spring Canyon

Bowknot
Bend

SAN RAFAEL
DESERT

Deadman
Point

Hell Roaring Canyon

Horseshoe Canyon

The
Spur

Mineral Canyon

T

Horsethief Point Road

To (24)

Mineral Bottom
Takeout

**HORSESHOE
CANYON UNIT,
CANYONLANDS
N.P.**

Horsethief Canyon

**CANYONLANDS
NATIONAL
PARK**

N

Great
Gallery
(rock art)

Deadman's
Trailhead

Green

Bluejohn

Horseshoe
Canyon

**GLEN CANYON
NATIONAL
RECREATION
AREA**

River

0   2.5   5

Miles

NPS
Ranger
Station

	Roadless Area
	Nat'l. Rec. Area
	National Park

in from view, and, seen from the opposite side of the river, they appear like three alcoves. We name this Trin-Alcove Bend."

At first, Navajo sandstone cliffs rise dramatically from desert flats, gradually becoming more formidable by the time Labyrinth Canyon is reached at Trin-Alcove Bend. Twisting canyons, plunging more than 600 feet deep, meet the river downstream. These canyons are flanked by high benches ending as dramatic overlooks above the river. By the time Labyrinth opens up at Mineral Bottom and around the corner at Canyonlands National Park, the buffs, oranges, and browns of Wingate sandstone are exposed on high cliff faces. This formation also lines the deeper side canyons. Upper reaches of these main drainages are marked by the red cross-bedded sandstone of the Kayenta formation.

The largest side drainage entering Labyrinth is Horseshoe Canyon, winding northward for 35 miles from Hans Flat to the river. As with Labyrinth, it also cuts through layers of Navajo and Wingate sandstone. The colorful Navajo formation is exposed at higher elevations, often in the form of arches, caves, buttes, and knolls.

Riparian plant communities of cottonwood, tamarisk, black greasewood, rabbitbrush, and snakeweed grow along the Green River and major tributaries. The higher ground is interspersed with a mix of grasses, sagebrush, and desert shrubs, such as Mormon tea and shadscale. The predominant impression is one of barren slickrock and sand. Significantly, the inaccessible cliff-faced mesa of Bowknot Bend (river miles 50 to 57) guards one of the few remaining relict desert-shrub communities.

In 1982 the Utah Division of Wildlife Resources reintroduced desert bighorn sheep into the nearby Orange Cliffs. Floaters in Labyrinth Canyon sometimes see desert bighorns on the east side of the river. Mule deer range from tamarisk thickets to steeper canyon breaks, and antelope gambol year-round on high rims and benches. Red foxes, bobcats, coyotes, and badgers live in a wide array of habitats, from the river to upper canyons and plateaus. Beaver build their lodges near the mouths of side canyons.

Bird species run the spectrum from vultures, golden eagles, prairie falcons, and red-tailed hawks to mourning doves and waterfowl along the river. At least a dozen kinds of fish fin the deep, slow waters of the Green, including the endangered Colorado squawfish, bony-tail chub, and humpback chub.

In middle Horseshoe Canyon a detached 2,500-acre unit of Canyonlands National Park protects one of the best and most puzzling displays of prehistoric rock art on the continent, known as the Great Gallery. Some of the mysterious forms are of armless human-like mummies and trapezoid-shaped antelope. Additional galleries of "Barrier Canyon" rock art unique to this area are located to the northeast another 2 miles down the canyon. Other nearby canyons harbor human-made artifacts more than 6,800 years old. Cowboy

Cave in the Upper Horseshoe Canyon country houses one of Utah's oldest and most extensive paleontological sites. The origin of some of these sites is believed to be Anasazi. Of far more recent vintage are signatures of early river explorers and trappers. Some of these writings are at the "Post Office," a rock with a visitor register in the saddle of Bowknot Bend. The remains of cabins used by Butch Cassidy and the Wild Bunch are located southeast of the river in the vicinity of Horseshoe Canyon.

RECREATIONAL USES: The sublime Green River corridor is the magnet that attracts the overwhelming majority of visitors to the Labyrinth Canyon Complex. An increasing number of people are discovering the "exquisite charm" and tranquility of this mellow stretch of the Green, just as John Wesley Powell did 130 years ago. Those seeking a peaceful float would do well to avoid the Memorial Day weekend when hundreds of motor craft join the annual Friendship Cruise down the Green to the Colorado River and from there up the Colorado to Moab.

Most floaters cover the 68-mile stretch to Mineral Bottom in three or four days, allowing little time for off-river exploration. Those who explore are well rewarded by the added adventure and solitude found in numerous side canyons. Several of the larger drainages, such as Horseshoe, have well-developed trails worn in place by previous hikers. In other cases, game trails are used by hikers to explore upper canyons. There are more than 60 miles of these informal trails in the vicinity of Labyrinth Canyon alone.

Several plateaus above the river are penetrated by primitive four-wheel-drive tracks that are well suited for horseback riding and mountain biking. An example is the 4.5-mile Deadman Trail primitive route that takes off from a road 13 miles north of the Hans Flat Ranger Station. First off, stop at the station and get a free backcountry permit required by Canyonlands National Park for both camping and hiking. Hans Flat is accessible by two-wheel-drive road from Utah Highway 24. The mountain bike route to the Deadman Trail in the detached Horseshoe Canyon unit of Canyonlands is described in Ride 71 of *Mountain Biking Utah* (Falcon Publishing).

From the Deadman trailhead a steep 1.5-mile trail drops into Horseshoe Canyon to the Great Gallery rock art panels. Those wishing a longer, extended backpack trip can hike Horseshoe Canyon in its entirety for 35 miles from Hans Flat to its confluence with the Green River, 61 river miles below the town of Green River. Large rock overhangs and grassy flats above the canyon bottom offer inviting campsites. The heads of Tenmile, Spring, and Horseshoe canyons can be entered from the top by way of low-standard roads. Although not easily accessible from the river, rims overlooking Labyrinth Canyon open up stunning vistas of cliffs, spires, river bends, and a 60-foot natural bridge.

HOW TO GET THERE: From Main Street in the town of Green River drive 0.25 mile southeast to the boat launch on the west shore of the river at Green River State Park (150 S. Green River Boulevard). The takeout is downstream at Mineral Bottom. To leave a shuttle car at Mineral Bottom, drive 20 miles east of Green River on I-70 to Crescent Junction. From this junction turn right (south) onto U.S. Highway 191 heading toward Moab. After another 20 miles turn right (west) on UT 313 and continue 13 miles to Horsethief Point Road leading to Mineral Bottom. Make another right (west) onto Horsethief Point Road and drive 15 miles down to Mineral Bottom. Coincidentally, the one-way shuttle distance is exactly the same as the river floating distance—68 miles!

Four- to eight-day river float with day hikes

Labyrinth Canyon–Green River to Mineral Bottom

Distance: 68 river miles plus variable distances for side hikes.
Starting and minimum elevations: 4,050 feet and 3,900 feet.
Difficulty: Easy floating with easy to moderate day hikes.
Best months: April through June; September through October.
Topo maps: Tenmile Canyon side hike: Tenmile Point-UT; Bowknot Bend saddle and Horseshoe Canyon hikes: Bowknot Bend-UT. Spring Canyon hike: Bowknot Bend-UT, Mineral Canyon-UT, and Dubinsky Wash-UT.

Floating the Green the full 68 miles from the state park to Mineral Bottom is a leisurely family style adventure through a world of soaring canyon walls, smooth water, and radiant golden light filtering into the depths of Labyrinth Canyon. Allow at least four days to reach Mineral Bottom, but if you've got the time we would surely recommend spending at least eight days through this stretch, as we did.

With slow-moving flat water most of the way, a canoe is the ideal craft for the Green, although rafts are popular for transporting additional people and gear. At 40 miles below the state park the mouth of Tenmile Canyon (left bank) provides a campsite as well as an interesting, serpentine canyon that can be explored for more miles than most day hikers could begin to cover. On the left bank at river mile 46 French trapper Denis Julien carved his name on a rock wall in 1836, 33 years before the Powell Expedition. At mile 50 pull over to the right bank and scramble up to the Post Office river register in the saddle of Bowknot Bend. The saddle sits 250 feet above the river and can be easily crossed over to where the river meets it on the other side—a mere 0.25 mile. The same point by boat (river mile 57) is reached by floating 7 miles in an almost 360 degree circle, wrapping around a mesa that towers 1,000 feet above the river. For a leg-stretcher along the way hike up Spring Canyon at mile 52.5

(left bank). The canyon is wildly scenic despite having a four-wheel-drive route in its lower reaches. Running straighter than most major tributaries, Spring Canyon tops out after only about 5 miles on the benchlands of Spring Canyon Point.

A day would be well spent on an out-and-back exploration of culturally rich Barrier Creek in 1,500-foot-deep Horseshoe Canyon (right bank, mile 61). If time is short a 3- to 4-mile loop can be hiked by taking the right fork 1 mile up Barrier Creek, which leads north another mile to a low divide. From there double back to the river by hiking down a 1.5-mile parallel side drainage that meets the Green about 0.5 mile above the mouth of Barrier Creek. The take-out for the Labyrinth Canyon float is another 7 miles down at Mineral Bottom (left bank).

Canyonlands Basin Complex 29

Location: 10 miles southwest of Moab (north end) and 8 miles northwest of
Monticello (south end), in southeast Utah.
Size: 669,970 acres.
Administration: NPS Canyonlands National Park and Glen Canyon National
Recreation Area; BLM Moab District, San Juan Resource Area; USDAFS Manti–La
Sal National Forest, Monticello Ranger District.
Management status: National park roadless land (275,920 acres); national
recreation area roadless land (161,950 acres in the Orange Cliffs); BLM wilderness
study areas (three units totaling 36,350 acres); unprotected BLM and state roadless
lands (125,750 acres); unprotected national forest roadless lands (70,000 acres).
Ecosystems: Colorado Plateau province ecoregion, potential natural vegetation is
pinyon-juniper woodland and blackbrush; Middle Rocky Mountain province,
Douglas-fir forest and western spruce-fir forest.
Elevation range: 3,750 feet (Colorado River) to 10,959 feet (Mount Linnaeus).
Established trails/routes: More than 130 miles of mostly primitive trails in
Canyonlands National Park and Glen Canyon National Recreation Area; plus
numerous primitive jeep tracks and unofficial trails in adjacent BLM wildlands
suitable for hiking and horseback riding.
Maximum core to perimeter distance: 4 miles (Canyonlands National Park,
Maze District).
Activities: River running, hiking, backpacking, canyoneering, rock climbing,
horseback riding, cross-country skiing, snowshoeing, photography, nature and
cultural study, hunting, fishing.
Maps: BLM 1:100,000 scale surface management/land ownership maps entitled
"Hanksville," "LaSal," and "Blanding;" 1989 USDAFS half-inch/mile planimetric map
for the Manti–La Sal National Forest, Monticello District. See Appendix E for a
listing of the 26 topo maps covering the complex.

OVERVIEW: The core of the 1,200-square-mile amphitheater of Canyonlands
Basin is protected by Canyonlands National Park, established in 1964. But
nearly 30 percent of the wildlands in the basin, mostly along its eastern and
southern edges, are BLM lands outside the park, along with 70,000 unprotected national forest acres high in the Abajo Mountains to the south.

Water and gravity have carved the sedimentary rocks of Canyonlands

29 CANYONLANDS BASIN COMPLEX

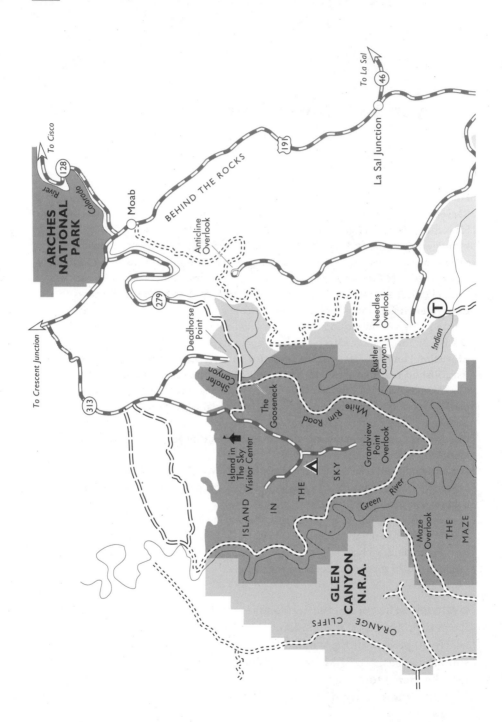

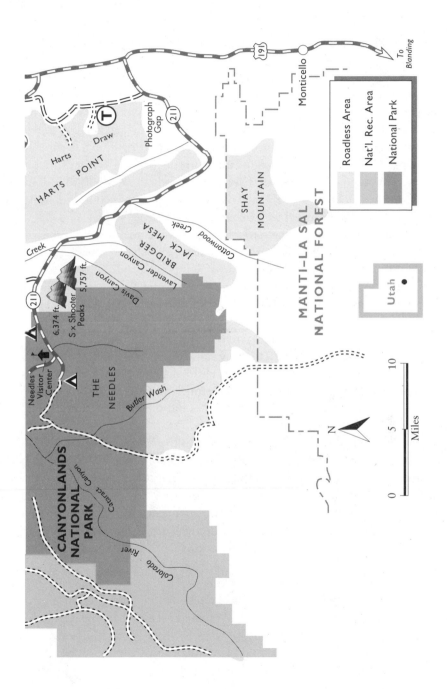

National Park into an overpowering landscape of colorful mesas, buttes, canyons, fins, arches, and spires. The great canyons of the Green and Colorado rivers split the park into the Island in the Sky, the Maze, and the Needles districts.

In the north end of the park, wedged into an inverted triangle by the Green and Colorado rivers, 104,235 acres of wildlands make up Island in the Sky. At 6,000 feet the broad mesa of the "island" is the park's observation tower. The foreground from this unequalled vantage point is the White Rim, which lies between the mesa and the river. The mid-ground is a sobering sweep of the Maze and the Needles. Beyond is the distant background of jagged peaks in the La Sal, Abajo, and Henry mountain ranges punctuating the flat-topped canyonscape. Narrow ledges leading down to and below the White Rim are favored by rarely seen desert bighorn sheep. The jagged-edged, 1,500-foot-deep crater of Upheaval Dome is probably the oldest geologic feature at Island in the Sky and may have been formed by a meteor.

On the southeast corner of the park the Needles includes 62,055 acres of wild country. The red and white banded sandstone and shale pinnacles of the Needles dominate this jumbled landscape of sculptured rock spires, arches, canyons, pot holes, and long parallel valleys called grabens. Grassy meadows, ranging in size from tiny to nearly 1,000 acres in Chesler Park, contrast with huge expanses of broken bare rock. A fin in a tributary to Salt Creek Canyon has eroded into 150-foot-high Angel Arch. Many other oddly shaped arches are hidden in secret side canyons. The Anasazi lived in virtually every canyon in the Needles. Tower Ruin, built high on a cliff ledge in a side draw of Horse Canyon, is a remarkable example of Anasazi stone and mud construction. The "Ancient Ones" also left a legacy of rock art as did the Archaic hunters and gatherers who preceded them.

West of the river, the 66,565 roadless acres in the Maze, plus other wildlands in the adjacent Orange Cliffs region of Glen Canyon National Recreation Area, constitute the wildest region in the basin—a remote and nearly inaccessible network of tortuous canyons aptly described as a "30-square-mile puzzle of sandstone." The puzzle is overlooked by the strangely shaped buttes, walls, and towers of the Fins, The Doll House, Emies Country, and the Land of Standing Rocks. Pigmy junipers dot mesas above a 600-foot plunge to the bottom of the Maze.

As the only major riparian habitat in this vast semi-desert corner of the Colorado Plateau, the Green and Colorado rivers are a lifeline for concentrations of wildlife. Cottonwood, willow, and tamarisk shelter deer, beaver, bobcats, foxes, hawks, eagles, and migratory waterfowl. Luxuriant hanging gardens of columbine, monkeyflower, and maidenhair ferns cling to water seeps on 1,200-foot cliffs. John Wesley Powell recorded his impressions of

Canyonlands while floating the river on his epic 1869 journey by writing, "We glide along through a strange, weird, grand region. The landscape everywhere, away from the river, is of rock."

West and below the Needles Overlook stretches BLM's Indian Creek wildland—a jumble of eroded red pinnacles and canyons. Formations are elaborately sculptured with the steep walls of four major canyons, truncated ledges, and rounded rock spires richly painted in tans, whites, pinks, dark reds, and purples. Bare slickrock sprinkled with desert shrubs affords habitat for bighorns and such rarities as peregrine falcons.

Southward, Harts Point is a 5-mile-wide plateau reaching north from the base of the Abajo Mountains 12 miles into Canyonlands Basin. Thousand-foot cliffs guard the point on 3 sides and its west face is the east wall of Indian Creek Canyon. Close by, the little known Harts Draw system is drained by narrow, watered canyons. The thick mantle of pinyon-juniper and sagebrush covering Harts Point serves as important mule deer winter range. A few elk also winter east of Harts Draw. The draw itself may be on the route of the Macomb Expedition, which made the first known exploration of Canyonlands Basin by white people in 1859.

To the west the mile-wide Bridger Jack Mesa runs for 10 miles, gradually dipping to the north. Rising 1,000 feet above the surrounding canyons this north end of the mesa abruptly ascends another 450 feet atop slickrock domes and knolls. Bridger Jack and other nearby mesas are crowned by pinyon-juniper woodland, broken occasionally by small sagebrush parks. A tiny relict stand of Douglas-fir is among the vegetative wonders found here. Wintering mule deer, coyotes, and bobcats are among the mesa's inhabitants. Lavender Canyon holds excellent examples of Anasazi and Fremont-style rock art.

The relatively shallow Butler Wash is an extension of the Canyonlands Park country, bordering the park on its south boundary. The upper ends of Salt Creek are lined by 600-foot red and white color-banded sandstone walls. Sagebrush parks and pinyon-juniper adorn mesas decorated with buff-colored buttes, knolls, and pinnacles similar to those found in the Needles region to the north. Butler Wash is a transition area between Fremont and Anasazi peoples. Rock art found here may help solve mysteries about the nature of contact between these cultures.

RECREATIONAL USES: To protect both solitude and the environment, permits are required for all overnight backcountry travel in Canyonlands National Park and the adjacent Orange Cliffs Unit of Glen Canyon National Recreation Area. The number of permits is limited in each of 19 backcountry zones, so making reservations is recommended. They are accepted only by mail or fax (801-259-4285). The reservation fee for backpacking is $10. The actual permit can then be picked up at the park visitor center the afternoon before the trip or up to an hour before the visitor center closes on the first day of the reservation. Not surprisingly, peak use occurs during the pleasant weather of spring and fall when average daytime highs are 60 to 80 degrees Fahrenheit.

Most Island in the Sky trails start on the mesa and switchback down to the White Rim bench, with some continuing on to the Green or Colorado rivers. The trails tend to be primitive and strenuous, with elevation changes of 1,000 to 2,000 feet. Hike 65 in *Hiking Utah* (Falcon Publishing) describes a strenuous trek around Upheaval Dome with an optional overnighter down Upheaval Canyon to the Green River.

In the Needles more than 60 miles of primitive hiking trails link canyons with routes through slickrock passes. Most of the trails can be hiked in a day by strong hikers, but longer trips are possible by connecting with other trails. Moderate elevation changes of only a few hundred feet are the rule, except for the Lower Red Rock Trail (4 miles one way), which drops 1,400 feet to the Colorado River. Another idea for a day hike is the 11-mile round trip to the Confluence Overlook on the Big Spring Trail. Backpackers can reach other park trails by descending the 1.7-mile, four-wheel-drive road down Cyclone Canyon to the Red Lake Canyon Trail. Those looking for a strenuous overnighter won't be disappointed with the 9.4-mile trail from Squaw Flat to Lower Red Lake.

The Maze and Orange Cliffs region of the park and national recreation area contains about 19 miles of primitive trails, some of which require climbing skills. The main vehicular access to rims above the Maze is on 46 miles of graded dirt road that leads east from Utah Highway 24 to the Hans Flat Ranger Station. Many of the routes involve maneuvering through and around deep sand, pouroffs, and steep slickrock. Other trails are exercises in basic rock climbing, such as segments of the Maze Overlook Trail. A 24-mile, out-and-back mountain bike route to the Maze Overlook is described in Ride 73 of *Mountain Biking Utah* (Falcon Publishing).

Keep in mind that mountain bikes are not allowed off-road or on park trails. However, the hundreds of miles of paved and dirt roads in the park offer an incredible variety of fat tire tours. Take for example the challenging mountain bike ride around the popular 100-mile White Rim loop. Most mountain bikers allow three to four days for this grand tour around and below the Island In The Sky mesa top.

River running and floating along with side canyon hikes is a joyous and at times exciting way to experience that portion of the basin most distant from a road. The confluence of the Green and Colorado rivers is in the heart of the park. Above the confluence both rivers are slow and peaceful, ideal for the contemplative enjoyment of canoeists and kayakers. Flat water boaters typically put in at Mineral Bottom on the Green or at Potash on the Colorado and float down to the confluence or a few miles farther downstream to Spanish

Bottom. A $10 flat water floaters permit is required by the park as is a pre-arranged jet boat shuttle upriver to the put-in. Of course, jet boats are more appropriate on Lake Powell than in the wild recesses of these river canyons. Gooseneck and Shafer Canyon BLM roadless lands enclose 10 miles of the Colorado River on the northeast boundary of the park. The rugged cliffs of the 3-mile long Gooseneck loop are especially scenic when viewed from nearly 2,000 feet above at the adjacent Dead Horse Point State Park.

Below the confluence the increased volume of water dramatically changes the river's character to a foaming 26-mile chute of whitewater in Cataract Canyon. This demanding series of class IV and V rapids requires experience, the right equipment, and a $25 permit fee from the Park Service. The first come, first served applications, which are drawn through a lottery system, should be sent in at least seven or eight weeks ahead of time.

Permits ($10) are also needed to use pack and saddle stock in the park (horses, mules, and burros only). The only at-large horse camping allowed is on the Orange Cliffs mesa top above 6,000 feet. Day trips on horseback can be taken on the west side hiking trail in Horseshoe Canyon and on all backcountry roads. Unless camping overnight, technical rock climbers need not obtain a permit in the park. All climbing must be free or clean aid and be at least 300 feet from archeological or cultural sites. A briefing at the visitor center on these and other applicable regulations, plus tips on minimum impact camping accompanies the issuance of backcountry permits.

The high Shay Mountain country in the Abajo Range epitomizes the incredible array of recreation activities in the complex. Beyond the Blue Mountain Ski Area west of Monticello, winter enthusiasts can cross-country ski in the morning and then travel north to lower elevations in the same canyons for afternoon hiking and canyoneering. A primitive USDA Forest Service trail (021) runs in the head of Indian Creek, the lower reaches of which wind along a deep, narrow canyon in a BLM wilderness study area bordering the east side of Canyonlands National Park.

Exceptional day and overnight trips with ample solitude can be experienced in Indian Creek and other nearby BLM wildlands within the basin. Butler Wash is one such place. This shallow, picturesque canyon winds northward through the wilderness study area for at least 10 miles before entering the park. The trailhead near House Park can be reached by way of Forest Roads 088 and 093 from North Cottonwood Wash and Utah Highway 211. To the north an out-and-back trip down Harts Draw could easily be extended into a two- or three-day backpack. Road access into the upper canyon is provided by dirt roads leading north and west from UT 211 just south of Photograph Gap. Harts Draw can also be reached by hiking down an old cattle trail on the west ridge of Bobbys Hole Canyon from the paved Needles Overlook Road just west of the Wind Whistle Campground, which drops into lower Bobbys Hole.

In the upper reaches, a pouroff that passes through a pothole arch blocks a direct descent down this canyon.

HOW TO GET THERE: Upper Harts Draw: From Moab drive 39 miles south on U.S. Highway 191 to Utah Highway 211. Turn right (west) on UT 211 and drive another 3 miles to just past Photograph Gap. Turn right (north) on the signed San Juan County Road 137 (North Flats Road), which is the first road beyond Photograph Gap. After about 2 miles on this improved dirt road, cross a cattleguard and immediately turn left (west) onto an unsigned, unimproved dirt road. Drive about 0.5 mile to the unmarked trailhead, which is just beyond a wash on a large flat of white sandstone with scattered juniper to the right. Pull over and park. The road continues to the west but quickly deteriorates to a four-wheel-drive route. The hike begins on the other side of the road to the south.

Upper Indian Creek: From the junction of US 191 and UT 211, about 39 miles south of Moab, turn right (west) on UT 211 and drive 19 miles past the end of state maintenance. Continue on the paved highway to just past mile marker 10 (2.7 miles east of the Canyonlands National Park boundary) and turn right (north) on the signed "San Juan County 122, Lockhart Road," which also has a BLM information board. Continue north on this improved dirt road 2 miles to Indian Creek, passing two BLM campgrounds. After crossing the creekbed drive 1 mile on a rougher, unimproved two-wheel-drive dirt road and turn left on a rough but short spur road that crosses the head of a shallow wash. Pull over and park after about 0.2 mile. The spur ends at a primitive car campsite below an overhang. The hike begins down the short side canyon, dropping westward to Indian Creek.

Day hike or overnighter

Upper Harts Draw

Distance: 12 to 14 miles out-and-back to Harts Spring or 8-mile loop via Lone Cedar.
Starting and minimum elevations: 6,320 feet and 5,620 feet (mouth of Harts Spring).
Difficulty: Moderate.
Best months: Mid-March through May; October through November.
Topo maps: Photograph Gap-UT (for out-and-back to Harts Spring Canyon). For explorations farther down Harts Draw add Harts Point North-UT and Hatch Rock-UT.

Harts Draw is the lifeline of the 62,800-acre Harts Point roadless expanse of canyons and mesas that the BLM dropped from wilderness study area status. This is a rarely explored part of Canyonlands Basin on its southeast corner—a secluded land visited more often by mountain lions than humans. And little wonder. The big cats make a good living with hundreds of mule deer relying on the undisturbed habitat for critical winter range. A distinctive Old West flavor in the upper draw offsets its initial lack of dramatic canyon topography. Harts Draw assumes classic canyon beauty downstream.

From the trailhead, cross the road in a southwesterly direction to a broad south-flowing wash that drains toward the Abajo Mountains and Harts Draw. This is a rolling landscape of white Navajo sandstone slab rock dotted with pinyon-juniper and sagebrush. Follow the draw, reaching a stock fence and pouroff after about 0.4 mile. Angle around to the right, walking on deer trails and sandstone in the shallow wash for another mile to the riparian bottom of Harts Draw. Turn right and head down the draw, taking note of the landmarks for the return trip. Soon the valley widens with rock rims pocketed with small caves rising on the right. An old jeep track winds along the left side of the draw, indented with fresh sign of deer, cougar, and bobcat.

Seasonal muddy water may be encountered in early spring, but most of the upper draw is dry. Two miles down, an old iron stockgate blocks the washed-out jeep track. Shelf rocks are broken by talus slopes of pinyon-juniper with an occasional gnarled old cottonwood along the bottom. Great flanges of overhanging ledges jut out from white sandstone rims. About 2.5 miles down Harts Draw two side canyons enter close to one another from the left (southwest). The first is a delight to explore with easy walking. The second is marked by a distinctive hole in the rock above a deep plunge pool and is worth exploring but brushy and more difficult to hike in. A short side loop of 2 to 3 miles can be made between these canyons across a ridge traversed by a primitive jeep track, but the climb into the more southern canyon requires route finding and moderately strenuous rock climbing.

Lone Cedar Canyon enters from the left another 0.5 mile down Harts Draw. An 8-mile loop is possible by way of an easy hike up Lone Cedar, followed by a gradual arc to the southeast back to the ridgetop road where the trailhead is located. The main Harts Draw canyon deepens as golden eagles soar overhead. The hiking is easy and pleasurable, even as the draw narrows below Lone Cedar Canyon.

Harts Spring flows from the right (east) another 1.5 to 2 miles down. This steep-walled canyon of Wingate sandstone overlain by the Kayenta formation is blocked by pools and a high pouroff only 0.25 mile above its mouth. With ample clear water in Harts Spring a base camp could be set up near its mouth, which is 6 to 7 miles below the trailhead. A day or two would be well spent exploring the deeper, more serpentine draw and its many interesting side canyons downstream.

For the return trip Harts Draw provides the easiest route back to the trailhead. The surrounding mesas are deeply incised and traversed by low-standard jeep tracks. A rough, dry, overland loop is feasible, however, by climbing above the lower Harts Spring waterfalls on the right side to the south rim of the canyon. Continue cross-country to the southeast, weaving up and down and in and out of side washes to the main ridge dividing Harts Spring and Lone Cedar canyons, meeting the end of a primitive jeep track. Follow the double track eastward about 1 mile to the head of a shallow draw draining south to a wide sagebrush valley. Head cross-country for about 2 miles by dropping south into the valley and climbing the far ridge where the trailhead and road are located. The loop trip distance is comparable to that of the recommended out-and-back route, but considerably more strenuous.

Two- to three-day backpack or long day hike

Upper Indian Creek

Distance: Variable, ranging from a 10-mile out-and-back to a 40-mile point-to-point.
Starting and minimum elevations: 4,650 feet and 4,440 feet (5 miles down), 3,900 feet (mouth of Indian Creek).
Difficulty: Moderate.
Best months: Mid-March through May; October through November.
Topo maps: North Six-Shooter Peak-UT (for out-and-back route); Monument Basin-UT; Lockhart Basin-UT; The Loop-UT; and North Six-Shooter Peak-UT (for extended point-to-point route).

This route explores the upper reaches of Indian Creek—the twisting main artery of a 27,000-acre roadless area adjoining the east-central boundary of Canyonlands National Park. Although wild and remote in its entirety, only 6,870 acres in lower Indian Creek are within the BLM wilderness study area. The perennial stream and its lush riparian plant community are a pleasing contrast to the adjacent dry Needles District of the park.

From the unmarked trailhead drop to the southwest down a red rock side draw, skirting to the right around a short pouroff, reaching Indian Creek after about 0.25 mile. For the return trip take note of the prominent rock spire marking the trailhead wash. A series of paths used by cattle and occasionally by off-road vehicles winds downstream to the right along the broad sandy bottom. En route down Indian Creek expect countless crossings, but stepping stones are well spaced for dry-foot hopping.

Off-road-vehicle tracks disappear about 3 miles downstream near an old woodcutter camp on the right. Cords of neatly stacked cottonwood and juniper firewood are slowly being covered by windblown sand. Another mile down, huge old mine timbers, cable, and debris are mute testimony to the dashed dreams of early prospectors in this rough and wild setting. The stream bottom is choked with dense brush, but the open creekbed affords easy walking on compacted mud. Although the valley is wide, the sense of isolation is deepened by multi-tiered layers of red rock cliffs crowned with severely eroded knobs, pillars, pinnacles, and buttes.

For overnighters, good campsites abound along Indian Creek. Once such place is about 5 miles down on a high south-side bench where major side canyons enter from the north and south directly opposite one another. The northern canyon is blocked by cliffs just around the bend. In contrast, the southern canyon is a joy to explore and can be climbed with a steep walkup all the way to the rim and mesa 500 feet above Indian Creek.

This upper Indian Creek route is easily retraced for a 10-mile, out-and-back day hike. The preferred option is to set up a base camp for one or two days of hiking down through the deeper and more narrow middle section of the canyon. A much longer point-to-point trip would be to backpack all the way down Indian Creek some 20 to 25 miles to its confluence with the Colorado River just inside the park. The return route heads back up a couple of miles to the mouth of Rustler Canyon and then about 8 miles up Rustler to its intersection with the Lockhart Basin Road (it's rough—four-wheel-drive recommended). This unsigned trailhead is 9 to 10 miles northwest of the upper Indian Creek trailhead on the same road, just beyond a landing strip below the Needles Overlook. One can fantasize about hiding a mountain bike to fetch the car if a second vehicle isn't available for the 20-mile round-trip shuttle between trailheads. A minimum of five days should be allowed for this moderately strenuous 30- to 40-mile exploration of Indian Creek and Rustler Canyon.

Behind the Rocks Complex   30

Location: 2 miles west and 1 mile south of Moab, in southeast Utah.
Size: 51,100 acres (four BLM roadless areas).
Administration: BLM Moab District, Grand Resource Area.
Management status: BLM wilderness study area (Behind the Rocks, 12,635
acres), plus 38,465 acres of unprotected BLM and state roadless lands.
Ecosystems: Colorado Plateau province ecoregion, with juniper-pinyon woodland
potential natural vegetation.
Elevation range: 4,000 to 6,530 feet (Moab Rim).
Established trails/routes: 4 to 5 miles of trail in Hatch Wash Unit; the Behind
the Rocks Wilderness Study Area contains about 3 miles of trail, 3.5 miles of double
tracks and four-wheel-drive tracks on the Moab Rim suitable for hiking and
horseback riding.
Maximum core to perimeter distance: 2 miles (Behind the Rocks Wilderness
Study Area).
Activities: Hiking, backpacking, rock climbing, canyoneering, horseback riding,
photography, geologic study.
Maps: BLM 1:100,000 scale surface management/land ownership maps entitled
"Moab" and "LaSal" (50 meter contour intervals). See Appendix E for a list of the
six topo maps covering the roadless area.

OVERVIEW: A dramatic but relatively bypassed backdrop just west of Moab,
the Behind the Rocks Complex functions as a wild and rugged bridge between
Arches and Canyonlands national parks. Hidden behind the 1,800-foot-high
Moab Rim are petrified sand dunes eroded along jointing fractures into a fantastic maze of domes, fins, arches, and deep canyons with springs, hanging
gardens, pools, and luxuriant riparian vegetation. From north to south the four
roadless sections of the complex are Goldbar Canyon (12,500 acres) north of
the Colorado River; Behind the Rocks (20,300 acres) and Hunter Canyon
(4,000 acres) south of the river and separated only by the Pritchett Canyon
four-wheel-drive track; and Hatch Wash (14,300 acres) west of Kane Springs
Canyon Road.

About half of the land surface is bare rock, consisting of either pale-orange
Navajo sandstone imbedded here and there with some red chert and sandy
limestone, or the more reddish-brown sandstone of the Kayenta formation.

30 BEHIND THE ROCKS COMPLEX

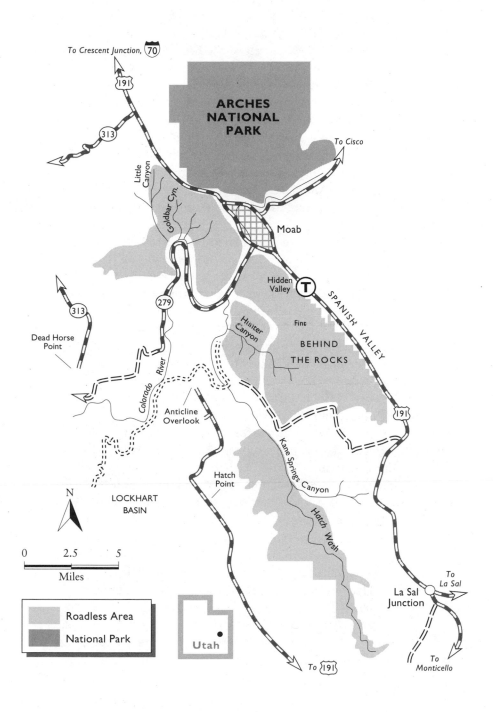

To Crescent Junction, (70)

191

313

ARCHES
NATIONAL
PARK

To Cisco

Little Canyon

Goldbar Cyn.

Moab

Hidden
Valley

T

SPANISH VALLEY

313

Hunter Canyon

Fins

BEHIND
THE ROCKS

279

Dead Horse
Point

Colorado River

Anticline
Overlook

191

N

LOCKHART
BASIN

Hatch
Point

Kane Springs Canyon

Hatch Wash

0   2.5   5

Miles

Roadless Area

National Park

Utah

To
La Sal

La Sal
Junction

To (191)

To
Monticello

Much of the wildland sits in the vast, northwest-trending Paradox Basin. This basin is framed by the northwest-trending collapsed salt anticline of the Spanish Valley on the northeast and the Kings Bottom syncline to the southwest.

Parallel joints in the Navajo sandstone have split vertically and weathered into huge slickrock fins, 100 to 500 feet high, 50 to 200 feet wide, and up to 1.5 miles long. Some of these closely spaced fins are only a few feet apart, pocketed with desert garden alcoves. The Behind the Rocks fins cover an area much larger than that of nearby Arches National Park. These wedges of sandstone are engraved with potholes, alcoves, terraces, and arches. Overall, the complex contains at least 48 named and unnamed arches, once again rivaling at least some of the arches of Arches. Upper Goldbar Canyon alone is a treasure trove of nameless arches, tunnels, and natural bridges. This most northern of the roadless units also features the magnificent Corona, Bowtie, Little, and Jeep arches. Another point of geologic interest is a prominent landmark known as the Vanishing Angel—a spire carved from the Wingate Cliffs near Moab Rim.

As the fins extend westward across Pritchett Canyon toward Hunter Canyon the landscape changes to one of ledges, domes, and a myriad of small canyons in the Kayenta formation before descending to Wingate cliffs. The greatest eroded depths expose both the Kayenta formation and Wingate sandstone, where canyon bottoms are bounded by sheer walls up to 1,000 feet high. Perennial springs in the Kayenta formation flow in Hunters and Hatch canyons. These and other nearby serpentine canyons are cloaked with dense riparian flora, providing an added dimension of remoteness and solitude.

Despite the predominance of bare rock, incessant winds have blown enough sand into sheltered niches to form patches of soil. From here a sparse cover of stunted pinyon pine, juniper, yucca, prickly pear, and blackbrush grows between fins and weathered sandstone forms. Hunter Canyon is a good place to look for hanging gardens clinging to seeps on vertical walls.

A small number of mule deer winter here, but lack of water forces most of them to migrate elsewhere during summer. With venison as its main staple the cougar also winters here. Coyotes, foxes, and cottontail rabbits live in these wildlands throughout the year. Observant travelers occasionally see desert bighorn sheep grazing on steep slopes above U.S. Highway 191 not far from Goldbar Canyon. Sheer canyon walls provide perches and secure nesting for raptors, such as red-tailed hawks, prairie falcons, and federally listed endangered peregrine falcons. Kestrels, wrens, and ravens are common, as are juncos during winter.

The complex is rich in prehistoric values. The Goldbar Canyon country contains a Kayenta formation rock slab with dinosaur tracks not far from the Poison Spider four-wheel-drive track. A mastodon petroglyph along the river road north of Moab likely represents a 10,000-plus-year-old sighting of the extinct animal by a Paleo-Indian. Other petroglyphs exist near Pritchett Canyon and in deep canyons near Hatch Wash. The Indian Fortress is a 5-acre Anasazi site with superb rock art and a two-room granary. A thorough cultural inventory of the complex would surely uncover dozens of other prehistoric sites.

During the 1830s early explorers and traders followed the Old Spanish Trail just east of the Moab River. Otho Arch, located on the west side of Behind the Rocks, is inscribed with historically significant graffiti. Today, a century-old cattle trail climbs the cliffs along Hidden Valley above Moab ending near the Indian Fortress.

RECREATIONAL USES: Day hiking is the most popular recreational pursuit here, in part because scarcity of water makes backpacking difficult, and the rugged jumble of sandstone formations poses an obstacle to extended horse travel. But limited backpacking and horseback riding can be enjoyable, especially during April through June. The best equestrian trips are on the several miles of jeep tracks and open mesas between rugged canyons. One note of caution for those seeking relief from the infernal combustion machine: Behind the Rocks should definitely be avoided during the peak Easter and Labor Day weekends. This is when quietude is shattered by hordes of off-road-vehicle enthusiasts converging on perimeter four-wheel-drive roads.

Hiker access up the western cliff face of Behind the Rocks is available on foot trails through Hidden Valley or past Jackson Reservoir. These routes, as well as some jumping off points from Pritchett Canyon, cross state or private lands. Utah Highways 163 and 279 provide good access to Goldbar Canyon where the most popular destinations are Corona and Bowtie arches and Poison Spider Mesa. The Poison Spider four-wheel-drive road is cherry-stemmed from the Goldbar Canyon roadless area boundary. This primitive doubletrack offers an invigorating, technically advanced mountain bike route to Portal's rim (5,000 feet elevation), as described in Ride 64 of *Mountain Biking Utah* (Falcon Publishing).

On the south end of the complex, the lower reaches of Hatch Wash may be entered from Kane Creek Canyon or by dropping into its head from upper side canyons. One of the only developed BLM trails in the vicinity follows Trough Springs Canyon along the north edge of the Hatch Wash roadless area. This canyon has water and is especially pleasant for spring hiking.

Behind the Rocks offers the full spectrum of hikes, from the intimacy of walking between tightly spaced fins and canyons to the exhilaration of commanding views of southeast Utah from points above 6,000 feet along Moab Rim. The Moab Rim trail, used at times by four-wheel-drive vehicles, takes off from Kane Creek Boulevard 1.5 miles down the Colorado River from Moab. The trail climbs northeast, steeply at first, for a couple of miles along tilted rocks of the Kayenta formation to the summit of the plateau. Once on top hikers can follow four-wheel-drive tracks southeast to the Hidden Valley trail, dropping to US 191 south of Moab for a point-to-point distance of about 6 miles. For those experienced in off-trail travel through rough country the fins can also be reached from the rim by heading south. Both Hunters and Pritchett canyons access a maze of formations and side canyons from the four-wheel-drive track along Pritchett Canyon or from Tunnel Arch or Moonflower Canyon via Kane Springs Canyon.

The fins and some of the canyon cliff walls provide excellent technical climbing, rappelling, and rock scrambling. Hunting during the fall is a minor use due to low populations of mule deer, chukar partridge, and mourning dove.

Serious photographers are apt to run out of film in this striking land so generously endowed with form and texture. Aided by the brilliance of sunrise and sunset, pink and buff rocks transform to glowing reds and purples. Shadows cast by fins move slowly across rock faces streaked with lines of dark desert varnish. Pools of sparkling water reflect the ever-changing light. And always there are the fins, with their limitless supply of hiking routes through interconnecting passageways.

HOW TO GET THERE: From Moab drive 3 miles south on U.S. Highway 191, just past mile marker 122, and then turn right on Angel Rock Road, which is also identified with a BLM trail sign for Hidden Valley. Drive a couple of blocks to a T intersection and turn right on Rimrock Lane for the final 0.3 mile to the signed trailhead and parking area at road's end.

Day hike, canyoneering

Behind the Rocks Fins

Distance: 5 miles round trip on trail, plus variable off-trail hiking, climbing, and canyoneering.
Starting and maximum elevations: 4,590 feet and 5,270 feet (pass) and up to 6,000 feet on the higher fins.
Difficulty: Moderate to moderately strenuous.
Best months: March through May; October through November.
Topo map: Moab-UT.

This rambling excursion behind the rocks of the Moab Rim, within a BLM wilderness study area, enters an unworldly place that is so strange and topographically complicated even the detailed topo map is virtually useless for route finding. The country is especially noteworthy for its blend of wild quietude in proximity to the bustling community of Moab. Once behind the rocks in Behind the Rocks the outside world is quickly shut off and forgotten.

The fabled fins can be accessed from several trails, but of these the Hidden

Looking down one of the countless fin-bound valleys behind the rocks of the Moab Rim.

Valley Trail is relatively short, direct, and free of motorized vehicles. The constructed rocky trail begins in a scattered juniper-sagebrush flat below the imposing east face of the Moab Rim. After a long series of switchbacks the trail reaches the lip of lower Hidden Valley, gaining 500 feet over the first mile. Lofty red cliffs to the south look over the elongated grassy basin of Hidden Valley. A low pass is reached at mile 1.8, but Hidden Valley goes on for another 0.5 mile to a more prominent 5,270-foot gap that opens to broad vistas westward to the canyon rims of the Colorado River.

From the pass a well-traveled, informal trail climbs steeply to the right and to the base of the cliffs. It then weaves up and down below the wall where an exceptional gallery of petroglyphs extends for a considerable distance. The main trail drops into a valley bound by high cliffs on both sides. About 0.25 mile below the pass the trail meets the southern terminus of a four-wheel-drive route. If you're willing to throw distance, direction, and destination to the wind, treat yourself to a roving ramble into the fins. Begin by following the four-wheel-drive trail about 0.25 mile down to the first swale and then cut left (south) toward the fins, which are close and clearly visible. They are oriented east-west, come in all shapes and sizes, and vary in spacing from wide valleys to a boot's width. The first valley can be hiked along parallel rock shelves, but it steepens rapidly and is difficult to climb at its head. The second fin-bound valley is wider and delightful to explore. And so it goes, with each set of parallel fins displaying its own unique personality. In some cases low passes between fins can be easily crossed to the next valley but most often they are guarded by formidable cliffs.

This is the kind of bewildering place where simply being there is everything, where speed and distance become irrelevant and you are lost in a fantastic geologic puzzle. When you're all "finned" out return to the four-wheel-drive trail by angling down and to the right (north) toward the major landmark of the petroglyph cliff face. Turn right on the trail for the 2.5- to 3-mile hike back down to the trailhead. With a car shuttle a point-to-point hike is possible to the Colorado River by following the Moab Rim four-wheel-drive trail northwest to its starting point on Kane Creek Boulevard 2.6 miles southwest of its intersection with U.S. Highway 191 in Moab.

La Sal Canyons Complex 31

Location: I mile east of Moab, in east-central Utah.

Size: 167,330 acres.

Administration: BLM Moab District, Grand Resource Area; USDAFS Manti–La Sal National Forest, Moab Ranger District.

Management status: BLM wilderness study areas (17,400 acres in 2 units); unprotected BLM roadless land (92,100 acres); unprotected national forest roadless land (57,870 acres).

Ecosystems: Colorado Plateau province ecoregion, from ponderosa pine–spruce-fir forests to pinyon-juniper woodland (potential natural vegetation) and sagebrush shrub, to riparian vegetation, with expanses of barren slickrock.

Elevation range: 4,200 feet (Mill Creek) to 12,721 feet (Mount Peale).

Established trails/routes: 65 miles of hiking trails within the national forest; former mining roads and canyon bottoms provide infinite hiking routes on BLM roadless lands.

Maximum core to perimeter distance: 1.5 miles.

Activities: Hiking, backpacking, cross-country skiing, canyoneering, rock climbing, horseback riding, mountain biking, photography, nature study.

Maps: BLM 1:100,000 scale surface management/land ownership maps entitled "Moab" and "LaSal" (50 meter contour interval); and 1989 USDAFS half-inch/mile planimetric map entitled "Manti–La Sal National Forest—Moab & Monticello Ranger Districts." See Appendix E for a listing of the 15 topo maps that cover the roadless area.

OVERVIEW: The La Sals are a beacon on the eastern horizon of central Utah. These are the second highest mountains in the state, falling behind only the Uintas. They were named by Spanish explorers for their snowy peaks, which looked salty from a distance. Thirty million years ago, the mountain range was created by an uplift of igneous rock that pushed beneath the overlaying red rock desert, twisting and turning it as it arose. Called a laccolith range, the La Sals share this igneous background with the Henrys, but the La Sals are considerably higher, with six peaks over 12,000 feet. Glacial valleys high on the mountainsides are reminders of the Pleistocene ice masses here on the Colorado Plateau.

31 LA SAL CANYONS COMPLEX

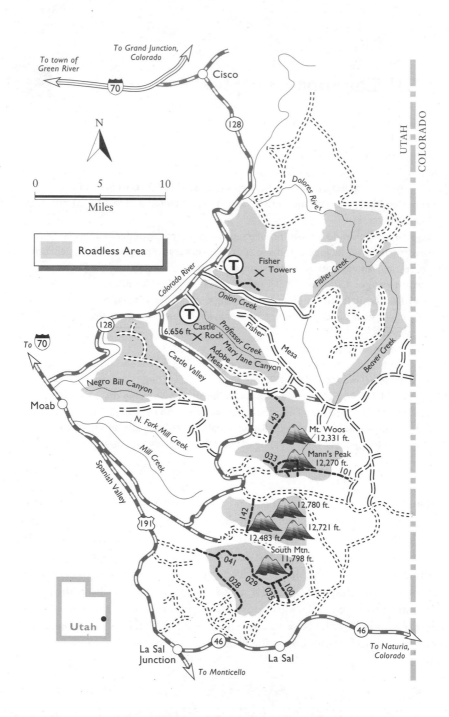

To town of Green River

To Grand Junction, Colorado

Cisco

70

128

N

0   5   10

Miles

Roadless Area

Dolores River

Colorado River

T Fisher Towers

Onion Creek

Fisher Creek

T Castle Rock
6,656 ft.

128

To 70

Fisher Mesa

Professor Creek

Mary Jane Canyon

Adobe Mesa

Castle Valley

Negro Bill Canyon

Beaver Creek

Moab

N. Fork Mill Creek

Mill Creek

143

Mt. Woos
12,331 ft.

033 Mann's Peak
12,270 ft.

101

Spanish Valley

142 12,780 ft.

12,721 ft.

12,483 ft.

191

041 029 South Mtn.
11,798 ft.

028 035 100

Utah

46

La Sal Junction

46

La Sal

To Naturia, Colorado

To Monticello

UTAH

COLORADO

Clear streams flow from highlands, cutting canyons in a radiating labyrinth around the mountain core. The topography is further complicated by collapsed salt domes that create eight valley swales emanating like rays from the shining mountain peaks. The uplift and then fractured collapse of these former domes, followed by extensive erosion, have left a mystical landscape of towers, flying buttresses, and fins, as well as countless arches and bridges, interspersed with sharp canyons.

Deer, elk, cougar, and black bear wander the La Sal complex, using the lower BLM lands for crucial winter range. Golden eagles ride the thermals off cliff faces and above canyons, watching for pikas, chipmunks, and other rodents below. Brown, brook, and perhaps even native cutthroat trout hide in the higher streams of the national forest.

The various sections of BLM land have distinct characteristics, but as a group they contribute to the balance of the La Sal wilderness complex. Left unprotected, their canyons, ridges, mountains, and mesas are jeopardized by roading, logging, and mining, which would forever destroy this valuable habitat.

Beaver Creek, flowing to the Dolores River on the northeast, and Negro Bill and Mill creeks on the west flank of the La Sals, are perennial streams, with waterfalls, swimming holes, and natural bridges. Hiking, hunting, and fishing opportunities are infinite for human visitors in these wild canyons; the wild residents also appreciate the riparian habitat. Mary Jane Canyon and Fisher Towers to the north attract climbers with awesome monoliths rising dramatically. The Titan, one of the most famous, soars 900 feet. Sewemup Mesa on the east continues on into Colorado. Wingate sandstone cliffs tower above the Dolores River Gorge, providing nesting sites for both golden and bald eagles.

Areas of old-growth ponderosa pine are hidden in the inaccessible reaches of the La Sal Wilderness. Pinyon-juniper forests blanket the mesas and slopes between huge expanses of barren sculptured slickrock. Riparian vegetation lies along the creek corridors; here, too, intermittent beaver ponds create important wetland habitat.

Numerous archeological sites from Archaic and Fremont cultures include dwelling sites and rock art. This area has not been systematically inventoried; hikers can make their own discoveries, taking care to leave all artifacts in place. Traces of Euro-American presence are also likely to be seen. The cowboy era, and the rustlers that went with it, are indicated by the stray wooden fencepost that seems out of place so far from any ranch. The remote mountain valleys made perfect hideouts for rustlers and others avoiding the law. The La Sals were the focus of a short-lived gold rush 90 years ago. Mining claims, cabins, and rusty hardware are all that was left by the grizzled prospectors.

Speaking of grizzled denizens of the Colorado Plateau, this area should be the Edward Abbey Wilderness. Abbey's *Desert Solitaire* contains innumerable passages indicating the spiritual value of the towering La Sals and their surrounding ramparts of canyons and fins. This desert warrior's writing has done more than any other to gain supporters for wilderness in the eastern Colorado Plateau.

RECREATIONAL USES: Close to Moab, the La Sal canyons have been the site of favorite canyoneering excursions for many visitors. Fisher Towers are a magnet for hikers, photographers, and climbers (see hike idea below). Reliable water makes Mill Creek a popular hiking route. Negro Bill, between Mill Creek on the south and Arches National Park across the Colorado River to the north, cuts a spectacular sandstone canyon that attracts hikers and campers from Moab with a perennial stream and cottonwood groves. Plus, 243-foot Morning Glory Natural Bridge across Negro Bill is the fifth-largest natural bridge in the United States.

From the maze of trails in the national forest to the unlimited hiking ways in the BLM lands, your trips are limited only by your time, energy, and water supply. From the wandering roads of the national forest, hikers can cross the benchland and explore the heads of the La Sal's canyons. Outings from the mouths of the several canyons near Moab are popular. Mill Creek and Negro Bill feature perennial streams, making them choice destinations even in summer months. Both Fisher Towers and Mary Jane (see below) were omitted by the BLM's wilderness process, but the Utah Wilderness Coalition supports their inclusion in the La Sal Wilderness.

The higher lands of the national forest are magnets for summer outings and are also popular with fall hunters. The roadless regions are centered on the higher lands around the peaks, so hiking trips here are more rugged. The Manti–La Sal Forest map provides information on trails and road access. The forest map is also essential in locating the trailhead for exploring the canyons northeast of the mountains, flowing down to the Dolores River. Beaver Creek and Cottonwood Creek both have exciting canyons for multi-day backpacks. There is enormous variety in this section of eastern Utah wilderness.

HOW TO GET THERE: Fisher Towers: Go north 23 miles from Moab on Utah Highway 128. At milepost 21 (21 miles north of the Utah Highway 191/128 junction), turn east at the BLM Fisher Tower sign. Go 3 miles on the improved dirt, two-wheel-drive, low-clearance road to the dead end at the trailhead. There is a small BLM campsite and picnic area at the trailhead. The hike begins at the information bulletin board and trail register.

Mary Jane Canyon: From UT 128, 20 miles north of Moab, turn east on Professor Creek Road, an improved dirt, two-wheel-drive, low-clearance road. The road is just before a sign reading "Onion Creek 2" at milepost 18. Immediately after turning onto Professor Creek Road there is a small homemade sign on the right that reads "Ranch Road Dead End." Drive east 2 miles, past the

Professor Valley Ranch gate on your left and a cement fenced irrigation diversion tank on your right. Park on the flat area just beyond the irrigation apparatus. The hike begins at Professor Creek, which is the second creek at the confluence below the parking area, heading southeast. The first creekbed, usually dry, leads south toward the Priest and Nuns rock formation.

Day hike

Fisher Towers

Distance: 4.4 miles round trip to overlook; additional mileage for exploration.
Starting and maximum elevations: 4,720 feet to 5,390 feet at overlook.
Difficulty: Moderate.
Best months: March through May; September through October.
Topo map: Fisher Towers-UT.

Before taking off at the parking area trailhead, pause to read up on the geologic background of these incredible towers, which you've probably seen in countless movies, videos, and ads. The well-marked and cairned trail is skillfully engineered, following the natural contours of the canyonland. It winds across the mesa south of the parking area, rises above one of the cleft canyons that shoot down from the towers, and hugs the sheer walls of the towers themselves. The destination, at 2.2 miles, is a lofty ridge with a magnificent view of the towers, Onion Creek Canyon, the La Sal Mountains, the Priest and Nuns formation, the winding Colorado River canyon, and the cliffed backside of Arches National Park.

Be sure to carry plenty of film. This short hike rates a 10 on the "wow" scale. The colors of the countryside are vibrant. The bright red mountains, towers, and slot canyons contrast sharply with the bright green of the juniper and Mormon tea, especially in the spring. Soaring above, the towers stand like medieval flying buttresses, extending from the mountain wall. Their dimensions are deceptive, for you will discover they are surprisingly skinny as you curve around and catch their profile. Titan Tower, the fourth one in the row, is the largest at 900 feet in height. On the USGS topo map, this name is given to another, smaller pinnacle in a canyon beyond the formation, but the BLM information confirms that this missile of stone is the true Titan. A favored site for courageous rock climbers, the towers usually echo with their calls; several permanent cables and fixed pieces of climbing hardware can be spotted with binoculars.

The canyons below the towers are a wonderland in their own right. Fanciful shapes of eroded red rock—spires, bridges, balanced rocks, pirouetting pinnacles—decorate each of the unnamed canyons that cut down to Onion Creek, dropping 500 feet in a little over a mile. Massive Fisher Mesa rises to

6,900 feet to the south, its 2,000-foot cliff face dwarfing the intricate valley canyons.

This short hike often takes a long time due to the many pauses you may make to enjoy the scenery. The details of the tower walls are enchanting. This is a gothic cathedral setting. Vertically fractured columns of harder rock are topped with softer stone, intricately eroded into fanciful gargoyles and chess pieces. It is reported that Fisher is a misnomer for the original Fissure Towers label. That such an area of geologic wonder has been omitted from wilderness study area designation is puzzling.

At trail's end the view of the towers 0.5 mile away is breathtaking. Large ravens swoop to their nests tucked into an alcove high on the tower wall. The peaceful Colorado River winds through its floodplain, with its mesas and pinnacles stretching into the distance. The hike back to the parking area provides an entirely new perspective on the towering landscape. For more adventuresome hikers, it is possible to continue to explore. Several unofficial trails peel off the main trail between the Titan and the overlook, heading northeast among the spires and pinnacles on the shelves above the diving canyons. Regretfully, at some point you will have to wind back to the trail and return to the trailhead.

Day hike

Mary Jane Canyon

Distance: 5 miles round trip to gorge; 10 to 12 miles for exploring.
Starting and maximum elevations: 4,320 feet and 5,041 feet (lookout).
Difficulty: Moderate.
Best months: March through April; September through October.
Topo map: Fisher Towers-UT.

This hike shares some common denominators with the Fisher Towers excursion: it too is close to Moab, and they're on the same topo map. But this trip into labyrinthine Mary Jane Canyon is very different because it is more typical of the La Sal Canyons complex. Here miles of eroded red rock canyons swirl and dive below the 7,000- to 7,500-foot mesas extending from the laccolith core of the La Sal Mountains. As with popular Negro Bill Canyon to the south, Mary Jane has a perennial stream flowing between deep red canyon walls, attracting hikers even during the hotter months.

The canyon commences high on the slopes of Adobe Mesa in a dense fir and spruce forest. Calculating the canyon miles in its tortuous course is nearly impossible, but it's safe to say that it is more than 10 miles long. The gorge is blocked by boulders, so it would be a wandering rim ramble to reach the headwaters. Exploring the lower reaches of Mary Jane is a more realistic goal.

The small stream in Mary Jane Canyon.

From the trailhead take a look over the bank at the flow in Professor Creek to get an idea of the appropriate footwear for your hike. With average flow you can hop across the stream. The winding stream course features dozens of crossings per mile. Numerous boulders and a gravel bottom make stream leaping pretty easy. Use a stout staff to vault across the water; bring your own because there are no tree limbs in the area. Many hikers choose to wear waders, especially in hot weather, and cruise up the canyon bottom with ease.

Follow Professor Creek up the middle of the valley. A clear hiking path along the creek cuts across the bends and repeatedly crosses the stream. There are numerous campsites in the first 2 miles of the hike. With the noisy stream these are delightful spots for desert camping, unless you are sensitive to the alkaline water that runs here. At about 2.5 miles the canyon narrows and deepens. The bright red walls make a side exit impossible. This is not a hike to take when flash flooding is possible. A major boulder blockage bars further travel in the gorge. This is the turn around for the short hike.

For a longer trip drop back out of the narrows and climb to the high bench to the south of the creek. A knob south of Mary Jane just before Hellroaring Canyon, labelled 5,041 feet on the topo map, is an excellent spot from which to survey the entire valley and surrounding canyons. Mid-valley knobs and ridges are numerous; only by getting above the canyon can you appreciate the intricate landscape you are penetrating. The bright red sandstone world stretches for miles, dotted with the vibrant green of pinyon, juniper, Mormon tea, and blackbrush. At the edges rise the sharp escarpments of Fisher Mesa to the northwest and Adobe Mesa to the southwest. The Priest and Nuns stand as high as the nearby mesa but seem much taller in their isolated setting on their sandstone pedestal. Beyond, to the southeast, rise the dominating La Sals, often snow covered, always stunning in their alpine beauty. The entire valley is cut with canyons. Off every indentation on the mesa cliff faces, another canyon slices its twisting way down to join Professor Creek. Most of these side canyons have only seasonal moisture. Mary Jane, with its constant stream, has eroded far below its tributaries, creating sheer 20- to 30-foot pouroffs at each stream's junction with the main canyon.

Located right in busy Moab's backyard, Mary Jane Canyon is an intricate wildland. The stream is too alkaline to drink, even when treated, but its rocky bed and clear water make it an enjoyable companion for a desert hike. You're far from the crowds as soon as you begin your outing in the Mary Jane unit.

Arches–Lost Spring Canyon Complex 32

Location: 3 miles north of Moab, in east-central Utah.
Size: 80,490 acres.
Administration: NPS (Arches National Park); BLM Moab District, Grand
Resource Area.
Management status: National park roadless land (63,590 acres, which includes
some state inholdings); BLM wilderness study area (3,880 acres); unprotected BLM
and state roadless lands (13,020 acres).
Ecosystems: Colorado Plateau province ecoregion, with potential natural
vegetation of pinyon-juniper woodland.
Elevation range: 3,960 feet (along Colorado River) to 5,653 feet (Elephant Butte
in Arches National Park).
Established trails/routes: 15 short interpretive, loop, and primitive trails totaling
15 miles within the park; most backcountry routes are off-trail; there are a few
miles of primitive jeep tracks within the BLM Lost Spring Canyon roadless area
suitable for nonmotorized travel.
Maximum core to perimeter distance: 2.5 miles.
Activities: Hiking, backpacking, horseback riding, rock climbing, photography,
nature study, spelunking (limited).
Maps: BLM 1:100,000 scale surface management/land ownership map entitled
"Moab" (50 meter contour interval). See Appendix E for a listing of the eight topo
maps covering the complex.

OVERVIEW: The 73,379-acre Arches National Park lives up to its name. Of its
more than 1,200 natural sandstone openings, more than 50 are major arches.
Superlatives abound. The park encompasses the largest concentration of arches
in the world. Landscape Arch in Devils Garden is one of the planet's longest
arches. Delicate Arch is internationally recognized as a major free-standing
arch eroded from what was once a complete fin.

The geologic history of today's arches began some 300 million years ago
when a salt deposit thousands of feet thick was left in Paradox Basin following evaporation of an inland sea. Over time wind-borne sediments covered the
salt, which later hardened into the predominant Entrada sandstone found here.
Uneven pressures forced the salt upward, bending the sediment layer in various places. These uplifts, or anticlines, later gave way when ground water dis-

32 ARCHES-LOST SPRING CANYON COMPLEX

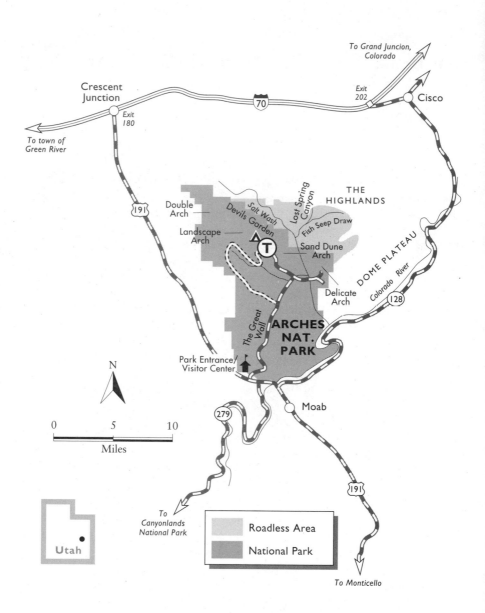

solved the supporting layer of salt. Faults and joints created by these repeated ups and downs were then eroded into hundreds of free-standing parallel fins. The long process of arch formation began once these sandstone fins were exposed to weathering. In some cases freezing and thawing peeled away layers of softer rock until holes formed in some of the fins. Gravity caused rocks to fall from weakened fractures within the holes, gradually enlarging them into the arches we see today. The wonderland of fins, arches, spires, and balanced rocks is thus the product of millions of years of complex geologic sculpturing.

The bare rock that distinguishes most of this high desert plateau country is interspersed with a sparse cover of evenly spaced blackbrush and other desert shrubs, grasses, and occasional clumps of stunted pinyon pine and juniper at higher elevations. Dark microbiotic crusts in the soil support fragile, specially adapted plant communities of bacteria, algae, fungi, and mosses. Springs and canyon wall seeps are decorated with intricate hanging gardens of columbine, maidenhair fern, orchids, and monkeyflowers.

Mule deer, coyotes, gray foxes, porcupines, and bobcats make a living here, relying for the most part on the sanctuary of pinyon-juniper woodland. However, you'll likely see only the tracks of these mostly nocturnal denizens. During the hot summer many deer migrate to higher, cooler ground on the Dome Plateau. During the day a variety of lizards common to the Colorado Plateau are seen darting across the slickrock. Other reptilian residents include the midget faded rattlesnake. With an eye to the sky be on the lookout for golden eagles, red-tailed hawks, ravens, canyon wrens, and great-horned owls.

More than one hundred archeological sites have been recorded in the complex, most of which are in the park, where cultural surveys have been more intensive. Most common are lithic scatters of flint artifacts. Among the numerous Indian pictographs and petroglyphs found within the park is an important rock art panel in Courthouse Wash. European influence dates back to the 1776 Dominguez–Escalante Expedition, followed by the Old Spanish Trail, which traversed Moab Canyon. Then came the French fur trappers during an overlapping period from 1810 to 1840. In 1844 one of the trappers, Denis Julien, left his inscription in what is now the park. The Wolfe Ranch, located at the start of the Delicate Arch trail, is a well-preserved remnant of late nineteenth-century ranching on the Colorado Plateau. Other historic old cabins and ranch ruins are located in and near Lost Spring Canyon just outside the park boundary.

RECREATIONAL USES: Despite being narrow, heavily visited, and bisected by a busy paved road, Arches National Park offers varied choices for quality day and overnight backcountry excursions, suitable for all experience levels. But even the most seasoned wilderness wanderers should begin their exploration by taking a guided ranger-led walk. This is an enjoyable source of valuable information, such as how to minimize impact by not walking on fragile, cryptobiotic crust. The park is open year-round, with the hot, dry summer being the least comfortable hiking season.

Anyone embarking on the popular 2-mile trailless loop through the towering fins and labyrinth of the Fiery Furnace must either be on a ranger-led hike or have a permit. Permits can be obtained by attending an orientation at the visitor center.

Another idea for a day hike is to take the 1.5-mile trail to Delicate Arch from the Wolfe Ranch parking area, crossing a swinging bridge over Salt Wash. To the northwest, Devils Garden is the trailhead for the longest maintained trail in the park—1 mile to Landscape Arch and another mile to Double O Arch. A 2.2-mile primitive trail suitable for experienced hikers winds through Fin Canyon for a 5.2-mile trail hiking loop. To prevent resource damage visitors must stay on designated trails in the vicinity of Landscape Arch.

Those camping overnight in the backcountry must obtain a backcountry permit at the visitor center. Permits will not be issued within one hour before sunset for the current date, so get there early. There are no formal backcountry trails or campsites in the park, so it is all the more important to strictly practice a no-trace camping ethic. Backcountry camps must be located at least 1 mile from and out of sight of any designated road, a minimum of 0.5 mile from and out of sight of designated trails, and out of view of any arch named on the USGS topo map. Also, to protect limited watering holes for wildlife, campsites

An old slickrock ranch corral just inside the Lost Spring Canyon Wilderness Study Area.

must be at least 300 feet from water sources, except along the Colorado River, where the required setback from water is 100 feet. These limits effectively close the interior of the park to camping, leaving open some backcountry in the southwest, southeast, and northeastern sections. Klondike Bluffs, Salt Valley, and Fiery Furnace are limited to day use throughout the year for visual and wildlife reasons. With all this in mind, be sure to stop at the visitor center for a copy of the informative leaflet on backpacking.

Some horseback riding takes place on several of the short trails in the park, mostly for guided horse trips. The park has a backcountry party size limit of 12 people and a maximum of 15 head of riding and pack animals per group. Stock parties are limited to one night at any one campsite.

Arches is surrounded by world class mountain bike opportunities, but within the park mountain bikes are allowed only on roads designated for vehicles. The fat tires are not permitted on any designated trails or off-trail in the park.

Technical rock climbers can find climbs suitable for all skill levels. Only two sites, the Bubo and Industrial Disease rock climbs, are closed to climbing between January 1 and June 30 each year to safeguard critical wildlife habitat.

Access into the adjacent BLM Lost Spring Canyon Wilderness Study Area/roadless area is available from Interstate 70 on the north, but the maze of roads in the Yellow Cat Mining District confuses directions and route finding. These highlands form the scenic backdrop for visitors at the high-use Devils Garden recreation facility. The best access to Lost Spring Canyon is from within the park, either from the vicinity of Devils Garden or by way of the Wolfe Ranch by heading north up Salt Wash from the Delicate Arch trailhead.

HOW TO GET THERE: From the visitor center in Arches National Park drive north on the main park road 16 miles to the signed Sand Dune Arch–Broken Arch trailhead and parking pullout on the right (east) side of the road.

Day hike

Lost Spring Canyon Loop

Distance: 12 miles.
Starting and minimum elevations: 5,300 feet and 4,480 feet.
Difficulty: Moderate.
Best months: February through April; October through November.
Topo map: Mollie Hogans-UT.

Arches National Park contains the greatest density of natural arches in the world. Understandably, this sculptured rock majesty also attracts a comparable density of visitors. A long day hike to Lost Spring Canyon within its namesake BLM wilderness study area allows visitors to savor the best of both worlds: the geologic splendor of the park and the solitude of its adjacent but lesser known backcountry. The wilderness study area borders Arches on the east, blending spacious open desert with the intimacy of hidden canyons.

Take the Sand Dune Arch trail north from the parking area. The trail junction to Broken Arch is quickly reached. Continue left another 0.1 mile to a buried gas pipeline, which is visible only as a faint doubletrack well suited for hiking. Turn right and head northeast along the pipeline route *cum* hiking trail. At first, Broken Arch is visible on the left. The sandy red path gradually descends through rolling pinyon-juniper woodlands. After 0.5 mile the trail opens to a broad vista of the Lost Spring Canyon country and The Highlands beyond. At 2 miles the trail crosses the shallow head of Clover Canyon, which has water in the early spring. Walk 0.1 mile to your right across white sandstone, to the abrupt lip of Clover Canyon. Sheer overhanging cliffs tower above a dense riparian community of cottonwood, willow, and tamarisk. The only way into this impassable box canyon is by hiking up from its mouth.

Continue on the pipeline trail, passing the park boundary at 2.7 miles, and then dropping down a deeply eroded track to the broad sagebrush bottom of Salt Wash at 3 miles. The stream is deep and muddy in early spring, but a giant cottonwood log provides a dry crossing. The route continues northeast across the wash to the top of the opposite rim, past a pump house, and across a flat mesa in The Highlands. After a long hot mile the main jeep track veers right from the buried pipeline corridor. Stay right on this route for 0.5 mile to the next junction, making another right after passing a mound of white rocks. Follow a primitive doubletrack as it drops into Lost Spring, which has a water trough and old corrals near the wilderness study area/vehicle closure sign.

Hike down the upper canyon wash, passing the mouth of Fish Seep Draw after about 0.3 mile. The left (east) side of the canyon is bound by sheer 300-foot Entrada sandstone walls and formations. Soon the valley widens with cow trails twisting through brushy bottoms. Red knobs and buttes border intimate little enclosures, enticing exploration. Fins resembling sharks' teeth punctuate the east rim above the open valley. Arches are slowing forming from rounded fins and alcoves. Two miles below Fish Seep Wash a large drainage enters from the left, pocketed with alcoves and bound by spires and knobs. A huge fin with a nearly formed arch juts out from the opposite rim. A 2-mile, out-and-back side trip is possible here.

A twin rock goblin on the right marks where well-worn cow paths angle to the right across the wide sagebrush flat to Salt Wash. Heading north (to the right) back up Salt Wash, walk along one of these paths at the base of the east-side cliff wall to avoid thick cryptobiotic crust. In a few places the rounded mounds of slickrock bordering Salt Wash can be climbed. After another 1.5 miles the buried pipeline is met, thereby completing the 6-mile Lost Spring Canyon–Salt Wash loop part of this lollypop-shaped route. Turn left and retrace the 3 miles back to the trailhead. If time and energy allow, visit both Sand Dune and Broken arches on short side trails near the trailhead.

This long day trip can be extended into an early season backpack by camping and treating the water at Lost Spring. This would allow time to explore Fish Seep Wash and other side canyons downstream. Pick up a backcountry permit at the visitor center and park at the nearby Devils Garden Campground. This would add about one mile round trip to the distance by hiking south on one of the arch trails to the buried pipeline.

Westwater Canyon Complex   33

Location: 50 miles east of Green River, along the east-central state line (Utah–Colorado border).
Size: 32,280 roadless acres in Utah; additional 72,440 acres on Utah–Colorado border and within Colorado under Colorado BLM administration.
Administration: BLM Moab District, Grand Resource Area; State of Utah.
Management status: BLM wilderness study area and unprotected BLM roadless land (31,160 acres); state roadless land (1,120 acres).
Ecosystems: Colorado Plateau province ecoregion, with pinyon-juniper woodland (potential natural vegetation), and saltbush and greasewood shrub.
Elevation range: 4,145 feet (Colorado River) to 6,496 feet (Coach Point).
Established trails/routes: No trails, but many miles of eroded jeep track on the ridges above the river.
Maximum core to perimeter distance: 2.5 miles.
Activities: River running, hiking, fishing, birdwatching, nature study, photography.
Maps: BLM 1:100,000 scale surface management/land ownership maps entitled "Westwater" and "Moab" (50 meter contour interval). See Appendix E for a list of the four topo maps covering the roadless area.

OVERVIEW: The mighty Colorado River enters Utah hundreds of miles below its headwaters in captive Lake Granby and the Rockies in Colorado. Just south of Interstate 70 at the state line, it follows a fairly gentle course. But almost immediately upon entering Utah it changes character and plunges into the immense canyon it has cut through the Uncompahgre Uplift of the Colorado Plateau. Here it begins dropping swiftly, an average 11 feet per mile. The river's powerful erosive force has cut through thousands of feet of the plateau's sedimentary layers, down to igneous bedrock. The dark gneisses in the deepest section of Westwater Canyon date from Precambrian times, 1.7 billion years ago. The contorted stripes of white quartz and dark granite that make up the gneiss give the canyon its nickname, Granite Canyon. This Precambrian baserock is visible again, many miles down the Colorado River, in the Grand Canyon.

Above the gneiss much younger sandstone sedimentary layers from Jurassic and Triassic periods (only 225 to 135 million years ago) show the fractures and folding of the gigantic Uncompahgre Uplift that formed the plateau. Early

33 WESTWATER CANYON COMPLEX

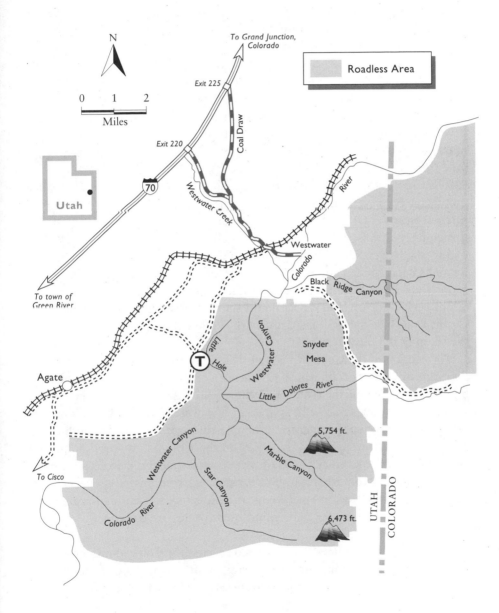

N

0 1 2
Miles

To Grand Junction,
Colorado

Exit 225

Roadless Area

Coal Draw

Exit 220

70

Utah

Westwater Creek

River

To town of
Green River

Westwater

Colorado

Black Ridge Canyon

Little Hole

Westwater Canyon

Snyder
Mesa

T

Little Dolores River

Agate

5,754 ft.

To Cisco

Westwater Canyon

Star Canyon

Marble Canyon

6,473 ft.

Colorado River

UTAH

COLORADO

explorers of the canyon called it Hades for the reddish walls. The campsite at river mile 120 retains this label.

Major side canyons—Little Dolores, Marble, and Star—enter Westwater Canyon from the south and the east. The power of the Colorado's flow has cut the main river's channel 100 to 200 feet below these side canyons, creating a gorge below stair-step cliffs to the rim. During heavy spring run-off the side canyons produce cascading falls to the river below.

The 13-mile river corridor is the focal point of the Westwater Wilderness Study Area. This dramatic stretch of whitewater has rapids rated class III to V, and has been proposed for wild river designation under the federal Wild and Scenic Rivers Act. It's not considered both wild and scenic because you can't drive along a road and enjoy the scenery from your vehicle. The federal designation would be an honor, but it does not protect the land farther than 0.25 mile from the river banks.

The Colorado's course forms the hypotenuse of the triangular Westwater unit. Some 80 percent of the roadless land lies southeast of the river. Access to this region is via Grand Junction and Glade Park in Colorado. Limited and difficult access has maintained the wild character of these sharp canyons, mesas, and ridges. These 30,000 untrammeled acres provide secluded habitat for mule deer, coyote, cougar, bobcat, and other small mammals. The Colorado Division of Wildlife has reintroduced bighorn sheep in the northern Wrigley Mesa region, and the herd now numbers three to four dozen animals. On the Utah side, the Utah Department of Wildlife Resources has reintroduced the sheep in the canyon as well.

The canyon of the Colorado is a hotbed of avian activity. Bald eagles and peregrine falcons enjoy hunting and soaring along the river. Golden eagles are reported to nest along the river's high cliffs; bald eagles that nest in the cottonwoods downstream can also be spotted in Westwater Canyon. Great blue herons likewise come up the river from their nesting areas just to the south of the wilderness study area. The canyon lies on the whooping cranes' migration route. In winter, migratory bands of waterfowl reside in the protected depths of Westwater Canyon. Mallards, blue-winged teal, mergansers, shovellers, and Canada geese will most likely have moved on before the rafting season commences in May. Common year-round bird species are canyon wrens, rock wrens, and killdeer.

The river itself harbors three protected species: the Colorado River squawfish, the humpback chub, and the bonytail chub. Carp, channel catfish, and bluegill are a few of the more common species a fisherman would find in these waters.

There is minimal riparian vegetation due to the river's narrow gorge. Elsewhere the semiarid uplands sport pinyon-juniper woodland, mixed with sagebrush, blackbrush, and short grasses.

Archeological investigations are incomplete in this area of the Colorado Plateau. There is evidence of use by Fremont peoples, consisting of rock art and small campsites. The inaccessibility of Westwater Canyon may have limited use by Paleo-Indians, but this same quality made the canyon a popular destination for outlaws in the early twentieth century. A cabin at river mile 124 as well as a cave at river mile 120 were havens for fugitives. A grave at 119.5 marks the final resting place for one of them.

RECREATIONAL USES: Westwater Canyon is one of the most challenging recreational areas on the entire Colorado. Since 1974 the BLM has operated a permit system to limit use, setting a cap of 14,000 visitor-days for the 150-day season from May to September. Contact the BLM office in Moab for information. A BLM ranger station just north of the wilderness study area at the put-in also assigns campsites, which are extremely limited and depend on the water level. Boaters put-in either at Westwater, or, for a longer float, at Loma, Colorado. The dozen rapids with catchy names like Funnel Falls, Sock-it-to-me Rapids, and Skull Rapid require skilled raftmanship or kayaking. This is not an outing for novices or the weak-hearted.

The unimproved dirt road along the unit's western boundary is part of Kokopelli's Trail, a popular route for mountain bikers. See *Mountain Biking Utah* (Falcon Publishing). Some hardy adventurers combine a bike ride with their boating, and pedal from Cisco back to Westwater for their shuttle.

Some of the boating parties explore the side canyons as they pause on the river's banks, but usually they pass on by, enjoying the excitement of the fast water. So even with thousands of people nearby, the Westwater canyons are quiet and lightly visited. It is possible to hike into the northwest edge of the roadless area, although there is some off-road-vehicle use that may detract from the wilderness experience. Westwater Wash at the canyon entrance and Little Hole Canyon (see below) and Big Hole Trail Canyon provide hiking routes to overviews of Westwater Canyon.

HOW TO GET THERE: The distance to the trailhead is 7 miles farther from the south (21 miles as opposed to 14 miles), but the road is much rougher from the north. High clearance is recommended for both routes; four-wheel drive is necessary for the northern route.

From the south: From Interstate 70 take Exit 202 and go south 3 miles on Utah Highway 128. Turn east on the old road and drive 3 miles to Cisco. Cisco, by the way, no longer exists as a town, so don't plan on stocking up on provisions here. From Moab go 40 miles north on UT 128, then turn east on the old Cisco road.

In the empty town turn right on the signed paved road to the Cisco Take-out. Go 3 miles to a Y intersection; turn left (north) with the sign to "Cisco Boat Launch." Another Y a mile further allows you to detour around an old bridge if you wish—the roads come together after the bridge so either way is fine. In one more mile you arrive at the takeout, with a BLM parking area and boat ramp. Just prior to the BLM facility, bear left on the improved dirt dry weather road. The dirt road just beyond the takeout is the wrong road, as the emphatic No Trespassing signs indicate. On the correct road, head north 3 miles. There you bear right at the ghost town of Agate, an old railroad town. The empty building foundations will be on your left. By now you will have noticed little brown BLM signs with arrows along the road marking the route of the Kokopelli bike trail. Continue another 3 miles beyond Agate to a Y intersection. Turn right, keeping south of the railroad tracks and traveling along the line of power poles. There is one wash to cross (shallow, with a firm gravel bottom) and one gate to open and then close after you pass through. About 4 miles beyond the Agate turn, turn right toward the Colorado River on an unimproved dirt doubletrack. You are leaving Kokopelli's Trail.

Just beyond this turn you will see on the left a rectangular block of cement, sitting alone on the sagebrush prairie. This is the remnant of a chimney, and around it is the foundation of the missing house. There's also a fenced exclosure a little bit further on the left, which verifies that you turned on the correct road. Continue east. There are no turns and no intersections, until at 2.5 miles you come to a T intersection, with the BLM wilderness study area marker straight ahead. This road is the western boundary of Westwater Wilderness Study Area. Turn right and go 0.5 mile to an old jeep track going left. Park east of the boundary road; this is the trailhead.

From the north: Take Exit 220 from I-70 and go south 5 miles on the paved road to Westwater. Dropping down to the Colorado River floodplain, the road makes a sharp left turn as it passes under the railroad bridge. Immediately after the bridge, turn right on an unimproved dirt, four-wheel-drive, high-clearance road, which is also the Kokopelli bike trail. Brown arrow markers appear intermittently along the route. Less than 20 feet after leaving the paved road, you encounter the first challenge: the wet crossing of Westwater Creek. The creek bottom is solid, but high water can make it impassable. Also, both banks are steep so a shorter wheel base is helpful. Drive south on the high-clearance rough road, parallel to the railroad tracks. One section of the track is abnormally rough where it crosses a section of railroad property south of the tracks. Here a hostile "No Trespassing" sign is designed to keep road traffic moving, so just pass on through. Two miles from the pavement bear left at the Y, departing from the railroad tracks and following the powerline and the brown Kokopelli arrows. Watch for an old bridge with a gaping hole; a well-used detour to the left avoids it. Continue 4 miles from the Y to turn left on an unimproved dirt road east to the Colorado River, leaving the powerline and the Kokopelli Trail. This is the only dirt road in the area. Continue by following the route starting at paragraph three of the directions from the south (above).

Day hike or backpack

Little Hole Canyon

Distance: 5 miles round trip.
Starting and minimum elevations: 4,711 feet and 4,280 feet (the Colorado River).
Difficulty: Easy.
Best months: March through April; September through October.
Topo map: Agate-UT.

Little Hole Canyon is a tiny pocket of exciting topography in a vast, high plateau prairie. Virtually invisible from the windswept plain above, the canyon descends to the Colorado River, with sheer cliffs, riparian greenery, and archeological reminders of ancient inhabitants. The world above, evident on either the north or south approach, in no way resembles the world in Little Hole Canyon.

From the trailhead on the wilderness study area boundary, follow the jeep track 0.5 mile down to the wash that leads to the head of the canyon. Off-road-vehicle operators have not heeded the tiny sign that forbids vehicles in the wilderness study area, so tire tracks are plentiful. Follow the wash down to the canyon rim, where you get an eagle's view of the Little Hole. From this overlook you can spot the trail down into the canyon. It's on your right, dropping

Nature has carved huge cave-like alcoves into the east wall of Little Hole Canyon.

down the canyon's west wall. You can also see the trail far below along the canyon's lower south slope. Circle around the slickrock of the canyon rim to pick up the trail to the bottom.

Little Hole is remote, a wild place with coyote, bobcat, and mountain lion in residence. Red-tailed hawks sail along the cliff walls. Huge concave rock shelters suggest that Fremont people found this a comfortable home. Several large alcoves sit high above the canyon floor on the cliff walls, facing south, with sweeping views of the approaches from the canyon and its mouth on the Colorado. The prehistoric inhabitants must have gained both physical and psychological comfort in these aeries. Watch for pictographs while exploring these sites.

The foot trail winds down to the sandy bank of the Colorado, avoiding the overgrown bottom of the canyon wash. A side canyon on the north invites exploration. Numerous footprints on the lower sections of the trail suggest that float parties use Little Hole as a leg-stretcher on the journey through Westwater Canyon, but they don't venture very far. Early spring, before river traffic gets busy, is an excellent season for this hike. During summer you are likely to encounter groups camped on the riverfront.

The mouth of the Little Hole at the Colorado is a spectacular display of geologic variety. Suddenly the sandstone of the canyon is interrupted by a granite intrusion that frames the canyon mouth and extends along the Colorado. The sinuous pastel sandstone contrasts with the angular fractures of the dark granite. From the Colorado's sandy beach a trail climbs to the top of the granite dike, providing an excellent vista of the Colorado, its stair-step cliffs, and the arches and obelisks along Westwater Canyon. Beyond the river, toward Colorado, is the more remote eastern region of this wilderness study area, inaccessible from Utah, except from the river, and seldom visited. You're looking at one of the wildest parts of the Colorado Plateau.

If it is not the busy floating season, the Colorado beach makes a perfect campsite for a backpack outing down the Little Hole. The remote Little Hole Canyon, far off the beaten track, possesses a quiet magic. A night under the stars here, with a small campfire of aromatic juniper, evokes the sense of eternity that wildlands embody.

Book Cliffs–Desolation Canyon Complex 34

Location: 33 miles east of Price and 5 miles north of Green River, in east-central Utah.
Size: 974,600 acres.
Administration: BLM Moab District, Price River and Grand resource areas (718,600 acres); Uintah and Ouray Indian Reservation (200,000 acres); State of Utah (55,000 acres).
Management status: BLM wilderness study areas (542,000 acres in seven units); unprotected BLM roadless land (176,600 acres); tribal roadless land (200,000 acres); state roadless land in Book Cliffs area (55,000 acres).
Ecosystems: Colorado Plateau province ecoregion with broad range of vegetation, from Douglas-fir forests in montane, to pinyon-juniper woodland (potential natural vegetation), saltbrush-greasewood shrub, and localized riparian zones.
Elevation range: 4,150 feet (Green River) to 9,510 feet (The Divide, East Tavaputs Plateau).
Established trails/routes: 100 miles of trails along Price and Green rivers; more than 160 miles of trail follow other drainages in Book Cliffs. Elsewhere, endless miles of informal trails, eroded jeep tracks, canyon bottoms, and ridgelines make suitable hiking routes.
Maximum core to perimeter distance: 5 miles (not including reservation lands); 15 miles (with reservation lands).
Activities: Hiking, backpacking, horseback riding, rafting and kayaking, rock climbing, canyoneering, photography, geology and wildlife study, fishing, hunting.
Maps: BLM 1:100,000 scale surface management/land ownership maps entitled "Price," "Seep Ridge," "Huntington," and "Westwater" (50 meter contour interval). See Appendix E for a listing of the 44 topo maps covering the roadless area.

OVERVIEW: The Book Cliffs are a 250-mile line of fluted, dissected cliffs that stretch from western Colorado to beyond the Green River in Utah. This massive rampart is the longest continuous escarpment in the world. The western end of the Book Cliffs, its last 50 miles, features even a second story—the Roan Cliffs—stair-stepping up to the Tavaputs Plateau. At the crest of the upper cliff walls the divide meets the southern extension of the Uintah and Ouray Indian Reservation; it also marks the parting of the waters, as the streams of the Tavaputs diverge from this ridgeline.

34 BOOK CLIFFS–
DESOLATION CANYON COMPLEX

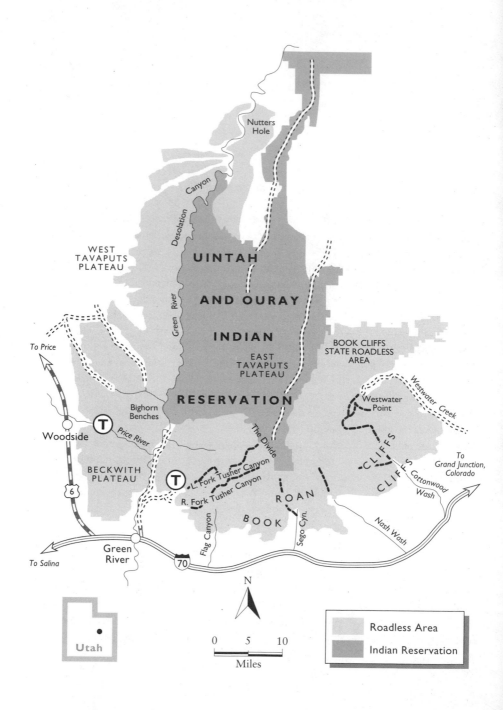

Nutters
Hole

Canyon

Desolation

WEST
TAVAPUTS
PLATEAU

Green River

UINTAH

AND OURAY

INDIAN

EAST
TAVAPUTS
PLATEAU

RESERVATION

BOOK CLIFFS
STATE ROADLESS
AREA

Westwater
Point

Westwater Creek

To Price

Bighorn
Benches

T
Woodside
Price River

The Divide

CLIFFS

To
Grand Junction,
Colorado

6

BECKWITH
PLATEAU

T
L. Fork Tusher Canyon

R. Fork Tusher Canyon

CLIFFS

S. Cottonwood
Wash

ROAN

BOOK

Sego Cyn.

Nash Wash

Flag Canyon

Green
River

70

To Salina

N

Utah

0   5   10
Miles

Roadless Area

Indian Reservation

The huge wild area of the Book Cliffs is well known—or at least frequently seen—by travelers on Interstate 70 just to the south. The other famous feature of the area is the Green River, which cut its canyon through the Tavaputs as the plateau gradually rose millions of years ago. From the south the cliffs display the edge of the plateau; from the Green River you get an 84-mile cross-section of the plateau's heart. The voyage down the Green is one of the most popular floats in the state.

The famous cliffs and the equally famous river represent two very different aspects of this wild area. The third wonderland, which river travelers and highway passers-by never see, is the Tavaputs Plateau above the cliffs. After the austere Roan Cliff, above the divide, a world of spruce, aspen, and fir replaces the sweeping barren rock face. On top, at 8,000-foot elevations, a slightly cooler and more moist climate supports montane vegetation. Grassy parks and riparian vegetation grow in the numerous valleys of gentle streams flowing north. This is the Hill Creek Extension of the Uintah and Ouray Indian Reservation. Hiking or hunting here requires a tribal permit. Traditionally a tribal hunting ground, the 300-square-mile East Tavaputs Plateau is being managed as a roadless area. Contiguous to tribal land on the east is a 55,000-acre unit of Utah State land. In recognition of the area's importance to wildlife, in 1975 the state closed these lands to development to protect habitat. Oil and gas and coal interests, however, continue to threaten the Book Cliffs region.

The plateau has been described as Utah's Serengeti. The expanse of forest and meadows supports a dwindling population of black bear. A herd of elk numbering over 400 lives here most of the year. Rocky Mountain bighorn sheep find the rocky crags of the plateau's rim comfortable habitat. One of the largest herds of mule deer in Utah, as well as antelope, coexists with a thriving cougar population. For obvious reasons, this is a favorite area for hunters who prefer to get off the road.

The intermediate cliff-zone of this three-tiered world is considerably more arid. Pinyon-juniper woodlands dot the less steep slopes and ledges between the vertical cliff walls. Some Douglas-fir manage to survive in the higher Roan Cliffs, along with scattered mountain shrubs. Grasses and sagebrush grow in the numerous drainages. The compound cliffs drop 4,500 feet in less than eight air miles. The upper Roan Cliffs are dry, but numerous springs dot the canyon heads of the lower Book Cliff canyons. The lower elevations and the protected canyons provide wintering areas for the ungulates of the plateau. On both sides of the Green River, the Book Cliffs provide habitat for mule deer, antelope, beaver, turkey, and both ruffed and blue grouse. There have even been sightings of the elusive and rare black-footed ferret.

While from a distance the cliff face appears monolithic, closer inspection on foot reveals its complicated and irregular topography. The sedimentary layers are a variety of hard and soft Cretaceous sandstones. The result is differential erosion, leaving shelves, tables, hoodoos, and giant steps.

Down below, in the canyon of the mighty Green River, the journey through these same strata provides a different geologic perspective. The uplift of the Tavaputs Plateau occurred after the Green had established its channel. So, similar to its journey through Split Mountain in Dinosaur National Monument 125 miles north of the Tavaputs canyon stretch, the persistent river ground a passage through the barrier that arose in its path, severing the plateau. The results are Desolation and Gray canyons, flanked by the East and West Tavaputs. The Powell expedition of 1869 labeled the austere barren river corridor Canyon of Desolation.

The river's meandering channel has cut amphitheaters in its wide-swinging tight curves. The sediments of the plateau, lain in place on the bottom of ancient Lake Uinta, are younger strata than the others of the Green or its companion the Colorado. The depth of Desolation Canyon, on the other hand, is on a par with the Grand Canyon. At Rock Creek the river-to-plateau height is greater than the Grand Canyon's at Bright Angel Trail. Reputed to be one of the best gorge floats in the nation, the 80-mile journey down the Green features 60 rapids for thrills, deep side canyons to explore, and spires, buttes, hoodoos, and arches to spark the imagination. The river's elevation at Sand Wash above Desolation is 4,615 feet; it drops 370 feet in the 60 miles through Desolation. In its descent through wider Gray Canyon, it falls another 145 feet in 24 miles by the Swasey's Rapid takeout.

The low riparian areas of cottonwood groves, willows, and tamarisk along the Green and its perennial tributaries form a corridor for migratory songbirds and waterfowl. Bald eagles winter along the canyon cliffs. During much of the year blue herons cruise the Green, while American avocets, with long legs and long bills, stalk their prey in the shallows. Flocks of cliff swallows jam their ball-shaped nests under cliff overhangs, creating an avian condominium. One wonders how they find the correct doorway to their own home.

The spring and summer insect hatch and the persistent summer mosquitoes provide a hearty diet for the bird population. Fish too thrive on the larvae. The Green is home for channel catfish and three endangered species: the bonytail chub, the humpback chub, and the Colorado squawfish. Rock Creek, flowing down from the West Tavaputs Plateau at river mile 54, has both rainbow and non-native brown trout in its clear waters. Gnawed willows are sign of the presence of beavers, which have returned after being trapped to the edge of oblivion in the mid-nineteenth century. Along the river the venomous midget faded rattlesnake is common but seldom seen. The striped whip snake, swift and harmless, is too shy to linger around human visitors. Look for tracks of black bear, mule deer, and cougar along the muddy riverbank. Florence Creek,

Hidden discoveries include Fremont petroglyphs high above the Price River.

Rock Creek, and Coal Creek, among others, provide corridors to the river bottom for these plateau residents.

The features that draw visitors to the Book Cliff wilderness today attracted early man also: water and wildlife. From Paleo-Indians through the Utes, people established semi-nomadic hunting camps both on the Green and its tributaries and on the Tavaputs Plateau. Traces can be found of their rock shelters, campsites, lithic scatters, middens, and burial sites. About one thousand years ago the Fremont people engaged in small-scale agriculture in wider valleys of the river bottoms. Hikers may discover stone ruins, projectile points, pottery fragments, and petroglyphs, all of which should remained untouched.

Leading the Euro-American tidal wave, the early explorer and hunter Denis Julien left his initials on the Green's canyon walls in the 1830s. During the same decade, beaver trappers were working all the streams of the mountainous west to harvest pelts for European hats. Fortunately haberdashery styles changed just before the beavers' extinction. In 1869 the Powell expedition made its way down the Green, suffering numerous crashes and close-calls on its rocks and rapids. His highly publicized reports on his journeys were intended to show this arid country was valuable only for its botanical and geologic wonders, that it should be set aside as a national preserve since it was basically uninhabitable for an agrarian nation. Ironically his writings and photographs only sparked interest, and he spearheaded the influx of visitors over the next century.

Oblivious to Powell's warnings about this American desert, ranchers followed. By the 1890s the McPhersons were established on Florence Creek. The Butch Cassidy gang passed by their place, often trading for fresh mounts in order to outrun the posse behind them. In the 1940s the ranch was sold to be added to the reservation.

Another turn-of-the-century ranch was on Rock Creek. Here the Seamonton family's corrals and sheds are gradually disappearing, although the fruit trees still stand where the family orchard grew. Grazing allotments exist on the BLM lands of the Book Cliffs–Desolation Canyon wilderness, but none exist in the lower Green River corridor to prevent riparian damage. Rogue cattle—or even remnants of former herds—sometimes find their way down to the Green's bottoms. North of Rain Canyon the allotments do run to the river's edge.

The river, the cliffs, and the plateau form a rare ecological unit. The streams, canyons, and washes provide essential links from plateau to river bottoms. The diverse habitat is an ideal environment for wildlife, which can meet its seasonal needs within this one enormous roadless wilderness.

RECREATIONAL USES: Desolation Canyon, designated a National Historic Landmark in 1969, is a magnet for thousands of visitors annually. The trip from Sand Wash to Swasey's Rapid north of the town of Green River is an 84-

mile, five- to seven-day float through Desolation and Gray canyons. Suitable for rafts and kayaks, the trip's rapids are rated class III. Several outfitting companies operate floats down the Green. A BLM lottery system to limit river use controls permits and launch schedules. Planning even years ahead is necessary. The meandering river bottom has about 50 campsites. Within the canyon, the Utes operate the Florence Creek Lodge on tribal land where the McPherson ranch once stood.

The second most popular use of the Book Cliffs wilderness is by hunters. The miles of pack trails on the southern and eastern edges of the roadless cliff area are used for their fall trips.

Hikers too can explore the wild regions of the Book Cliffs. The south-facing cliffs are hot and dry in the summer, but with adequate water in your pack you can explore several canyons. Both Tusher canyons provide access to the higher reaches of the cliffs. The right fork of Tusher Canyon goes up to the basin below the divide. The left fork can become a loop trip over into Rattlesnake Canyon. On the eastern rampart, Nash, Cottonwood, and Diamond canyons have trails to their headlands high in the Book Cliffs. The forbidding cliffs entice intrepid explorers.

Hiking on top of the plateau east of the Green River requires a permit from the tribal offices in Duchesne. Inquire at the BLM office in Price for further regulations before commencing your adventure.

HOW TO GET THERE: Price River–Water Canyon: Take U.S. Highway 191/6, driving either 22 miles north of Exit 156 on Interstate 70, or 36 miles south of Price. Turn east at Woodside onto a graded dirt road. This road is 0.1 mile north of the highway bridge over the Price River at milepost 279. The improved dirt road has a few low spots that could be muddy in rainy weather; in the first 0.25 mile the first one occurs when the road dips down to cross a wash that is impassable when wet. The road continues to wind along the Price into the Book Cliffs canyon. At 5 miles you may decide to park in one of the flat areas because the road can be muddy; at 6 miles rock falls have nearly erased the road. There are several cottonwood flats for camping and parking before you reach these challenging sections. The dicey off-road-vehicle track continues until mile 7 at the mouth of Trail Canyon where the BLM wilderness study area signs are, but most vehicles would not go that far.

Left Fork Tusher Canyon: From Main Street in Green River, take Hastings Road, the first street east of the river, north 5 miles. Just as the pavement ends, a green sign directs you to bear right to Swasey's Rapid, Nefertiti Rock, and The Beach. Take this improved dirt road. The BLM campground at Swasey's Rapid is 5 miles north on this two-wheel-drive, low-clearance road. The Tusher Canyon turnoff, on the other hand, occurs almost immediately, 0.3 mile after the road begins, bearing right after the cattleguard. Disregard the first dirt road to the right; it deadends in a gravel pit. Follow the second improved dirt road across the mesa and down into Tusher Wash. For 6 miles it winds up dramatic Tusher Canyon. Spots can be sticky when wet; it also drops to cross side washes that could be impassable in flash floods. The narrow wash-road in Tusher Canyon is also hazardous for flash flooding, so use caution in planning your trip. At the Y, 6 miles from the pavement, bear left and continue up the Left Fork of Tusher Canyon for 2 miles, or sooner if your vehicle and conditions suggest stopping. Begin your hike from there.

Day hike

Price River–Water Canyon

Distance: 12 miles round trip from two-wheel-drive, high-clearance parking; 10 miles round trip from dry weather, four-wheel-drive, high-clearance parking.
Starting and minimum elevations: 4,500 feet and 4,360 feet.
Difficulty: Moderate.
Best months: March through May; September through October.
Topo map: Jenny Canyon-UT.

The topo map for this hike may be alarming. It indicates a pack trail winding back and forth across the Price. During high spring run-off, the best season for this hike, crossing the Price would be impossible. Luckily a footpath stays along the northern bank of the Price. In early spring the southern exposure assures you a relatively snow-free trail, while the south side of the river remains in winter's icy grasp.

After hiking down the rock-strewn old road you arrive at the intersection with Trail Canyon. The BLM sign forbidding motorized use has been blatantly ignored in this side canyon, while the terrain along the Price has successfully kept it protected from vehicles. Here the winding pathway, running high and low along the bank, travels through intermittent riverside meadows of sage flats, old gnarled willows, and tamarisk groves. Many suitable campsites exist along the river; most have plenty of downed firewood courtesy of long-gone beavers.

The constantly winding Price with its hairpin bends provides new vistas at each bend. The striped cliffs of red, orange, beige, and black rise in their horizontal layers 1,000 to 1,500 feet, topped by pinnacles of limestone and junipers. In the spring, songs of canyon wrens echo from the cliffs. From microbiotic soil to mountain lions, the Price River area is home to both extremes of the biotic community. In addition to watching for signs and sightings of wildlife, vigilant hikers will also find both pictographs and petroglyphs. The feeling of immeasurable time is a product of the awesome geologic forces in evidence as well as the sense of ancient humans whose spirit remains.

The Price River Valley begins to narrow just below Water Canyon.

Three miles down the Price, Water Canyon appears on the left. Although the side trip into Water Canyon is shortened by a 50-foot pouroff at 0.5 mile, the stroll is well worth the surprise that lies at the end. Here you find the source of its name! At the mouth of Water Canyon are plenty of flat sandy tent sites; this would be an excellent overnight spot from which to explore further down the Price. The river trail beyond is less traveled, at times primitive, at times even obscure. When the water in the Price is low, a long three-day backpack could be done to the Green, and then, crossing the Price, on downstream to the trailhead north of the town of Green River. High run-off in the spring makes the Price a potential kayak run in its 20 miles down to the Green, and on down to the Swasey's Rapid takeout.

More likely, the out-and-back hike on the Price provides adventure enough. The huge amphitheaters cut by the Price allow you to catch glimpses of the Beckwith and Tavaputs plateaus that bracket the river. Watch for mountain sheep on these high meadows. The return hike to the trailhead is a different journey. We saw panels of rock art we had missed on our way in, as well as even more signs of mountain lions.

The hike on the Price samples only a tiny fraction of the Book Cliffs–Desolation Canyon Wilderness. It's just a teaser, encouraging further exploration.

Day hike

Left Fork Tusher Canyon

Distance: 6 miles round trip.
Starting and maximum elevations: 4,940 feet and 5,200 feet.
Difficulty: Easy.
Best months: March through May; September through October.
Topo map: Butler Canyon-UT.

Evidence of off-road-vehicle use here in Tusher Canyon impacts the wilderness experience of this outing. But the quality of the vast country reduces the effect of the tire tracks underfoot. The BLM has taken no steps to limit vehicle use, not even indicating where the wilderness study area boundary should be. Nevertheless, the wildness of the region is overwhelming; silence and space dominate. Blackbrush, Mormon tea, and sage proliferate on sandy benches in the canyon's bends. While tamarisk groves dominate the lower wash, junipers become more common as you climb. High above pinyon pines peek over the ridge from the high plateau. In high snow years, spring melt sends a torrent down the canyon, erasing tracks in the gravelly wash; summer thunderstorms can do the same.

The gentle amble up the wash would be a suitable excursion for horseback. The wash remains firm, with only a few sandy spots.

Venturing deep into the solitude and wildness of the Book Cliffs provides a new perspective on the role of wildlands. The inaccessibility of the Book Cliffs for recreational users is not a suitable argument against its wilderness values. It is simply egocentric of humans to look at land as theirs to use. This remoteness, instead, embodies a biocentric value, for wildlife, for its pristine primitive qualities, for its eternal testimony to our transitory life on earth.

White River   35

Location: About 36 miles southeast of Vernal, in northeastern Utah.
Size: 10,600 acres.
Administration: BLM Vernal District, Book Cliffs Resource Area (9,700 acres);
State of Utah (900 acres).
Management status: BLM and state roadless lands.
Ecosystems: Colorado Plateau province ecoregion of sagebrush shrub and riparian
vegetation along the river.
Elevation range: 4,760 feet (White River) to 5,986 feet.
Established trails/routes: 4 miles of trail; 3 miles of eroded jeep track and the
river bottom are suitable for hiking.
Maximum core to perimeter distance: 1 mile.
Activities: Floating, fishing, birdwatching, hiking.
Maps: BLM 1:100,000 scale surface management/land ownership map entitled "Seep
Ridge" (50 meter contour interval). See Appendix E for the topo map covering the
roadless area.

OVERVIEW: The White River begins its journey in Colorado, 100 miles east of
Utah, in the White Mountain range of the Rockies. The White River wilderness unit lies near Bonanza, 10 miles from the Utah–Colorado border, on the
river's final section, where it zigs and zags southwest, then west, and then
northwest through the Uintah and Ouray Indian Reservation to join the Green
River three miles south of Ouray. A 40-mile stretch of the White is a popular
river float, suitable for canoes, rafts, and kayaks. The wilderness unit encompasses a 10-mile section by river miles (or 6 land miles) in the first half of the
float, from river mile 43 to mile 33.

The White River, unrelated to White Canyon country 160 miles to the
south, is a scenic gentle float, perfect for families or beginner canoeists. There
are a few rapids to make it interesting, but nothing too hazardous. The White
has cut a broad river channel 600 to 800 feet below ridges of sandstone. The
highest point in the roadless unit (5,986 feet) is 1.5 miles south of the river. Not
a gorge, the White River valley has plenty of sky showing and consequently
allows wildlife viewing from the river.

The wilderness unit is bracketed by the Southman Canyon and Rock House

35 WHITE RIVER

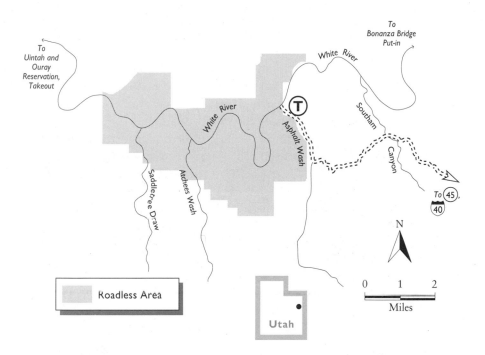

Gas Fields. Gas wells and drill holes lie at the end of rough jeep roads both north and south of the river, up on the ridges and out of sight. The Uintah Mountain Club, based in Vernal, has promoted designating the section of the White River as wilderness, in spite of the BLM's rejection of the roadless area in the wilderness study area process. This avid group of backcountry recreationists recognizes the special niche of the river's meandering valley for its botanic and wildlife diversity.

Small enough to fit on a single 7.5-minute topo map, the White River Wilderness is a green stripe through the beige world of the Colorado Plateau. Totally lacking woodlands, the White's high rolling ridges feature cactus and desert primrose. In the spring, wildflowers abound here as well as on the lower benchlands and parks closer to the river, where scrub juniper, sagebrush, and desert shrubs hold the thin soil against the powers of erosion. Along the river corridor itself, cottonwood groves, tamarisk, and willow provide stunning greenery in the spring and a display of orange and yellow in the fall.

Beaver and mule deer are plentiful. Migratory waterfowl can be found during the appropriate season. Both golden eagles and peregrine falcons swoop from the hillsides and cliffs. This piece of wildland may be obscure, small, and off the beaten track, but it holds immense importance to the species that call it home.

RECREATIONAL USES: This popular section of the White provides a gentle family route without the blood-curdling features of the Green or the Westwater stretch of the Colorado. In spite of its name, there is no whitewater. Parents of young children can bring the whole family and relax on a two- to three-day outing. The put-in is on the Bonanza–Duck Rock highway bridge. Takeout is at the only other bridge, which is on the Uintah and Ouray Indian Reservation. A tribal permit (and fee) is required to park at the bridge. If you want to float further down the White, you also need a tribal permit. The Ute Tribal Office is in Fort Duchesne (801-722-5511). A no-fee takeout at the Enron Oil and Gas Company gas well is at mile 24, about 3 miles above the bridge. Spring run-off is the prime season for the trip. This usually occurs from mid-May through June, about the same time the wildflowers are in bloom. The BLM does not require permits, but the BLM office in Vernal does have information and a helpful pamphlet about the trip, including a schematic river map.

Hikers can also enjoy this stretch of the river. Upstream access is via the gravel road in West Asphalt Canyon to the south side of the river. Other en-

A westward view of high rims, mesas, and rock formations above the secluded White River Canyon.

try points for hikers are at the ends of long gas exploration roads down Atchees Wash and West Saddletree Draw, both to the south. Just downriver from Atchees Wash, a popular campsite on the south bank marks the beginning of the trail to Goblin City, a geologic fantasyland that caught the attention of the 1871 Powell expedition. A two-hour hike up the ridge ends at an enchanting overlook of sandstone spires and pillars that resemble a town, especially in the late afternoon sun.

HOW TO GET THERE: From U.S. Highway 40, some 11 miles east of Jensen, turn south on the paved road to Bonanza. Drive south 17 miles to the junction with Utah Highway 45 and turn left. In 4 miles you will pass through Bonanza, though you may hardly notice it: it is only an industrial oil storage and shipping site, with no services. Continue 3 miles south of Bonanza on UT 45 and look for the BLM river access launch site, which is signed to the right before the road's descent to the White River bridge. For a hike in the roadless area, continue on UT 45. At the Y, 4 miles south of Bonanza, bear right. Here a BLM sign indicates that it is 4 miles to Southman Canyon and 10 miles to Asphalt Wash. Shortly after this right turn, an ominous sign announces that the highway will end at a barricade; a defunct shale oil plant is at the end of UT 45. A signed dirt road on the left leads to Southman Canyon and on to the right turn down Asphalt Wash, 8 miles from the pavement. Continue down Asphalt Wash 1.5 miles to end above the White River's southern bank. A gas well is at road's end.

Day hike

White River Hike

Distance: 8 miles round trip.
Starting and minimum elevations: 4,920 feet and 4,920 feet.
Difficulty: Easy.
Best months: April through May; September through October.
Topo map: Asphalt Wash-UT.

A hike along the White, after this drive, illustrates the value of this roadless area amid the roaded industrial gas fields of the Uinta Basin. The sandstone cliffs step back to form a broad canyon. Cottonwood groves cluster along the river corridor and junipers provide patches of dark green high on the ridges. Elsewhere expanses of barren sandstone outcroppings contribute their muted orange to this riparian palette. The shaley porous soil provides sufficient growth medium for sage and grasses.

Little has changed here while oil wells and gas lines have spread through the surrounding countryside. Traditional sheepmen (BLM permittees) still winter their flocks in the draws south of the river, as they have for decades. This is coyote habitat; both shepherd and his dogs keep a vigilant watch for these sheep fanciers. The sheep are moved back to higher pasture in Colorado in the spring before the black gnats hatch. The pesky gnats also mean spring is the season for a White River hike. The shaley soil becomes gooey, vehicle-encumbering mud in early spring; by late March the roads are usually passable.

From the trailhead, you can hike downstream along the river's huge hairpin meander. About 2 miles from the trailhead, at the southern bend of the meander, a short draw invites exploration. The cliffs are highest, to 5,634 feet, along the northern bank, whereas the south is rolling, with washes instead of canyons.

Along the White, you can hike for almost 10 miles. Floating parties often stop to stretch their legs here as well, but they are not so numerous as to disturb your solitude. Deep in the White River country wilderness still exists, a reminder of what this land was like hundreds of years ago.

Greater Dinosaur Complex 36

Location: 10 miles east of Vernal, on the northeastern edge of Utah on the Colorado border.

Size: 61,000 acres in Utah (total roadless area in Utah and Colorado 300,000 acres).

Administration: BLM Vernal District, Diamond Mountain Resource Area; NPS Dinosaur National Monument.

Management status: BLM wilderness study areas (Utah portion 14,346 acres) and unprotected roadless land (6,754 acres); NPS roadless land recommended as wilderness (186,114 acres total, about 40,000 of which are in the Utah portion of the monument).

Ecosystems: Rocky Mountain forest province ecoregion; potential natural vegetation is sagebrush steppe, with pinyon-juniper, mountain mahogany, and greasewood.

Elevation range: 4,750 feet (Green River) to 9,006 feet (Zenobia Peak on Douglas Mountain in Dinosaur National Monument).

Established trails/routes: 40 miles of trail; abandoned jeep tracks make excellent hiking routes in BLM lands.

Maximum core to perimeter distance: 2 miles.

Activities: Hiking, backpacking, horseback riding, river running, photography, geology study, paleontology and archeology study, hunting.

Maps: BLM 1:100,000 scale surface management/land ownership maps entitled "Dutch John" and "Vernal" (50 meter contour interval). See Appendix E for a listing of the seven topo maps covering the roadless area in Utah.

OVERVIEW: Gnarled pinyon and juniper, dwarfed by the wind, stand high on the 5,600-foot rim above the Green River where it enters Utah after its side trip to Colorado and the Gates of Lodore. These old trees have witnessed the passing centuries of migratory waterfowl, transient bands of Paleo-Indians, the Powell expedition of 1869, and countless boat-loads of thrill seekers who have braved Whirlpool Canyon. The Green settles in to a mellow float through Island Park and Rainbow Park. After this 7-mile interlude, excitement returns. The river dives through Split Mountain Canyon for an exciting run of the rapids, dropping at the rate of 20 feet per mile. After this screaming 7-mile ride, the Green returns to its mellow behavior.

36 GREATER DINOSAUR COMPLEX

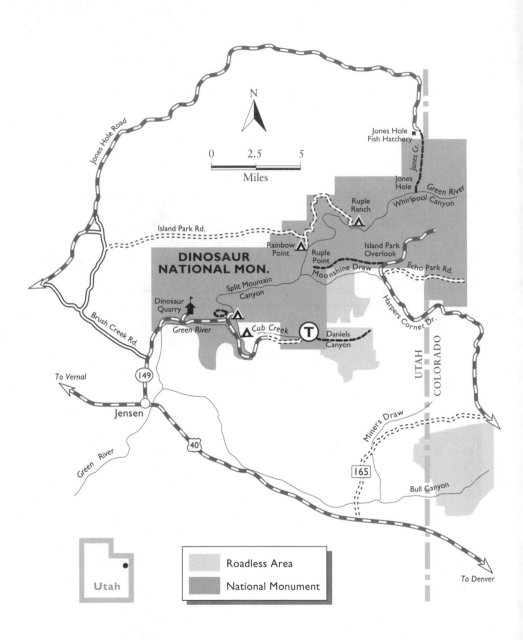

Jones Hole Road

N

0   2.5   5
Miles

Jones Hole
Fish Hatchery

Jones Cr.

Jones
Hole

Green River

Whirlpool Canyon

Ruple
Ranch

Island Park Rd.

Rainbow
Point

Ruple
Point

Island Park
Overlook

Echo Park Rd.

**DINOSAUR
NATIONAL MON.**

Split Mountain
Canyon

Moonshine Draw

Dinosaur
Quarry

Harpers Corner Dr.

Green River

Cub Creek

T

Daniels
Canyon

Brush Creek Rd.

UTAH

COLORADO

To Vernal

149

Jensen

40

Green River

Miners Draw

165

Bull Canyon

To Denver

Utah

Roadless Area

National Monument

The Green and its tributary in Colorado, the Yampa, form the core of Dinosaur National Monument. The thrills of river running are just one of the attractions of this small region of wild country on Utah's eastern border. Long before Hollywood discovered the powerful draw of dinosaurs, in 1909 a Pittsburgh paleontologist, Earl Douglass, found brontosaurus bones in the Jurassic sediment here on the eastern end of the Uintas. About 145 million years ago a sandbar on the banks of an ancient stream was the destination of jumbled dinosaur bones swept downstream. Since buried by thousands of feet of sediment, then uplifted 70 million years ago in the formation of the Uintas and the Rockies, the sandbar is now called the Dinosaur Quarry. It features *in situ* presentation of fossilized bones of the ancient reptiles. A visit to the Carnegie Museum in Pittsburgh is necessary to see the prime reconstructed specimens.

Publicity regarding Douglass' finds was intense, resulting in the first 80-acre unit of the national monument being set aside in 1915. Although no more dinosaur bone beds have been located, the larger monument today, at 200,000 acres, straddles the Utah–Colorado boundary to incorporate the confluence of the Green and Yampa rivers and their exotic canyons. Although the name preserves its paleontological origins, the monument today has a broader purview. Of its 200,000 acres the National Park Service has recommended 186,114 acres for wilderness designation. The Park Service would also like to include in the monument 5,818 adjacent acres of BLM roadless land.

These wild lands that lie around Dinosaur are indeed valuable in preserving the viewshed, the varied habitat, and the canyons that form an ecological unit with the monument. These surrounding lands are, in addition, valuable in their own right.

To the south of Dinosaur, the BLM units of Daniels Canyon and Moonshine Draw lie entirely within Utah. Bull Canyon, also in the south, and the fragmented roadless areas of Wild Mountain, Diamond Breaks, and Cold Springs, all north of Dinosaur, straddle the state line. Most of their acreage lies within neighboring Colorado where their eastern boundaries coincide with the monument's borders.

From the 7,600-foot Yampa Plateau, the canyons of Cub Creek and Moonshine Draw cut through the Weber sandstone. The towering cream-colored walls create a contrast with the ridges and shelves of Moenkopi red rock. In the rain shadow of the Uintas, this arid land supports only sparse vegetation. It is barren sagebrush steppe according to its botanical category, but even with an annual average of only 9 inches of precipitation a diversity of plants ekes out an existence. On the higher slopes, particularly north-facing ones, mountain mahogany, serviceberry, big sagebrush, and pinyon pine can be found, with infrequent stands of ponderosa pines. At lower levels, pinyon-juniper woodlands, shrubs, and grasses grow wherever they can find soil amid the stretches of barren rock. The flat canyon bottoms harbor greasewood, big sagebrush, and grasses. Near springs and along perennial streams box elders, cottonwood, tamarisk, and willow flourish.

This austere land supports a surprising diversity of wildlife too. The broad valleys, high parks, and gentle slopes of the northern BLM units provide important winter range for mule deer, antelope, and elk. Deer and sage grouse are popular game in hunting season. Reintroduced Rocky Mountain bighorn have flourished; the Colorado Division of Wildlife contemplates limited hunting eventually. It is unlikely that you will spot the elusive mountain lions, but you may see their big paw prints in damp stream bottoms. Be on the lookout for black bear tracks in the remote Diamond Breaks unit. While the coyote chorus has been rare in recent years due to an active predator control program to protect livestock grazing on BLM allotments, the primeval song can still be heard on evenings in the backcountry. Cottontails, jackrabbits, deer mice, and kangaroo rats flourish, and provide a tasty diet for the eagles (both bald and golden) and peregrine falcons that pass along the Green River corridor.

Here, as elsewhere in the Colorado Plateau, wherever there is water there is archeological evidence of Paleo-Indian presence. Within the monument, cave habitation sites and rock art lie along the Green and the Yampa. Even along the little trickle in Daniels Canyon rock shelters and petroglyphs indicate Anasazi bands were in the area from 500 to 1250 A.D. Cub Creek is also the site of Morris Ranch cabin, in use from 1914 into the 1960s. These early residents were tenacious, but not prosperous. The region evidently had a damper climate during Paleo-Indian times. Today there are only two perennial springs and several seeps in Daniels Canyon. Hikers are advised to carry water and not rely on nature.

RECREATIONAL USES: There are endless hiking opportunities within Dinosaur National Monument. Nature trails and hikes to vista points are described in the pamphlet available at the visitor center. Off-trail journeys of exploration can follow canyons or washes. Check at the monument visitor station for regulations. Backcountry permits are required for overnight camping; this is one of the few Park Service areas where campfires are permitted in the backcountry. Camping is restricted, however, in certain areas, such as around Cub Creek.

River trips within the monument also require permits, and also considerable navigational skill. Several licensed river running companies operate trips on the Green and the Yampa. Contact the River Unit at Dinosaur National Monument for further information.

The hike in Daniels Canyon (see below) is just one of the many day hikes that this country has to offer. Frequented by horseback riders and birders, the Daniels Canyon unit attracts diverse backcountry users. Bull Canyon, easily accessible from the monument's entrance road, is also a popular destination for hikers, as is the hike to Jones Hole on the Green River.

To the north, the Diamond Breaks and Cold Springs Mountain units bracket Browns Park National Wildlife Refuge in Colorado. From the 8,000-foot ridges in Diamond Breaks you can enjoy breathtaking views of the Uintas and the Canyon of Lodore south on the Green. Cold Springs Mountain is a popular destination for hunters, attracted by its elk, deer, and antelope.

HOW TO GET THERE: From the Dinosaur National Monument visitor center turn-off, continue straight on Utah Highway 149 (Blue Mountain Road) for 7 miles, passing turn-offs to Split Mountain and Green River campgrounds. The paved road ends, but continue for 2 miles on the unimproved dirt road to its end at the parking area at Josie Morris' ranch. The red clay road has a few low spots that can be sticky when wet, but it does not require a high-clearance vehicle.

Day hike

Daniels Canyon

Distance: 10 miles round trip.
Starting and maximum elevations: 5,363 feet and 7,185 feet.
Difficulty: Moderate.
Best months: Late March (depending on snow) through late May; September through October.
Topo maps: Split Mountain-UT; Stuntz Reservoir-UT-CO.

Before embarking on the hike up Daniels Canyon it is worth your while to poke around the Morris ranch. The National Park Service has erected a roof over Josie's old cabin to prevent further deterioration. She lived here, ranching in the valley, for the first half of the twentieth century, leaving in 1964. You can admire her handiwork in the intricate fencing, the canal system, and the coyote-proof chicken coop. Just north of the parking area a short box canyon (0.5 mile out-and-back) is an idyllic warm-up for the hike.

For the main attraction follow the beaten footpath southeast past the chicken coop through the hikers' maze, winding east past a low ridge to the mouth of Hog Canyon. An NPS sign here mentions an exotic orchid that was discovered in this surprising location. Josie used this large box canyon to keep her swine enclosed; fenced off now from the cows and horses that graze in the surrounding meadows, Hog Canyon is a lot lovelier than its name suggests. The deep dramatic box canyon in the pale Weber sandstone is a 1.5-mile round trip, another good side trip before or after the main outing.

Continue past Hog Canyon to an old barbed wire fence. Cross the fence, turn right, and follow it south toward Cub Creek. As you near the creek after 0.2 mile, veer left to the cottonwood grove, a favorite spot of the cattle in hot

Looking north across Daniels Canyon to the Yampa Plateau.

weather. Here you can easily find the shallow creek crossing and pick up the cattle trail through the tamarisk and sage on the south bank. Rising to the sage bench, follow any of the several cowpaths east-southeast. They converge to pass through an open gate in the antique barbed wire fence; look for the high posts on either side of the gate as a visual reference as you head across the bench.

From the gate continue east, staying high on the sage bench close to the pinyon-juniper slope on the south canyon wall. An intermittent, ancient jeep trail will become the hiking path as you gradually rise above Daniels Canyon. The mid-slope trail provides panoramic rim-to-rim views of the Cub Creek drainage. For explorers who want to have a more hands-on experience, it is possible to bushwhack up the north side of the creek bottom from Hog Canyon until rimmed out; then you can hop across the stream and claw your way up the steep, vegetated south bank, joining the trail a mile up the canyon.

Although long closed to vehicles, the hiking route resembles a jeep trail and becomes very easy to follow once it rises above the sage bottoms to wind through the junipers. At about 1.5 miles the trail bends slightly to the south and begins to parallel a side canyon, while the major Cub Creek drainage lies below a second ridge north. At one of the numerous crests in the rolling trail you will cross the Park Service boundary; here the Daniels Creek Wilderness Study Area begins.

The long escarpment of the Yampa Plateau rises 2,000 feet above Cub Creek. Huge amphitheaters have been cut into the north canyon wall. Golden eagles circle over the edge of the cliff, while mule deer drift along the sage meadows of the lower trail. The sage becomes more scarce and the juniper larger and more dense as you ascend the sloping trail. At 6,500 feet pinyon pine begin to appear. Old gnarled tree trunks weathered like driftwood decorate the edges of the trail.

At 4 miles the trail rises to curve around the high ridge below the Yampa Plateau's corrugated edge. Looking back now, down canyon, the view is breathtaking: the valley and beyond to the Tavaputs Plateau of the Book Cliffs wilderness, the snow-covered peaks of the Wasatch Front in the distance.

While the trail continues east-northeast, it crosses a private inholding and eventually joins the maze of roads on the Yampa Plateau, so the head of the canyon (7,185 feet) is an excellent place to soak up the splendor of the wild country, then head back down to Josie's place.

NORTH-CENTRAL

MIDDLE ROCKY MOUNTAINS · CENTRAL PLATEAUS

Introduction

A great flange of high peaks and isolated mesas within the Wasatch Range, Uinta Mountains, and central mountain plateaus comprises the dramatic alpine grandeur of Utah's wild heartland. This lofty land has been carved by glaciers, leaving lake-studded cirques, knife ridges, horned peaks, and U-shaped valleys—protected in large part by their remoteness and ruggedness.

The narrow Wasatch uplift extends 200 miles from the northern boundary to central Utah. Movement along the Wasatch Fault has produced the spectacular sheer west face of the range, making it one of the most formidable upthrusts on the continent. The northeast corner of the state is dominated by the 150-mile rise of the High Uintas—"Utah's Rooftop"—where some 1,400 sparkling tarns are spread across glacial moraines punctuated with 24 peaks above 13,000 feet. To the south, an elevated, forested province of central mountains and plateaus forms an ecological transition between basin and range country and the Colorado Plateau.

Most of the wildlands of the Middle Rocky Mountains and Plateaus lie within the Canadian life zone (8,000 to 10,000 feet above sea level), Hudsonian life zone (10,000 to 11,000 feet), and Arctic-alpine life zone (above 11,000 feet). In the Canadian life zone deer and elk feed in grassy parks interspersed with lodgepole pine, limber pine, white fir, blue spruce, and aspen. In the Hudsonian life zone deep snows bury lakes and subalpine meadows nestled in thickets of gnarled Engelmann spruce and subalpine fir, forcing most wildlife to lower elevations during winter. Only grasses, sedges, mosses, and annual plants have adapted to the extreme conditions of the Arctic-alpine life zone, where freezing snow squalls can blast the high country anytime of the year.

Virtually all of the wildlands here are administered by the USDA Forest Service, with nine designated "islands" of wilderness. The remaining majority of national forest roadless areas described in *Wild Utah* lack formal protection but provide the full spectrum of beyond-the-road recreational activities along with clean water, undisturbed wildlife habitat, and stunning scenery.

Mount Naomi Wilderness Complex   37

Location: Immediately adjacent to and northeast of Logan, in north-central Utah.
Size: 77,950 acres in Utah with another 29,000 contiguous roadless acres
extending north into Idaho.
Administration: USDAFS Wasatch–Cache National Forest, Logan Ranger District.
Management status: Mount Naomi Wilderness (44,350 acres), plus about 33,600
acres of contiguous unprotected national forest, state, and private roadless lands.
Ecosystems: Middle Rocky Mountain ecoregion, with potential natural vegetation
types of Douglas-fir; western spruce–fir coniferous forest.
Elevation range: 4,800 feet to 9,980 feet (Mount Naomi).
Established trails/routes: About 100 miles of national forest system trails.
Maximum core to perimeter distance: 3 miles.
Activities: Hiking, backpacking, horseback riding, cross-country skiing,
snowshoeing, mountaineering, caving, photography, nature study, fishing, hunting.
Maps: 1994 USDAFS half-inch/mile map entitled, "Wasatch–Cache National
Forest—Ogden & Logan Ranger Districts" (50 meter contour interval). See
Appendix E for a listing of the six topo maps covering the area.

OVERVIEW: The highest peaks in Northern Utah's Bear River Mountains are
encompassed within the 44,350-acre Mount Naomi Wilderness—a product of
the 1984 Utah Wilderness Act. Bounded by Logan Canyon, additional roadless
land south and east of the wilderness boundary brings the total size of the
contiguous wildland to around 78,000 acres, with additional wild country
extending north into Idaho. A large block of unroaded land near the northeast
side of the wilderness, within and above Franklin Basin, was originally excluded from wilderness consideration because it is owned by the State of Utah.
These lands may eventually be acquired by the Forest Service through land
exchanges with the State of Utah. These and other wildlands to the south are
an integral part of the wilderness as well as crucial summer and winter range
for moose and elk. During winter large numbers of elk feed on south-facing
slopes directly above lower Logan Canyon. Bobcats, cougars, and golden eagles
are fairly common in the Bear River Range. Several streams support cutthroat
trout.

The Bear River Range is characterized by extremely steep slopes on the west
with rolling plateaus and a more moderate east-side gradient. At 9,979 feet,

Mount Naomi is the apex of its namesake wildland. Another half dozen nearby peaks rise above 9,500 feet. Elaborate caverns and depressions near the top of these mountains are the result of water eroding limestone and dolomite rock formations. This rough-hewn landscape is referred to by geologists as "karst" topography. Similar forces of erosion have cut numerous canyons into this rugged alpine terrain, many of which carry perennial streams bordered by monkeyflowers, cottonwood trees, and, a bit higher up, maple and aspen. During late spring and early summer, visitors can enjoy the music of mountain water along with the high pitched sounds of yellow warblers, hermit thrushes, and warbling vireos. With increases in elevation the montane Douglas-fir forest gradually changes to subalpine fir, lining bowl-shaped meadows generously sprinkled with columbine, alpine buttercup, lupine, and penstemon. Rock wrens and Clark's nutcrackers are commonly seen and heard in these upper alpine forests and grassy parks.

RECREATIONAL USES: The Mount Naomi country is big and rugged enough to challenge the most ardent backpacker and mountaineer, yet close enough to good year-round access for short, easy day trips. U.S. Highway 89 extends up Logan Canyon for more than 22 miles, making a huge half-circle around the southern and eastern periphery of the wildland, from the mouth of Logan Canyon upstream to Franklin Basin. From this point, further access into the roadless country takes off from Forest Road 006, which continues northwest up the Logan River into Idaho.

Most visitors to the backcountry start off from the Logan Canyon corridor, whether by foot, ski, horse, or mountain bike. There are nine Forest Service campgrounds (both fee and no fee) in Logan Canyon from Spring Hollow on up to Red Banks. Several trailheads invite short day hikes or longer trips connecting to trails that lead north or west into the higher reaches of the Mount Naomi Wilderness.

The Wind Caves trailhead is 5 miles above the mouth of Logan Canyon. The 1.5 mile path gains 1,100 feet in elevation to a triple arch overlooking the canyon. The arch was formed by wind and water erosion and is part of the "China Wall" rock formation halfway up the canyon wall, which runs for about half the length of the canyon. The Jardine Juniper trail takes off from US 89 another 5 miles up Logan Canyon. It climbs 1,800 feet in 4.4 miles to Old Jardine, a venerable 3,000 year-old Rocky Mountain juniper. With a circumference of about 27 feet this 45-foot tall juniper is well worth the 9-mile round trip. Refer to Ride 3 in *Mountain Biking Utah* (Falcon Publishing) for the details of this popular hiking and mountain biking out-and-back trip just south of the wilderness boundary. Logan Cave is adjacent to the highway 12 miles above the canyon mouth. This limestone cavern is about 2,000 feet long and can be explored easily with the aid of headlamps. The cave is seasonally

37 MOUNT NAOMI WILDERNESS COMPLEX

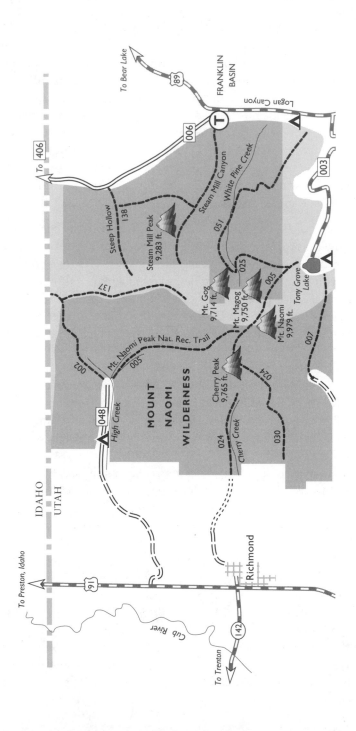

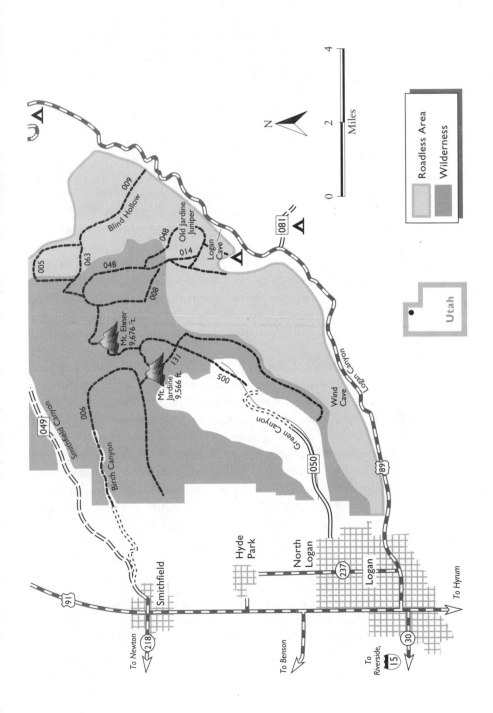

closed to within 150 feet of its mouth to protect a rare and special community of Townsend's big-eared bats, which are especially vulnerable to human disturbance during hibernation from October 1 to May 15.

For the technical rock climber, Logan Canyon offers a myriad of climbs on limestone rock ranging in difficulty from 5.6 top-roped climbs to 5.14 bolted sport climbs. All of the cliffs, including the China Wall formation, support sensitive plants, such as king aster and Conquist daisy, as well as the federally listed threatened Maguire primrose. Climbing and rappeling within 50 feet of these plants is not allowed, nor are climbing bolts within wilderness. Climbing ethics and general route information are described in an introductory brochure to Logan Canyon climbs published by the Logan Ranger District and the Cache Valley climbing community.

A campground is located at Tony Grove Lake 7 miles west of US 89 by way of Forest Road 003. At 8,100 feet the campground is open only during summer. From here the Mount Naomi National Recreation Trail (005) climbs northwest, skirts around the north end of 9,979-foot Mount Naomi, and connects with other trails in the wilderness. The one-way hiking distance to the peak is 2.9 miles with a vertical gain of 2,000 feet. The lake is also the jumping off point for Trail 025, which heads 3.4 miles north to White Pine Lake, a sublime talused tarn nestled in an alpine basin between two 9,700-foot peaks. This 7-mile round trip is a pleasant summer day hike with wonderful displays of wildflowers; the route can be extended into peak climbs for the more energetic.

To get away from the more beaten track of Logan Canyon, head up Birch Creek Canyon Road northeast of Smithfield on the west side of the wilderness. Here a trail follows lovely Birch Creek up into 9,000-foot saddles and ridges leading to 9,566-foot Mount Jardine. In general, open country on the higher ridges lends itself to off-trail hiking for peak climbing or to complete trailless segments of a high-country backpack route. An example is the 2 miles of open, trailless ridgeline south of Mount Naomi. Because some off-trail routes involve steep sidehilling on loose rock, horseback riders are advised to ride on the network of existing trails that offer a variety of day and overnight equestrian options. In the north, Trail 005 to High Creek Lake is especially popular with horseback riders. A popular point-to-point, 12-mile hiking traverse up and over the crest of the Bear River Range begins at the Green Canyon trailhead and ends at Tony Grove Lake.

HOW TO GET THERE: From the center of downtown Logan (the intersection of U.S. Highways 91 and 89) take US 89 to the mouth of Logan Canyon. Continue up the canyon on US 89 about 22 miles to the winter recreation Franklin Basin Trailhead and parking area on the left side of the highway. From downtown Logan the distance to the trailhead by way of the paved, all-weather highway is about 25 miles.

Day or overnight ski or snowshoe

Steam Mill Canyon day trip or Steam Mill Canyon–Steep Hollow overnight loop

Distance: 6 to 8 miles day touring; 18-mile loop.
Starting and maximum elevations: 6,637 feet and 9,537 feet (Bear River Range divide) or 9,879-foot Doubletop Mountain.
Difficulty: Moderate day tour to strenuous overnight loop.
Best months: January through March, with March generally being the best month.
Topo maps: Naomi Peak-UT; Tony Grove Creek-UT.

Aspen parks, spacious open hillsides, and stringers of lodgepole pine, spruce, and fir in the wild country northeast of the wilderness boundary offer varied and challenging out-and-back and short to long loop ski or snowshoe tours. March is usually the best time to ski into the high country west of the Logan River above Franklin Basin. Of course, at any time during the winter on into early spring a storm can dump two or more feet of fresh powder. When this happens, unconsolidated snow can make skiing difficult and can affect avalanche conditions. Before setting out, check on local avalanche and mountain weather conditions by calling the Logan number for the Utah Avalanche Forecast Center at 801-797-4146. To find out about the snow base and other trail conditions call the Logan Ranger District at 801-755-3620.

Slogging through an aspen park at 7,800 feet elevation on the Steam Mill Creek Trail.

Begin the trip by skiing north on the groomed snowmobile trail about 0.3 mile across the bridged Logan River, which is a small stream at this point. After reaching the top of a small rise in another 0.1 mile, turn west across an open flat to the forest edge. From here the trail makes a moderate but steady 5.5-mile ascent to Steam Mill Lake at 8,650 feet. After the first 2 miles the trail intersects the ridge at about 7,800 feet. Cross the ridge to the north and look for an old wagon road cut that climbs northwest along the south side of Steam Mill Canyon to Steam Mill meadow and lake. The trail isn't blazed but is noticeable for the most part as a swath through the forest. At any point along the trail below 8,200 feet travelers can make an enjoyable short return loop by angling left (south) to the mostly open ridge above White Pine Creek. Ski traversing and telemarking can be superb during this return descent through open aspen parks and moderately steep slopes. After skiing toward the southwest to a relatively gentle bench at about 7,800 feet, gradually cut back to the left (north) to intersect the Steam Mill Canyon trail near the open flat starting point. The other return option is to double back on the uphill trail for some exciting runs through the trees, zigzagging down the stream bottom.

For those well-versed in ski-mountaineering and avalanche safety this day tour route can be extended into a strenuous two- to three-day, 18-mile loop. From Steam Mill Lake continue climbing northwest up a steep draw, gaining 900 feet in about 1 mile to the 9,500-foot crest of the Bear River Range. Sheer cliffs and steep, rocky slopes plunge dramatically to the west in the Mount Naomi Wilderness. The divide can be skied, or sometimes hiked on its wind-swept crest, 2 miles northward to 9,873-foot Doubletop Mountain. To continue the loop, drop and angle left (northeast) around Point 9,018 feet (as shown on the topo map) into the narrow head of Steep Hollow. After about 1.5 miles look for signs of an old four-wheel-drive roadbed in the notch of Steep Hollow at around 8,400 feet. The old road grade moderately descends Steep Hollow for another 4 to 5 miles to the Logan River at 7,300 feet. From there turn right (south) and ski the groomed snowmobile trail 3 to 4 miles back down the Logan River to the trailhead. You'll appreciate the relative ease of completing the loop on a hard-packed trail after the previous 15 miles of steep terrain and untracked powder!

Wellsville Mountain Wilderness   38

Location: One mile north of Brigham City and 1.5 miles west of Wellsville, in north-central Utah.
Size: 23,847 acres.
Administration: USDAFS Wasatch–Cache National Forest, Logan Ranger District.
Management status: Wilderness.
Ecosystems: Middle Rocky Mountain province; potential natural vegetation of Douglas-fir forest.
Elevation range: 4,680 feet (southwest corner) to 9,372 feet (Box Elder Peak).
Established trails/routes: About 15 miles of system trails.
Maximum core to perimeter distance: 2 miles.
Activities: Hiking, photography, nature study (raptor watching), limited backpacking and horseback riding.
Maps: 1994 USDAFS half-inch/mile map entitled "Wasatch–Cache National Forest—Ogden & Logan Ranger Districts" (50 meter contour interval). See Appendix E for a listing of the four topo maps covering the Wellsville Mountain Wilderness.

OVERVIEW: High, narrow, and handsome—the Wellsville Mountains are a genuine Utah conservation success story. Early twentieth-century overgrazing and rampant burning eroded the Wellsvilles bare, causing widespread flooding. Finally, in 1941 concerned local people raised contributions, bought the mountain range, and turned it over to the USDA Forest Service for rehabilitation. In 1984 this mostly successful initiative was reinforced by designation of the Wellsville Mountain Wilderness as part of the Utah Wilderness Act. Going from an abused land stripped of soil-holding vegetation to a largely recovered, federally protected wilderness within the same century is a wonderful success story that can serve as a model elsewhere.

The Wellsvilles have been described as "the steepest mountains in the world," for rarely does a range ascend so high, so fast, from a base so narrow. This impressive north-south trending uplift is less than 20 miles long with an average width of only 3 to 4 miles. At elevations between 7,500 feet and nearly 9,400 feet, the main dividing ridge towers as much as 5,000 feet above Cache Valley to the east and the Great Salt Lake on the west.

38 WELLSVILLE MOUNTAIN WILDERNESS

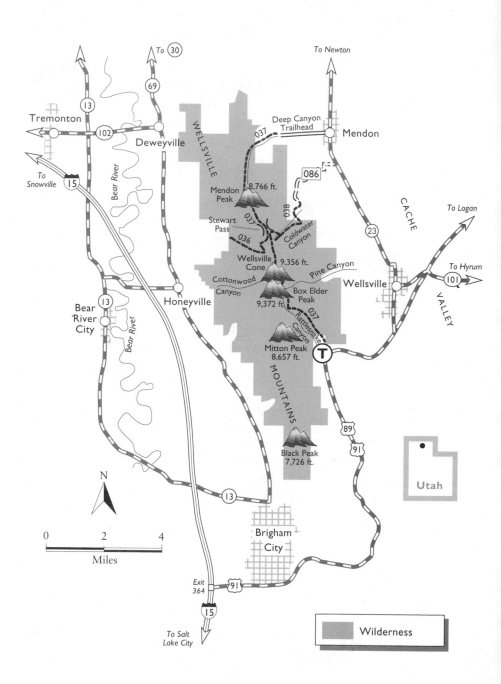

To 30

To Newton

69

13

Tremonton

102

Deweyville

Deep Canyon
Trailhead

Mendon

037

WELLSVILLE

086

To Snowville

15

Bear River

8,766 ft.

Mendon
Peak

038

CACHE

To Logan

Stewart
Pass

037

Coldwater
Canyon

036

23

Bear
River
City

13

Honeyville

Wellsville
Cone

9,356 ft.

Pine Canyon

Wellsville

To Hyrum

101

Cottonwood
Canyon

Bear River

Box Elder
Peak

9,372 ft.

Rattlesnake Canyon

037

VALLEY

Mitton Peak
8,657 ft.

T

MOUNTAINS

89

91

N

Black Peak
7,726 ft.

Utah

0   2   4

Miles

13

Brigham
City

Exit
364

91

15

To Salt
Lake City

Wilderness

91

Lower canyon entrances are marked with a mix of mountain ash and maple. An exceptionally large maple tree is a point of interest near the east side in Coldwater Canyon. The mid-slopes are typically mantled with oak woodlands and open grassland, lending a spacious look to the countryside. Douglas-fir and quaking aspen grace small, intimate pockets near the crest of the mountains. Hardy limber pine cling tenaciously to rocky perches along and near the high divide. Late spring and early summer heralds the advent of a dazzling display of such wildflower beauties as Indian paintbrush, blue penstemon, mountain clover, and glacier lilies.

Mule deer and mountain lion are among the larger wild denizens making their home in these overly steep highlands. The Wellsville Mountains are perhaps best known as *the* place to see fall raptor migrations, with hundreds of hawks riding the air currents near Mendon Peak in the north end of the range.

RECREATIONAL USES: Backpacking is possible but rarely attempted here due to the absence of water and suitable, protected campsites. High winds often produce brutal windchill temperatures along the exposed main ridge. The steepness of terrain and fall-line pitches of trails curtail or severely limit winter travel and horseback riding, although some horse use occasionally takes place.

With one undeveloped and two developed trailheads connecting a dozen or so miles of constructed trails, the Wellsvilles are a good choice for late spring to late fall hiking. The trailheads are located on the more rugged and rocky east side of the mountains. The main trailhead is Deep Creek on the northeast edge of the wilderness, 2 miles west of Mendon.

The Deep Canyon Trail (087) starts out at 5,400 feet, reaching an 8,100-foot saddle in only 3 miles for a vigorous vertical gain of 2,700 feet. An 8,585-foot unnamed peak about 0.75 mile northwest of the pass is a prime location from which to witness fall hawk migrations. It may be that there is no other place in the world where so many raptors can be observed flying so close to a ridgetop viewing site. This hike to the Wellsville divide can be done as an out-and-back trek or as a longer 8-mile loop by continuing south along the crest to 8,376-foot Stewart Pass and down the steep Coldwater Lake Trail (038), which loses 2,100 feet in only 1.5 miles to Coldwater Lake. The high point of the range, 9,372-foot Box Elder Peak, is another 2 miles south of Stewart Pass. For a detailed description of the Deep Canyon–Coldwater Canyon Loop and points in between see Hike 2 in *Hiking Utah,* from Falcon Publishing.

Getting to the summit ridge of the precipitous Wellsvilles is tough and demanding, but the views from the top more than make up for the effort expended. Much of northern Utah spreads out before you like a giant map, with the twisting oxbows of the Bear River a vertical mile below and to the west, and the even higher Bear River Range directly east.

HOW TO GET THERE: From Interstate 15 take exit 364 at Brigham City and follow U.S. Highway 91 as it goes east through Box Elder Canyon, turning north toward Wellsville. After about 14 miles the busy four-lane highway makes a sharp bend to the right (east). Slow down and look carefully for an unmarked dirt road on the left side of the bend of the highway immediately east of a large green power pole. The road ends within 10 yards at a fence with a Forest Service "Rattle Snake Trail" sign and a locked gate posted "No Vehicles." From the opposite direction the trailhead is only about 3 miles southwest of Wellsville from the junction of US 91 and Utah Highway 23. If no one else is there park in the shade next to the fence. Otherwise, there is ample parking space in the open toward the power pole.

Day trail hike and climb
Box Elder Peak Climb

Distance: 9 to 10 miles (out-and-back).
Starting and maximum elevations: 5,640 feet and 9,372 feet (Box Elder Peak).
Difficulty: Strenuous.
Best months: June to early July, September through October.
Topo maps: Honeyville-UT; Wellsville-UT; Brigham City-UT; and Mount Pisgah-UT.

Gird your loins for this demanding high and dry trail hike to the rooftop of the Wellsvilles. With precious little shade it is important to get an early start and to carry lots of water. From the locked gate hike northward up the doubletrack road, which climbs 350 feet in 0.5 mile through privately owned grassy parklands. As the old road swings to the right (east) a Forest Service "Rattle Snake Trail" sign marks the otherwise obscure beginning of the trail to Box Elder Peak. The national forest boundary lies just beyond. The somewhat primitive path is overgrown with ferns and box elder but easy to follow as it climbs steadily up the bottom of Rattlesnake Canyon. Soon the canopy changes to aspen with a thick understory of wild rose, sunflower, and lupine. After about 2.5 miles the trail reaches a bench above the main Rattlesnake Canyon next to a clump of Douglas-fir. A dry campsite on this level, 7,500-foot overlook is ringed by a garden of early summer wildflowers with panoramic views to the east and south.

The trail is surprisingly brushy for a dry south-facing slope, but the grand vistas are unobstructed by mostly low brush. After about 3.5 miles the trail meets the main Wellsville divide in a grassy saddle at 8,400 feet. Early season visitors sometimes camp in this gap when snowbanks linger as a water source. Wildflowers abound along with big sagebrush. Just before reaching the saddle the trail makes a sharp turn to the right that is usually buried by a snowbank into early July. If you miss the trail at this tricky spot simply aim for the main north-south Wellsville divide to your right and you'll soon intercept the clear path.

As the trail climbs the spine of the ridge toward centrally located Box Elder Peak it passes through stringers of limber pine and Douglas-fir. Several castle rock outcrops on the east slope, framed by gnarled old snags, overlook secluded basins that feed into Pine Canyon. Small hanging valleys are perched above the narrow V-shaped chute of the drainage. Blue penstemon and scarlet gilia are especially prolific along this upper stretch. From here the hiking is easy across open grassy slopes to the rounded 9,372-foot summit of Box Elder Peak.

From this apex of the range the options include continuing north along the open crest for a point-to-point trek to either the Coldwater Canyon trailhead (another 5 or 6 miles) or another 9 miles to Deep Canyon if a car shuttle has been arranged. Otherwise, limber up your knees for the long 4,000-foot descent back to the Rattle Snake trailhead. An intermediate option is to follow the trail from Box Elder Peak northward about 0.75 mile to the 9,356-foot Wellsville Cone. The trail plunges nearly 500 feet to the saddle between the two peaks, but time, energy, and water permitting, the view north toward Stewart Pass makes this additional 1.5-mile round trip more than worthwhile.

Uinta Mountains Wilderness Complex   39

Location: 10 miles north of Vernal and 12 miles northeast of Heber City, in northeast Utah.
Size: 659,000 acres.
Administration: USDAFS Wasatch–Cache National Forest, Kamas, Evanston, and Mountain View ranger districts; and Ashley National Forest, Duschesne, Roosevelt, Vernal, and Flaming Gorge ranger districts.
Management status: High Uintas Wilderness (460,000 acres) plus 199,000 acres of unprotected national forest roadless land.
Ecosystems: Rocky Mountain Douglas-fir forest ecosystem, with western spruce–fir forest, Douglas-fir forest, alpine meadows, mountain mahogany/oak scrub, and sagebrush community vegetation.
Elevation range: 7,200 feet to 13,528 feet (Kings Peak).
Established trails/routes: More than 1,000 miles of national forest trails.
Maximum core to perimeter distance: 11 miles.
Activities: Hiking, backpacking, hunting, fishing, wildlife study, photography, horseback riding, rock climbing, cross-country skiing, snowshoeing.
Maps: BLM 1:100,000 scale surface management/land ownership maps entitled "Salt Lake City," "Kings Peak," and "Dutch John;" USDAFS 1994 half-inch/mile map entitled "Wasatch–Cache National Forest-Kamas, Evanston, and Mountain View Ranger Districts" (50 meter contour interval) and 1982 three-eighths-inch/mile planimetric map entitled "Ashley National Forest-Utah & Wyoming." See Appendix E for a listing of the 47 topo maps covering the roadless area.

OVERVIEW: The Uinta Mountain Wilderness Complex evokes superlatives. It is the highest mountain range in Utah, with more than a dozen peaks above 13,000 feet; King's Peak, on the Uinta divide, is the highest mountain in the state. This is the only major mountain range in the lower 48 that runs east-west. The Uinta roadless area is the largest in Utah. The core-to-perimeter distance (11 miles) enables the intrepid hiker to be farther from a road here than in any other Utah wilderness.

But this is also the largest national forest roadless area that is not entirely protected by wilderness designation. In 1984, Congress set aside the 460,000-acre mountainous core as the High Uinta Wilderness. The medium and low Uintas, another 199,000 acres, were not included. In the High Uintas Wilder-

39 UINTA MOUNTAINS WILDERNESS COMPLEX

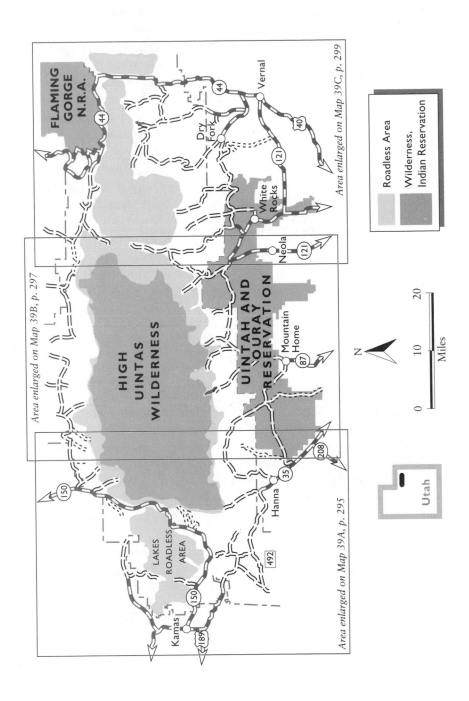

FLAMING GORGE N.R.A.

Vernal

Dry Fork

White Rocks

Neola

HIGH UINTAS WILDERNESS

UINTAH AND OURAY RESERVATION

Mountain Home

Hanna

LAKES ROADLESS AREA

Kamas

Area enlarged on Map 39C, p. 299

Area enlarged on Map 39B, p. 297

Area enlarged on Map 39A, p. 295

Roadless Area

Wilderness, Indian Reservation

N

0   10   20

Miles

Utah

ness, 80 square miles of rocks and ice form the core of the mountain range, with high alpine basins and glaciated valleys. Left out, but necessary to wildlife, were lower elevation winter ranges for elk, mule deer, and moose: the wet meadows and aspen parks. The higher elevations receive more than 40 inches of precipitation annually, mainly as snow. Several thousand feet lower, the landscape receives half that much, making it more hospitable for wintering wildlife.

High elevation makes this one of the wettest areas in Utah, with more than 2,000 alpine lakes. The region provides 90 percent of the state's water supply, and thus attracts the interest of water-starved cities in the drier lowlands. Numerous reservoirs and pipeline projects have erupted on the Uinta perimeter to tap the coveted water supply. The lakes and wetlands also create a bumper crop of mosquitoes, eager to greet visitors during the short summer season.

The dramatic mountain range that is the "high" of the Uinta Wilderness is a 60-mile crest of Precambrian rock. Quartzite, with sandstone and shale, is exposed on the rocky pinnacles from Hayden Peak to Leidy Peak. These formations date back 600 million years and are evidence of the enormous subterranean pressure that forced these rocks to the surface. Fault lines on the exposed peaks also testify to tectonic activity here. Naked ridges reveal tightly compressed sedimentary layers standing vertically, jammed by the powerful thrust of the earth's crust. John Wesley Powell, among other early geographers, was fascinated with this anomalous range and wrote about it extensively. Its east-west orientation is rare; tectonic plates and the fault lines of North America tend to create north-south ranges.

U-shaped basins, created by the glaciers of the Pleistocene Era, descend from the long crest. From lakes high in these basins, rivers wind through the bottoms, occasionally halted by moraine dams; beaver are also busy in some drainages. Natural bogs in the high mountain meadows are 12,000 year-old remnants of warm spells in the glacial era. The rivers feed several drainages. On the north slope west of the Elizabeth Pass divide (10,353 feet), they flow to Wyoming to join the Bear River. East of the pass, the Uintas drain to the Green River in Wyoming, returning to Utah via Flaming Gorge. The rivers of the Uinta south slope drain to the Uinta Basin, to the Duschesne River, which joins the Green River at Ouray.

This wet region of Utah supports a wide variety of vegetation. Above 11,000 feet the peaks and ridges consist of barren rock and talus, with vast stretches of alpine tundra. Here dwarfed alpine wildflowers display brilliant colors during their abbreviated season. Engelmann spruce, limber pine, and subalpine fir coat the high elevations, merging with ponderosa and lodgepole pine on lower slopes. Aspen groves and wetlands vegetation are common in the lower meadows; here too the wildflowers put on a colorful show featuring lupine,

39 A UINTA MOUNTAINS WILDERNESS COMPLEX

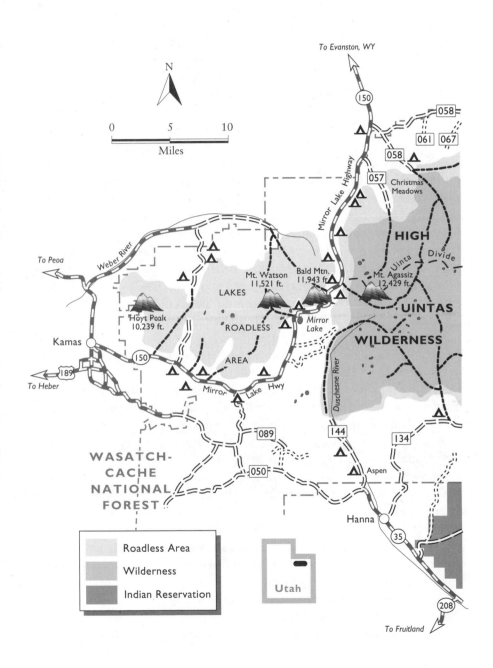

N

0   5   10
Miles

To Evanston, WY

150

058

061 067

058

057

Christmas
Meadows

HIGH

Uinta Divide

UINTAS

WILDERNESS

To Peoa

Weber River

Mirror Lake Highway

Mt. Watson
11,521 ft.

Bald Mtn.
11,943 ft.

Mt. Agassiz
12,429 ft.

LAKES

Hoyt Peak
10,239 ft.

ROADLESS

Mirror
Lake

Kamas

150

AREA

189

To Heber

Mirror Lake Hwy

Duchesne River

144

134

089

WASATCH-
CACHE
NATIONAL
FOREST

050

Aspen

Hanna

35

Roadless Area

Wilderness

Indian Reservation

Utah

208

To Fruitland

larkspur, paintbrush, and Colorado columbine. Sagebrush, grasses, and pin-yon-juniper are common in the foothill prairie ecosystem at lowest elevations.

The Uinta range is a Noah's ark of Rocky Mountain wildlife. The vast roadless areas beyond the wilderness core provide plentiful winter range, en-abling large herds of ungulates to flourish. A large moose population of more than 400 animals is the southernmost natural (that is, not introduced) repre-sentative of this species on the continent. Heavy snows force the moose to lower elevations during long winters. Utah's largest elk herd also is driven from the high country, along with the sizeable mule deer population. The Uintas are also home to black bear, bighorn sheep (reintroduced), mountain lions, pine martens, weasels, skunks, mink, and river otters. Rare sightings of lynx, tim-ber wolf, and wolverine have been reported. Beaver flourish and exercise their engineering skills in the alpine meadows. Beaver Dam Park, below Spirit Lake in the northeast quadrant of the range, is an excellent display of their ingenu-ity and teamwork. Rare goshawk, saw-whet owls, and pileated woodpeckers find refuge in old-growth forest on high mountain slopes. Ruffed, blue, and sage grouse are common game birds. The introduced white-tailed ptarmigan has found comfortable habitat below Gunsight Pass. Brook, golden, brown, and rainbow trout dart through stream riffles and congregate in the lakes, at-tracting multitudes of fishermen. Competition from these exotic trout species has virtually eliminated the native cutthroat population of the Uintas.

Except for the missing grizzly bear and a substantial drop in the numbers of furbearers and carnivores, the wildlife web is virtually the same as when the Fremont, Uintas, and Shoshone hunted here centuries ago. They were followed by trappers in the 1820s, and the trade flourished until the 1840s when the demand for fur declined. In 1868 and 1869, the Union Pacific's thirst for wood as it proceeded westward not far north of the Uintas resulted in heavy logging activity. The use of 5,000 railroad ties a mile, as well as hefty timbers for trestles, meant intense logging along the route. Only the rugged terrain of the High Uintas kept its virgin forests intact on steep interior slopes; the lower slopes along the route on the north were cut bare.

Mormon calls for settlers and the pre-World War I homestead rush brought optimistic pioneers to the Uinta region. With a short growing season and in-sufficient moisture during those critical months, farm efforts were doomed. Ranching proved more successful, although year-round residency was—and remains—out of the question. Sheep and cattle still use grazing allotments in the mountain meadows for summer range.

While the high core of the Uintas remains relatively untouched by the hand of man, the edges are being gnawed away by clearcuts and oil and gas devel-opment. By virtue of its east-west alignment, the range is not sliced by roads. Trains, highways, and travelers bypass the mountains. Only the Mirror Lake Highway (Utah Highway 150) penetrates the mountains, crossing at dramatic

39 B UINTA MOUNTAINS WILDERNESS COMPLEX

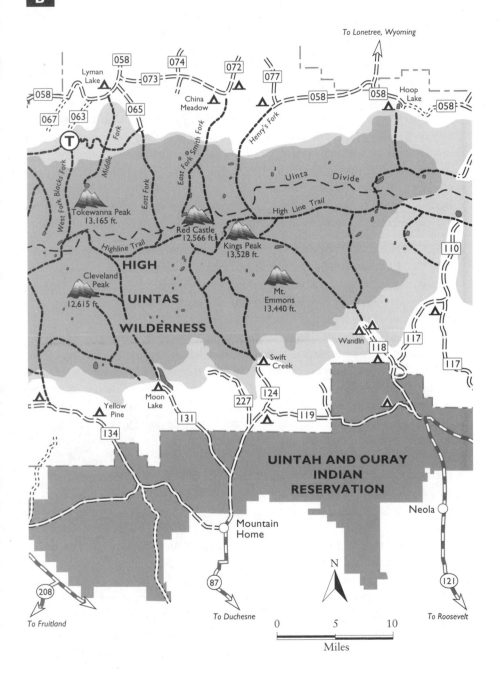

To Lonetree, Wyoming

058 074 072 077

Lyman Lake

073

058

067 063 065

China Meadow

Henry's Fork

Hoop Lake

058 058 058

T

Middle Fork

East Fork Smith Fork

Uinta Divide

West Fork Blacks Fork

East Fork

High Line Trail

110

Tokewanna Peak 13,165 ft.

Red Castle 12,566 ft.

Kings Peak 13,528 ft.

Highline Trail

HIGH

Cleveland Peak

12,615 ft.

UINTAS

Mt. Emmons 13,440 ft.

WILDERNESS

Wandln

118 117

117

Swift Creek

Yellow Pine

Moon Lake

124

227 119

131

134

UINTAH AND OURAY INDIAN RESERVATION

Neola

Mountain Home

N

208

87

121

To Fruitland

To Duchesne

To Roosevelt

0   5   10

Miles

Hayden Pass. This is a rare, unfragmented integrated roadless ecosystem, the largest unprotected area in the entire national forest system. The largest roadless unit outside of the Uinta Wilderness is the Lakes Roadless Area (104,709 acres), on the western end of the mountains. The Wasatch–Cache National Forest manages this area of peaks and alpine lakes as a semi-primitive nonmotorized area. Other roadless units are scattered around the perimeter of the wilderness. Under the administration of both the Wasatch–Cache and Ashley national forests, these lower elevation areas are heavily impacted by motorized recreationists; the doctrine of multiple-use development governs the management of these important wildlife zones. Only eventual inclusion in the wilderness system will ensure the health of the entire Uinta ecosystem. Two decades of development since the RARE II evaluation have significantly reduced the roadless acres on both the north and south slopes of the Uintas; industrial interests have targeted the Uintas for intensive development. Only an impassioned citizenry can save what's left.

RECREATIONAL USES: Located 50 air miles from Salt Lake City, the Uintas attract a multitude of visitors during the brief summer season from July 1 to mid-September. Hunters are numerous from then until early November. Late season hikers are advised to wear neon hunter's orange prominently; any pets should likewise be dressed appropriately.

Road access to this spectacular mountain range is relatively convenient. From Kamas, the paved Mirror Lake Highway (Utah Highway 150) rises from 6,500 feet in town to an elevation of 10,678 feet at Bald Mountain Pass. In winter the road is plowed as far as Soapstone (mile 15.5), allowing access for snowmobilers and cross-country skiers. Throughout the 50 miles of this scenic byway, the scenery is breathtaking and hiking opportunities are plentiful. Lakes, both nearby and distant, are readily accessible; trailheads into the backcountry are marked and have information boards and large parking areas. Hikes to Notch Mountain (at mile 25.4), Bald Mountain (at mile 29.1), and Lofty Lake (at mile 32.1) are just a few of the options. At 10,200-foot Hayden Pass (mile 34.2) the Highline Trail along the crest of the Uintas takes off east of the highway, winding 100 rocky miles to end at East Park Reservoir north of Vernal. The Highline Trail gets a lot of use, particularly by horse parties; this is not surprising since the trip is magnificent. Heavy use along the entire length of the Mirror Lake Highway corridor has led the Forest Service to institute a permit program. If you intend to leave your vehicle overnight at any trailhead, you must stop at a ranger station and purchase a recreation pass to display on your dashboard. This new Mirror Lake Recreation Area fee program is experimental; check at the ranger station before embarking on your outing.

U.S. Highway 40 parallels the mountains on the south; from this paved highway a dozen rough roads lead to trailheads on the north side of the Uintah

39 C UINTA MOUNTAINS WILDERNESS COMPLEX

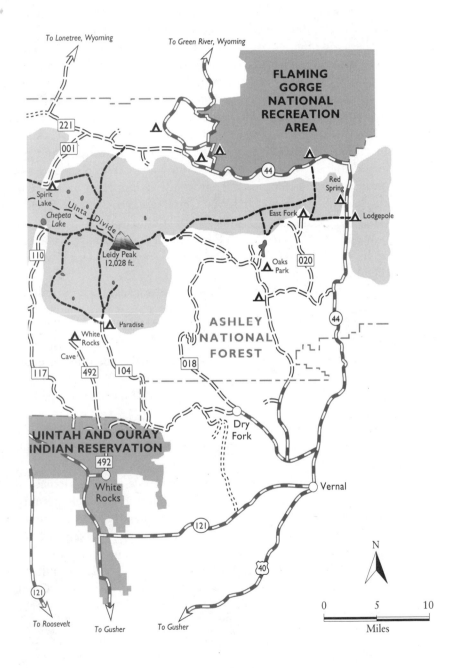

and Ouray Indian Reservation. On the north side of the Uintas, the North Slope Road is a wiggly, rough, long forest road. Side roads lead south to trailheads, which are less visited the further east you go. The vast lake area northeast of the wilderness is a bouncy 6-hour drive from Mirror Lake Highway, but you will run into fewer backcountry users as a result!

Due to the large number of visitors compressed into a short season, the Forest Service enforces numerous regulations designed to reduce environmental damage. In the wilderness, backcountry regulations limit party size to 14 people and 15 head of stock. Weed-free feed is required. Some areas may be posted as temporarily closed to stock use to encourage revegetation. The Chain Lakes Basin in the Roosevelt District of the Ashley National Forest is such an area. Wilderness campsites must be 200 feet away from trails and water sources. In addition, local restrictions cover individual areas regarding campsites and prohibition of campfires. The most heavily impacted areas are indicated on the Trails Illustrated Map *(High Uintas Wilderness)*. Check with the ranger district for specific rules. Trailhead bulletin boards also provide information about heavily impacted areas. For example, in Naturalist Basin campfires are prohibited—except in designated, marked locations—to prevent further destruction of trees for firewood.

The Wasatch–Cache and Ashley forests have a large network of trails, both within the wilderness and in the adjacent roadless areas. They wind toward peaks, link lakes, and follow river drainages. Well marked and usually maintained, the trail system is easy to follow, with a map. At high elevations the rough terrain causes a high percentage of Uinta hikes to be rated strenuous. Variable summer weather can produce freezing temperatures at night and possible snowstorms at any time. Explorers of these mountains need to be ready for anything!

The Lakes Roadless Area, west of Mirror Lake Highway, is a popular destination and receives heavy use. With a dozen peaks 10,000 feet and higher, and countless alpine lakes, it is a miniature Switzerland. The Wasatch–Cache National Forest administers the 110,000-acre unit as a quasi-wilderness, forbidding motorized use during most of the year but unfortunately permitting snowmobiles in the winter. The trailheads clustered near Bald Mountain summit are crowded with vehicles, particularly on summer weekends, but the multitude of trails and lakes spreads out the visitors. A loop outing that avoids the congestion takes off at the North Fork Provo River trailhead (mile 23.5) on Trail 075. Hike upstream 8 miles to the intersection with Lakes Country Trail 066. Hike west 6 miles on this mainline trail to Big Elk Lake. Near the intersection with the Big Elk Trail (068), which goes south, drop left into the Boulder Creek drainage. Follow this trailless creek 8 miles back to the trailhead. Solitude is ensured on the final segment of this two- to three-day trip. Off-trail travel gets you away from the crowds.

At the far eastern end of the mountain range, the Spirit Lake region provides respite from the hordes of visitors elsewhere in this cool corner of Utah in the summer. Although it is not as scenic as the North Slope Road, Interstate 80 in Wyoming is a faster route to the east Uintas. Take Wyoming Highway 414 south from Fort Bridger. About 3 miles past Burntfork turn south on a gravel road (Forest Road 221). Drive 14 miles and turn right to Spirit Lake. The rough road (FR 001) to Spirit Lake is 6 miles. From the Spirit Lake area (at 10,240 feet) trails go both north and south; from either direction a loop trip can be enjoyed as a several days backpack up to the 12,000-foot Uinta Divide. Basins both north and south of the divide are dotted with clear alpine lakes.

With a little ingenuity and a good map and compass, the vastness of the Uinta complex makes it possible to enjoy solitude in the backcountry. Even on the busiest summer weekend it is possible to find a remote basin with no human footprints. Spreading usage and abiding by leave-no-trace guidelines will preserve this mountain Eden.

HOW TO GET THERE: From the Mirror Lake Highway (Utah Highway 150), 48 miles northeast of Kamas, turn right on FR 058. Continue on this wide but very bumpy and washboarded improved dirt road 17 miles to turn right at the Lyman Lake intersection. Take the immediate hairpin right just beyond the Lyman turn, going back west on FR 063. This bumpy road goes 6 miles to the West Fork crossing. High clearance will make the journey less stressful, but a passenger vehicle could make the trip with care. An undeveloped campground at the West Fork crossing is the trailhead. All-terrain vehicle users, anglers, and horseback riders congregate at the shady campsites on the hillside above the river on weekends. Find a shady parking place and begin the hike at the river crossing.

Backpack loop

Bob's Lake

Distance: 22 to 24 miles.
Starting and maximum elevations: 9,320 feet and 11,512 feet (loop trip); 13,165 feet (Tokewanna Peak).
Difficulty: Strenuous.
Best months: July to September.
Topo maps: Lyman Lake-UT, WY; Red Knob-UT; Mount Lovenia-UT.

OVERVIEW: A remote wilderness getaway, this loop trip through unprotected roadless lands on the northern slopes of the High Uintas Wilderness Complex provides solitude even on the busiest summer weekend. A four-day, three-night backpack allows three leisurely days of travel, with a layover day at Bob's Lake to climb 13,165-foot Tokewanna Peak. The loop consists of well-marked trail, primitive or faint trail, cross-country bushwhacking, and several miles of jeep road. The terrain is equally varied, featuring a canyon, mountain meadows, stream bottoms, an alpine lake, mountain ridges, and an optional peak climb.

At the trailhead on the West Fork Blacks Fork, cross the river. This is the only wet-foot crossing of the basic loop, so you could stash your wet waders in the willows for your return slog across the river. Follow the beaten dirt road for a mile south through a forest of subalpine fir and lodgepole pine. At the signed intersection for the Bear River–Smiths Fork Trail (091), turn left. This steep trail to the 10,700-foot ridge climbs 1,300 feet in 1 air mile. The route involves many sharp switchbacks, a highly appreciated feature: it lessens the impact of the elevation gain and it effectively closes the trail to motorized users.

At the pass it will be a welcomed relief to drop your pack and scamper up the 10,911-foot rise south of the trail to survey the country. Continuing the trip to the Middle Fork the trail becomes indistinct in the broad mountain meadow at the head of Brush Creek. To pick it up again, follow the meadow's slope down to the drainage straight east. The trail exits the meadow immediately north of the streambed. There is an old silvery wooden trail signpost, with no sign, leaning at the spot where the trail is discernible on the eastern edge of the meadow, as well as several rock cairns to mark the route there. If you move with stealth across this grassy wonderland, you may spot elk grazing among the trees.

From the meadow the trail is clear to the Middle Fork. The descent on this eastern side of the ridge is more gradual than the climb on the west. Along the way you pass a decades-old logging unit on the north side of the trail. The clearcut is on a half-section of private land in this checkerboarded region of the north Uintas.

About 6 miles from the trailhead, the trail reaches the Middle Fork at 9,760 feet. Here there are nearly a dozen log cabins—a village in the forest—and the remnants of an ambitious turn-of-the-century tie-hacking operation that evidently wasn't successful. Gargantuan logs piled along the river suggest that transporting these massive trees was where the business failed.

Campsites are plentiful in the area along the Middle Fork, either at the intersection with Middle Fork Trail, or on up the Middle Fork Trail (096). Bring plenty of mosquito repellent.

There is no sign at the intersection. This is not a maintained trail, nor is it heavily used. The trail is not shown on the topo maps (dated 1967), but it is on the Trails Illustrated map. On the ground, the trail fades in and out. The best way to find it is to look for the overgrown blazes on the trees. The invisible path goes up the Middle Fork, staying on the west side. Whenever it enters a boggy meadow, which is often, keep to the wooded area on the right and you'll pick up the trail again.

Watch for elk and moose as you travel. Theirs are the only footprints you're likely to see on the trail. You'll pass the wilderness boundary sign in one of the wooded sections of the trail. Continuing up the main drainage for 4.5 miles, the faint trail gets even more invisible as the altitude increases and tree trunks for blazes grow more scarce. Continue on your course of bearing right along the stream bank.

Bob's Lake sits in a glaciated basin below the naked hump of Tokewanna Peak. The lake, however, is not straight up the Middle Fork, but is 0.3 mile west, just west of a low ridge running down from Tokewanna. When you reach the intermittent meadows of the upper Middle Fork, bear west on the side drainage that comes from Bob's Lake. From the upper meadow, hike toward this low ridge to intersect both the stream and the trail. The trail is on the southern side of the stream and is quite visible along the wooded streambank. Follow the stream or the trail as it hooks around and climbs to Bob's Lake's basin. Another topographical landmark to guide you is the saddle in the lofty ridge running north-northwest from Tokewanna. This saddle is directly above Bob's Lake's outlet. It is also the cross-country route back to the West Fork valley on the final loop segment.

Bob's Lake sits in a cirque at 11,200 feet. Camping is impossible at the lake itself since the sloping basin has no flat spots that are more than 200 feet from water. About 200 vertical feet below a hill of glacial moraine sits a grassy hanging valley. This alpine bench has numerous flat tent sites protected by scattered spruce and subalpine fir. Here campers can enjoy early morning sunshine, as well as water from the stream below. Early in the season melting snowbanks that circle the basin provide water. This is a great spot for a layover day, to enjoy the solitude, or to climb Tokewanna Peak. Trout in Bob's Lake tantalize anglers. The ridge above the lake affords sweeping views of the upper Middle Fork valley. Its winding streams and extensive willow patches are choice habitat for moose.

For the peak climb, two options exist: either scramble directly up the sloping face above the lake, or, preferably, hike to the saddle west of the lake and then up along the peak's northwest ridge. Your reward for the 2,000-foot climb includes a magnificent view of the Uinta divide 6 miles to the south. Mount Beulah (12,557 feet) rises with a jagged peak to the southwest; Red Knob (12,108 feet), Wasatch (13,156 feet), and Mount Lovenia (13,219 feet) soar to meet the sky to the south. To the southeast, 12,990-foot Squaw Peak and the spires of Red Castle (12,566 feet) rise 2 miles away, with Kings Peak (13,528 feet) behind them.

It will be hard to leave this pristine valley, but the return leg of the loop trip is challenging enough to be interesting. Cross Bob's Lake outlet stream and zigzag 500 feet up the steep slope on the west to the 11,512-foot saddle.

Regardless of whether you climbed Tokewanna Peak, you'll enjoy the vista of the Uintas from the saddle.

The 2,000-foot drop to the West Fork valley is via the ridge directly west of the saddle. The descent is gentle at first, down the grassy pass. Keep angling to the left (south) of the gully to avoid hitting the brushy bottom too soon. Intermittent game trails are useful. Numerous streams course down the mountainside in the spring. The descent through the open forest on the steep slope is rapid. Quickly you reach the meadows above the stream bottom and then emerge at Buck Pasture on the West Fork. Look for delicate elephant's head blooming in the pasture.

Stay on the east side of the West Fork if you want to avoid two extra crossings. A clear game trail follows the riverbank north. Within a mile, at the wilderness boundary, the trail (now a road) crosses to the east side. Motorized traffic uses this jeep track right up to the wilderness boundary in spite of the fact that the forest travel plan indicates a closure 2 miles farther north. Thus the final 4 miles of the hike are on a dirt road. Especially on weekends, the route is used by four-wheelers of all sizes.

The traffic on this part of the loop makes the wildness of the Middle Fork even more precious. It also is a reminder of the need to protect these lands from the spreading intrusions of motorized use. The conservation-minded hiker should take note that the Forest Service has proposed to road and log, as well as lease for oil and gas development, most of lower to mid-elevation land in the Middle Fork drainage. Citizen action is the only force that will protect this wild country.

Central Wasatch Wilderness Complex   40

Location: North end: 1 mile southeast of Salt Lake City (Mount Olympus Wilderness). South end: 2 miles northeast of Provo (South Fork Provo River roadless area); in north-central Utah.
Size: 116,440 acres.
Administration: USDAFS Wasatch–Cache National Forest (Mount Olympus and Twin Peaks wildernesses) and Uinta National Forest (Lone Peak and Mount Timpanogos wildernesses plus the South Fork Provo roadless area).
Management status: Wilderness (four units totaling 69,938 acres); unprotected national forest roadless land (48,502 acres).
Ecosystems: Middle Rocky Mountain province, with potential natural vegetation of Douglas-fir and western spruce–fir coniferous forest.
Elevation range: 5,000 feet (western edge of Mount Olympus Wilderness) to 11,750 feet (Mount Timpanogos).
Established trails/routes: About 120 miles of national forest system trails.
Maximum core to perimeter distance: 2.5 miles (Lone Peak Wilderness).
Activities: Hiking, backpacking, mountaineering, rock climbing, horseback riding, fishing, cross-country skiing, snowshoeing, photography, nature study, hunting.
Maps: North end: 1994 USDAFS half-inch/mile map for the Wasatch–Cache National Forest, Salt Lake District (50 meter contour interval). South end: 1993 USDAFS half-inch/mile planimetric map for the Uinta National Forest. See Appendix E for a listing of the nine topo maps covering the complex.

OVERVIEW: The dramatic upsweep of northern Utah's Wasatch front forms the eastern rim of the Great Basin, running north to south for 200 miles from the Bear River to Mount Nebo. Wasatch is an Indian word meaning "high mountain pass." Indeed, countless high passes connect this monumental uplift of neck-craning mountains and canyons at Salt Lake City's eastern doorstep. The range has a jumbled foundation of ancient ocean sediments intruded with granite along with overthrusting of younger rocks on top of older rocks. The stunning alpine landforms visible today are the result of 500,000 years of glacial activity, carving rocks into horns and knife ridges and scouring out hanging valleys, cirques, and U-shaped drainages. The glaciers are long gone, but several year-round snowfields remain below high peaks.

With an astounding elevation range of up to 7,000 feet, the central Wasatch

40 A CENTRAL WASATCH WILDERNESS COMPLEX NORTH

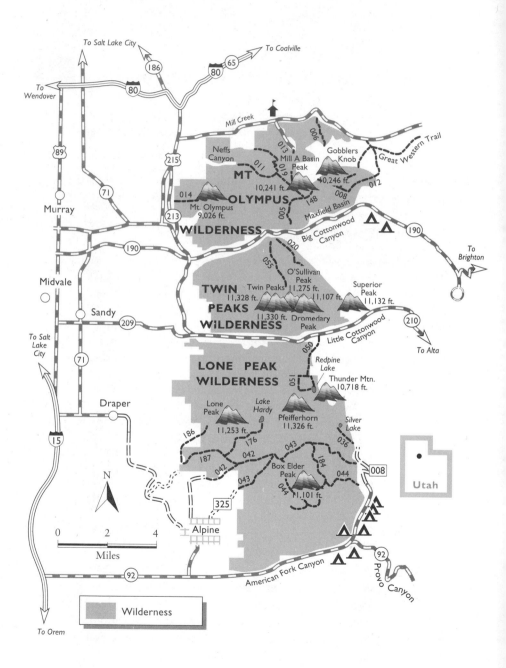

To Salt Lake City

To Coalville

186

80   65

To Wendover

80

89

215

71

Murray

213

Mill Creek

Neffs Canyon

014

Mt. Olympus
9,026 ft.

MT OLYMPUS
10,241 ft.

WILDERNESS

190

Midvale

Sandy

190

209

71

To Salt Lake City

Draper

15

006

013
011
019
005
148

Mill A Basin Peak

Gobblers Knob
10,246 ft.

Great Western Trail

012
008

Maxfield Basin

Big Cottonwood Canyon

190

To Brighton

020

055

O'Sullivan Peak
11,275 ft.

TWIN PEAKS
11,328 ft.

Twin Peaks

11,107 ft.

11,330 ft.   Dromedary Peak

Superior Peak
11,132 ft.

210

Little Cottonwood Canyon

To Alta

PEAKS WILDERNESS

050

LONE   PEAK
WILDERNESS

Redpine Lake

051

Thunder Mtn.
10,718 ft.

Lone Peak
11,253 ft.

Lake Hardy

Pfeifferhorn
11,326 ft.

Silver Lake

036

186

176
187   042
042   043

043

184
044

008

Box Elder Peak
044   11,101 ft.

Utah

N

0   2   4

Miles

325

Alpine

92

Provo Canyon

92

American Fork Canyon

To Orem

Wilderness

supports an equally wide span of habitats. Grasslands, juniper, pinyon pine, maple, and scrub oak grow up to the 7,500-foot level. Timberline continues on up to 11,000 feet with dense forests of aspen, ponderosa pine, Douglas-fir, limber pine, white fir, spruce, and subalpine fir. Alpine plant communities above timberline are a matted mix of grasses, sedges, mosses, and annuals that have adapted to powerful winds and arctic cold. By summer mountain meadows are ablaze with lupine, primrose, and at least 100 other kinds of wildflowers.

Within these diverse habitats lives a variety of Rocky Mountain wildlife, such as mule deer, elk, an occasional moose, transplanted mountain goats, black bear, coyote, badger, foxes, and flying squirrels. The high-pitched squeak of pikas, a tiny member of the rabbit family, is a special delight in the alpine zone, where marmots and pocket gophers leave tunneled trails.

The central Wasatch front harbors 70,000 acres of protected wilderness in four areas in addition to a 37,302-acre block of unprotected national forest roadless land in and adjacent to the South Fork Provo River drainage, which includes about 2,000 acres of uninventoried roadless land in Dry Fork. These five precious gems of wildness seem at first glance to be an anomaly next to a huge, rapidly growing urban complex. A closer look reveals that its proximity to civilization makes the contrast of its wildness all the more dramatic. Perhaps nowhere on earth is there a more accessible alpine wilderness that still retains its essential wild character. Equally divided between the Wasatch–Cache and Uinta national forests, this stretch of the Wasatch Range receives the heaviest national forest recreation use in the nation. Fortunately, wilderness values are protected by the combination of steep rugged terrain, vigilance by the USDA Forest Service, and an aware public. This means that these closely accessible wildlands still offer exceptional wilderness experiences in settings of solitude and natural grandeur.

On the north end of the complex the 16,000-acre Mount Olympus Wilderness is truly a home for the gods with its craggy namesake peak rising to a snowy 9,026 feet, along with Mount Raymond to the east at 10,241 feet. As part of the compromise to win passage of the 1984 Utah Wilderness Act the highest point of Gobbler's Knob (10,246 feet) was left out of the wilderness to accommodate high-altitude heli-skiing.

Just across Big Cottonwood Canyon to the south is the 13,100-acre Twin Peaks Wilderness. Quartzite, slate, and granite on the Twin Peaks (11,328 feet and 11,330 feet) bear the polished signatures of glaciers. Several other peaks exceed 11,000 feet along the main east-west ridge that dominates this alpine wilderness. Trout fin the icy, clear waters of lakes Lillian and Blanche, nestled on the north-facing basins below Superior and Dromedary peaks.

In 1978, 30,088 acres surrounding Lone Peak became Utah's first designated wilderness as part of the Endangered American Wilderness Act. The namesake 11,253-foot pinnacle of quartz monzonite jabs the sky south of Little Cottonwood Canyon less than 5 miles from Twin Peaks. Lone Peak is within a granite intrusion that occurred 24 million years ago when molten magma intruded into the limestone and quartzite rocks. Later the intrusion was uplifted, eroded, and glaciated into the sheer cliff face of the peak. Hard-to-catch cutthroat cruise the clear waters of trailless Upper Red Pine Lake below the 11,000-foot crest that runs across the north end of the wilderness.

Continuing southward across American Fork Canyon we next come to a 21,950-acre roadless area encompassing the 10,750-acre Mount Timpanogos Wilderness, from the Ute for "rocky stream." The namesake peak spans five life zones from desert to arctic, towering 7,000 feet above the Utah Valley and making it the most distinctive mountain in the Wasatch Range. Mount Timpanogos is the apex of a 7-mile-long ridge that resembles the reclining profile of a legendary Indian princess. Glaciers have scoured the steep northern and eastern faces of the peak from horizontally bedded layers of sedimentary limestone and quartzite. The resulting hanging valleys, cliffs, and waterfalls of "Timp's" east face are especially impressive.

Provo Canyon separates the Mount Timpanogos Wilderness from the fifth and only unprotected roadless block of national forest land in the Central Wasatch Complex—37,302 acres straddling the divide above the South Fork Provo River watershed. The dominant feature is the huge sweeping arc of 10,908-foot Cascade Mountain, which sends snow melt plummeting north to the South Fork and west into Pole and Rock canyons. The rough terrain is marked by rocky cliff faces and sharp, narrow drainages. Several deep, craggy canyons on the steep west slope entice exploration of the more remote highlands beyond. The more moist east-side slopes are mantled with spruce and fir; oak brush and maple cover the drier, rocky western faces.

RECREATIONAL USES: Spectacular and often vigorous hiking, backpacking, or cross-country ski trips are available throughout most of the year in the alpine gems of the central Wasatch. Outings can last one to four days without overstaying your welcome. The prime hiking season is usually from early summer to mid-fall. Most trails that climb to the 11,000-foot crest of the range average at least 1,000 feet per mile over a distance of 4 or 5 miles. But the country is equally inviting to those who prefer less physically demanding pursuits. There are plenty of opportunities for short, easy walks to contemplate the wonder of country so close and yet so wild.

The Tolcats Canyon Trailhead (014) into the Mount Olympus Wilderness, literally in the suburbs of Salt Lake City on busy Wasatch Boulevard, provides quick access into the high country. Another trip idea involves a strenuous point-to-point ski or hiking traverse across the wilderness from Big Cotton-

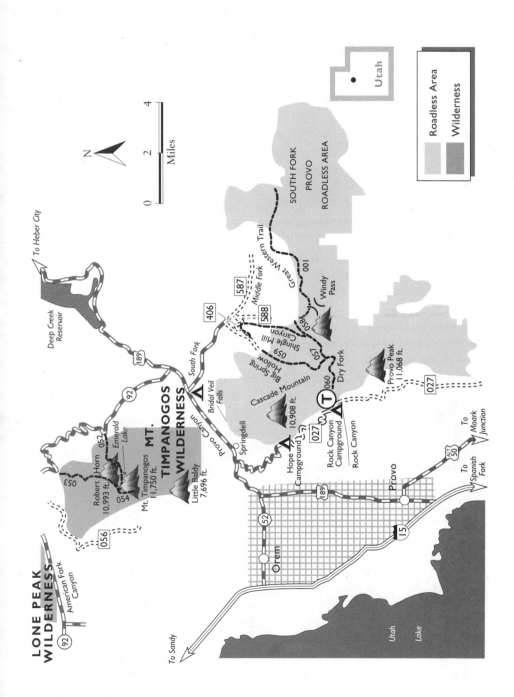

wood Canyon north to Mill Creek. Begin on the Butler Creek Trail (012) at 7,100 feet, forking left after about 0.5 mile onto Trail 008. Trail 008 connects to the Desolation Trail (019), which climbs into the head of Mill A Basin. From this point take a left on the Bowman Fork Trail (007), which wraps around the south side of Mount Raymond. Contour around to the north into a 9,350-foot saddle at the head of Porter Fork and ski the relatively gentle (but still plenty steep) slope 3 to 4 miles down the Porter Fork to Terrace Campground on Mill Creek—a distance of about 8 miles with a gain of about 2,300 feet and loss of 3,000 feet. This trip is definitely for experienced ski mountaineers during stable snow conditions. Anyone who attempts this or any other backcountry route in the Wasatch on skis must be constantly aware of avalanche danger and take all necessary precautions. For other ideas take a look at hikes 6, 7, and 8 in *Hiking Utah* (Falcon Publishing), which describe day or overnight hikes to Mount Raymond, Gobbler's Knob, and Alexander Basin in the east end of the wilderness.

The Twin Peak Wilderness is popular with rock climbers. "Temple" granite outcrops and rock ledges test the skill of technical climbers along the southern flank cliffs below the main Twin Peaks–Superior Peak divide. For most people it's adventure enough just to watch the climbers from Little Cottonwood Canyon.

Numerous nontechnical ascents of Lone Peak are possible, with the final 0.25-mile rock scramble gaining 450 feet on an exposed ridge. The peak can be summitted in a long, tough day, but the better choice is to savor its grandeur by taking two days. An approach from the north takes off from Little Cottonwood Canyon by way of the Bells Canyon Trail (070) or from Alpine on the south via the Lake Hardy Trail (176). See hikes 10 and 11 in *Hiking Utah* for route details.

The most popular peak climb in the Wasatch is likely Mount Timpanogos, which is described in Hike 15 of *Hiking Utah*. Despite being strenuous, with a 1,300-foot vertical gain in the final 0.5 mile, this climb is a wonderful family outing. It is not unusual to encounter three generations hiking and smiling together as they trudge up the steep trail. A 14.5-mile point-to-point loop hike is possible between the Timpooneke and Aspen Grove trailheads. The two trails (053 and 052) join just below the north summit ridge, so a scramble to the peak on Trail 054 should be done along the way. Trail distance to the peak from the Timpooneke trailhead is 9.4 miles compared with 9.0 miles from Aspen Grove.

The South Fork Provo River roadless area lies just south of Provo Canyon. The glaciated but dry cirques on the east side offer challenging opportunities for cross-country hiking and rock climbing, although public access across private lands is limited on this side. Two Forest Service campgrounds are adjacent to the western boundary of the roadless area. Of these the Rock Canyon

Campground (south of U.S. Highway 189 on Forest Road 027) is closest to the Dry Fork trailhead (Trail 060), which allows access to Cascade Mountain, Lightning Peak, and other trails to the north.

Please keep in mind that the Forest Service has special regulations for the four small Wasatch front wildernesses. The regulations are designed to encourage visitors to help protect the fragile wilderness resource from the effects of overuse. For example, to safeguard water quality, camps must be located at least 200 feet from the closest water source. Other regulations allow only day use in certain locations, limit camping duration, or prohibit campfires, dogs, and horses from specific areas. Party sizes cannot exceed ten people for overnight stays in the Mount Olympus, Twin Peaks, and Lone Peak wildernesses. Rather than trampling pristine areas, make your camp in an already established campsite. Be sure to check with the USDAFS Salt Lake Ranger District for the latest regulations concerning the Mount Olympus and Twin Peaks wildernesses and with the Pleasant Grove Ranger District with respect to Lone Peak and Mount Timpanogos.

HOW TO GET THERE: From Interstate 15 take Exit 275 at Orem and head east on Utah Highway 52. After about 3.5 miles the highway swings left and merges into U.S. Highway 189 as it enters Provo Canyon. Continue into the canyon another 2 miles on US 189 and look carefully for the first paved road on the right, which is just past a series of water facilities and just before Springdell.

From the main divide, the central Wasatch range stretches far to the north.

This paved road is unsigned so drive slowly in the right-hand lane to avoid missing the turnoff. If approaching from the east on US 189 this road takes off to the left about 5 miles southwest of the junction with UT 92.

The road switchbacks steeply past a popular overlook, reaching the Forest Service Hope Campground after 5 miles. At this point the pavement turns to improved dirt (Forest Road 027) and gradually becomes rougher over the next 6 miles to Rock Canyon Campground. The unsigned Dry Fork Trail (060) begins at Rock Canyon Campground (from the top of the left-hand loop) and climbs up a draw, crossing FR 027. To avoid crossing the road on foot, drive left on FR 027 past the campground turnoff for about 0.5 mile to where the trail crosses the road. Find a wide spot to pull off and park. The Dry Fork Trail is unsigned but obvious where it crosses the road.

Day hike and climb

Wasatch Crest–Cascade Mountain

Distance: 10 to 16 miles round trip.
Starting and maximum elevations: 7,000 feet and 9,800 feet (Wasatch crest) or 10,908 feet (Cascade Mountain).
Difficulty: Moderately strenuous (Wasatch crest); Strenuous (Cascade Mountain).
Best months: Mid-June through October, with deep green conifers and color-banded rock formations. Aspens are especially colorful in the fall.
Topo map: Bridal Veil Falls-UT.

This vigorous high-country exploration, so near and yet so far from the hustle and bustle of the Wasatch front, offers a variety of beyond-the-road choices. The basic 10-mile out-and-back trail hike to and along the lofty Wasatch crest is a full enough day outing for most folks. With an early start, well-conditioned climbers can put in an even longer day of at least 16 rugged miles round trip to the rocky pinnacles of Cascade Mountain. And those with the time and desire to savor more of this alpine south end of the complex can base camp in a high east-side basin for peak climbing both north and south.

The clear Dry Fork Trail climbs steadily up an active avalanche chute, alternating through aspen groves and thick brushfields. After a couple of miles it breaks out into steep open meadows with peaks and buttresses soaring dramatically to nearly 11,000 feet southward. After the trail winds through the upper Dry Fork basin it switchbacks up a series of old constructed terraces to the 9,800-foot Wasatch crest. The monumental sweep of massive Cascade Mountain dominates the northwest horizon as does Mount Timpanogos and Lone Peak beyond. Provo and Lake Utah can be seen far below through the V-shaped wedge of Rock Canyon. Perfectly symmetrical cone-shaped peaks rise to the south. To attain this vantage point the trail gains nearly 3,000 vertical feet over a distance of about 4 miles from the trailhead.

From the signed three-way trail junction just below the crest, Trail 059 follows the divide northwest a short ways and then drops steeply to the open, upper reaches of Big Spring Hollow. The Shingle Mill Canyon Trail (057) heads straight up the hillside and then descends a dividing ridge to grassy meadows at the head of Shingle Mill Canyon. Unlike the more rounded ridges of adjacent Big Spring Hollow, this drainage is bound by rugged cliffs, spires, talus slopes, and dense pockets of coniferous forest. Two secluded hanging valleys in the eastern upper end of the basin offer remote campsites for those willing to backpack off-trail across rough terrain. A 10- to 12-mile Big Spring Hollow–Shingle Mill Canyon trail loop is possible by starting from FR 406 near Big Spring Hollow about 4 miles up the South Fork Provo River Road.

Another option from the three-way trail junction is to hike the crest northwest for an easy mile to Point 10125. From here, hiking the ridge is slowed by steeper, more rugged terrain for the next 3 to 4 miles to the northern 10,908-foot apex of Cascade Mountain. This massif is flanked by cliffs on all sides with scenery to match. It is completely exposed to whatever the winds may bring and should only be attempted during fair weather. Windswept bristlecone pines cling tenaciously to this stretch of the crest, which is also adorned with fields of Indian paintbrush and blue penstemon during early summer. Dropping back down to the trailhead brings to mind that both the Dry Fork and nearby Lightning Peak are aptly named. Carry lots of water and keep a watchful eye out for approaching storms.

Mount Nebo–
Golden Ridge Wilderness Complex   41

Location: 2 miles northeast of Nephi in north-central Utah.
Size: 69,480 acres (two units).
Administration: USDAFS Uinta National Forest, Spanish Fork Ranger District.
Management status: Mount Nebo Wilderness (28,170 acres) plus 41,310 acres of
unprotected national forest roadless land.
Ecosystems: Middle Rocky Mountain province, with potential natural vegetation of
mountain mahogany–oak brush.
Elevation range: 5,300 to 11,928 feet (Mona Summit/Mount Nebo).
Established trails/routes: About 50 miles of USDAFS system trails.
Maximum core to perimeter distance: 2 miles (in both Mount Nebo and
Golden Ridge).
Activities: Hiking, backpacking, rock climbing, horseback riding, cross-country
skiing, snowshoeing, photography, nature study, hunting, fishing.
Maps: 1993 USDAFS half-inch/mile planimetric map for the Uinta National Forest.
See Appendix E for a listing of the six topo maps covering the complex.

OVERVIEW: The apex of the Wasatch Range is also its southernmost named
peak—11,928-foot Mount Nebo. This pyramid-shaped pinnacle is the crown-
ing centerpiece and namesake of a 28,170-acre wilderness designated in the
1984 Utah Wilderness Act. Early Indians built signal fires on the peak, which
was later named by Mormon pioneers after Mount Nebo in Palestine. One of
the settlers, W. Phelps, made the first recorded ascent in 1869. The wilderness
is split in two by an old jeep trail that runs up Pole Canyon (Forest Road 109)
north of Mount Nebo. FR 109 then connects to the Privateer Mine road (FR
160), which leads southeast to the Nebo Loop Road (FR 015). This old roadway serves better as a trail than as a vehicular route, having been washed out
in 1983 and later closed by the USDA Forest Service.

East of the Nebo Loop Road sits the 32,180-acre Golden Ridge roadless
area. In contrast to the high, sharp Wasatch crest in the adjacent wilderness,
Golden Ridge is a broad, more diverse topographical mix of open grassy parks,
long forested ridges, and steep, rocky canyons. Its lack of classic alpine scenery is more than compensated by its abundance of critical deer, elk, and black

41 MOUNT NEBO–GOLDEN RIDGE WILDERNESS COMPLEX

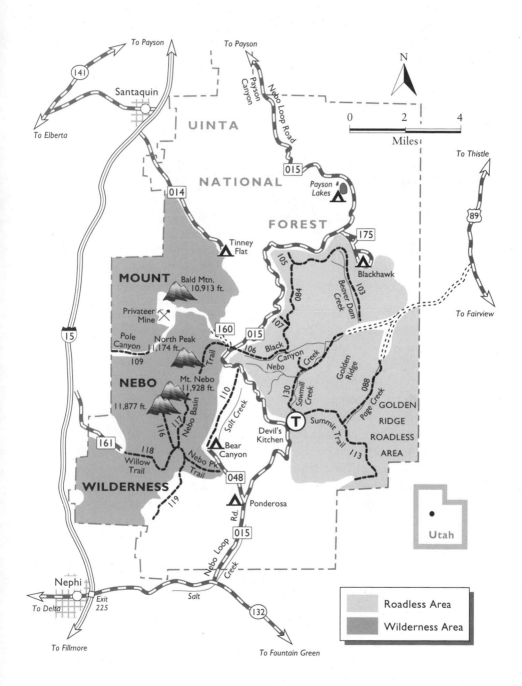

bear habitat. As such, Golden Ridge is a logical extension of the Mount Nebo Wilderness. Its main artery of Nebo Creek is an excellent trout fishery thanks, in part, to its relative remoteness from roads.

Before the formation of the Wasatch Range some 80 million years ago active erosion deposited soil and gravel at canyon mouths. These depositions were then buried, cemented, and oxidized into red conglomerate. As the mountains rose along the Wasatch Fault so too did the conglomerate. Today's formations of cones, hoodoos, columns, and banded layers are the result of erosion and weathering of these red conglomerate rocks, with notable examples at Devil's Kitchen and above Nebo Creek.

At lower to mid elevations the complex is characterized by sagebrush grasslands and oak, maple, and Douglas-fir forests. Hardy limber pine cling to high, windswept ridges in a subalpine zone ablaze with lupine, bluebell, Indian paintbrush, and columbine. The surrounding forest is a coniferous blend of mostly white fir and spruce. The highest ridges on and near the major peaks support a sparse alpine mantle of lichens and matted tundra grasses.

Golden eagles and sharp-shinned hawks cruise the air currents above peaks and ridges. Grassy slopes and thick aspen-fir forests give food and secure cover to one of Utah's largest elk herds. Most of Mount Nebo provides summer range for deer and elk along with some critical winter range on the dry western slopes.

RECREATIONAL USES: Both sides of the scenic Nebo Loop Road access numerous jumping off points for hikes, climbs, backpacks, horseback rides, cross-country ski tours, hunts, and fishing trips into both the wilderness and Golden Ridge country. Most of these excursions are day trips, with deer and elk hunting attracting the largest number of visitors. Four Forest Service campgrounds border the edges of the two roadless areas (Ponderosa, Bear Canyon, Tinney Flat, and Blackhawk). Hiking and horseback riding is especially popular from Blackhawk Campground on the northern boundary. The Devil's Kitchen Picnic Area (9 miles north of Utah Highway 132 on the Nebo Loop Road) has a 0.25-mile, wheelchair-accessible nature trail ending at a spectacular overlook of "mini-Bryce Canyon" formations. The Golden Ridge roadless area is crisscrossed with a well-distributed trail system. One possibility is to hike or ride horseback 15 miles from the Summit Trailhead down Sawmill Fork, ending at Blackhawk Campground. Another idea for an extended two- to four-day backpack or horse trip is to take a 25-mile trail loop from the Summit Trail to Blackhawk, down Beaver Dam Creek, and back up Nebo Creek to the Summit trailhead.

An ascent of Mount Nebo can be accomplished as a one-night backpack or as a demanding 12-mile round-trip day climb. The route gains an average of 1,000 feet per mile over a distance of 5 trail miles from the Nebo Peak

Trailhead (Trail 117) to the south summit at 11,877 feet. The final mile to the main 11,928-foot peak requires off-trail rock-scrambling along a knife ridge. See Hike 17 in *Hiking Utah* (Falcon Publishing) for the details on climbing Mount Nebo. Snowfields linger well into summer, and those who summit this apex of the Wasatch crest earn a 360-degree vista of Basin and Range desert, the vertical sweep of Nebo Ridge, and central plateau canyons and mountains fading to the southeastern horizon.

HOW TO GET THERE: From the south: from Interstate 15 take Exit 225 at Nephi and head 6 miles east on Utah Highway 132 to the signed Nebo Scenic Loop Road (FR 015). Turn left (north) on this good paved road (open from mid-June to late October) and drive about 9 miles to the signed Summit Trail trailhead and parking area, which is bound by a corral fence on the right (east) side of the road. The trailhead is about 0.5 mile below (south) of the Devil's Kitchen picnic area and nature trail.

From the north: from I-15 take Exit 254 at Payson and follow 600 East to the northern beginning of the paved Nebo Scenic Loop Road (FR 015). Follow FR 015 about 29 miles to the signed Summit Trail trailhead and parking area on the left (east) side of the road.

Trail and off-trail day hike

Golden Ridge Loop

Distance: 12-mile loop.
Starting, minimum, and maximum elevations: 8,300 feet, 6,700 feet, and 8,453 feet.
Difficulty: Moderate (out-and-back); strenuous (loop).
Best months: Mid-June to mid-October.
Topo map: Nebo Basin-UT.

A diversity of terrain and hiking conditions distinguishes this full day excursion through the heart of the Golden Ridge roadless area, combining high ridge on-and-off-trail hiking. The clear Summit Trail 113 climbs eastward through a forest of mature aspen and huge veteran white fir. During early summer the route is graced by a profusion of white Colorado columbine. A signed trail junction at mile 0.5 points left to Sawmill-Nebo Creek Trail 130. Continue to the right on the Summit Trail, which soon opens to 360-degree views of the entire complex and beyond. The ridgeline rolls delightfully up and down but is dry, so carry lots of water. For miles the summit ridge is complemented by the imposing majesty of the Nebo Peak ridge, behind and to the immediate west. The lofty summit route blends open vistas with ample shade due to pockets of fir and aspen along the crest. A stock fence parallels much of the trail, which is also used for driving cattle in early summer.

At mile 3 (according to the Forest Service, but it's closer to mile 4) the trail runs up to a signed junction with the Page Fork Trail (088). A spring seeps out some 250 feet below at the head of Page Fork, but don't rely on this mudhole for water. For a moderate and highly scenic trail hike of 7 to 8 miles round trip retrace your route back to the trailhead on the Summit Trail.

To start the off-trail segment of the loop along Golden Ridge, double back about 0.25 mile to the gate, turn right, and follow the fenceline north to a rounded 8,453-foot knoll, which happens to be the apex of the hike. At this point the fence swings westward. Continue north on a primitive game trail as it drops steeply to a saddle mantled with scattered Douglas-fir, chokecherry, and a dazzling display of wildflowers in early summer. Follow the faint path another 0.75 mile to the third hill (elevation about 8,340 feet) and then zigzag downslope through the brush to the northwest, dropping 400 feet to an old cow camp in a grassy flat. The loop continues on this long, relatively gentle northwest-trending ridge for about 2 miles, passing above the Upper Pasture en route to Nebo Creek. Surprisingly, this dry ridge is ablaze with wildflowers in early summer, including such beauties as Nuttal's sego lily and the flaming red flowers of cushion cacti. At times travel is impeded by dense Gambel oak, manzanita, and mountain mahogany, but numerous grassy glens break up the bushwhacking.

From Point 7,362 the ridge plummets 600 feet between colorful columns of red conglomerate to the green meadows of Nebo Creek. After miles of waterless ridge running this cottonwood-lined stream bottom is truly an oasis, where trout dart in shady dark pools. The drainage is grazed heavily by cattle so be sure to purify all drinking water. Upon reaching Nebo Creek turn left and head upstream. The trail (130) is primitive and intimate yet easy to follow as it weaves through a lush spruce bottom. After about 1 mile a sign at the Blackhawk Trail junction indicates 2 miles to the Nebo Loop Road, but 3 miles is more accurate. Turn left on the Sawmill Fork Trail, which gains 500 feet per mile to its junction with the Summit Trail. Make a right and retrace the final 0.5 mile to the trailhead. An overnight option would be to backpack down Sawmill Fork and base camp in the upper reaches of Nebo Creek for exploring side ridges and canyons.

A base camp on upper Nebo Creek would also be an ideal starting and ending point for the 20-mile loop described in the "Recreational Uses" section above to Black Canyon, Beaver Dam Creek and back up Nebo Creek.

Wasatch Plateau Complex ■ 42

Location: Immediately east of Manti, in central Utah.
Size: Eight units of roadless national forest designated for nonmotorized recreation totalling 55,000 acres.
Administration: USDAFS Manti–La Sal National Forest, San Pete, Ferron, and Price ranger districts.
Management status: Unprotected national forest roadless land.
Ecosystems: Douglas-fir section, Rocky Mountain province, semi-arid steppe of the dry domain.
Elevation range: 6,550 to 11,285 feet (South Tent Mountain).
Established trails/routes: More than 70 miles of trails in nonmotorized-use units.
Maximum core to perimeter distance: 2 miles (Fish Creek unit).
Activities: Hiking, camping, horseback riding, hunting, fishing, cross-country skiing, snowshoeing, mountaineering.
Maps: USDAFS 1995 half-inch/mile Manti–La Sal National Forest, San Pete, Ferron, and Price ranger districts, (50 meter contour interval) and 1989 Manti–La Sal, San Pete, Ferron, and Price ranger districts travel map. See Appendix E for a listing of the 31 topo maps covering the roadless pieces.

OVERVIEW: Rising from the heart of Utah, the 70-mile long Wasatch Plateau is a southern extension of the Wasatch Range. It is not a traditional table-top plateau, but an extended mountain range jutting above a 10,000-foot plateau. From 8,789-foot Brown's Peak in the north to 10,984-foot Mary's Nipple in the south, the plateau has more than a dozen peaks above 10,500 feet; the highest is 11,285-foot South Tent Mountain in the midsection of the plateau. Steep canyons drop east and west from the plateau ridge. This forested finger is bracketed both east and west by highways and agricultural development; its mountain waters are dammed, channeled, and piped to the Castle Valley on the east and the San Pete Valley on the west.

The public lands of the plateau are under the jurisdiction of the Manti–La Sal National Forest. While the original number of roadless acres was substantial (328,218 acres), this sum is deceptive. Since the roadless inventory of RARE II, these lands have been fragmented by roads. The area has been further reduced by revegetation projects, logging, coal, oil and gas development, and ambitious water projects. Originally there were 20 roadless units in excess

42 WASATCH PLATEAU COMPLEX

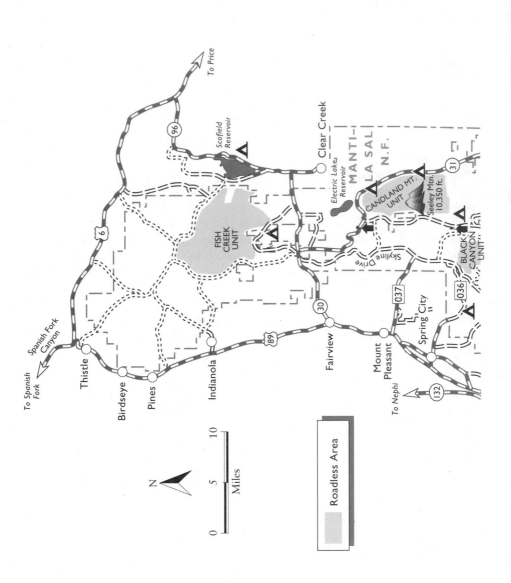

To Price

96

Scofield Reservoir

Clear Creek

MANTI-LA SAL N.F.

Electric Lake Reservoir

CANDLAND MT. UNIT

Seeley Mtn. 10,350 ft.

31

6

FISH CREEK UNIT

Skyline Drive

BLACK CANYON UNIT

037

036

Spring City

30

Fairview

89

Mount Pleasant

132

Spanish Fork Canyon

To Spanish Fork

Thistle

Birdseye

Pines

Indianola

To Nephi

N

10

5

Miles

0

Roadless Area

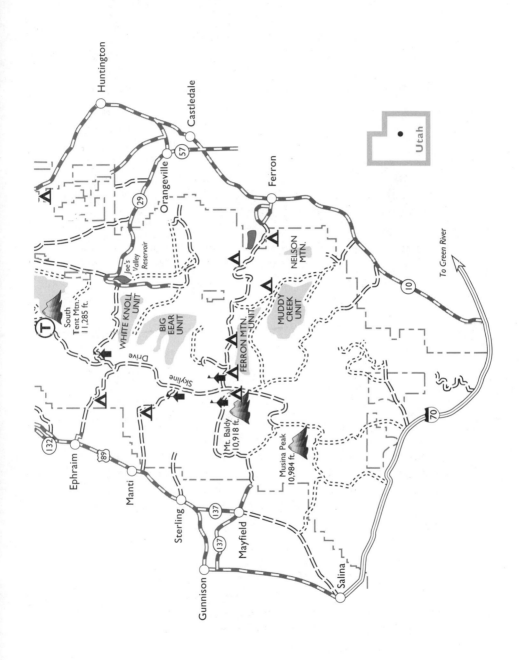

of 5,000 acres, ranging in size from 50,403 acres in the Muddy Creek–Nelson Mountain unit to the 5,741 acres of Black Mountain. Now, after two decades of development, the plateau is covered by a cobweb of roads zigzagging up drainages, down ridges, and across meadows.

The forest travel plan (released in 1989) has identified 8 remnant areas that are closed year-round to motorized use. At 22,450 acres, the Fish Creek unit is the largest remaining vestige of wild country on the plateau. Candland Mountain (10,880 acres) and Black Canyon (8,320 acres) are also large enough to encompass entire drainages within the complex plateau topography. The rest (Big Bear at 6,400 acres; White Knoll at 2,000 acres; Ferron Mountain at 2,000 acres; Muddy Creek at 1,500 acres; and Nelson Mountain at 1,000 acres) are oddly shaped, lacking physiographic integrity. The smallest two are the sole survivors of the largest original RARE II unit, illustrative of the level of activity in this national forest. Fortunately some of these units have more actual roadless acres than the travel map illustrates.

As fragmented as these lands are, the terrain and vegetation retain the splendor of the plateau. The intrepid hiker can find undeveloped basins and drainages wholly out of sight of intrusive roads and far from the roar of internal combustion engines. The plateau's numerous peaks tickle the clouds that hang along the 10,000-foot escarpment above the San Pete Valley, bringing up to 30 inches of annual precipitation as either rain or snow. The huge laccolith uplift that created the plateau has been modified over eons of geologic time by faulting as the Earth's crust shifts. Erosion and glaciation have further eaten away at the interbedded sandstone to create the rough topography of abrupt peaks, shaggy canyons, and jagged ridges.

The vegetation of the region reflects varying doses of moisture received at different elevations and aspects. Scattered pinyon-juniper is the climax vegetation at lower elevations. On north facing slopes this sparse cover shifts to white fir, subalpine fir, and spruce communities with increasing altitude. The south facing slopes are host to aspen, forb-grass, and mountain brush communities, shifting to sagebrush and forb-grass communities at highest elevations.

Deer and elk abound. The lower country on the eastern edge of the Manti–La Sal National Forest provides much-needed winter range. Herds of ungulates rely on the remote canyons and meadows within the plateau during summer and fall. Bobcat, mountain lion, and various smaller mammals prowl the forests of the plateau. Widespread fishing activity reflects a flourishing trout population in the streams. Many of their flows have been modified, however, as dams and reservoirs channel irrigation water and community water supplies for the bustling towns in the valleys both east and west of the national forest.

No archeological surveys have been done in the Wasatch Plateau. Both Paleo-Indians and historical tribes used the lower reaches of the plateau in the warmer summer months, but no sites have been identified.

RECREATIONAL USES: The Wasatch Plateau's central location and dramatic topography make it an attractive destination for a variety of recreational users. Skyline Drive (Forest Road 150) follows the plateau's north-south axis for 80 miles. To reach Skyline Drive take Exit 71 from Interstate 70, about 18 miles east of Salina. FR 009 goes up Salina Creek to meet Skyline Drive at the southern end of the plateau. From there the improved dirt road heads north on the 10,000-foot plateau, winding between peaks and lakes. Skyline Drive is a popular mountain bike route (see Gregg Bromka's *Mountain Biking Utah,* Falcon Publishing). The newly designated Great Western Trail also follows the Skyline Drive route through this part of Utah. Forested sections are interspersed with meadows providing magnificent panoramas of the mountains and buttes of this high country.

This road along the plateau's crest also offers access to infinite hiking possibilities, either dropping into the canyons to the east, or climbing the peaks that punctuate the route. Hikers wishing to avoid motorized use will want to consult the forest travel map to locate the quiet trails. Black Canyon (see below), Candland Mountain, and Fish Creek are the largest nonmotorized roadless units remaining along the plateau; each is accessible from Skyline Drive. At the southern end of the national forest the White Knoll, Big Bear, Ferron Mountain, Muddy Creek, and Nelson Mountain roadless remnants are smaller. But each of these out-of-the-way nooks is from 1 to 10 miles east of the Skyline corridor, therefore offering greater solitude. In the fall hunters abound, so bright orange garb is necessary for hikers who enjoy the mountain aspens' fall colors.

Winter brings both snowmobilers and cross-country skiers to the high plateau, with the motorized powderhounds being the more numerous of the two. The forest travel map will help with the planning of a winter outing for those skiers and snowshoers seeking silence and solitude on the plateau.

HOW TO GET THERE: From Spring City, 1.5 miles east of U.S. Highway 89 in the San Pete Valley, go east from Main Street on 100 South East. There's a sign for Spring City Canyon at the intersection. The road east to the plateau is paved for 1 mile, then gravel for the next 5 miles. Bear left at the only Y, about 1 mile out of town. Upon entering the Manti–La Sal National Forest the road is designated Forest Road 036. As the road climbs higher the surface changes to improved dirt with some gravel. This road is suitable for passenger vehicles if driven carefully. Dicey muddy spots can be challenging if there's any rain, however. At 15 miles from the town you reach Skyline Drive on the top of the Wasatch Plateau. This mid-point of the plateau country is clear of snow before the higher areas north or south. Skyline Drive, at 10,000 feet and higher, is often blocked by lingering snowbanks late in the spring.

An important footnote to this travel information is to NOT take FR 037 out of Mount Pleasant. Although this latter route looks inviting on the map (it appears shorter, more direct), the road is eroded, full of boulders, narrowed by landslides, and gutted by washouts. It is only suitable for all-terrain vehicle riders who enjoy such challenges.

When the snow is gone, Skyline Drive is accessible from the north via Utah Highway 31, 9 miles east of Fairview. Turn right on Skyline and drive south 12 miles on the improved dirt road to the Spring City Road intersection.

To reach the trailhead, drive south 1.5 miles from the intersection. Turn east on the second unmarked dirt road on the left. This road descends gradually to a flat below Reeder Ridge. The road crosses a wet spot created by a spring. Park your car beyond the damp crossing, about 0.3 mile from Skyline. Going further only means you have to do more climbing to get to the ridge. This spur road (FR 103) to the trailhead may be difficult for a low-clearance vehicle. Park just off Skyline Drive if you have any doubts about clearance and rough terrain and begin your hike from there.

Loop day hike

South Tent Mountain–Black Canyon Loop

Distance: 9 to 10 miles.
Starting and maximum elevations: 10,480 feet and 11,285 feet (South Tent Mountain).
Difficulty: Moderate (out-and-back to peaks); strenuous (loop trip).
Best months: July through October.
Topo map: South Tent Mountain-UT.

Deep in the heart of the roaded Wasatch Plateau, this Black Canyon unit provides refuge for people seeking quiet woods and meadows, panoramic views, and intimate streams. This loop trip can be done as a moderate 7-mile out-and-back hike along Reeder Ridge to South Tent Mountain. Or it can be extended into a strenuous loop trip with an off-trail descent of 2,000 feet into Black Canyon, followed by a gradual climb by trail and road back to the trailhead. The longer journey can be done as a 2-day backpack. There are campsites along the streams in Black Canyon.

From your parking spot, hike west to ascend the ridge. Follow the ridge crest south. Scattered limestone boulders require some skillful footwork. In early summer Parry's primrose decorates the boulder mounds with its dazzling purple and yellow blooms. Within the first mile, the route provides vantage points from which to scan the surrounding mountains and meadows for elk. Below the ridge to the east are lush pristine meadows with wildflowers and gooseberry. Gnarly subalpine fir cling to the ridge, providing respite from the winds that whip across this high country. From the rooftop of central Utah, you can see the Big and Little Horseshoe basins carved into the west side of the

Snow cornices remain into early July along the high ridge connecting North and South Tent mountains.

plateau. To the northwest Mount Nebo pierces the skyline of the Wasatch front range.

Continue hiking south along the ridge to gradually ascend to North Tent Mountain. This tent is a two-pole model, with a sagging 0.2-mile ridge between the peaks. The lower first summit (11,230 feet) affords a view of Black Canyon below. If you're planning the loop trip you can see your return to the trailhead from the dirt road that runs down into the head of Black Canyon from Skyline Drive. Where the road switchbacks sharply to the southwest you will continue hiking up the side drainage, taking a direct route back to your vehicle below the spring. Speaking of vehicles, after North Tent Mountain there are no more all-terrain-vehicle tracks beneath your feet. They don't appear again until the road begins in the upper reaches of Black Canyon.

Continuing the journey, follow the ridgeline as it drops 200 feet to the saddle before the gradual walk up South Tent to its 11,285-foot peak. A survey marker pinpoints the summit of this highest peak of the Wasatch Plateau. This is a good spot for lunch, and it is the turn-around for the out-and-back hike. On a clear day you can see the Uintas on the northern horizon. The rugged silhouette of the San Rafael Swell rises to the east. The Henry Mountains are in the distance to the southeast.

From the peak the loop route follows the ridgeline down to 10,940-foot Little Mountain. Intermittent game trails head in the right direction. This high point along Reeder Ridge is forested with fir and aspen, interspersed with protected mountain meadows of wildflowers. With map and compass, plan your descent to Black Canyon via the ridge to the northwest. This route to the confluence of Brough Fork and the Black Canyon stream is steep, but allows the most direct line of travel. Expect to detour around areas of heavy windfall on the densely forested northwest slope. The ridge has a steep pitch at the top, eases somewhat midslope, and then drops sharply to the canyon floor at 9,200 feet.

The Black Canyon stream can be crossed on convenient rocks. Pick up the overgrown ancient jeep trail on the north side of the stream and follow it upstream. Gently sloping meadows stretch between stately aspen groves. Campsites are plentiful. A pile of wood debris marks the site of a long-gone dwelling. The evidence of past beaver residents is more permanent, with gnawed stumps and remnants of dams still blocking the stream and creating shallow ponds in the bottom.

The jeep trail is easy to follow and is a relief after route finding a way down the ridge. The trail leads up through cool spruce thickets. An old stock fence marks the end of the hiking trail at the road to the exploratory drill hole in upper Black Canyon. Here you pick up the road for the 2-mile hike up to the point on the switchback where another cross-country segment takes you to your car. Although the road is closed to vehicles in the lower 1-mile stretch, no sign or gate discourages motorized use. On your way up, after a mile, look for a water diversion project on your right. This is the inlet of the tunnel that transports the plateau's water to the thirsty San Pete Valley.

At the point of the final switchback going southwest, continue on up the side draw to return to your vehicle. Climbing sharply to your right (north) is a mistake, for the slope is steep and the shrubbery dense. Select the more gradual route up the valley.

Upon returning to Skyline Drive you will have gained new insight into the wildness of the Wasatch Plateau. This rugged terrain protects itself from development. Wildlife has succeeded in finding protected pockets. Horned owls, elk, black bear, and mountain lions are at home in this patchwork wilderness.

Pahvant Range Complex   43

Location: 3 miles east of Fillmore and 1 mile north and west of Richfield, in west-central Utah.
Size: 225,628 acres (nine national forest roadless areas).
Administration: USDAFS Fishlake National Forest, Fillmore Ranger District.
Management status: Unprotected national forest roadless land.
Ecosystems: Middle Rocky Mountain province, with potential natural vegetation of juniper-pinyon woodland, spruce-fir, Douglas-fir, and western spruce-fir forest ecosystems.
Elevation range: 5,500 feet (Beehive Peak east-side canyon mouths) to 10,222 feet (Mine Camp Peak in the Pahvant roadless area).
Established trails/routes: About 80 miles of national forest system trails.
Maximum core to perimeter distance: 2.5 miles (Beehive Peak area).
Activities: Hiking, backpacking, horseback riding, cross-country skiing, snowshoeing, hunting, fishing.
Maps: USDAFS 1993/1994 Fishlake National Forest Travel Map, half-inch/mile. Refer to Appendix E for a listing of the 18 topo maps covering the complex.

OVERVIEW: Sandwiched between Interstates 15 and 70 near Richfield is a 50-mile sweep of the Pahvant Range—a mountainous plateau of 10,000-foot summits, high ridges, steep slopes, and deep, narrow canyons. Surprisingly, much of this land remains wild—not because of wilderness designation but by virtue of remoteness, steepness, and lack of developable resources.

Small to medium-size roadless areas are strung like pearls across this otherwise heavily roaded expanse of the Fishlake National Forest. From north to south the nine individual roadless areas within the complex are North Pahvant (49,306 acres); Beehive Peak (56,572 acres); Flat Canyon (8,324 acres); Copleys (12,026 acres); Pahvant (43,898 acres); Ferguson (6,344 acres); Joe Lott (22,389 acres); Pyramids (14,142 acres); and Dog Valley (12,627 acres).

The colorful Pahvant Mountains are a source of abundant water as reflected by their Ute name which means "much water." The west slope of the range is a contorted mix of very old shales, sandstones, quartzites, and limestones that were originally deposited in a slowly sinking sea bed. Compression then forced these marine deposits over other layers to form gray and tan colored moun-

43 PAHVANT RANGE COMPLEX

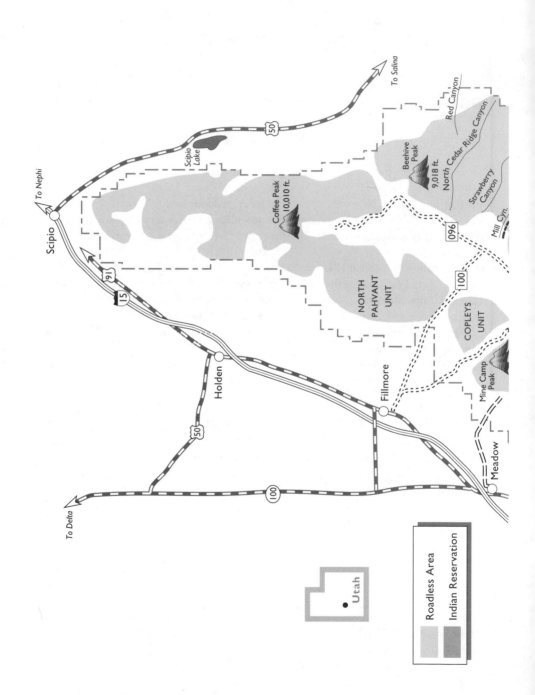

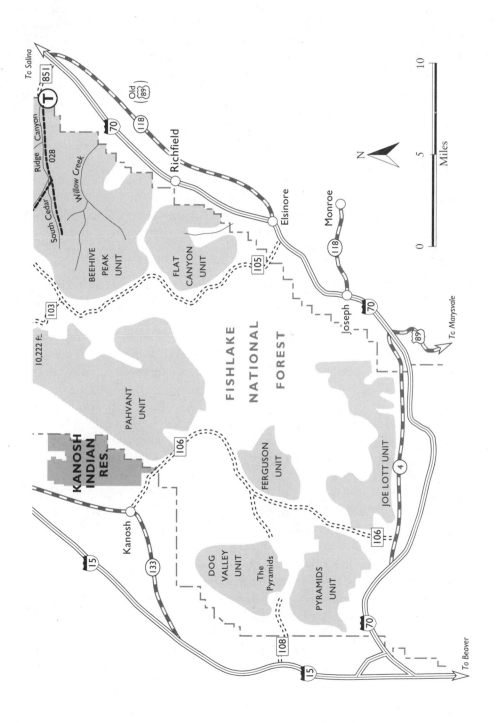

tains. The younger and more colorful east side shales, sandstones, and conglomerates were laid down at the foot of these mountains. Uplifting then began along block faults and continues to this day.

Elevations in North Pahvant rise from 7,000 to 10,000 feet in only 2.5 miles, forming a landscape of high peaks, mountain parklands, and steep canyons with perennial streams. Lower slopes are clad with pinyon-juniper and sagebrush-grass along with white fir, aspen, and alpine meadows in the higher country. Separated from North Pahvant only by the Willow Creek Road (Forest Road 102), Beehive Peak is the largest unroaded expanse in the Pahvant Range. Draping the eastern slopes, Beehive Peak is a continuation of similar rounded ridges, pointed peaks, open meadows, and steep cliffs falling into deep canyons. Many of the cliffs are terraced with short vertical drops of 30 feet or less. Vegetation is similar with the added ecological attraction of bristlecone pine near 9,018-foot Beehive Peak and upper Red Canyon. Little Valley Road (FR 096) splits Beehive Peak from Flat Canyon—a dry, lower elevation roadless area immediately west of Richfield. The mostly bare slopes between 6,000 and 7,000 feet are broken by patches of pinyon-juniper, grasses, and mountain brush.

Roads and development have fragmented the originally inventoried Pahvant roadless area into four pieces. The first, Copleys, is a small, triangular unit with long ridges, up to 10,000 feet high, dropping into steep-walled canyons with narrow bottoms. Varied vegetation includes pinyon-juniper, sagebrush-grass, mountain mahogany, Douglas-fir, and white fir. The turning fall colors of deciduous aspen, mountain maple, and Gambel oak are spectacular. Across the Sand Rock Ridge Road (FR 103) stretches the still sizable Pahvant roadless area. From its apex at 10,222-foot Mine Camp Peak long ridges plunge abruptly into narrow canyons. High-country coniferous plant communities are similar throughout the Pahvant Range. The Pahvant unit is distinguished more by its geologic features, such as the pocketed walls of Hell Hole Canyon and the conglomerate rock of the Devil's Armchair.

Several miles of developed national forest sequester the next unit, the tiny Ferguson roadless area. Comparable topography and vegetation are found here along with the added diversity of riparian cottonwood trees and curly leaf mountain mahogany. Of special interest are the volcanic remnants of an ancient crater on the divide between Cottonwood and Cummings creeks. Joe Lott is the fourth and most southerly chunk of the original Pahvant roadless area. The landscape is similar to the other units—long ridges separating steep, narrow canyons. A few of its hidden treasures include a huge rock formation in the left fork of Joe Lott Creek, a large cottonwood spring up Whiskey Creek, and the Three Creek Calderas of the Marysvale volcanoes.

On the south end of the Pahvant Range the Pyramids roadless area is named for a jumble of rock pinnacles called the Pyramids (7,961 feet). Varied vegetative types include open sagebrush flats, steep pinyon-juniper side hills, narrow canyons with springs lined by red cedars, and an abundance of Gambel oak. A constructed four-wheel-drive trail from Bull Valley splits off Dog Valley, the southernmost unit in the complex. Landforms and plant communities are a similar extension of those found in Pyramids.

Working back to the north, Dog Valley and Pyramids provide winter range for elk and mule deer along with some spring and fall habitat. Mountain lions are rare, but are more apt to be living in the Dog Valley country. In the central reaches of the range, mule deer roam throughout the Joe Lott area. The least likely residents here are the Bonneville cutthroat trout that have been planted in Sam Stowe Creek. The Pahvant unit supports a good population of elk and mule deer, and also cutthroat and rainbow trout in several small streams. To the immediate north, Copleys also harbors cutthroat in small creeks. Mule deer summer here in the higher country and also find winter refuge at lower elevations. Much of the Beehive Peak country is also good summer range for elk and deer. This vital summer habitat extends well into the North Pahvant; a few mountain lions roam here as well. Bald eagles are known to visit during winter.

These nine surviving vestiges of unroaded terrain function as islands in the sea of surrounding roads and development most people associate with the Pahvant Range. As such, rewarding discoveries await those who venture beyond the roads.

RECREATIONAL USES: The fall deer hunting season attracts the heaviest overall use, which is localized but scattered throughout the Pahvant Range. Despite the dryness of the country, quality hiking can be enjoyed in several of the roadless tracts, notably in North Pahvant, Beehive Peak, Copleys, Joe Lott, Pyramids, and Dog Valley. One trip idea for the Pyramids is to hike several miles up Widemouth Canyon, where water flows seasonally in the spring, all the way to the Pyramids rock formations. In the North Pahvant most of the canyon bottoms and several ridges are traversed by low-standard trails.

Due to their larger size and the presence of water, the North Pahvant, Beehive Peak, Pahvant, and Joe Lott roadless areas are better suited for backpacking and horseback riding. With a scarcity of live streams, fishing is a limited and localized activity in these mostly parched mountains. There are some angling opportunities in the Pahvant roadless area and in short, trailless stretches of Pioneer Creek and the North Fork of Chalk Creek within the North Pahvant.

HOW TO GET THERE: From the south: From Main Street in Richfield, head east on 300 North to the east end of town and turn left (northeast) on Utah Highway 118 (Old U.S. Highway 89). Continue 4.3 miles and turn left (north) on an improved gravel road signed 4200 East. Cross Substation Road after 1.5

miles, continuing straight north. After another 0.4 mile the road crosses over Interstate 70, changing to an unimproved two-wheel-drive dirt road 0.1 mile beyond the overpass. During the next 0.7 mile the road crosses several irrigation ditches. Turn left immediately after the third ditch (2.7 miles from old US 89) and follow the main dirt road 1.1 miles into the mouth of the canyon. Here the road ends on the north side of the creek just past a wide turn-around and parking area, which is the unsigned trailhead. Another road access is the south side of the canyon entrance.

From the north: From I-70 south of Salina take Exit 46 and drive 1 mile south, passing the turnoff to Sigurd. Turn right (west) on North Bastian Lane. Continue past the Vermillion Cemetery and turn right again onto an improved dirt road that crosses over I-70. Angle left toward the mouth of South Cedar Ridge Canyon after passing under the powerlines, and then branch to the right for the final mile to the unsigned trailhead and parking area at the canyon entrance and road's end.

Day horseback or hike, or overnighter

South Cedar Ridge Canyon

Distance: 10 miles out-and-back, or up to a 30-mile "lollypop" loop.
Starting and maximum elevation: 5,680 feet and 6,400 feet (mouth of Strawberry Canyon), 8,800 feet (head of South Cedar Ridge Canyon below Forest Road 096).
Difficulty: Moderate (out-and-back day trip) to moderately strenuous (for extended options).
Best months: Mid-May through June; September through October.
Topo maps: Richfield-UT (for basic out-and-back day trip). Richfield-UT; White Pine Peak-UT (for extended trip).

This deep, narrow canyon provides a colorful route through the eastern slopes of the Pahvant Range. The Forest Service manages a sizable portion of the 56,572-acre Beehive Peak roadless area just north of South Cedar Ridge Canyon for nonmotorized recreation. Most visitors to the canyon come on foot or horseback, limiting their journey to the lower reaches. Key attractions include a rushing perennial stream interspersed with pools and short waterfalls wedged into a red rock canyon.

During early spring high water, hikers should carry a walking stick for the countless crossings of this steeply plunging stream. From the trailhead cross to the left side of the creek and head up the wide trail. High buff and red multi-layered cliffs tower above a rocky pinyon-juniper bottom with Gambel oak and cottonwood, and alcoves eroded deeply into the canyon walls. In places honeycombed shelf rock is thinly supported by white sandstone pillars. The canyon deepens dramatically as the trail climbs. After 1.5 to 2 miles the rocky trail becomes more primitive and is used more by equestrians than hikers.

A horseback rider heads up South Cedar Ridge Canyon.

The broken, twisting nature of the main canyon accounts for a high density of closely spaced side canyons. Most of them are blocked by stair-step pouroffs, but every so often one opens to white rims 1,000 feet above. As the canyon floor climbs to 6,200 feet, overhangs and narrows create a feeling of intimacy. The high, cold water of early spring may not make this the most comfortable time for hiking, but it is certainly the most dramatic, with the roar of the rapid stream resounding against rock walls. Near the mouth of Strawberry Creek, which enters from the north (right) 4 to 5 miles up, Douglas-fir and spruce begin to appear. A primitive trail extends a short distance up Strawberry Creek and quickly becomes steep, rocky, and brushy—enticing the determined hiker.

The actual trail continues left up the main canyon and can be traveled westward for another 10 to 15 miles to the head of the drainage near the 9,000-foot dividing ridge of the Pahvant Range just below FR 096. A "lollypop" loop from the top is possible by returning down Mill Canyon to the north or by hiking 4 to 5 miles down the prominent South Ridge to the confluence of South Cedar Ridge and Mill canyons. These longer options of about 30 miles round trip would require at least one overnight camp. Benches above the stream offer good campsites in the main canyon. As with so many wild Utah canyons, the return down South Cedar Ridge Creek is like a brand new trip with impressive views of pink, red, white, yellow, and gray cliffs curving around great amphitheaters.

A varied 15- to 18-mile point-to-point route begins from the mouth of Willow Canyon and ends at the South Cedar Ridge Canyon Trailhead. The unsigned Willow Creek Canyon trailhead is reached by driving 1.8 miles northeast of Richfield on old U.S. Highway 89. Turn north onto 2200 East (an improved gravel road) and drive 2.9 miles to the trailhead, which is 0.3 mile before road's end on the north (right) side of the canyon. An old wagon road used mostly by horses and all-terrain vehicles climbs to the rim and continues another 3 or 4 miles northwest to a high point directly above the south rim of South Cedar Ridge Canyon. From here look for an old primitive trail that drops 1,000 feet to the canyon floor, ending about 1 mile below and east of the foot of South Ridge. Follow the trail 10 to 12 miles downstream to the South Cedar Ridge Canyon trailhead. A second scenic hiking option (off-trail) from the high point above the south rim of South Cedar Ridge Canyon is to follow the rim eastward for about 4 miles to a high mesa (Point 7,780 on the topo map). Double back to the old wagon road trail for the return trip to the mouth of Willow Creek Canyon.

Sevier Plateau Complex 44

Location: 6 miles southeast of Panguitch and 5 miles southeast of Fremont, in south-central Utah.
Size: 160,245 acres (four roadless areas).
Administration: USDAFS Dixie National Forest, Powell Ranger District.
Management status: Unprotected national forest roadless land.
Ecosystems: Middle Rocky Mountain province, with potential natural vegetation of pinyon-juniper woodland, Douglas-fir forest, western spruce-fir forest.
Elevation range: 6,800 to 10,426 feet (Adams Head).
Established trails/routes: About 50 miles of national forest system trails.
Maximum core to perimeter distance: 3 miles (Deer Creek roadless area).
Activities: Hiking, backpacking, horseback riding, cross-country skiing, snowshoeing, hunting.
Maps: USDAFS 1995 half-inch/mile Dixie National Forest, Powell, Escalante, and Teasdale ranger districts, (50 meter contour interval). See Appendix E for a listing of the 11 topo maps covering the roadless area.

OVERVIEW: The heart of the Sevier Plateau is contained within its largest roadless area—the 93,440-acre Casto Bluff country. Elevations average 8,000 feet across a variable landscape of gentle plateaus, deep rocky canyons, and steep slopes. Most of the average annual precipitation of 20 inches falls in the form of snow. Water is scarce, but several of the larger canyons have small year-round streams. Lower foothills are vegetated with pinyon-juniper and sagebrush grading to spruce, fir, and aspen in the higher country. A blend of aspen parks, grassy slopes, and dense stringers of conifers provide summer range and escape cover for a large number of deer and elk from the Mount Dutton herd. A Powell Expedition survey cairn is just southeast of the high point of 10,426-foot Adams Head about 1 mile by trail from the South Fork of Cottonwood Creek.

The South Fork and a major forest road (Forest Road 125) separates Casto Bluff from the 44,285-acre Deer Creek roadless area to the east. On average, this country is drier, rougher, and steeper with numerous rock outcrops and only intermittent streams in the larger canyons. Higher elevations in the upper drainages support a mix of spruce, fir, and aspen. Downstream and closer to the forest boundary, scattered pinyon-juniper give way to sagebrush grasslands.

44 SEVIER PLATEAU COMPLEX

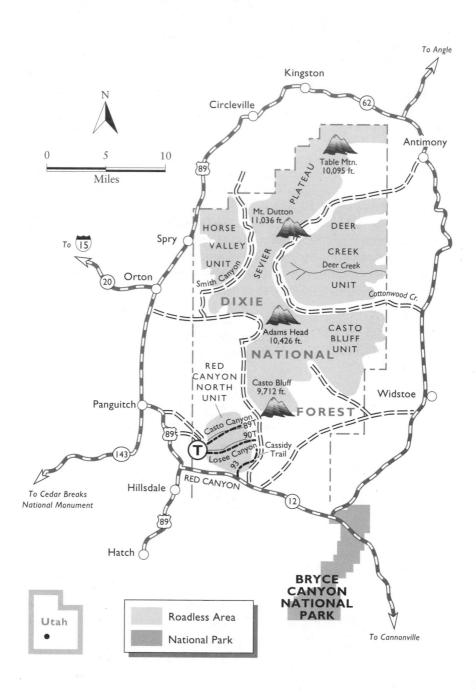

N

0   5   10
Miles

To Angle

Kingston

Circleville

62

Antimony

Table Mtn.
10,095 ft.

89

SEVIER PLATEAU

To 15

Spry

Mt. Dutton
11,036 ft.

HORSE

DEER

VALLEY

CREEK

Orton

20

UNIT

Deer Creek

Smith Canyon

UNIT

Cottonwood Cr.

DIXIE

Adams Head
10,426 ft.

CASTO
BLUFF
UNIT

NATIONAL

RED
CANYON
NORTH
UNIT

Casto Bluff
9,712 ft.

Panguitch

FOREST

Widstoe

Casto Canyon

89T

89C

143

90T

Cassidy
Trail

T

Losee Canyon

93

Hillsdale

RED CANYON

12

To Cedar Breaks
National Monument

89

Hatch

BRYCE
CANYON
NATIONAL
PARK

Utah

Roadless Area

National Park

To Cannonville

On the west side, the 13,420-acre Horse Valley roadless area is separated from Casto Bluff by Smith Canyon Road (FR 129). Horse Valley is a lower elevation continuation of Casto Bluff with dry, rocky pinyon-juniper mountain slopes and gentle sagebrush-covered foothills. Deer and other wildlife rely on the secluded open hillsides for winter range.

The southwest corner of the Sevier Plateau consists of the 9,100-acre Red Canyon North roadless area, which also averages close to 8,000 feet elevation and around 20 inches of annual precipitation. The colorful, deeply dissected topography is characterized by pink and white limestone cliffs crowned with sandstones and conglomerates of the Wasatch Formation. Most of the sparse tree cover is ponderosa pine along with a scattering of bristlecone pine, spruce, Douglas-fir, and pinyon-juniper.

RECREATIONAL USES: Backcountry recreation in the four roadless islands of the Sevier Plateau is light throughout most of the country during most of the year. The exception comes in the fall when big game hunters pursue mule deer and elk from the Mount Dutton elk herd. Low visitation is due primarily to the obscurity of these dry hills, plateaus, and canyons combined with poor vehicle access. Most of the rough roads are dry weather routes requiring high-clearance vehicles. Some of these peripheral forest roads offer great mountain biking with a variety of loop trips possible. Utah Highway 12 provides the only all-weather, year-round access near the complex, accessing the Red Canyon North roadless area in the southwest corner. But even here there are few official USDA Forest Service trails, although a wide path suitable for hiking, horseback riding, and mountain biking extends about 5 miles up Casto Canyon. The northwest corner of the complex in the Horse Valley roadless area is trailless. A number of trails bisect the larger blocks of wild country in the Casto Bluff and Deer Creek units.

The southern end of the Casto Bluff roadless area offers a 15- to 20-mile, two- to three-day hiking or horseback riding loop with a short side trip to the apex of the complex—10,426-foot Adams Head. Begin from Forest Road 123 (a four-wheel-drive track requiring high clearance) on the East Fork of Hunt Creek where a pack trail joins the jeep trail at 8,255 feet as shown on the topo map. Head north directly up the East Fork Trail toward Adams Head. Or take a slightly longer route following the four-wheel-drive tracks to the West Fork of Hunt Creek Trail, which climbs north to a junction with the Rock Creek Trail. Adams Head rises 850 feet from less than 1 mile north of this trail junction. From the Adams Head cutoff trail continue the loop by traveling along a high ridge at 9,500 feet and then descending Rock Creek to the east. After 6 or 7 miles look for a trail taking off to the right below Window Rock just past a spring. The trail winds up and down side drainages in a southwesterly direction for 7 or 8 miles back to the starting point, thereby completing a varied loop through the heart of the Sevier Plateau.

HOW TO GET THERE: From the south on Utah Highway 12, a little less than 0.5 mile west of Red Canyon, turn north at milepost 2. Continue north for 3 miles on this good dirt and gravel road to the Casto Canyon Trailhead and parking area. From the north at Panguitch drive about 4 miles south on U.S. Highway 89 and turn left (east) onto unsigned Forest Road 118, which is 0.5 mile south of mile post 128. The road crosses the Sevier River on a concrete bridge and continues another 4 miles to the signed Casto Canyon Trailhead, which has no water but does feature a restroom, large parking area, and unloading ramps for horses. Camping is not allowed at the trailhead. This northern route may become impassable when wet, during which time the directions from the south should be followed.

Day hike or horseback riding loop

Casto Canyon–Losee Canyon Loop

Distance: 13 miles.
Starting and maximum elevations: 7,070 feet and 8,000 feet (Little Desert).
Difficulty: Moderate.
Best months: Mid-April through October.
Topo map: Casto Canyon-UT.

This is a long and highly scenic trail loop from red rock canyon bottoms to forested highlands, with a bit of western folklore thrown in for good measure, all within a 9,100-acre national forest roadless area known as Red Canyon

Turrets and hoodoos grace the north side of lower Casto Canyon.

North. The recommended direction of the loop is clockwise, from the Casto Canyon trailhead to the Losee Canyon Trailhead. Only a mile of flat dirt road separates these two developed trailheads.

From a wilderness standpoint the trails are oversigned. In addition, the first 4 miles in Casto Canyon are maintained as a wide multi-purpose trail (Trail 89) shared by visitors on foot, horse, mountain bike, and off-road vehicles under 40 inches wide. Accordingly, the trip is not so much a remote wilderness experience as it is a grand scenic loop sampling the backcountry flavor of the Sevier Plateau.

The spectacular red rock formations at the entrance to Casto Canyon never let up. With its dazzling display of bright red hoodoos, spires, and turrets, Casto is a miniature Bryce Canyon without the crowds. At 0.4 mile the wide gravelly canyon bottom passes a stock fence. The roadless area is closed to livestock grazing, but Casto Canyon is still used for driving cattle. Up canyon the effects of wind and water erosion are dramatically displayed with intricate rock shapes, alcoves, and shallow cave openings inviting exploration. Later in the season the loop and adjacent trails are used by guided horse parties. The guides have colorful names for many of the equally colorful features along the route; a few are signed and shown on the Forest Service Red Canyon Trail Map brochure. Water is scarce but horses can be watered at the small Casto Canyon spring midway through the loop. Early season camping is possible before ephemeral streams dry up, which usually occurs by June.

Vertical lines distinguish Casto Canyon for several miles with spires, snags, and stately ponderosa pines that escaped early logging. At mile 4 turn right at a signed trail junction toward "Losee Canyon-5 miles." Soon the country begins to open up with slate gray limestone cliffs rising to the east. Mexican Hat Peak (8,095 feet) can be seen up canyon. For the next 5 miles the trail is well marked with cairns and tree blazes all the way to Losee Canyon. As the trail climbs to 7,600 feet pockets of spruce begin to appear, followed by sagebrush and ponderosa pine just before the second signed trail junction at Casto Canyon spring 5 miles above the trailhead. Keep to the right (south) on the Cassidy Trail (Trail 93), which was used by the notorious outlaw Butch Cassidy. A sparse spruce forest, old snags, and the Mexican Hat formation combine for a southwest desert feel mixed with an alpine flavor. The trail continues between Mexican Hat Peak and Black Rock, gradually descending through spacious parks of old-growth ponderosa pine. Vistas northeast of rugged peaks, cliffs, and serrated ridges are overwhelming. The trail climbs more steeply as it circles around the huge 8,482-foot mesa of Lon's Knoll.

At mile 8 the trail winds across the Little Desert, where mounds of shale lend a classic "western" look beneath limestone cliffs and red, pink, orange, and gray badlands dotted with juniper and ponderosa pine. Expect slick walking or riding if this trail is wet. After the trail plummets 300 feet into a side draw at mile 9 it meets the Losee Canyon Trail (Trail 90). Stay right and head down the Losee Canyon Trail for the final 3 miles to the Casto Canyon Road and trailhead. The Cassidy Trail continues left (south) another 5 miles to Red Canyon. Hoodoos capped with sandstone line the watercourse near the junction.

Upper Losee is comparable to Casto, with its dizzying array of intricate formations, caves, and alcoves, plus the added allure of a good but more primitive trail and the intimacy of a narrower canyon. In places, goblins, hoodoos, pillars, and fins rise 50 to 100 feet above the ground. Every so often a hole in the rock brings to mind Butch Cassidy and his infamous Hole In The Wall gang. Side canyons invite short scrambles and explorations of small hidden valleys leading to higher ridges. Upon reaching the Losee Canyon Trailhead at mile 12, turn right and hike or ride the Casto Canyon Road 1 mile north to the Casto Canyon Trailhead, thereby completing this exhilarating loop through the southwest corner of the Sevier Plateau.

Cedar Breaks–
Ashdown Gorge Wilderness Complex **45**

Location: 7 miles east of Cedar City, in southwestern Utah.

Size: 11,580 acres.

Administration: NPS Cedar Breaks National Monument; USDAFS Dixie National Forest, Cedar City Ranger District.

Management status: NPS roadless area in Cedar Breaks (4,830 acres); USDAFS wilderness area (6,750 acres).

Ecosystems: Middle Rocky Mountain province ecoregion, ranging from ponderosa pine, fir, and spruce to pinyon-juniper woodland (potential natural vegetation), desert scrub, and riparian zones.

Elevation range: 7,379 feet (Ashdown Creek Canyon) to 10,606 feet (Cedar Breaks rim).

Established trails/routes: About 12 miles of trail; additional miles of canyon bottom and former jeep tracks suitable for hiking routes.

Maximum core to perimeter distance: 1.25 miles.

Activities: Hiking, cross-country skiing, snowshoeing, canyoneering, geology, and nature study.

Maps: BLM 1:100,000 scale surface management/land ownership map entitled "Panguitch" (50 meter contour interval) and USDAFS 1995 half-inch/mile map entitled "Dixie National Forest-Pine Valley and Cedar City Ranger Districts" (50 meter contour intervals). See Appendix E for a listing of the four topo maps covering the roadless area.

OVERVIEW: The Cedar Breaks–Ashdown Gorge wilderness complex, only 9 miles east of Interstate 15, is a readily accessible geologic fantasy land. The National Park Service administers the higher land of the breaks. The 6,400-acre monument was transferred from the national forest by President Franklin Roosevelt in 1933. With only one roadway, curving in an arc along the eastern rim of the vast basin, the park service has recommended that the roadless 75 percent of the monument be designated as wilderness. Fitting next to it like a puzzle piece, Ashdown Gorge wraps around three sides of the monument. The core area of Ashdown Gorge is a private inholding, but the surrounding creeks, canyons, and ridges were included in the 1984 Utah Wilderness Act.

45 CEDAR BREAKS–ASHDOWN GORGE WILDERNESS COMPLEX

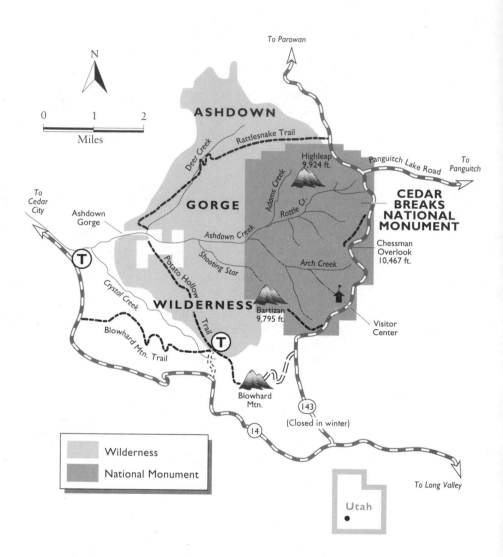

N

0   1   2
Miles

To Parowan

ASHDOWN

Deer Creek

Rattlesnake Trail

Highleap
9,924 ft.

Panguitch Lake Road

To Panguitch

To Cedar City

Ashdown Gorge

GORGE

Adams Creek

Rattle Cr.

CEDAR BREAKS NATIONAL MONUMENT

Ashdown Creek

Shooting Star

Arch Creek

Chessman Overlook
10,467 ft.

T

Potato Hollow Trail

WILDERNESS

Bartizan
9,795 ft.

Visitor Center

Crystal Creek

Blowhard Mtn. Trail

T

Blowhard Mtn.

143

(Closed in winter)

14

To Long Valley

Wilderness

National Monument

Utah

Originally mapped by both the Wheeler and Powell surveys of 1872, the breaks consist of a giant amphitheater carved into the western edge of the Markagunt Plateau. 10,000-foot cliffs of multi-colored Wasatch limestone drop sharply into canyons 2,500 feet below. The 3-mile wide basin is penetrated by ridges and ramparts—Orange Ridge, Chessman Ridge, Wasatch Rampart—and punctuated by monoliths, left like huge exclamation points, rising to 9,924 feet (Highleap), 8,610 feet (Meadow Hill), and 9,795 feet (Bartizan) around the semicircle facing west. The rainbow of rock layers resembles the formations in Bryce Canyon, 40 miles to the east on the parallel Paunsaugunt Plateau. Called the "Circle of Painted Cliffs" by Paiutes, the jagged cliff walls of the breaks exhibit yellows, reds, and purples as the minerals oxidize in the high desert air.

Markagunt is a Paiute word for "highland of trees," an apt name for the high country in Cedar Breaks. Oddly, there is not a cedar in sight. Forests of ponderosa pine, aspen, Douglas-fir, and Engelmann spruce coat the rim of the breaks. Tenacious junipers grow at middle elevation, wherever they can find enough soil. Early visitors mistook them for cedars, hence the name. Patches of ancient bristlecone pines can be found. Look for them at Spectra Point in the monument. Another major stand of these ancient trees is on the northern corner of Ashdown Gorge Wilderness in an area appropriately known as the Twisted Forest. Some of these trees are 2,000 years old. The summer months bring a startling display of wildflowers to the breaks' high country, as well as numerous visitors to view them.

The edges of the breaks provide habitat to wildlife found elsewhere in this large region of the Dixie National Forest below nearby Brian Head (11,307 feet) and Hancock Peak (10,598 feet). Mule deer silently thread their way through the forests and glens, while porcupine and grouse putter around on the forest floor trying to be inconspicuous.

A separate world exists in the creek bottoms far below. There, stripes of bright green riparian vegetation break up the pastel hues in the palette of the cliff walls. The canyons that begin on the walls of the breaks 5 miles to the east converge in the gorge. Rattlesnake Creek, Ashdown Creek, and Cedar Canyon Creek join in a majestic canyon to become Coal Creek. Continuing the dramatic claystone and limestone cliff formations of the breaks, the spires, pinnacles, and ragged cliffs create magnificent panoramas.

The Ashdown Gorge Wilderness is an entirely different world from the national monument. Although only 7 miles from Cedar City, and on the Markagunt Scenic Byway (Utah Highway 14), this rugged patch of wilderness is relatively obscure. Barely mentioned in guidebooks, not listed in the "points of interest" on the forest map, and without signed trailheads, conspicuous parking areas, or official trails, Ashdown Gorge is close to—but off— the beaten track.

Venturing up Coal Creek through the gorge provides an Alice-in-Wonderland entrance to a world of winding canyons. From above, on the other hand, the overlooks along the high rim of the breaks provide no access for hikes down into the miles of canyons; the abrupt cliffs prevent that. Although this is a tiny wilderness area by Utah standards, it has plenty of intricate canyons to explore.

RECREATIONAL USES: Skiing and hiking are the primary recreational uses of the breaks and gorge, respectively. In winter the closed roads of Cedar Breaks attract cross-country skiers and snowmobilers from the Brian Head ski area, 1 mile north of the monument. At other times of the year, visitation in the monument occurs primarily along the road that skirts the dramatic amphitheater. A 4-mile round-trip trail to Spectra Point and the 2-mile loop Alpine Pond Trail are hiking options from the roadway. The visitor center, open from Memorial Day to Labor Day, is at the southern end of this scenic byway. There is a campground near the visitor center.

Other than these short trails, there are no other hiking routes in the monument. The Park Service, in recognition of the fragile nature of the breaks and its vegetation, has no developed trails down from the rim. One unmaintained Forest Service trail does lead from the high country to the gorge. Immediately north of the monument, in the Dixie National Forest, a lightly marked trail goes west to Stud Flat and down Rattlesnake Creek to Ashdown Creek in the gorge. This is a strenuous 10-mile point-to-point hike. See *Hiking Zion and Bryce Canyon National Parks* (Falcon Publishing) for details on this trip.

The Forest Service also wishes to keep the wilderness primitive, and has no established trailheads that provide quick access to this remarkable gorge that is so close to a major highway. The Forest Service Cedar Canyon Campground is 1.5 miles south of the wilderness on Utah Highway 14. Open from June to mid-September, its 8,100-foot elevation ensures relatively cool summer evenings. The trail down into the gorge via Potato Hollow begins at the end of Crystal Spring Road, northeast of the campground. The trail crosses the private H-shaped inholding located on Ashdown Creek in the heart of the wilderness. There is a four-wheel-drive access road to this property. It lies outside of the wilderness boundary, and is not open to vehicles, but hikers may use the road. Hikers may also travel across the private land in the wilderness, but may not camp there.

All hikers who plan to venture into the gorge need to check with either the ranger station at Cedar Breaks or at the Forest Service office in Cedar City regarding water levels and the weather report. The narrow gorge is hazardous during high water and is subject to flash flooding. The narrow channel drains a lot of country!

Dixie National Forest is engaged in a major effort to provide recreational opportunities for mountain bikers in the Ashdown Gorge–Cedar Breaks region.

While mountain bikes cannot be ridden off paved roads in the monument, and may not enter the wilderness, they are permitted in the national forest. Just south of the forbidden zone, the Blowhard Mountain Trail was recently developed for bikers. This 10-mile bike trail starts near the Federal Aviation Administration dome south of the wilderness area at the end of Blowhard Mountain Road. It follows Trail 047 steeply down a series of switchbacks, crosses the Crystal Spring Road, curves north of Wood Knoll, and then drops sharply again to emerge in Moots Hollow on UT 14 in Cedar Canyon. Contact the Forest Service in Cedar City for details on the route.

HOW TO GET THERE: From Utah Highway 14, there are two trailheads for venturing into Ashdown Creek. About 0.4 mile east of Cedar Canyon Campground, turn north on Crystal Spring Road (closed in winter) and drive 1 mile to end at Potato Hollow Trail parking area. When water is low in the gorge, and there is no flash flood danger, it is possible to hike up the gorge from the west. There is an unmarked pullout along UT 14 just west of the gorge's mouth near milepost 8. Watch for it on the north side of the highway next to a protective roadside barrier. Park here. The gravel road drops down from the highway to the bench above Coal Creek. From here it is a 1-mile hike to the gorge. A pullout also exists at Martin's Flat, near milepost 7. A hairpin turn around a highway barrier on the north side of the road puts you in a broad, unmarked gravel parking area. Beyond a locked gate, a deserted jeep track serves as a trail up Coal Creek to the gorge, about 2 miles to the southeast.

Day hike

Ashdown Gorge Canyons

Distance: 8 to 10 miles.
Starting and minimum elevations: 8,950 feet (Crystal Spring trailhead) to 7,320 feet (Gorge).
Difficulty: Moderate.
Best months: May through June; September.
Topo maps: Flanigan Arch-UT; Brian Head-UT; Webster Flat-UT.

Whether entering this deep canyon wonderland through the gorge or dropping into it from the Potato Hollow Trail, visitors experience the magnificent hidden wilderness away from the bustle of Cedar City and the traffic of UT 14. Hiking through the 2-mile gorge involves wading the creek. If the water is cold, which it always is in the spring, or if it is too deep, also likely in the spring, the trail route is the preferred one. Since camping is not permitted outside of the campground in the monument and campsites are limited in the small wilderness, we suggest that hikers explore the canyons on a long day outing.

The Potato Hollow Trail leaves from the parking area at the end of Crystal Spring Road. It drops steadily, sometimes steeply, through aspen and fir on the way down to Ashdown Creek. Above the creek the trail joins and then crosses a jeep road before descending to the streambed. Here it crosses private land, an inholding within the wilderness. The gorge itself, a 2-mile section of the Ashdown Creek bottom, and lower Calf Hollow are not part of the wilderness. Exercise appropriate courtesy when crossing private land where you are a guest.

From the bottom of the trail you can explore this hidden valley. The gorge is just downstream. Its jagged walls and winding path extend for more than 2 miles. Soaring pinnacles and even an arch adorn its rising walls. The soaring tight canyon of Ashdown Creek is a dramatic exit for this stream that drains more than 30 square miles of this high plateau. With flash flood danger a possibility, check with the visitor center at Cedar Breaks or the Forest Service in Cedar City before doing the gorge trip.

The monument boundary is less than 2 miles upstream from the trail crossing. The vegetated benches make going tough; the easier hiking route is the streambed. Shooting Star Creek and Spring Creek might tempt you to wander off on side hikes, but your destination should be The Quarry, just inside the monument. The vastness of this amphitheater is overwhelming when viewed from the bottom. It is humbling. The colorful ridges and canyons dwarf human visitors when viewed from 2,000 feet below the rim.

On your way back to the trailhead, pause often to look back at the world you have explored. This is a piece of Earth that has been virtually untouched by the modern world.

The urge to develop is a powerful instinct in our society, so it is refreshing to visit this wilderness area that has been kept primitive. Keeping visitation low is a valid management policy here where use is funnelled into a narrow sensitive area. Both the gorge and the breaks are isolated and wild, and need to stay that way. Travel especially lightly here.

AFTERWORD

"Why would you want to ruin this country by writing a book about it?" asked the seasoned backcountry explorer. It was a tough and pointed question, demanding our immediate attention and thoughtful response. The question was especially compelling because it caught us during a magical slickrock sunset that was softly lighting up color-banded rock formations and canyon rims in a deepening display of multi-hued radiance, reaching to infinity. As we revelled in the wildness and solitude of this blank spot on the map, we were challenged that all of our hard work to produce a comprehensive guide to Utah wildlands could compromise the very values that lured us to this awe-inspiring landscape.

The spectrum of these values includes uncluttered horizons, scenic majesty, topographic wonder, varied wildlife, and reservoirs of answers to as yet unthought-of questions. As the preceding pages attest, this place we call Utah yields some of the highest quality outdoor recreation remaining on the planet, where we can truly re-create ourselves with the timeless tonic of wildness.

Our ensuing and very positive discussion with our provocative friend is worth recounting. It is true that Utah's bigger-name wilderness areas are already being loved to death by an ever-increasing number of visitors. One could argue that we don't need another guidebook to the Utah backcountry. Certainly this was our concern before beginning this project as we pondered our own ethics and motivations. At the same time we recalled the words of wilderness writer Ed Abbey, who said wilderness needs no defense, just more defenders. In truth both are needed, but the strongest defense of wild country comes from defenders who have a heartfelt passion for the land they love. This feeling can be developed vicariously by those with a broad appreciation of the ecological need for wilderness. It also emanates from the personal experiences people have when they paddle, ski, hike, backpack, climb, or ride horseback into natural, wild landscapes.

Wilderness will endure in our industrialized society only if there is public support. This book is presented in hopes that you will join or increase your involvement with the ranks of wilderness defenders, regardless of whether you ever set foot in any of the 45 Utah wild areas and complexes featured in the previous pages. Wilderness defense can take many forms, from political advocacy to a leave-no-trace camping ethic to quietly setting an example of respect for wildlands for others to follow.

Our second reason for writing this book and believing that it should be written is our conviction that redistributing recreational use in our wildlands is desirable. The vast majority of backcountry recreation takes place on a small percentage of the wildland base, with many of the same locations receiving heavier use with each passing year. Most folks would agree that Grand Gulch in the San Juan-Anasazi Complex or the lower Paria River Canyon in the Grand Staircase doesn't need more visitors. If *Wild Utah* helps some of these backcountry enthusiasts find new places to explore, it will have provided an important benefit. Most of the suggested trips described in this book go to lightly visited places that can absorb sensitive use without losing their essential wildness.

It all boils down to respect for untrammeled land, for those wild denizens that live there, for other visitors who go there for the same reasons, and for those yet unborn who will retrace the journeys we make today into the next millennium and beyond.

APPENDIX A

Recommended Equipment for Hiking, Skiing, and Backpacking Beyond the Roads

Core essentials for day trips:

GEAR / ACCESSORIES

- ❑ day pack (or "day-and-a-half," climbing-style pack, if needed)
- ❑ water: 2 quarts to 1 gallon per person per day (depending on season), in sturdy, screw-top, plastic containers
- ❑ matches in a waterproof case, fire starter (commercially available fire sticks or pitch scraped off a dead tree and stored in a reclosable plastic bag)
- ❑ small first aid kit: tweezers, band-aids, antiseptic, moleskin, snakebite kit
- ❑ insect repellent (in season)
- ❑ bee sting kit (over the counter antihistamine or epinephrine by prescription)
- ❑ sun glasses, sunblock, and lip sunscreen
- ❑ pocket knife
- ❑ whistle and mirror (for emergency signalling)
- ❑ flashlight with extra batteries and bulb (for those after-dark returns)
- ❑ lunch or snack, with baggie for your trash
- ❑ toilet paper, with a plastic zipper bag to pack it out
- ❑ large-scale topo map and compass (be sure to adjust for magnetic declination)
- ❑ your FalconGuide

CLOTHING

- ❑ sturdy, well-broken-in boots (normally light to medium weight)
- ❑ shirt, sweater, pants, and jacket suitable to the season
- ❑ socks: wool outer; light cotton, polypropylene, or nylon inner
- ❑ rain gear that can double as wind protection (breathable, water-repellent parka and/or rain suit with pants or chaps)
- ❑ warm skiing-style hat (balaclava, headband, or stocking cap)
- ❑ hat, windproof with broad brim (for sun protection)
- ❑ gloves (weight depends on the season)
- ❑ belt and/or suspenders

If you're staying in the wilderness for one night or longer, add the following:

GEAR AND ACCESSORIES

- ❑ backpack, pack cover, extra set of pack straps
- ❑ plastic bags (including a large garbage bag) with ties

❑ web strap, 30 to 40 feet long (for raising and lowering packs on steep slickrock faces)

❑ tent with fly and repair kit (including rip-stop tape)

❑ sleeping bag (rated to at least 10 degrees F or as season requires)

❑ sleeping pad (self-inflating type is best)

❑ stove, fuel bottle (filled), repair kit including cleaning wire

❑ candle lantern with spare candle

❑ cooking kit, pot gripper, cleaning pad

❑ eating utensils, including a bowl (12 to 15 ounces, with cover), cup, fork, spoon

❑ several small drawstring grab bags for miscellaneous items

❑ trowel

❑ biodegradable soap and small towel for (drying clothes, etc.)

❑ toothbrush, toothpaste, dental floss

❑ drugs: prescriptions and antibiotics

❑ zinc oxide (for treatment of sunburn)

❑ eye drops

❑ aspirin or ibuprofen

❑ throat lozenges

❑ laxatives

❑ decongestant medicine

❑ antacid tablets

❑ salt tablets

❑ scissors, safety pins, and small sewing kit

❑ moleskin (use to prevent blistering), second skin (use to treat blister)

❑ extra bandages

❑ water filter designed and approved for backcountry use

❑ sharpening stone

❑ nylon cord (50 to 100 feet for hanging food, drying clothes, etc.)

CLOTHING

❑ wading sandals or old running shoes that can double for use around camp and in wading streams

❑ hiking shorts, swim suit (summer)

❑ gaiters (especially for winter trips)

❑ undershirt and longjohns (polypropylene or capilene)

For winter trips add or substitute:

❑ internal frame backpack (lowers the center of gravity for skiing)

❑ space blanket

❑ extra shirt

❑ extra socks and underwear (3 to 5 pair for a weeklong trip)

❑ bandana/handkerchiefs

❑ lightweight cotton or polypropylene gloves

❑ avalanche cord

❑ special ski poles that can be threaded together to probe for avalanche victims

❑ closed-cell foam pad (for insulation against the snow)
❑ foam pad for stove
❑ four-season tent
❑ sleeping bag rated to at least -10 degrees F (down-filled bag is best during winter)
❑ snow shovel
❑ ski accessories (extra tip, skins, wax, cork, and scrapper)

❑ transceivers (at least two in the party)
❑ warm, waterproof clothing that can be layered
❑ Two gallon-size plastic food storage bags (wear them in your boots over your socks to keep feet dry in slushy conditions)

Optional for any day or overnight trip:

❑ compact binoculars
❑ camera, film, lens brush, and paper
❑ walking stick (especially useful for probing muddy stream bottoms)

❑ notebook and pencils
❑ book
❑ field guides
❑ fishing tackle (fly and/or spin)

So there you have it—80 pounds of lightweight gear! Actually, most people can get along safely and comfortably with 35 to 50 pounds of gear and food, depending on the duration of the trip. Your pack will weigh 8 to 10 pounds more during winter with four-season gear and heavier clothing.

APPENDIX B

Trips At a Glance

Trip Name	Area	Type	Distance	Difficulty
WEST: BASIN & RANGE				
Cat Canyon	King Top (12)	Day hike	12 miles	Moderate
Corral Canyon	Wah Wahs (8)	Day hike	5–6 miles	Moderate/ strenuous
Muskrat Canyon	Stansburys (3)	Day hike	6 miles	Moderate
Needle	Mountain Home (9)	Day hike	9 miles	Strenuous
North Willow	Stansburys (3)	Day hike	6–8 miles	Strenuous
Pyramid Peak	Dugways (5)	Day hike	5 miles	Moderate
Ridge Ramble	Cedars (2)	Day hike	2–5 miles	Easy
Robbers' Roost– Tatow Knob	House Range (6)	Day hike	10-12 miles	Moderate/ strenuous
Scotts Basin	Deep Creek (4)	Day hike/ overnight	12 miles	Strenuous
Silver Ramble	Silver Islands (1)	Day hike	2–5 miles	Moderate
Wah Peak	Wah Wahs (8)	Day hike	7–8 miles	Moderate/ strenuous
SOUTHWEST: HOT DESERT				
South Boundary	Cougar Cnyn (10)	Day hike/ backpack	10 miles	Moderate
Joshua Tree	Beaver Dam (11)	Day hike	4–8 miles	Easy/ Moderate
Red Mountain	Red Mountains (12)	Day hike	10 miles	Moderate/ strenuous
SOUTHEAST: COLORADO PLATEAU				
Beaver Wash Cyn	Dirty Devil (26)	Day hike	6 miles	Moderate
Bullfrog Canyons	Henrys (21)	Day hike/ backpack	10–14 miles	Moderate
Cheesebox Canyon	White Canyon (24)	Day hike	7–10 miles	Moderate/ strenuous
Cliff Climb	Upper Kanab (17)	Day hike	4–6 miles	Strenuous
Crack Canyon	San Rafael Swell (27)	Day hike	10 miles	Moderate/ strenuous
Daniels Canyon	Greater Dinosaur (36)	Day hike	10 miles	Moderate
Dark Canyon	Dark Canyon (25)	Backpack	6–20 miles	Moderate/ strenuous
Diana's Throne	Upper Kanab (12)	Day hike	1 mile	Moderate
Fins	Behind the Rocks (30)	Day hike	5 miles	Moderate/ strenuous

Trip Name	Area	Type	Distance	Difficulty
Fisher Towers	LaSal Canyons (31)	Day hike	4.4 miles	Moderate
Fools Canyon– Coyote Gulch	Escalante (20)	Backpack	35 miles	Moderate/ strenuous
Labyrinth Canyon	Labyrinth Canyon(28)	Float trip	68 miles	Easy
Left Hand Tusher	Book Cliffs (34)	Day hike	6 miles	Easy
Little Hole Canyon	Westwater (33)	Day hike	5 miles	Easy
Lost Spring Canyon	Arches (32)	Day hike	12 miles	Moderate
Mary Jane Canyon	LaSal Canyons (31)	Day hike	5–10 miles	Moderate
Muddy Creek– Poor Canyon	San Rafael Swell (27)	Day hike/ backpack	12 miles	Moderate
Oak Grove	Pine Valley Mountains (14)	Day hike	7 miles	Strenuous
Owl Creek & Fish Creek	San Juan–Anasazi (23)	Backpack	15 mile	Moderately strenuous
Paria–Hackberry Hogeye	Grand Staircase (18)	Backpack	25 miles	Moderately strenuous
Price River– Water Canyon	Book Cliffs (34)	Day hike	12 miles	Moderate
Pysert Hole	Henrys (21)	Day hike	2–5 miles	Moderate/ strenuous
Quail Creek	Cottonwood (13)	Day hike	2 miles	Moderately strenuous
Rim Ramble	Moquith Mountain (16)	Day hike	10–12 miles	Moderate
Rogers & Basin Canyons	Kaiparowits (19)	Day hike/ backpack	12–14 miles	Moderately strenuous
San Juan River	San Juan–Anasazi(23)	Float trip	84 miles	Moderate
Squirrel– Water Canyon	Zion (15)	Day hike/ backpack	10–12 miles	Moderately strenuous
Studhorse Peaks	Escalante (20)	Day hike	1 mile	Moderate
Ticaboo Canyon– Peshliki Canyon	Glen Canyon (22)	Backpack	30–50 miles	Moderately strenuous
Upper Harts Draw	Canyonlands Basin (29)	Day hike/ backpack	12–14 miles	Moderate
Upper Indian Creek	Canyonlands Basin (29)	Day hike/ backpack	10 miles	Moderate
White River	White River (35)	Day hike	8 miles	Easy

NORTH-CENTRAL: MIDDLE ROCKY MOUNTAINS AND PLATEAUS

Ashdown Gorge	Cedar Breaks– Ashdown Gorge (45)	Day hike	8–10 miles	Moderate
Bob's Lake	High Uintas (39)	Backpack	22–24 miles	Strenuous

Trip Name	Area	Type	Distance	Difficulty
Box Elder Peak	Wellsville Mtn.(38)	Day hike	9–10 miles	Strenuous
Casto Canyon– Losee Canyon	Sevier Plateau (44)	Day hike	13 miles	Moderate
Golden Ridge	Mount Nebo (41)	Day hike	12 miles	Strenuous
South Cedar Ridge	Pahvant Range (43)	Day hike/ backpack	10 miles	Moderate
South Tent Mtn– Black Canyon	Wasatch Plateau (42)	Day hike	9–10 miles	Strenuous
Steam Mill Canyon	Mount Naomi (37)	Cross- country ski	6–8 miles	Moderate
Wasatch Crest– Cascade Mountain	Central Wasatch (40)	Day hike	10–16 miles	Strenuous/ moderately strenuous

APPENDIX C

Federal and State Land Management Agencies in Utah

Unless noted otherwise, all phone numbers are in area code 801.

Federal Agencies

BUREAU OF LAND MANAGEMENT

Bureau of Land Management
Utah State Office
324 South State, Suite 301
Salt Lake City, UT 84111-2303
539-4001

Salt Lake City District
2370 South 2300 West
Salt Lake City, UT 84119
977-4300

Bear River Resource Area
2370 South 2300 West
Salt Lake City, UT 84119
977-4300

Pony Express Resource Area
2370 South 2300 West
Salt Lake City, UT 84119
977-4300

Cedar City District
176 East D.L. Sargent Drive
Cedar City, UT 84720
586-2401

Beaver River Resource Area
176 East D.L. Sargent Drive
Cedar City, UT 84720
586-2401

Dixie Resource Area
345 Riverside Drive
St. George, UT 84770
673-4654

Escalante Resource Area
P.O. Box 225
Escalante, UT 84726
826-4291

Kanab Resource Area
318 North First East
Kanab, UT 84741
644-2672

Richfield District
150 East 900 North
P.O. Box 768
Richfield, UT 84701
896-8221

Sevier River Resource Area
150 East 900 North
P.O. Box 768
Richfield, UT 84701
896-8221

House Range Resource Area
P.O. Box 778
Fillmore, UT 84631
743-6811

Warm Springs Resource Area
P.O. Box 778
Fillmore, UT 84631
743-6811

Henry Mountain Resource Area
P.O. Box 99
Hanksville, UT 84734
542-3461

Moab District
82 East Dogwood
P.O. Box 970
Moab, UT 84532
259-6111

Grand Resource Area
82 East Dogwood
P.O. Box 970
Moab, UT 84532
259-6111

Price River Resource Area
125 South 600 West
Price, UT 84501
636-3600

San Rafael Resource Area
125 South 600 West
Price, UT 84501
636-3600

San Juan Resource Area
435 North Main
Monticello, UT 84535
587-2141

Vernal District
170 South 500 East
Vernal, UT 84078
781-4400

Diamond Mountain Resource Area
170 South 500 East
Vernal, UT 84078
781-4400

Book Cliffs Resource Area
170 South 500 East
Vernal, UT 84078
781-4400

**Grand Staircase–Escalante National
    Monument**
337 South Main Street
Cedar City, UT 84720
865-9214

NATIONAL PARK SERVICE

Arches National Park
P.O. Box 907
Moab, UT 84532
259-8161

Bryce Canyon National Park
Bryce Canyon, UT 84717-0001
834-5322

Canyonlands National Park
2282 South West Resource Blvd.
Moab, UT 84532-2995
259-3911

Capitol Reef National Park
HC 70 Box 15
Torrey, UT 84775-9602
425-3791

Cedar Breaks National Monument
82 North 100 East
Cedar City, UT 84720-2606
586-9451

Dinosaur National Monument
4545 Highway 40
Dinosaur, CO 81610-9724
(970) 374-3000

Glen Canyon National Recreation
  Area
P.O. Box 1507
Page, AZ 86040-1507
(520) 608-6200

Natural Bridges National
  Monument
Box 1-Natural Bridges
Lake Powell, UT 84533-0101
692-1234

Timpanogos Cave National
  Monument
RR 3, Box 200
American Fork, UT 84003-9803
756-5239

Zion National Park
Springdale, UT 84767-1099
772-3256 or 772-0157

U.S. FISH & WILDLIFE SERVICE

Ecological Services
Lincoln Plaza 145 East 1300 South
Suite 404
Salt Lake City, UT 84115
524-5001

USDA FOREST SERVICE

Intermountain Region
324 25th Street
Ogden, UT 84401
625-5182

Forest Service Information Office
2501 Wall Avenue
Ogden, UT 84403
625-5306

Ashley National Forest
355 North Vernal Avenue
Vernal, UT 84078
789-1181

Flaming Gorge Ranger District
P.O. Box 279
Manila, UT 84046
784-3445

Vernal Ranger District
355 North Vernal Avenue
Vernal, UT 84078
789-1181

Roosevelt Ranger District
244 West Highway 40
Box 333-6
Roosevelt, UT 84066
738-2482

Duchesne Ranger District
P.O. Box 981
Duchesne, UT 84021
738-2482

Dixie National Forest
82 North 100 East
P.O. Box 580
Cedar City, UT 84721-0580
865-3700

Pine Valley Ranger District
345 East Riverside Drive
St. George, UT 84771-2288
652-3100

Cedar City Ranger District
82 North 100 East
P.O. Box 0627
Cedar City, UT 84721-0627
865-3200

Powell Ranger District
225 East Center
P.O. Box 80
Panguitch, UT 84759
676-8815

Escalante Ranger District
270 West Main
P.O. Box 246
Escalante, UT 84726
826-4221

Teasdale Ranger District
138 East Main
P.O. Box 99
Teasdale, UT 84773
425-3702

Fishlake National Forest
1125 North Main, Suite 301
Richfield, UT 84701
896-9233

Fillmore Ranger District
390 South Main
P.O. Box 265
Fillmore, UT 84631
743-5721

Loa Ranger District
138 South Main
P.O. Box 129
Loa, UT 84747
836-2811

Beaver Ranger District
575 South Main
P.O. Box E
Beaver, UT 84713
438-2436

Richfield Ranger District
115 East 900 North
Richfield, UT 84701
896-9233

Manti–La Sal National Forest
599 West Price River Drive
Price, UT 84501
637-2817

Sanpete Ranger District
540 North Main 32-14
Ephraim, UT 84627
283-4151

Ferron Ranger District
115 West Canyon Road
P.O. Box 310
Ferron, UT 84523
384-2372

Price Ranger District
599 West Price River Drive
Price, UT 84501
637-2817

Moab Ranger District
2290 South West Resource Blvd.
P.O. Box 386
Moab, UT 84532
259-7155

Monticello Ranger District
496 East Central
P.O. Box 820
Monticello, UT 84535
587-2041

Uinta National Forest
88 West 100 North
P.O. Box 1428
Provo, UT 84601
377-5780

Heber Ranger District
125 East 100 North
P.O. Box 190
Heber City, UT 84032
342-5200

Pleasant Grove Ranger District
390 North 100 East
P.O. Box 228
Pleasant Grove, UT 84062
342-5240

Spanish Fork Ranger District
44 West 400 North
Spanish Fork, UT 84660
342-5260

Wasatch–Cache National Forest
8230 Federal Building
125 South State Street
Salt Lake City, UT 84138
524-5030

Salt Lake Ranger District
6944 South 3000 East
Salt Lake City, UT 84121
542-5042

Kamas Ranger District
50 East Center Street
P.O. Box 68
Kamas, UT 84036
783-4338

Evanston Ranger District
1565 Highway 150, Suite A
P.O. Box 1880
Evanston, WY 82931-1880
(307) 789-3194

Mountain View Ranger District
Lone Tree Road, Highway 44
P.O. Box 129
Mountain View, WY 82939
(307) 782-6555

Ogden Ranger District
507 25th Street
Odgen, UT 84401
625-5110

Logan Ranger District
1500 E. Highway 89
Logan, UT 84321
755-3620

STATE OFFICES AND LAND MANAGEMENT AGENCIES

Governor's Office
210 State Capitol
Salt Lake City, UT 84114
538-1000

State Division of Wildlife Resources
1596 West North Temple Street
Salt Lake City, UT 84116
538-4700 or 596-8660

State Parks & Recreation Division
1596 West North Temple Street
Salt Lake City, UT 84116
538-7221

School & Institutional Trust Lands
   Administration
675 East 500 South, Suite 500
Salt Lake City, UT 84102
538-5100

Utah Geological Survey
1594 West North Temple Street
Salt Lake City, UT 84116
537-3300

Utah Travel Council
Council Hall
Capitol Hill
300 North State Street
Salt Lake City, UT 84114
538-1030

Utah Travel & Recreation
   Information Center
Council Hall
Capitol Hill
300 North State Street
Salt Lake City, UT 84114
538-1467

APPENDIX D

Public Lands Conservation Groups in Utah

High Uintas Preservation Council
P.O. Box 72
Hyrum, Utah 84319
(801) 245-6747

Southern Utah Wilderness Alliance
1471 South 1100 East
Salt Lake City, Utah 84105
(801) 486-3161

Uintah Mountain Club
P.O. Box 782
Vernal, Utah 84078

Utah Chapter Sierra Club
2273 South Highland Drive #2
Salt Lake City, Utah 84106
(801) 467-9297

Utah Wilderness Coalition
P.O. Box 11446
Salt Lake City, UT 84147
(801) 532-5959

Wasatch Mountain Club
888 South 200 East, Suite 207
Salt Lake City, Utah 84111

Wilderness Watch
P.O. Box 9175
Missoula, Montana
(406) 542-2048

Wild Utah Forest Campaign
1264 East 24th Street
Ogden, Utah 84401
(801) 399-5411

APPENDIX E

Topographic map lists

Finding the Right Map: Topo Maps by Wildland Area (1:24,000)

Note: All of the following 1:24,000-scale topo maps (2.6 inches/mile) are listed line-by-line from left to right, beginning on the most northern line and ending with the most southeastern map title covering the area. For the best results, consult the USGS map index for Utah. The map index is free.

1. **SILVER ISLAND RANGE:** Graham Peak-UT; Floating Island-UT; Bonneville Racetrack-UT.

2. **CEDAR MOUNTAINS:** Arogonite-UT; Hastings Pass-UT; Aragonite Quincy Spring-UT; Wig Mountain NE-UT; and Tabbys Peak-UT.

3. **STANSBURY MOUNTAINS WILDERNESS COMPLEX:** Timpie-UT; Flux-UT; Salt Mountain-UT; North Willow Canyon-UT; Deseret Peak West-UT; Deseret Peak East-UT; Terra-UT; and Johnson Pass-UT.

4. **DEEP CREEK MOUNTAINS:** Ibapah-UT; Clifton-UT; Goshute-UT; Goshute Canyon-UT; Ibapah Peak-UT; Indian Farm Creek-UT; Skinner Canyon-NV UT; Partoun-UT; and Trout Creek-UT.

5. **DUGWAY MOUNTAINS:** Dugway Range NW-UT; Dugway Range NE-UT; Dugway Range SW-UT; Dugway Pass-UT.

6. **HOUSE RANGE COMPLEX:** Sand Pass SE-UT; Swasey Peak NW-UT; Swasey Peak-UT; Whirlwind Valley NW-UT; Swasey Peak SW-UT; Marjum Pass-UT; Whirlwind Valley SW-UT; Notch Peak-UT; Miller Cove-UT; Hell 'n Maria Canyon-UT; and Skull Rock Pass-UT.

7. **KING TOP:** Thompson Knoll-UT; Bullgrass Knoll-UT; Hell 'n Maria Canyon-UT; Pyramid Knoll-UT; King Top-UT; The Barn-UT; Warm Point-UT.

8. **WAH WAH MOUNTAINS COMPLEX:** Middle Mountain-UT; Crystal Peak-UT; Pine Valley Hardpan North-UT; Grassy Cove-UT; Fifteenmile Point-UT; Pine Valley Hardpan South-UT; Wah Wah Summit-UT; Lamerdorf Peak NW-UT; Sewing Machine Pass-UT; Wallaces Peak-UT; Pine Grove Reservoir-UT; Lamerdorf Peak-UT; and Frisco SW-UT.

9. **MOUNTAIN HOME RANGE:** Miller Wash-NV-UT; Mountain Home Pass-UT; Hamlin Well-NV-UT; Lopers Spring-UT.

10. **COUGAR CANYON-DOCS PASS COMPLEX:** Pine Park-NV-UT; Water Canyon

Peak-UT; Docs Pass-NV-UT; Gold Strike-UT; Dodge Spring-NV-UT; Motoqua-UT.

11. BEAVER DAM SLOPES WILDERNESS COMPLEX: Terry Benches-NV-UT; Castle Cliff-UT-AZ; Jarvis Peak-UT-AZ; and White Hills-UT-AZ.

12. RED MOUNTAIN: Gunlock-UT; Veyo-UT; Shivwits-UT; Santa Clara-UT.

13. COTTONWOOD CANYON: Washington-UT; Harrisburg Junction-UT.

14. PINE VALLEY MOUNTAINS WILDERNESS COMPLEX: Grass Valley-UT; New Harmony-UT; Saddle Mountain-UT; Signal Peak-UT; Pintura-UT.

15. GREATER ZION COMPLEX: Kanarraville-UT; Kolob Arch-UT; Kolob Reservoir-UT; Cogswell Point-UT; Pintura-UT; Smith Mesa-UT; The Guardian Angels-UT; Temple of Sinawava-UT; Clear Creek Mountain-UT; Virgin-UT; Springdale West-UT; Springdale East-UT; The Barracks-UT; Smithsonian Butte-UT.

16. MOQUITH MOUNTAIN: Yellowjacket Canyon-UT-AZ; and Kanab-UT-AZ.

17. UPPER KANAB CREEK: Orderville-UT; Glendale-UT; Mount Carmel-UT; White Tower-UT; Cutler Point-UT.

18. GRAND STAIRCASE WILDERNESS COMPLEX: Bryce Canyon-UT; Tropic Canyon-UT; Pine Lake-UT; Upper Valley-UT; Tropic Reservoir-UT; Bryce Point-UT; Cannonville-UT; Henrieville-UT; Canaan Peak-UT; Death Ridge-UT; Podunk Creek-UT; Rainbow Point-UT; Bull Valley Gorge-UT; Slickrock Bench-UT; Butler Valley-UT; Horse Mountain-UT; Deer Spring Point-UT; Deer Range Point-UT; Calico Peak-UT; Nephi Point-UT; Eightmile Pass-UT; Fivemile Valley-UT; Lower Coyote Spring-UT; Pine Hollow Canyon-UT-AZ; West Clark Bench-UT-AZ; and Bridger Point-UT-AZ.

19. KAIPAROWITS PLATEAU COMPLEX: Canaan Creek-UT; Dave Canyon-UT; Tenmile Flat-UT; Henrieville-UT; Canaan Peak-UT; Death Ridge-UT; Carcass Canyon-UT; Seep Flat-UT; Sunset Flat-UT; Butler Valley-UT; Horse Mountain-UT; Petes Cove-UT; Collet Top-UT; Basin Canyon-UT; Big Hollow Wash-UT; Horse Flat-UT; Fourmile Bench-UT; Ship Mountain Point-UT; Needle Eye Point-UT; East of the Navajo-UT; Blackburn Canyon-UT; Sooner Bench-UT; Lower Coyote Spring-UT; Nipple Butte-UT; Tibbet Bench-UT; Smoky Hollow-UT; Sit Down Bench-UT; Mazuki Point-UT; Navajo Point-UT; Bridger Point-UT; Glen Canyon City-UT; Lone Rock-UT.

20. ESCALANTE CANYONS WILDERNESS COMPLEX: Bicknell-UT; Twin Rock-UT; Fruita-UT; Government Point-UT; Blind Lake-UT; Grover-UT; Jacobs Reservoir-UT; Deer Creek Lake-UT; Lower Bowns Reservoir-UT; Bear Canyon-UT; Posy Lake-UT; Roger Peak-UT; Boulder Town-UT; Steep Creek

Bench-UT; Lamp Stand-UT; Bitter Creek Divide-UT; Wide Hollow Reservoir-UT; Escalante-UT; Calf Creek-UT; King Bench-UT; Pioneer Mesa-UT; Wagon Box Mesa-UT; The Post-UT; Tenmile Flat-UT; Red Breaks-UT; Silver Falls Bench-UT; Horse Pasture Mesa-UT; Deer Point-UT; Sunset Flat-UT; Egypt-UT; Scorpion Gulch-UT; Stevens Canyon North-UT; Hall Mesa-UT; Big Hollow Wash-UT; King Mesa-UT; Stevens Canyon South-UT; The Rincon NE-UT; Sooner Bench-UT; Davis Gulch-UT; The Rincon-UT; and Nasja Mesa-UT.

21. HENRY MOUNTAINS COMPLEX: Caineville-UT; Town Point-UT; Steamboat Point-UT; Noton NE-UT; Stevens Mesa-UT; Dry Lakes Peak-UT; Bull Mountain-UT; Sandy Creek Benches-UT; Steele Butte-UT; Mount Ellen-UT; Raggy Canyon-UT; Bitter Creek Divide-UT; Cave Flat-UT; Mount Pennel-UT; Cass Creek Peak-UT; The Post-UT; Ant Knoll-UT; Copper Creek Benches-UT; Deer Point-UT; Clay Point-UT.

22. UPPER GLEN CANYON COMPLEX: Black Table-UT; Hite North-UT; Mount Holmes-UT; Hite South-UT; Lost Spring-UT; Ticaboo Mesa-UT; Good Hope Bay-UT; Bullfrog-UT; Knowles Canyon-UT; Mancos Mesa-UT; Chocolate Drop-UT; Fry Spring-UT; Halls Crossing-UT; Halls Crossing NE-UT; Burnt Spring-UT; Clay Hills-UT; and Red House Spring-UT.

23. SAN JUAN–ANASAZI NORTH COMPLEX: Kigalia Point-UT; Cream Pots-UT; Moss Back Butte-UT; Kane Gulch-UT; South Long Point-UT; Hotel Rock-UT; Halls Crossing-UT; Halls Crossing NE-UT; Burnt Spring-UT; Clay Hills-UT; Red House Spring-UT; Pollys Pasture-UT; Cedar Mesa-UT; Snow Flat Spring Cave-UT; Bluff NW-UT; The Rincon-UT; Alcove Canyon-UT; Nokai Dome-UT; Mikes Mesa-UT; Whirl Wind Draw-UT; Slickhorn Canyon West-UT; Slickhorn Canyon-East-UT; Cedar Mesa South-UT; Cigarette Spring Cave-UT; Bluff SW-UT; Nasja Mesa-UT; Wilson Creek-UT; Deep Canyon North-UT; No Mans Mesa North-UT; Goulding NE-UT; The Goosenecks-UT; Mexican Hat-UT; and San Juan Hill-UT.

24. WHITE CANYON–NATURAL BRIDGES COMPLEX: Copper Point-UT; Indian Head-UT; Jacobs Chair-UT; The Cheesebox-UT; Moss Back Butte-UT; Kane Gulch-UT.

25. DARK CANYON WILDERNESS COMPLEX: Bowdie Canyon West-UT; Bowdie Canyon East-UT; Indian Head Pass-UT; Black Steer Canyon-UT; Warren Canyon-UT; Poison Canyon-UT; Woodenshoe Buttes-UT; Kigalia Point-UT.

26. DIRTY DEVIL COMPLEX: Point of Rocks West-UT; Point of Rocks East-UT; Angel Cove-UT; Angels Point-UT; Robbers Roost Flats-UT; Baking Skillet Knoll-UT; Burr Point-UT; The Pinnacle-UT; Gordon Flats-UT; Turkey Knob-UT; Stair Canyon-UT; Fiddler Butte-UT; Hite North-UT; Sewing Machine-UT.

27. SAN RAFAEL SWELL-CAINEVILLE DESERT COMPLEX: Horn Silver Gulch-UT; Sids Mountain-UT; Bottleneck Peak-UT; Devils Hole-UT; Mexican Mountain-UT; Sid and Charley-UT; The Blocks-UT; The Wickiup-UT; Drowned Hole Draw-UT; Spotted Wolf Canyon-UT; Walker Flat-UT; Mesa Butte-UT; Big Bend Draw-UT; Copper Globe-UT; San Rafael Knob-UT; Twin Knolls-UT; Arsons Garden-UT; Greasewood Draw-UT; Willow Springs-UT; Mussentuchit Flat-UT; Ireland Mesa-UT; Tomsich Butte-UT; Horse Valley-UT; Temple Mountain-UT; Old Woman Wash-UT; Geyser Peak-UT; Solomons Temple-UT; Salvation Creek-UT; The Frying Pan-UT; Hunt Draw-UT; Little Wild Horse Mesa-UT; Goblin Valley-UT; Lyman-UT; Flat Top-UT; Cathedral Mountain-UT; Fruita NW-UT; Caine Springs-UT; Factory Butte-UT; Skyline Rim-UT; The Notch-UT; Bicknell-UT; Torrey-UT; Twin Rocks-UT; Fruita-UT; and Caineville-UT.

28. LABYRINTH CANYON COMPLEX: Moonshine Wash-UT; Tenmile Point-UT; Dubinsky Wash-UT; Keg Knoll-UT; Bowknot Bend-UT; Mineral Canyon-UT; Whitbeck Knoll-UT; Sugarloaf Butte-UT; Horsethief Canyon-UT; Robbers Roost Flats-UT; and Head Spur-UT.

29. CANYONLANDS BASIN COMPLEX: Horsethief Canyon-UT; Upheaval Dome -UT; Musselman Arch-UT; Shafer Basin-UT; Cleopatras Chair-UT; Turks Head-UT; Monument Basin-UT; Lockhart Basin-UT; Elaterite Basin-UT; Spanish Bottom-UT; The Loop-UT; North Six-Shooter Peak-UT; Harts Point North-UT; Hatch Rock-UT; Teapot Rock-UT; Cross Canyon-UT; Druid Arch-UT; South Six-Shooter Peak-UT; Harts Point South-UT; Photograph Gap-UT; Fable Valley-UT; House Park Butte-UT; Cathedral Butte-UT; Shay Mountain-UT; Monticello Lake-UT; and Mount Linnaeus-UT.

30. BEHIND-THE-ROCKS COMPLEX: Goldbar Canyon-UT; Moab-UT; Trough Springs Canyon-UT; Kane Springs-UT; Eightmile Rock-UT; LaSal Junction-UT.

31. LA SAL CANYONS COMPLEX: Cisco SW-UT; Dewey-UT; Blue Chief Mesa-UT; Steamboat Mesa-UT-CO; Big Bend-UT; Fisher Towers-UT; Fisher Valley-UT; Dolores Point North-UT-CO; Moab-UT; Rill Creek-UT; Warner Lake-UT; Mount Waas-UT; Dolores Point South-UT; Mount Tukuhnikivatz-UT; Mount Peale-UT.

32. ARCHES-LOST SPRING CANYON COMPLEX: Klondike Bluffs-UT; Mollie Hogans-UT; Cisco SW-UT; Merrimac Butte-UT; The Windows Section-UT; Big Bend-UT; Goldbar Canyon-UT; Moab-UT.

33. WESTWATER CANYON COMPLEX: Agate-UT; Westwater-UT-CO; Big Triangle-UT; Marble Canyon-UT-CO.

34. BOOK CLIFFS–DESOLATION CANYON COMPLEX: Duches Hole-UT; Nutters Hole-UT; Cedar Ridge Canyon-UT; Firewater Canyon North-UT; Dog Knoll-UT; Summerhouse Ridge-UT; Steer Ridge Canyon-UT; Firewater Canyon South -UT; Wolf Flat-UT; Flat Rock Mesa-UT; Wolf Point-UT; Lighthouse Canyon-UT; Chandler Falls-UT; Moonwater Point-UT; Chicken Fork-UT; Black Knolls-UT; Tenmile Canyon North-UT; Cedar Camp Canyon-UT; Woodside-UT; Turtle Canyon-UT; Three Forks Canyon-UT; Lion Canyon-UT; Walker Point-UT; Supply Canyon-UT; Tenmile Canyon South-UT; Preacher Canyon-UT; Dry Canyon-UT; Cliff-UT; Jenny Canyon-UT; Butler Canyon-UT; Bobby Canyon North-UT; Floy Canyon North-UT; Bogart Canyon-UT; Tepee Canyon-UT; Flume Canyon-UT; Antone Canyon-UT; Blue Castle Butte-UT; Tusher Canyon-UT; Bobby Canyon South-UT; Floy Canyon South-UT; Sego Canyon-UT; Calf Canyon-UT; Cisco Springs-UT.

35. WHITE RIVER: Asphalt Wash-UT.

36. GREATER DINOSAUR: Island Park-UT; Jones Hole-UT-CO; Dinosaur Quarry-UT; Split Mountain-UT; Stuntz Reservoir-UT; Cliff Ridge-UT; Snake John Reef-UT-CO.

37. MOUNT NAOMI WILDERNESS COMPLEX: Richmond-UT; Naomi Peak-UT; Tony Grove Creek-UT; Smithfield-UT; Mount Elmer-UT; Temple Peak-UT.

38. WELLSVILLE MOUNTAIN WILDERNESS: Honeyville-UT; Wellsville-UT; Brigham City-UT; and Mount Pisgah-UT.

39. UINTA MOUNTAINS WILDERNESS COMPLEX: Deadman Mountain-UT; Elizabeth Mountain-UT; Lyman Lake-UT; Bridger Lake-UT; Gilbert Peak NE-UT; Hole in the Rock-UT; Hoop Lake-UT; Hidden Lake-UT; Slader Basin-UT; Whitney Reservoir-UT; Christmas Meadows-UT; Red Knob-UT; Mount Lovenia-UT; Mount Powell-UT; Kings Peak-UT; Fox Lake-UT; Chepeta Lake-UT; Whiterocks Lake-UT; Leidy Peak-UT; Elk Park-UT; East Park Resevoir-UT; Hoyt Peak-UT; Erickson Basin-UT; Mirror Lake-UT; Hayden Peak-UT; Explorer Peak-UT; Oweep Creek-UT; Garfield Basin-UT; Mount Emmons-UT; Bollie Lake-UT; Rasmussen Lakes-UT; Paradise Park-UT; Marsh Peak-UT; Taylor Mountain-UT; Woodland-UT; Soapstone Basin-UT; Iron Mine Mountain-UT; Grandaddy Lake-UT; Tworoose Pass-UT; Kidney Lake-UT; Lake Fork Mountain-UT; Burnt Mill Spring-UT; Heller Lake-UT; Pole Creek Cave-UT; Ice Cave Peak-UT; Lake Mountain-UT; Dry Fork-UT.

40. CENTRAL WASATCH WILDERNESS COMPLEX: Sugarhouse-UT; Mount Aire-UT; Draper-UT; Dromedary Peak-UT; Lehi-UT; Timpanogos Cave-UT; Aspen Grove-UT; Orem-UT; and Bridal Veil Falls-UT.

41. MOUNT NEBO WILDERNESS COMPLEX: Santaquin-UT; Payson Lakes-UT; Birdseye-UT; Mona-UT; Nebo Basin-UT; and Spencer Canyon-UT.

42. WASATCH PLATEAU: Birdseye-UT; Thistle-UT; Mill Fork-UT; Tucker-UT; Indianola-UT; C Canyon-UT; Scofield Res-UT; Fairview-UT; Fairview Lakes-UT; Scofield-UT; Huntington Res-UT; Candland Mountain-UT; Watts-UT; Spring City-UT; South Tent Mountain-UT; Rilda Canyon-UT; Hiawatha-UT; Ephraim-UT; Danish Knoll-UT; Joe's Valley Res-UT; Mahogany Pt-UT; Black Mountain-UT; Ferron Res-UT; Ferron Canyon-UT; The Cap-UT; Woods Lake-UT; Heliotrope Mountain-UT; Flagstaff Peak-UT; Ferron-UT; Acord Lakes-UT; Emery West-UT.

43. PAHVANT RANGE: Scipio Pass-UT; Scipio South-UT; Coffee Peak-UT; Scipio Lake-UT; Fillmore-UT; Mount Catherine-UT; Beehive Peak-UT; Kanosh-UT; Sunset Peak-UT; White Pine Peak-UT; Richfield-UT; Dog Valley Peak-UT; Red Ridge-UT; Joseph Peak-UT; El Sinore-UT; Cove Fort-UT; Trail Mountain-UT; and Marysvale Canyon-UT.

44. SEVIER PLATEAU: Junction-UT; Phonolite Hill-UT; Bullrush Peak-UT; Mount Dutton-UT; Deep Creek-UT; Blind Spring Mountain-UT; Adams Head-UT; Cow Creek-UT; Casto Canyon-UT; Flake Mountain West-UT; and Wilson Peak-UT.

45. CEDAR BREAKS–ASHDOWN GORGE WILDERNESS COMPLEX: Flanigan Arch-UT; Brian Head-UT; Webster Flat-UT; and Navajo Lake-UT.

FINDING THE RIGHT MAPS: To explore the country described in *Wild Utah* you need two basic types of maps: the detailed U.S. Geological Survey (USGS) 1:24,000-scale topographic (contour) maps listed above for on-the-ground route-finding; and Bureau of Land Management (BLM) surface management/ land ownership maps or USDA Forest Service national forest visitor maps (usually scaled at one half-inch to the mile on a contour or planimetric base) for trip planning and for vehicular access to the trailhead. In some cases a special wilderness or recreation map may be available from the land management agency. These smaller-scale maps are listed under "Maps" in the Trip Planning Chart for each Utah wildland. At this writing the USGS topo maps as well as the smaller-scale BLM and Forest Service maps cost $4 each. Appendix C lists addresses to which you can write to the BLM or Forest Service maps you need. If you are ordering more than one map from the BLM it would be more efficient to purchase them from the Utah State Office in Salt Lake City. In the case of a multiple map order of Forest Service maps contact the Information Assistant for the Regional Office in Ogden. USGS maps may be purchased from USGS Information Services, Box 25286, Denver, CO 80225, or by calling 1-800-USA-MAPS or 1-800-HELP-MAP. The USGS charges a handling fee of $3.50 for each order mailed.

Other maps that will help you in getting to the lands described in *Wild Utah* are the series of 1:357,000-scale multipurpose maps published by the Utah Travel Council. The five maps covering Utah show points of interest, land ownership, and special land-use designations, and are entitled "Northern," "Northeastern," "Southeastern," "Southwestern," and "North Central." They can be purchased for $2 each from the Utah Travel Council (see Appendix C for address).

Of particular value is the Utah series of maps published by Trails Illustrated. These waterproof, tear-resistant topo maps are specially designed for the backcountry traveler, with information on trails, trailheads, and applicable backcountry regulations. For a free catalog or to order specific Utah map titles contact: National Geographic Maps/Trails Illustrated, P.O. Box 3610, Evergreen, CO 80439, or call 1-800-962-1643.

ROADLESS AREA UPDATE
and Visitation Record

Please send a completed copy of this form to Bill Cunningham and Polly Burke c/o Falcon Publishing, P.O. Box 1718, Helena, MT 59624. Feel free to copy as needed.

1. Name of area visited _____

2. Management agency _____

3. Location of visit (legal description: section, township, range, if possible; name of drainages, trail numbers, etc.) _____

_____

_____

4. Date of visit _____

5. Condition of access to trailhead or beginning of trail _____

_____

6. Status and condition of trails used by name/number _____

_____

_____

7. Brief description of area visited _____

_____

_____

8. Is the trail (area) used by both motorized and nonmotorized recreationists? _____

If yes, is there any evidence of user conflict or resource damage? _____

_____

_____

9. If the area or trail segment visited has been changed by roads or resource development, describe the **location** and **type** of development and its impact on the roadless area _____

_____

_____

10. Action taken (if applicable) _____

_____

11. Name, address, telephone _____

_____

_____

Note: This information will serve as a record of your visit to a wildland and may also be used for future updates of this book. Also, with your permission, the information may be shared with the land management agency and/or the local conservation group concerned with the area in order to assist in its protection and stewardship.

About the Authors

Bill Cunningham has been a lifelong "wildernut," as a wildlands studies professor, an outfitter, and a conservation activist. Bill, who lives in Missoula, Montana, has written several books and numerous articles about wilderness areas based on his extensive on-the-ground knowledge. Bill is the author of *Wild Montana,* the first in Falcon Publishing's series of guidebooks to wilderness and unprotected roadless areas. He has been exploring portions of wild Utah on annual trips for more than 20 years. As a lobbyist for The Wilderness Society during the late 1970s he played a modest role in the passage of the Endangered American Wilderness Act of 1978, which contained Utah's first designated wilderness, Lone Peak.

Polly Burke, formerly a history teacher in St. Louis, Missouri, now makes her home in Montana and is pursuing a career as a free-lance writer. As one of Bill's fellow instructors in San Francisco State's Wildlands Studies program, she shares his passion for wilderness. Polly has hiked and backpacked extensively throughout many parts of the country.

Polly and Bill recently co-authored Falcon's *Hiking California's Desert Parks* (1996). *Wild Utah* is their second co-authorship for Falcon, in what they hope will be a long series of joint exploration and writing projects.

Index

get FALCON GUIDED

FALCON GUIDES ® are available for where-to-go hiking, mountain biking, rock climbing, walking, scenic driving, fishing, rockhounding, paddling, birding, wildlife viewing, and camping. We also have FalconGuides on essential outdoor skills and subjects and field identification. The following titles are currently available, but this list grows every year. For a free catalog with a complete list of titles, call FALCON toll-free at 1-800-582-2665.

HIKING GUIDES

Hiking Alaska
Hiking Alberta
Hiking Arizona
Hiking Arizona's Cactus Country
Hiking the Beartooths
Hiking Big Bend National Park
Hiking California
Hiking California's Desert Parks
Hiking Carlsbad Caverns &
    Guadalupe Mtns. National Parks
Hiking Colorado
Hiking the Columbia River Gorge
Hiking Florida
Hiking Georgia
Hiking Glacier & Waterton Lakes National Parks
Hiking Grand Canyon National Park
Hiking Great Basin National Park
Hiking Hot Springs
    in the Pacific Northwest
Hiking Idaho
Hiking Maine
Hiking Michigan
Hiking Minnesota
Hiking Montana
Hiking Nevada
Hiking New Hampshire
Hiking New Mexico
Hiking New York
Hiking North Carolina
Hiking North Cascades

Hiking Northern Arizona
Hiking Olympic National Park
Hiking Oregon
Hiking Oregon's Eagle Cap Wilderness
Hiking Oregon's Three Sisters Country
Hiking Pennsylvania
Hiking South Carolina
Hiking South Dakota's Black Hills Country
Hiking Southern New England
Hiking Tennessee
Hiking Texas
Hiking Utah
Hiking Utah's Summits
Hiking Vermont
Hiking Virginia
Hiking Washington
Hiking Wyoming
Hiking Wyoming's Wind River Range
Hiking Yellowstone National Park
Hiking Zion & Bryce Canyon National Parks
The Trail Guide to Bob Marshall Country

BEST EASY DAY HIKES

Beartooths
Canyonlands & Arches
Best Hikes on the Continental Divide
Glacier & Waterton Lakes
Glen Canyon
Grand Canyon
North Cascades
Yellowstone

■ *To order any of these books, check with your local bookseller*
or call FALCON ® *at **1-800-582-2665**.*

Visit us on the world wide web at:
www.falconguide.com

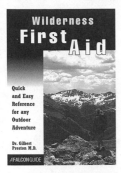

WILDERNESS FIRST AID

By Dr. Gilbert Preston M.D.
Enjoy the outdoors and face the inherent risks with confidence. By reading this easy-to-follow first-aid text, all outdoor enthusiasts can pack a little extra peace of mind on their next adventure. *Wilderness First Aid* offers expert medical advice for dealing with outdoor emergencies beyond the reach of 911. It easily fits in most backcountry first-aid kits.

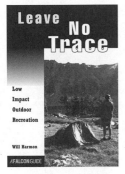

LEAVE NO TRACE

by Will Harmon
The concept of "leave no trace" seems simple, but it actually gets fairly complicated. This handy quick-reference guidebook includes all the newest information on this growing and all-important subject. This book is written to help the outdoor enthusiast make the hundreds of decisions necessary to protect the natural landscape and still have an enjoyable wilderness experience. Part of the proceeds from the sale of this book go to continue leave-no-trace education efforts. The Official Manual of American Hiking Society.

BEAR AWARE

by Bill Schneider
Hiking in bear country can be very safe if hikers follow the guidelines summarized in this small, "packable" book. Extensively reviewed by bear experts, the book contains the latest information on the intriguing science of bear-human interactions. *Bear Aware* can not only make your hike safer, but it can help you avoid the fear of bears that can take the edge off your trip.

MOUNTAIN LION ALERT

By Steve Torres
Recent mountain lion attacks have received national attention. Although infrequent, lion attacks raise concern for public safety. *Mountain Lion Alert* contains helpful advice for mountain bikers, trail runners, horse riders, pet owners, and suburban landowners on how to reduce the chances of mountain lion-human conflicts.

To order these titles or to find out more about this new series
of books, call FALCON® at **1-800-582-2665.**